Federal Courts

AF869017

WEST ACADEMIC PUBLISHING'S EMERITUS ADVISORY BOARD

JESSE H. CHOPER
Professor of Law and Dean Emeritus
University of California, Berkeley

LARRY D. KRAMER
President and Vice Chancellor and Professor of Law
The London School of Economics and Political Science

GRANT S. NELSON
Professor of Law Emeritus, Pepperdine University
Professor of Law Emeritus, University of California, Los Angeles

JAMES J. WHITE
Robert A. Sullivan Emeritus Professor of Law
University of Michigan

WEST ACADEMIC PUBLISHING'S LAW SCHOOL ADVISORY BOARD

MARK C. ALEXANDER
Arthur J. Kania Dean and Professor of Law
Villanova University Charles Widger School of Law

JOSHUA DRESSLER
Distinguished University Professor Emeritus
Michael E. Moritz College of Law, The Ohio State University

MEREDITH J. DUNCAN
Alumnae College Professor of Law
Assistant Dean for Strategic Opportunities, Pedagogy, and Faculty, Student, and Community Engagement, University of Houston Law Center

RENÉE HUTCHINS LAURENT
Dean & Professor of Law
University of Maryland Carey School of Law

RENEE KNAKE JEFFERSON
Joanne and Larry Doherty Chair in Legal Ethics and Professor of Law, University of Houston Law Center

ORIN S. KERR
William G. Simon Professor of Law
University of California, Berkeley

JONATHAN R. MACEY
Professor of Law
Yale Law School

DEBORAH JONES MERRITT
Distinguished University Professor
John Deaver Drinko/Baker & Hostetler Chair in Law Emerita
Michael E. Moritz College of Law, The Ohio State University

ARTHUR R. MILLER
University Professor and Chief Justice Warren E. Burger Professor of Constitutional Law and the Courts, New York University

A. BENJAMIN SPENCER
Dean & Trustee Professor of Law
William & Mary Law School

BLACK LETTER OUTLINES

Federal Courts

SIXTH EDITION

Donald L. Doernberg
Professor of Law *Emeritus*
Elisabeth Haub School of Law
Pace University

Richard D. Freer
Dean and Charles Howard Candler Professor of Law
Emory University School of Law

Martin H. Redish
Louis and Harriet Ancel Professor of Law and Public Policy
Northwestern University

BLACK LETTER SERIES®

WEST ACADEMIC

The publisher is not engaged in rendering legal or other professional advice, and this publication is not a substitute for the advice of an attorney. If you require legal or other expert advice, you should seek the services of a competent attorney or other professional.

Black Letter Series is a trademark registered in the U.S. Patent and Trademark Office.

COPYRIGHT © 1985, 1991 WEST PUBLISHING CO.
© 2004 West, a Thomson Business
© 2017, 2021 LEG, Inc. d/b/a West Academic
© 2025 LEG, Inc. d/b/a West Academic
860 Blue Gentian Road, Suite 350
Eagan, MN 55121
1-877-888-1330

West, West Academic Publishing, and West Academic are trademarks of West Publishing Corporation, used under license.

Published in the United States of America

ISBN: 979-8-89209-748-2

Summary of Contents

■ PART TWO: THE STRUCTURE OF FEDERAL JURISDICTION

Table of Contents

PART THREE: FEDERAL COURTS, FEDERALISM AND THE STATES

NAVIGATING THIS BOOK

There are two types of hyperlinks in this book. External links (*e.g.*, to cases and statutes) are doubtless familiar to you and always appear underlined. Where you see a citation to a particular page, clicking on the main part of the citation (*i.e.* the full citation or the date) will take you to the beginning of the case in Westlaw. Clicking on the *page* (pin cite) citation will take you to that page of the case in Westlaw. For example, the hyperlinks for *Cohens v. Virginia*, 19 U.S. (6 Wheat.) 264, 404 (1821), are subdivided. Clicking on 19 U.S. (6 Wheat.) 264 or (1803) will take you to the first page of the case, but clicking on 404 will take you to the page on which the relevant language appears, saving you 180 pages of scrolling through WestLaw. (There are a few instances in which WestLaw does not have a citation to the relevant page within the opinion. Those appear with the individual page number not as a hyperlink, *e.g.* *Marbury v. Madison*, 5 U.S. (1 Cranch) 137, 176 (1803).)

Internal links—cross references—are also familiar. They appear in with gray backgrounds. Typically, internal links suffer one drawback: after you have gotten to your destination page, you have to scroll through the document again to return to your original page—possible, to be sure, but a nuisance. Not so here. After each reference to another page or section of the book, you will see *[R]* (for "Return") followed by a number, *e.g. [R1]*, *[R2]*, etc. They will always appear *italicized*, but not underlined—not appearing as hyperlinks on your original pages because they are not hyperlinks; they are bookmarks. *Make a mental note* of that bookmark number before you jump to your destination page. At the end of the passage, paragraph, or set of pages that is your destination, you will see a hyperlink corresponding to the bookmark number on your original page, *e.g.* [R1], [R2], etc. That will appear as a hyperlink, and clicking on it will take you back to the place on your original page where you began, eliminating the need to scroll so much.

EDITING CONVENTIONS

We have used some editing conventions to avoid cluttering up the text with detail unrelated to the Black Letter's purpose. We do not include the subsequent history of cases when it is unrelated to the principle of Federal Courts that the case articulates. Accordingly, if the Supreme Court overrules a case "on other grounds," that subsequent history does not appear. Therefore, do not take the citations here to be complete

Bluebook explications of the courts' treatment of the cases. References to articles, sections, and clauses of the United States Constitution appear without the words "of the Constitution," to save space. We refer to diversity-of-citizenship jurisdiction simply as diversity jurisdiction. We try to avoid cumbersome phrases such as "defendant or defendants" and references such as "defendant(s)." Unless otherwise indicated, a general noun may refer to singular or plural entities, according to the context.

It often is very helpful to diagram cases, particularly multiparty cases. Diagrams appear particularly in Chapters V, VI, and VII (concerning diversity and alienage jurisdiction, supplemental jurisdiction, and removal) and are probably similar to diagrams that you and your professors used. The only perhaps unusual notation we have employed involves arrows indicating claim directions. A solid arrow (⟶) indicates a claim over which the court has stand-alone subject-matter jurisdiction. A dotted arrow (----------→) denotes a claim over which the court lacks a stand-alone basis of subject-matter jurisdiction but may have supplemental jurisdiction.

PERSPECTIVE

■ APPROACH TO FEDERAL COURTS

Studying federal courts includes considering the internal structure and operation of the federal judiciary, its relationship to the other branches of the federal government (separation-of-powers principles), and its interaction with the judicial and political segments of the state governments (federalism principles). The subject is a unique blend of highly technical and detailed statutory analysis on one hand and the study of broad theoretical issues of federalism and separation of powers on the other. It is this combination of very different modes of thought—of detail and of "big picture"—that makes the study of federal courts so interesting.

To gain the most from the course, recognize the importance of both the intricate detail and the broad themes without emphasizing either over the other. For example, you must be able simultaneously to comprehend the highly theoretical issues surrounding the controversy over congressional power to regulate the jurisdiction of the federal courts and the technicalities of removal. In all areas, always attempt to relate the practical legal doctrines to the policies behind the development of the federal judiciary and its role as part of a dynamic federal system that must reconcile often competing interests of state and federal governments.

There are many resources to aid in understanding the complexities of the subject. Judges and lawyers routinely consult two multi-volume treatises available in law school libraries: WRIGHT & MILLER, FEDERAL PRACTICE AND PROCEDURE and MOORE'S FEDERAL PRACTICE. In addition, very helpful single-volume resources include: CHEMERINSKY, FEDERAL JURISDICTION (8th ed. 2021); MULLENIX, REDISH & VAIRO, UNDERSTANDING FEDERAL COURTS AND JURISDICTION (2d ed. 2016); WRIGHT & KANE, THE LAW OF FEDERAL COURTS (8th ed. 2017); LARRY YACKLE, FEDERAL COURTS (3d ed. 2009), LARRY YACKLE, FEDERAL COURTS: THE CURRENT QUESTIONS (2017), and DOERNBERG, FEDERAL COURTS IN A NUTSHELL (6th ed. 2021).

■ APPROACH TO EXAMINATIONS

In deciding how to prepare for an examination in federal courts, a great deal may depend on whether the test will include short answers, or will consist exclusively of essay questions. If the examination contains numerous short answer questions, it is likely that the professor is interested in the students' knowledge and understanding of specific legal doctrines and statutory structure. Preparation for such an examination should emphasize the details of the various jurisdictional statutes and judge-made principles and should consider closely the specific elements of each. If the examination is open-book, there is less need for rote memorization. Given the limited time generally available during an examination, however, it is always better to avoid relying too heavily on access to books. There is no time to take the course during the examination.

If the examination is primarily or exclusively of the essay variety, be prepared to deal with some of the many unresolved policy issues in the field. As in most law school examination questions of this variety, it is likely that there is no one "right" answer, and it is important both to explain the thought process that leads to your conclusion and to your rejecting opposing arguments. But while it is important to include broad policy analysis in such questions, it is also important to demonstrate familiarity with detailed statutes and doctrines that are applicable. Particularly in an essay question, the two modes of analysis—detail and "big picture"—are not mutually exclusive.

■ EDITING CONVENTIONS

We have used some editing conventions to avoid cluttering up the text with detail unrelated to the Black Letter's purpose. We do not include the subsequent history of cases when it is unrelated to the principle of Federal Courts that the case articulates. Accordingly, if the Supreme Court overrules a case "on other grounds," that subsequent history does not appear. Therefore, do not take the citations here to be complete Bluebook explications of the courts' treatment of the cases. References to articles, sections, and clauses of the United States Constitution appear without the words "of the Constitution," to save space. We refer to diversity-of-citizenship jurisdiction simply as diversity jurisdiction. We try to avoid cumbersome phrases such as "defendant or defendants" and references such as "defendant(s)." Unless otherwise indicated, a general noun may refer to singular or plural entities, according to the context.

It often is very helpful to diagram cases, particularly multiparty cases. Diagrams appear particularly in Chapters V, VI, and VII (concerning diversity and alienage jurisdiction, supplemental jurisdiction, and removal) and are probably similar to diagrams that you and your professors used. The only perhaps unusual notation we have employed involves arrows indicating claim directions. A solid arrow (⟶) indicates a claim over which the court has stand-alone subject-matter jurisdiction. A dotted arrow (⇢) denotes a claim over which the court lacks a stand-alone basis of subject-matter jurisdiction but may have supplemental jurisdiction.

Capsule Summary

■ Chapter I. PROBLEMS OF JUDICIAL REVIEW

I. THE INSTITUTION OF JUDICIAL REVIEW

Article III, § 1, provides many federal judges with lifetime tenure and ensures that Congress cannot reduce their compensation. It accords this extraordinary protection to ensure that federal judges can make decisions without fear of political reprisal. *Marbury v. Madison*, 5 U.S. (1 Cranch) 137 (1803), established that the federal judiciary has the constitutional power to invalidate unconstitutional acts of the other branches of government. Judicial review allows the judiciary to monitor the proper functioning of the government, but creates tension between it and the political branches. Several related doctrines—the justiciability doctrines—limit the federal judicial power and, therefore, judicial review.

II. FEDERAL COURTS CANNOT ISSUE ADVISORY OPINIONS

Article III, § 2, extends the judicial power of the federal courts to "cases" and "controversies" of various types. The judicial power can operate only if a true dispute exists and thus does not allow advisory opinions—opinions that can have no dispositive effect on an actual dispute properly before the courts. Despite occasional requests for advisory opinions from the other branches of government, the Supreme Court has adhered steadfastly to the prohibition.

III. STANDING

A party may not litigate in federal court unless she has "standing." Article III's case-or-controversy requirement has three requirements, which every plaintiff must satisfy in every case, as "an irreducible minimum" for standing. First, the plaintiff must show that she personally suffered actual or imminently threatened injury as a result of the defendant's putatively illegal conduct. Second, the injury must be fairly traceable to (caused by) the challenged action. Third, the litigation must be likely to redress the injury if the plaintiff prevails. These requirements support separation of-powers by confining the federal courts to performing the traditional judicial function of resolving disputes.

In addition to the three constitutional requirements for standing, the Supreme Court at one time imposed three "prudential" limitations on standing as a matter of sound judicial administration. First, the plaintiff must have asserted her own interest, not that of a third-party. Second, the plaintiff's interest must have been within the "zone of interests" protected by the relevant law. Third, the plaintiff must not have asserted a "generalized grievance." Congress could have overridden these limitations but never did. The Court has now turned its back on prudential standing, recharacterizing the first two as going to whether the plaintiff states "a claim upon which relief may be granted" rather than to standing. The Court now sees the generalized-grievance concern as part of the constitutional case-or-controversy inquiry.

One subset of the standing problem concerns the extent to which taxpayers can sue to challenge the constitutionality of government spending programs. Federal taxpayers have standing only if they can demonstrate a "necessary stake as taxpayers" to satisfy Article III. That exists only (1) in suits that challenge statutes passed pursuant to Congress's power under the Taxing and Spending Clause, Article I, § 8, cl. 1, and (2) if the taxpayer can establish a nexus between that status and the constitutional infringement. Thus far, only one case has qualified.

IV. RIPENESS

The ripeness doctrine provides that the federal courts may not adjudicate when it is unclear whether the plaintiff will suffer actual injury. The dispute must be mature enough to require adjudication. This reflects Article III's case-or-controversy requirement; until a dispute ripens, there is no case or controversy. Ripeness focuses on the fitness of the issues for judicial decision and the hardship to the parties of withholding a determination. If the court says a case is not ripe, it means that it is *too soon* for litigation.

V. MOOTNESS

Mootness also concerns the timing of litigation, but it addresses whether the case is pending when it is *too late* for the court to act. For instance, if Congress repeals a challenged statute, the case becomes moot. That also reflects Article III's case-or-controversy requirement; if a change in circumstances means that judicial resolution would be meaningless, there is no longer a justiciable controversy, and an opinion would be merely advisory.

There are important exceptions to the mootness doctrine, including one that applies when a claim is "capable of repetition, yet evading review." This concerns harms that may pass before litigation can remedy address them. Federal courts may hear such claims if (1) there is a reasonable expectation or demonstrated probability that the same controversy will recur and (2) the harm will be complete before litigation can be effective.

VI. POLITICAL-QUESTION DOCTRINE

The political-question doctrine rests upon the proposition that some issues of constitutional law are simply beyond the federal judiciary's competence. It undeniably reflects separation of powers. By declining to adjudicate political questions, the federal bench avoids potentially dangerous confrontations between it and the other federal branches. The Court has identified several factors as earmarks of such non-justiciable political questions. These factors seem to include (1) exclusive constitutional commitment of the matter to another branch of the federal government, (2) concern that courts should stay out of policy areas in which there are no clear judicial standards, and (3) prudential concerns of comity with coordinate branches of the federal government. For example, the federal bench will not intervene in any aspect of impeachment, for which the Constitution vests sole responsibility in the House of Representatives and the Senate.

■ Chapter II: CONGRESSIONAL POWER TO REGULATE FEDERAL JURISDICTION

I. DISTINCTION BETWEEN CONGRESSIONAL POWER OVER JURISDICTION OF THE SUPREME COURT AND OF THE LOWER FEDERAL COURTS

Article III, § 1, mandates having the Supreme Court of the United States and permits Congress to determine whether there will be any lower—known as inferior—federal courts. Common sense dictates that the power to create the lower courts includes broad power to regulate their jurisdiction. Section 2 vests in the Supreme Court original—trial—jurisdiction over two types of cases: (1) those affecting ambassadors, other public ministers and consuls and (2) those in which a state is a party. In all other matters, it has appellate jurisdiction "with such Exceptions" as Congress makes. The Exceptions Clause gives Congress considerable power to tailor the Supreme Court's appellate jurisdiction.

II. CONGRESSIONAL POWER TO REGULATE LOWER FEDERAL COURT JURISDICTION

The traditional theory is that because Congress has the constitutional authority to create lower federal courts, it also has plenary power to prescribe their jurisdiction. Congress has, for example, limited district courts' jurisdiction in the Antiterrorism and Effective Death Penalty Act, the Illegal Immigration Reform and Immigrant Responsibility Act, and the Prison Litigation Reform Act.

III. CONGRESSIONAL POWER TO REGULATE SUPREME COURT ORIGINAL JURISDICTION

The Constitution requires a Supreme Court of the United States, so Congress cannot abolish it. Consequently, it lacks the plenary power to restrict Supreme-Court Jurisdiction that Congress has over the lower federal courts. The constitutional grants of original jurisdiction are self-executing; the Supreme Court has trial jurisdiction over such cases without congressional action. On the other hand, the Constitution does not say that the Supreme Court's original jurisdiction is exclusive, so Congress may grant concurrent original jurisdiction over such cases to the lower federal courts and has done so in 28 U.S.C. § 1251, reserving only "controversies between two or more States" to the Supreme Court.

IV. CONGRESSIONAL POWER TO REGULATE SUPREME COURT APPELLATE JURISDICTION

The Constitution also gives the Supreme Court appellate jurisdiction in all other cases within the judicial power, subject to congressional exceptions. *Ex parte McCardle*, 74 U.S. (7 Wall.) 506 (1868), upheld a statute removing appellate jurisdiction; Congress feared the result the Court might reach. Though *McCardle* seems to imply nearly unfettered congressional authority to restrict the Supreme Court's appellate jurisdiction, some have argued against such expansive legislative power. One theory is that Congress may not make exceptions to appellate jurisdiction that would rob the Supreme Court of its essential role in the constitutional plan.

V. LIMITATIONS ON CONGRESSIONAL POWER DERIVING FROM OTHER CONSTITUTIONAL PROVISIONS

There are theories that other constitutional provisions limit Congress's power to regulate federal court jurisdiction. One is that equal protection prevents Congress from limiting access to the federal courts for specific fundamental rights. Another is that due process requires an independent judicial forum as a prerequisite to taking either liberty nor property from an individual. This requirement does not necessarily require *federal* adjudication of constitutional rights; litigation in state courts satisfies due process. Another theory, with more discussion in case law, is that separation-of-powers principles operate as a brake on Congress's authority to restrict federal court jurisdiction. Thus, Congress may not prescribe a rule for deciding a case in a particular way, *United States v. Klein*, 80 U.S. (13 Wall.) 128 (1871), nor can it pass a statute that effectively converts an earlier Supreme Court holding into an advisory opinion. *Plaut v. Spendthrift Farm, Inc.*, 514 U.S. 211 (1995).

VI. CONGRESSIONAL POWER TO VEST ARTICLE III FEDERAL COURTS WITH NON-ARTICLE III POWERS

Article III judges have the life tenure and salary protection under Article III, § 1. The federal district courts, courts of appeals, and the Supreme Court are Article III courts. Article III extends judicial power of the United States only to "cases" or "controversies." Congress has occasionally vested Article III courts with responsibilities beyond adjudicating cases or controversies. For instance, the United States District Court for the District of Columbia used to perform administrative functions such as setting utility rates. The Supreme Court considered such tribunals "hybrid" courts; thus, they were Article III courts when they adjudicated cases or controversies and were not Article III courts when they performed non-judicial tasks. Congress ended hybrid courts by creating local courts for the District of Columbia, which are not Article III courts. Congress also clarified other situations by abolishing the Court of Claims and the Court of Customs and Patent Appeals and creating the Court of International Claims, the Court of Federal Claims and the Court of Appeals for the Federal Circuit. In sum, Congress can—but rarely does—require an Article III court to perform some administrative tasks.

But can Congress permit Article III courts to adjudicate cases that do not fall within the judicial power of the United States? The answer seems clearly to be no. Article III courts can adjudicate only cases and controversies falling within the judicial power that Article III, § 2, cl. 1, creates.

■ CHAPTER III: NON-ARTICLE III COURTS

I. ARTICLE III COURTS AND NON-ARTICLE III COURTS

This Chapter discusses the converse of one of the issues in Chapter II: whether courts Congress created under Articles I or IV can perform judicial tasks falling within Article III. Article I permits Congress to create "tribunals inferior to the Supreme Court," and Article IV allows Congress to govern United States territories. In 1828, *The American Insurance Company v. 356 Bales of Cotton*, 26 U.S. (1 Pet.) 511 (1828) (usually cited as *The American Insurance Company v. Canter*) Chief Justice Marshall's opinion for the Court recognized Congress's power to create what he termed "legislative Courts, created in virtue of the general right of sovereignty which exists in the government, or in virtue of that clause which enables Congress to make all needful rules and regulations, respecting the territory belonging to the United States." Non-Article III courts have been a fixture ever since. There are disputes about the extent of their power, but none about their legitimacy. Because they are not Article III courts, neither Article III's protections for judicial tenure and salary nor its justiciability requirements apply. Territorial courts, military courts, the tax court, and the local courts for the District of Columbia are examples of non-Article III courts. Note, however, that territorial courts, courts Congress creates to hear public-rights cases, and military courts are exceptions to the general rule that non-Article III courts cannot adjudicate Article III matters.

II. CONSTITUTIONAL LIMITS ON CONGRESSIONAL POWER TO VEST NON-ARTICLE III COURTS WITH AUTHORITY TO DECIDE ARTICLE III MATTERS

No one doubts that Congress can create non-Article III courts, but there is serious debate over whether Congress can vest them with authority to determine matters falling within Article III's judicial power. If Congress can, that could eviscerate a central goal of Article III—to ensure that judges protected from retaliation by the political branches of government hear such cases or controversies. Early precedent suggested that there was no limit to Congress's authority to vest authority to decide Article III matters in non-Article III courts.

In recent years, however, the Supreme Court has said that there are two areas in which Congress may not vest Article III adjudicative power in non-Article III courts. First, private rights cases—disputes between private litigants—in federal court are "inherently judicial" and must ordinarily go to Article III courts. But in 2015, the Supreme Court declared the entitlement to an Article III court to be a personal constitutional right of the litigants, who may consent—at least in bankruptcy proceedings—to non-Article III adjudication of private disputes.

By contrast, public rights cases—between the government and persons subject to its authority regarding the legislative or executive performance of constitutional functions—need not go to Article III courts, but (and this is the second exception) Article III courts must determine "constitutional facts"—facts that form the underlying basis for the claim that a governmental act is unconstitutional. *Crowell v. Benson*, 285 U.S. 22 (1932).

III. ADJUDICATION BY ADJUNCTS TO ARTICLE III COURTS

Non-Article III courts operate independently of Article III courts. There are also various adjunct decisionmakers that Congress often creates to assist Article III courts. They, too, are non-Article III officers or bodies. They can adjudicate even matters considered "inherently judicial," provided an Article III court can substantially review their decisions.

Both the executive and the legislative branches of the federal government create administrative agencies. Typically, they have rulemaking and adjudicative authority. *Crowell v. Benson* requires that Article III judicial review be available for administrative findings of constitutional facts. In general, Congress has permitted a party to an administrative adjudication to petition for review in the Courts of Appeals, which are Article III courts.

Bankruptcy judges are Article I officers and serve as adjuncts to the district court. Their jurisdiction extends only to core bankruptcy issues (except for litigants' right to consent to determination of private-rights cases). The district court (an Article III court) retains jurisdiction over plenary matters. Magistrate judges are not Article III judges. District judges within the district appoint them, and they serve a term of years. A statute strictly defines magistrate judges' authority, and provides review by district judges. Magistrate judges can decide non-dispositive matters, subject to review by district judges for "clear error." They can decide dispositive matters subject to *de novo* review. They can try cases only with the consent of the parties, who thereby waive their right to an Article III judge.

■ CHAPTER IV: FEDERAL-QUESTION JURISDICTION

I. CONSTITUTIONAL AND POLICY BASES FOR FEDERAL-QUESTION JURISDICTION

Article III, § 2, cl. 1, extends the federal judicial power, *inter alia*, to cases "arising under this Constitution, the Laws of the United States, and treaties made, or which shall be made, under their authority." That is federal-question jurisdiction. The Supreme Court has interpreted the constitutional provision very broadly. So long as any issue of federal law "might form an ingredient" in a case, it is within Article III. Thus any case in which a federal issue might arise—even if it never does—is an Article III federal-question case. This opens the door to federal courts determining cases involving state-law issues, even in the absence of diversity-of-citizenship (diversity) jurisdiction, as long as a federal issue could arise in the case. It has also opened the door to academic theories for vastly expanding federal-court power to decide cases based upon state law.

"Protective jurisdiction" describes two distinct theories to justify vesting authority in the federal courts (under the federal-question language) to hear cases involving only state law. Congress has never attempted to vest such authority in the federal courts, so these theories' validity is unclear. One version of protective jurisdiction, associated with Professor Herbert Wechsler, suggests that if Congress possesses constitutional authority to legislate substantively in an area, it can take the lesser step of choosing not to enact substantive law but simply vesting jurisdiction in the federal courts to apply relevant state law. The other version, which Professor Paul Mishkin developed, suggests that when Congress has a preexisting active and articulated policy in a substantive area, it may protect its program from potential undermining by state court adjudication by allowing the federal courts to adjudicate even pure state law cases in areas related to the federal program. That idea clashes with the concept of parity of state and federal courts.

The policy bases for federal-question jurisdiction are clear and undisputed. Federal judges can develop expertise in interpreting federal law and may be sensitive to policies underlying federal law. (Note the parity concerns again.) In addition, there seems to be no dispute, even in an era of overloaded dockets, that federal-question jurisdiction is salutary. Adjudication and protection of federal rights is arguably the federal courts' primary function.

II. THE STATUTORY GRANT OF FEDERAL-QUESTION JURISDICTION

Article III's federal-question provision is *not* self-executing. It vests no jurisdiction in courts inferior to the Supreme Court for the simple reason that it creates no inferior federal courts. It only permits Congress to create them. Thus, the inferior federal courts only have jurisdiction to hear federal-question cases if Congress grants it in a jurisdictional statute. Congress has long done so. The present statute, 28 U.S.C. § 1331, appears to mirror the constitutional grant of federal-question jurisdiction by granting jurisdiction over cases "arising under" federal law, but the Supreme Court has interpreted the statutory grant of federal-question jurisdiction far more narrowly despite the identical operative language. Though it creates uncertainty at times, the narrow interpretation of the statutory grant helps docket control. If all cases satisfying the constitutional grant of federal-question jurisdiction actually could be in federal courts, it would inundate them.

The Supreme Court has limited statutory federal-question jurisdiction in two ways. First, the "well-pleaded-complaint" rule provides that courts may look only at the plaintiff's claim to determine whether a case arises under federal law. The complaint cannot use an anticipated federal defense as a predicate for jurisdiction. Only the plaintiff's assertion that some federal law supports the relief demanded satisfies § 1331.

The second statutory limitation is more difficult to label, but concerns whether the federal law is sufficiently important. The Supreme Court has adopted different tests for this aspect of federal-question jurisdiction. The decisions have not been consistent, and the law is unclear. As a general rule, if federal law creates the claim plaintiff asserts, the case qualifies for federal-question jurisdiction. A much more difficult situation exists when state law creates the claim, but incorporates federal law as a decisional standard. In 1986, the Court appeared to rule (five-to-four) that incorporating a federal standard in the state-law private action did not necessarily render the action one arising under federal law for purposes of § 1331, but it has since ruled that sometimes such incorporation can make a federal-question case, so if you see such a situation on an examination, be sure to discuss factors that cut in favor of federal-question and factors that cut against it. Your primary references will be *Grable & Sons Metal Products, Inc. v. Darue Engineering & Manufacturing*, 545 U.S. 308 (2005), and *Gunn v. Minton*, 568 U.S. 251 (2013). *See infra* pages 104-106 *[R1]*.

■ CHAPTER V: DIVERSITY AND ALIENAGE JURISDICTION

I. CONSTITUTIONAL, STATUTORY, AND POLICY BASES FOR DIVERSITY AND ALIENAGE JURISDICTION

Article III, § 2, cl. 1, extends the judicial power of federal courts, *inter alia*, to cases between citizens of different states (diversity jurisdiction), and to cases between citizens of a state and foreign citizens or subjects (alienage jurisdiction). These Article III provisions are not self-executing either; legislation must confer jurisdiction on the federal courts. Congress provides diversity jurisdiction in 28 U.S.C. § 1332(a)(1) and alienage jurisdiction under § 1332(a)(2). The statutory grant imposes a requirement that such cases involve an amount in controversy exceeding $75,000.

Historically, diversity jurisdiction rests on a desire to provide a federal forum for cases involving citizens of different states, for fear that state courts might be biased against out-of-state litigants. Federal judges are politically insulated. They serve life terms, and Congress cannot reduce their pay. State judges, by contrast, are often elected and may be susceptible to local political pressure. The need for diversity jurisdiction has been the subject of spirited debate for more than a century.

By contrast, alienage jurisdiction is not controversial. It provides a federal forum for many cases in which an alien opposes a citizen of a state of the United States, either as plaintiff or defendant. In part, the federal forum exists to permit the alien to avoid any local bias in state courts. In part, the Framers intended it to assure other countries that their citizens or subjects have ready access to the national courts.

II. DETERMINING WHETHER THE CASE INVOLVES APPROPRIATE LITIGANTS

Diversity cases under § 1332(a)(1) must satisfy the complete-diversity rule: each plaintiff must be of diverse citizenship from each defendant. An alienage case under § 1332(a)(2) must be between a citizen of a state of the United States on one side and a foreign citizen or subject on the other. Applying those rules requires determining the litigants' citizenships.

A human citizen of the United States is a citizen of the state in the United States where her domicile is. Only humans have domiciles, and they may have only one domicile at a time. Domicile requires physical presence in the state combined with the intent to make that state one's home for an unbounded period of time. A United States citizen domiciled in a foreign country is not a citizen of any state, because she is not domiciled in one of the states. Neither is she an alien, because she is not a citizen or subject of a foreign country; she is still a citizen of the United States. Such a person cannot be a party in either a diversity or an alienage case.

Section 1332(c)(1) defines a corporation's citizenship: all states in which the corporation has a charter (usually there is only one) and the state in which the corporation has its principal place of business, which the Supreme Court now defines as the corporation's "nerve center"— "the place where a corporation's officers direct, control, and coordinate the corporation's activities."

No statute defines the citizenship of a unincorporated association, such as a partnership or a union. Rather, courts look to the citizenship of each member of the association. For example, a partnership is a citizen of all states of which its partners are citizens. In litigation by a fiduciary on behalf of decedents, minors, or incompetents, § 1332(c)(2) considers only the citizenship of those represented, not the fiduciary's citizenship. On the other hand, § 1332(c)(2) does not apply to class action litigation; courts determine the citizenship of the class by looking only at the citizenship of the named class representatives.

III. DETERMINING WHETHER THE REQUIRED AMOUNT IN CONTROVERSY EXISTS

Section 1332 also requires that diversity and alienage cases involve an amount in controversy exceeding $75,000, not counting interest on the claim or recoverable costs of litigation. The amount-in-controversy requirement serves a docket-control function, limiting the number of cases in federal court and ensuring that federal courts not become small-claims tribunals. The amount the plaintiff claims controls unless it is clear to a legal certainty that she cannot recover more than $75,000. That is extraordinarily difficult to show unless there is some legal limit on the amount recoverable.

To determine the amount in controversy, courts aggregate all claims asserted by a single plaintiff against a single defendant, even if the claims are unrelated legally or factually. Aggregation does not occur if there are multiple plaintiffs or defendants. On the other hand, claims involving joint liability or joint rights are assessed by viewing the total value of the claim, regardless of how many parties there are.

> **Example:** A plaintiff suing joint obligors under a contract for $100,000 satisfies the amount-in-controversy requirement. The court does not divide the amount of the action by the number of obligors.

Claims for equitable relief present special problems. Most courts consider such claims from the plaintiff's viewpoint, and uphold jurisdiction if the defendant's behavior that equitable relief would modify harms the plaintiff by more than $75,000. Other courts consider the matter from the defendant's viewpoint; if it would cost the defendant more than $75,000 to comply with the equitable decree sought, that satisfies the requirement.

IV. EXCEPTIONS TO DIVERSITY AND ALIENAGE JURISDICTION

Even if a diversity-of-citizenship or alienage case satisfies § 1332's requirements, federal courts have long refused to entertain domestic relations (divorce, alimony, or child custody) cases or to probate decedents' estates. Ecclesiastical, not common-law, courts historically heard such cases, so they are not within § 1332's grant of jurisdiction over "civil actions."

Section 1359 prohibits jurisdiction in cases involving collusive joinder of parties to create subject-matter jurisdiction. (It says nothing, however, about joinder of parties to *defeat* diversity jurisdiction.) Cases involving assignments of claims often fall under this section. If the plaintiff-assignee of a claim is merely a collection agent for the assignor, without any real interest in the case, § 1359 directs courts to ignore the assignment and to consider only the assignor's citizenship. That precludes a would-be plaintiff from creating diversity jurisdiction by assigning her claim to someone diverse from the defendant.

■ CHAPTER VI: SUPPLEMENTAL JURISDICTION

I. POLICY ISSUES

Supplemental jurisdiction permits federal courts to hear claims that do not qualify for diversity, alienage, federal-question, or any other stand-alone form of federal subject-matter jurisdiction. Courts have supplemental jurisdiction only if the supplemental claim is so closely related to a claim over which there is subject-matter jurisdiction that the claims are part of the same overall controversy. Supplemental jurisdiction is discretionary, and courts may refuse to exercise it in narrow circumstances Congress has spelled out in 28 U.S.C. § 1367.

II. HISTORICAL DEVELOPMENT OF SUPPLEMENTAL JURISDICTION

Federal courts long recognized that they could entertain claims that were closely related to a claim that qualified for subject-matter jurisdiction, even when that other claim standing alone lacked any independent basis of subject-matter jurisdiction. In cases antedating 1990, courts referred to "pendent" and "ancillary" jurisdiction. *United Mine Workers v. Gibbs*, 383 U.S. 715 (1966), is the leading statement of the constitutional authority to exercise those forms of jurisdiction, holding that a federal court had power to hear claims that shared a "common nucleus of operative fact" with a jurisdiction-invoking claim because the claims constitute "one constitutional case" within the meaning of Article III, § 2.

III. THE SUPPLEMENTAL-JURISDICTION STATUTE

In 1990, Congress substantially—but not completely—codified *Gibbs* in § 1367 and substituted the term "supplemental jurisdiction" for "pendent" and "ancillary" jurisdiction. Congress enacted § 1367 in reaction to the unfortunate result and some loose language in *Finley v. United States*, 490 U.S. 545 (1989). In addition to overruling *Finley*, the statute purported to codify the entire areas of pendent and ancillary jurisdiction as they existed before *Finley*.

Section 1367 suffers in some ways from poor drafting and unanticipated consequences. Section 1367(a) grants supplemental jurisdiction to the full extent of the Constitution, clearly embodying *Gibbs*'s common-nucleus standard. The last sentence of that subsection makes clear that the grant applies even to claims involving separate parties (known as "pendent parties") from those against whom the initial, jurisdiction-invoking claim lies.

Section 1367(b) carves out exceptions from the grant of supplemental jurisdiction, but only in pure § 1332 diversity or alienage cases. The exceptions preserve the complete-diversity rule and pre-*Finley* limits of pendent and ancillary jurisdiction. Section 1367(b) prohibits supplemental jurisdiction over claims asserted (1) by plaintiffs joined under Federal Rule 19, (2) by plaintiffs seeking to intervene under Federal Rule 24, *and* (3) by plaintiffs against parties joined under Federal Rules 14, 19, 20, or 24.

Section 1367(c) lists four discretionary factors that may allow a court refuse to exercise supplemental jurisdiction. *Gibbs* discussed the discretionary nature of then-pendent and ancillary (now supplemental) jurisdiction and suggested factors counseling against its exercise. Section 1367(c) codifies some of the *Gibbs* factors. For instance, if the federal court dismisses the federal-question claim early in proceedings, the court ordinarily will refuse to exercise supplemental jurisdiction over transactionally related state law claims. Discretion under *Gibbs* was broader than under § 1367; the statute makes exercising supplemental jurisdiction the default, with specified narrow limits on the court's discretion.

Section 1367(d) tolls the statute of limitations for thirty days for any claim invoking supplemental jurisdiction under § 1367(a) "and for any other claim in the same action that is voluntarily dismissed at the same time as or after the dismissal" of a claim invoking supplemental jurisdiction. The subsection also recognizes that state law may require a longer toll. *Jinks v. Richland County*, 538 U.S. 456 (2003), rejected a constitutional challenge to this subsection.

Whether § 1367 overturns the longstanding principle that each member of a diversity class action must claim more than $75,000 was in doubt for some time, generating a significant circuit split. *Exxon Mobil Corp. v. Allapattah Services, Inc.*, 545 U.S. 546 (2005), resolved the question. As long as at least one named plaintiff satisfies the amount-in-controversy requirement and the class satisfies the other diversity requirements, supplemental jurisdiction exists over claims of other class members (named or not) that would otherwise be too small.

■ CHAPTER VII: REMOVAL: A METHOD OF INVOKING JURISDICTION

I. GENERAL PRINCIPLES OF REMOVAL

Removal permits a defendant in a case filed in state court to switch the case to a federal court. It operates only in that direction: from state to federal court. If removal is improper, either procedurally or because the federal court lacks subject-matter jurisdiction, the federal court remands the case to state court. Thus, the combination of original jurisdiction statutes and removal statutes provide both the plaintiff and the defendant with a right to have a federal court decide appropriate cases. All parties-defendant in the state case must join in the notice of removal. And, obviously, a defendant may remove the case only if the case comes within some basis of federal subject-matter jurisdiction, such as diversity, alienage, or federal-question jurisdiction. ***N.B.*** "Removal" is not a type of jurisdiction; it is a procedural device that allows a defendant to invoke the jurisdiction of the federal court under some grant of jurisdiction, *e.g.* 28 U.S.C. §§ 1331, 1332, 1338. The general removal statute, 28 U.S.C. § 1441, does not vest jurisdiction in any federal court.

II. GRANTS OF REMOVAL

No constitutional provision mentions removal; it is purely statutory. Title 28, § 1441(a), which permits the defendant or defendants to remove a civil action qualifying for original jurisdiction, covers removal for most civil cases. All of the requirements for invoking federal jurisdiction as an original matter apply to removed cases as well. Thus, for example, because federal-question jurisdiction exists only for a plaintiff's claim that arises under federal law, removal of a federal-question case cannot rest on a federal defense or even a counterclaim arising under federal law.

Congress can deny removal even of cases that would otherwise arise under federal law and qualify for federal-question jurisdiction under 28 U.S.C. § 1331. It has done so in several particulars in 28 U.S.C. § 1445. For example, a case under the Federal Employers' Liability Act (FELA), which authorizes railroad employee negligence suits against employers, is not removable.

Section 1441 authorizes removal for diversity cases, but "only if none of the parties in interest properly joined and served as defendants is a citizen of the State in which such action is brought." Thus, cases in which the plaintiff could have invoked diversity jurisdiction if she had sued in federal court are not removable if any defendant is a forum citizen. This is in service of the underlying purpose of diversity jurisdiction: protecting *out-of-state* litigants from potential bias in state courts.

III. PROCEDURES FOR REMOVAL AND REMAND

Pursuant to 28 U.S.C. § 1446(a), the defendant wishing to remove files a "notice of removal," signed under Federal Rule 11, in the federal court. The notice must contain "a short and plain statement of the grounds for removal (note the parallel to Rule 8(a)(2)), together with a copy of all process, pleadings, and orders served upon [the defendant] in such action." Promptly after filing the notice of removal in federal court, the defendant must give written notice to all adverse parties and must file a copy of the notice with the clerk of the state court. Filing the copy of notice "shall effect removal and the State court shall proceed no further unless and until the case is remanded." 28 U.S.C. § 1446(d). In a civil case, the defendant must file the notice of removal in federal court within thirty days after her receipt, "through service or otherwise," of a copy of the initial pleading or within thirty days "after the service of summons upon the defendant if such initial pleading has then been filed in court and is not required to be served on the defendant, whichever period is shorter."

If the plaintiff believes removal was improper, she can move to remand to state court. She might do so either because the federal court lacks subject-matter jurisdiction or because of a procedural defect in the removal. If the motion to remand rests upon "any defect other than lack of subject-matter jurisdiction," the plaintiff must move to remand no later than thirty days after the defendant filed the notice of removal. 28 U.S.C. § 1447(c). In other words, defects in removal other than lack of subject-matter jurisdiction are waivable. Obviously, however, lack of federal subject-matter jurisdiction is not waivable, and the plaintiff (or the court on its own motion or even the defendant) may raise the issue at any time. If there is no federal subject-matter jurisdiction, the federal court must remand. 28 U.S.C. § 1447(c).

■ CHAPTER VIII: SUPREME-COURT JURISDICTION

I. CONSTITUTIONAL AND STATUTORY STRUCTURE

Under Article III, § 2, the Supreme Court shall have "original jurisdiction" over two kinds of cases: (1) those "affecting Ambassadors, other public Ministers and Consuls" and (2) those in which "a State shall be a party." Original jurisdiction is trial jurisdiction, so the Constitution allows the Supreme Court to try such cases. In all other cases falling with the judicial power of the United States, in Article III, § 2, paragraph 1, the Supreme Court "shall have appellate Jurisdiction. . . ." The Court's appellate jurisdiction extends over cases from the lower federal courts or from the highest court in each state that could hear a particular case (usually, but not always, the state's highest court).

II. ORIGINAL JURISDICTION

The Supreme Court has original jurisdiction over cases in which a state is a party. Congress has subdivided such cases; the Court's original jurisdiction is exclusive when the case is "between two or more states" (usually involving boundary disputes and water rights). 28 U.S.C. § 1251(a). Notwithstanding, the Court on occasion has refused to hear such cases—a *de facto* type of abstention that leaves the disputing states with no judicial forum. In other cases in which a state is a party, the Court's original jurisdiction is not exclusive. 28 U.S.C. § 1251(b). Thus, a federal district court can try such disputes, assuming, of course, that they otherwise qualify for subject-matter jurisdiction.

The Supreme Court also has original jurisdiction over cases involving ambassadors and other public ministers or consuls. It exercises this jurisdiction very rarely, not least because foreign ambassadors and public ministers (but not consuls) have diplomatic immunity from suit in the United States. The Court's original jurisdiction in such matters is not exclusive. A federal district court may hear them.

III. APPELLATE JURISDICTION

The Supreme Court has jurisdiction by writ of certiorari—an entirely discretionary review device—to review some final decisions of state courts. It is important to understand that § 1257 authorizes review only of a decision by the highest court of the state in which review was possible (not always the state's highest court). If review by that state court is discretionary, the case cannot go to the Supreme Court until a litigant has sought whatever discretionary state review exists. In addition, the Supreme Court can review only "final" judgments of the state court. The Court has recognized exceptions to this requirement and has great discretion in determining whether a judgment in which review is sought was final. Three kinds of state cases qualify for Supreme Court review: (1) cases raising constitutional challenges to a federal law, (2) cases challenging state law as repugnant to federal law (supremacy violations), or (3) cases claiming any title, right, privilege or immunity under federal law. 28 U.S.C. § 1257. In addition, the Court may review any decision of a federal court of appeals by certiorari or by certification from a circuit court of a particular question. 28 U.S.C. § 1254(1).

The Court has long held that it lacks authority to review state-court interpretations of state law. It is not clear whether the Constitution requires this rule, but it is clear in practice. A corollary to this principle refuses review if the state decision rests on "adequate and independent" state-law grounds. Thus, if the state decision rests upon both federal and non-federal substantive grounds, the Court cannot review if the non-federal ground, standing alone, fully supports the judgment. This ensures that the Supreme Court does not issue essentially advisory opinions on federal law. The burden rests on the state court to be clear that state, not federal, law, drives its decision.

If the state court refused to adjudicate a federal issue because the litigant failed to comply with a legitimate state procedural rule, the Court will rarely review the federal issue; the Court wants to avoid undermining legitimate state-court procedures. But the Court has recognized several circumstances in which a state procedural bar will not preclude appellate review. In *Henry v. Mississippi*, 379 U.S. 443 (1965), the Court seemed especially willing to ignore a state procedural rule and undertake appellate review, leading some to believe that it had markedly diluted the procedural bar to review of state decisions. More recent cases suggest otherwise.

■ CHAPTER IX: CONGRESSIONAL AND JUDICIAL RESTRICTIONS ON EXERCISING FEDERAL JURISDICTION

I. CONGRESSIONAL RESTRICTIONS

A. THE ANTI-INJUNCTION ACT

The Anti-Injunction Act, 28 U.S.C. § 2283, has existed in some form since 1793. Today, with three narrow exceptions, it prohibits a federal court from enjoining state-court proceedings, and the Supreme Court has recognized a fourth exception for cases the United States brings. If an exception applies, a party may seek an injunction from a federal court to enjoin other parties from litigating in state court. Though the original motivations for the statute are unclear, it is now understood to be a cornerstone of federalism aimed at avoiding unnecessary friction between state and federal courts. Because the statute generally prohibits injunctions of state court "proceedings," it does not apply if a federal court issues an injunction before any state action commences.

The Anti-Injunction Act limits a federal-court power to enjoin state-court proceedings. It does not apply to enjoining federal-court proceedings. Such an injunction does not implicate federalism concerns because it does not affect state courts. As a general rule, the federal district in which *in personam* litigation is pending may enjoin the litigants from proceeding in another federal district on the same or a related matter. A state court in which related *in personam* litigation is pending has no authority to enjoin proceedings in federal court, but a state court that has attached property (*rem* jurisdiction) may enjoin parties from proceeding in federal court concerning that property if that would interfere with state-court jurisdiction.

First, Congress may "expressly authorize" injunctions against state-court proceedings. There are several examples, including statutory interpleader under 28 U.S.C. § 2361. The Supreme Court also recognized an exception for cases under 42 U.S.C. § 1983 as expressly authorized *Mitchum v. Foster*, 407 U.S. 225 (1972), notwithstanding the statute's complete silence about whether federal courts should be able to enjoin state proceedings. Second, federal courts may issue injunctions against state-court proceedings when "necessary in aid of [federal] jurisdiction." The Court has interpreted this exception quite narrowly: it generally applies only in cases involving the federal court's seizure of property as the basis for jurisdiction over the defendant (*rem* jurisdiction). Third, to "protect or effectuate" federal judgments, federal courts may enjoin parties from proceeding in state court. This "relitigation" exception is also narrow. Ordinarily, the Court prefers litigants to rely on claim or issue preclusion, as appropriate. Congress added the relitigation exception in 1948 to overrule a particular case.

B. THE JOHNSON ACT OF 1934

The Johnson Act forbids district courts sitting in diversity cases from interfering with public utility rates as long as they do not interfere with interstate commerce and include procedures for "plain, speedy, and efficient" remedies in the state courts.

C. THE TAX INJUNCTION ACT OF 1937

This statute forbids district courts from interfering with assessment, levy, or collection of state taxes provided that "a plain, speedy, and efficient remedy" is available in the state courts.

II. JUDICIAL RESTRICTIONS: ABSTENTION

A. INTRODUCTION

Since at least 1888, federal courts have on occasion declined to exercise subject-matter jurisdiction that they clearly have. There are five distinct categories of abstention. Four of them get little use, but *Younger v. Harris* abstention is frequent and widespread. Despite a strong argument that federal courts have no authority to abstain when they have subject-matter jurisdiction, abstention doctrines exist but do not automatically apply.

B. SOURCES OF THE ABSTENTION DOCTRINES

Abstention is a generic term referring to judge-made (*i.e.* common-law) doctrines allowing federal courts to refuse to exercise subject-matter jurisdiction. Mainly, considerations of federalism justify abstention and counsel deference to state decision-making bodies in circumstances in which federal court involvement might disrupt or show lack of respect for state governments. Each abstention doctrine has different requirements, justifications, and procedures.

C. COMPARATIVE ASPECTS OF THE DIFFERENT FORMS OF ABSTENTION

Four of the doctrines carry the name of the case that introduced them; hence, we have *Pullman*, *Burford*, *Thibodaux*, and *Colorado River* abstention. *Younger* abstention is the outlier; it originated in 1888 in *In re Sawyer* but saw little use until *Younger v. Harris* in 1971, which was the doctrine's Great Leap Forward. It is critically important to keep the criteria and justifications for each doctrine distinct in your mind. That is not always easy, because some cases overlap more than one type of abstention.

D. *PULLMAN* ABSTENTION

1. Substantive requirements

The Supreme Court ordered abstention in *Railroad Commission of Texas v. Pullman*, 312 U.S. 496 (1941). Plaintiffs challenged a state-agency order as racially discriminatory. There was a serious question as to whether state law gave the agency authority to enter the order. If it did, there was a serious constitutional issue. If it did not, there was no constitutional issue. In such circumstances—when the federal court could avoid having to decide a constitutional issue if the state's courts interpreted unclear state law in a particular way—the Court held that federal courts should give the state courts an opportunity to construe the state law. The federal court stays proceedings while the litigants go to state court for a definitive interpretation of the state-law issue. If the party seeking abstention properly reserves the federal constitutional issue for the federal court, the litigation can return to federal court for ultimate determination if the state-court judgment leaves the constitutional issue in place. State statutes allowing federal courts to certify questions of state law to the state's highest court for resolution have greatly reduced *Pullman* abstention's utility.

2. Procedural Aspects

Pullman abstention requires the federal court to stay its proceedings while the parties secure a definitive state-court interpretation of state law. The procedure is cumbersome, requiring the party seeking the state interpretation preserve his right to return to the federal court for determination of federal constitutional issues. In many states, a federal court may "certify" an issue of state law to the state's highest court for interpretation. This streamlines *Pullman* abstention considerably by obviating the need for a separate state-court action. Under the remaining abstention doctrines, the federal court dismisses the case. State courts then decide the federal issues, subject only to review by the United States Supreme Court.

E. *BURFORD* ABSTENTION

Burford v. Sun Oil Co., 319 U.S. 315 (1943), counsels that a federal court should abstain when a state has established a complex regulatory scheme for dealing with an issue of local import. Abstention avoids federal disruption of state efforts to maintain coherent policy for the underlying substantive area. *Burford* held that a federal court should not intervene in allocating oil drilling rights in Texas, which were subject to extensive state regulation and oversight. Mere existence of a state mechanism for dealing with an important local issue does not usually require abstention. The court must determine whether federal resolution of the claim asserted would enmesh the federal court into a complex area of state mechanisms for decision and review. If the federal court abstains under *Burford*, it dismisses the case rather than staying the federal proceedings as under *Pullman*.

F. *THIBODAUX* ABSTENTION

The basis and scope of this form of abstention is unclear. The Supreme Court reached apparently opposite results in two cases on the same day—*Louisiana Power & Light Co. v. City of Thibodaux*, 360 U.S. 25 (1959), and *County of Allegheny v. Frank Mashuda Co.*, 360 U.S. 185 (1959). Each involved a challenge to a municipality's exercise of eminent domain. *Thibodaux* upheld abstention, emphasizing the "special nature of eminent domain proceedings," which it saw as intimately involved with a "sovereign prerogative," and noting (reminiscent of *Pullman* abstention) that the state law was not clear. In *Frank Mashuda*, however, the Court rejected abstention, saying that eminent domain—at least where the state law is clear—does not involve any particular "sovereign prerogative."

G. *YOUNGER* ABSTENTION: "OUR FEDERALISM"

"Our Federalism," which *Younger v. Harris*, 401 U.S. 37 (1971), espoused, restricts the power of federal courts similarly to the Anti-Injunction Act. It reflects not only comity, but also a long-followed maxim that a court of equity will not act if a party has an adequate remedy at law. Thus, for example, a federal court should not issue an injunction or declaratory relief concerning an ongoing state criminal judicial proceeding if the criminal defendant can raise constitutional challenges in the state-court defense. Because the Anti-Injunction Act does not apply to cases brought in federal court under 42 U.S.C. § 1983, restriction on federal judicial power in such cases comes only from "Our Federalism." Since *Younger*, the Supreme Court has also applied the doctrine to civil proceedings "closely in aid of criminal statutes," civil proceedings concerning other intense state interests, some administrative proceedings, some executive actions, and some purely civil proceedings between private parties, although most recently it seems to have limited the doctrine.

H. *COLORADO RIVER* ABSTENTION

Unlike other forms of abstention, this one is not rooted in a concern for federalism. Rather, it rests upon "wise judicial administration" and a desire to avoid overlapping litigation in federal and state courts. It is thus potentially the most far-reaching and controversial type of abstention. *Colorado River Water Conservation District v. United States*, 424 U.S. 800 (1976), upheld dismissal of a federal case that concerned water allocation already the subject of litigation in state court. It identified four relevant abstention factors: (1) whether either the federal or state court had assumed jurisdiction over property; (2) geographical inconvenience of the federal forum, (3) the desirability of avoiding piecemeal litigation, and (4) the sequence in which the federal and state courts obtained jurisdiction. The Court emphasized that abstention on the grounds of "wise judicial administration" was extraordinary, though many commentators thought the facts were not extraordinary. At first glance, *Colorado River* abstention may seem to resemble *Burford* abstention, but note that the criteria are different, though they may produce similar results.

■ CHAPTER X: CLAIM AND ISSUE PRECLUSION IN THE FEDERAL SYSTEM

I. INTRODUCTION

Claim and issue preclusion (a/k/a res judicata and collateral estoppel, respectively) operate in the federal system much as you learned in Civil Procedure. Both limit relitigation, either of claims or particular issues. The formal difference is that the federal courts often are dealing with successor cases to actions originally litigated in a state court. Of course, on the state-court level, courts frequently confront prior judgments from *other* state-court systems. In such situations, the Full Faith and Credit Clause, art. IV, § 1, dictates how state courts must handle such problems, but the Clause does not apply to the federal government. Congress addressed that problem in the Full Faith and Credit Act, 28.U.S.C. § 1738, which essentially parallels the command of the constitutional provision.

II. FULL FAITH AND CREDIT AND RELATED COMMON-LAW DOCTRINES

In Civil Procedure, you studied claim and issue preclusion. These doctrines often prevent parties from relitigating claims or some issues in subsequent cases. The states and the federal government have their own principles of claim and issue preclusion. The question here is whose law of claim or issue preclusion applies to determine a judgment's preclusive effect. The issue becomes complicated in our federal system, because different judicial systems—federal/state or state/state—may end up adjudicating sequential cases. The Full Faith and Credit Clause (art. IV, § 1), the Full Faith and Credit Statute (28 U.S.C. § 1738), and common law all address this area.

Article IV, § 1, provides, in part, that "Full Faith and Credit shall be given in each State to the . . . judicial Proceedings of every other State." This provision applies only to cases in state courts, and so does not restrict federal courts. The requirement that the state courts in one state accord "full faith and credit" to the judgment of the courts of another state (Forum 2) generally means that the court of the second state must apply the claim and issue preclusion rules of the state that entered the judgment in the first case (F1).

The Full Faith and Credit Act, provides, in part, that "judicial proceedings" of a "State, Territory, or Possession of the United States" shall have "the same full faith and credit in every court within the United States and its Territories and Possessions as they have by law or usage in the courts of each State, Territory, or Possession from which they are taken." This provision applies not only to the state-to-state situation Article IV addresses, but also to situations where a state court enters the first judgment and the second case is pending in a federal court.

■ CHAPTER XI: FEDERAL COMMON LAW

I. THE DIFFERENCVE BETWEEN FEDERAL COMMON LAW AND "FEDERAL GENERAL COMMON LAW"

Erie Railroad v. Tompkins, 304 U.S. 64 (1938), requires that federal courts exercising diversity jurisdiction often must apply state substantive law. It established that there is no "federal *general* common law"—common law in areas the Constitution does not assign to the federal government. Federal common law often exists in areas—most found in art. I, § 8—where there is constitutional authorization for the federal government to act.

II. ENGLISH COMMON LAW, COMMON-LAW METHOD, AND THE CONSTITUTION

Common-law judges did not see themselves as *making* law. The common law was an abstract, universally true collection of rational legal principles not of human formulation, a kind of natural law. Common-law judges "discovered" these principles; they did not formulate them. The United States inherited this common-law method.

III. COMMON LAW IN THE UNITED STATES, 1789 to 1938

Until 1938, the English method ruled. *Swift v. Tyson*, 41 U.S. (1 Pet.) 1 (1842), confirmed that federal judges were just as able to discover common-law principles as state judges and therefore need not follow state judges' opinions on common law. *Swift* interpreted the Rules of Decision Act's reference to the "laws of the several states" to exclude state common law, leaving federal judges free to make their own common-law discoveries.

IV. *ERIE* AND THE JURISPRUDENTIAL SHIFT

Erie overruled *Swift*, requiring federal courts to apply state common law in areas where the Constitution grants no power to the federal government, such as property and torts, both involved in *Erie*. *Swift*'s doctrine was unconstitutional because it purported to allow federal courts to create federal common law in the absence of any constitutional grant of federal power. *Erie* did *not* say there was no federal common law at all; it merely implicitly limited it to areas in which the Constitution does create federal power. *Erie* also rejected natural-law theory, upon which *Swift* rested, in favor of legal positivism—the idea that all law comes from a government, whether through the legislative, executive, or judicial process.

V. HOW, WHEN, AND WHY FEDERAL COMMON LAW EXISTS

Federal common law does exist. *Clearfield Trust Co. v. United States*, 318 U.S. 363 (1943), applied federal common law to an issue about rights and duties that flow from banks' handling federal-government checks. The Court noted the Constitution does authorize disbursement of federal funds, thus distinguishing *Erie*. More generally, federal common law exists to protect important federal interests; the more important the interest, the more likely the federal courts are to create federal common law if Congress has not spoken. *Erie* stands for the proposition that the Constitution, by implicit exclusion, declares that there are areas of law in which the federal government cannot have any interest.

VI. DECIDING WHETHER TO CREATE FEDERAL COMMON LAW: THE EVOLVING PROCESS

Federal courts create federal common law in four ways: (1) spontaneous generation, (2) construing a jurisdictional grant to be an implicit congressional direction to create common law, (3) recognizing private rights of action in constitutional provisions and statutes that create individual rights, and (4) filling in statutory interstices. There must be an underlying dominant federal interest that justifies creating federal common law; that principle undergirds all four techniques. That interest may not always require the federal common law to be different from the state law that would otherwise apply, so the federal courts often adopt state law as the content of federal common law. This permits the federal courts to vary from state law if applying state law would produce results incompatible with the dominant federal interest.

■ CHAPTER XII: STATE COURTS AND FEDERAL POWER

I. THE ROLE OF THE STATE COURTS IN THE FEDERAL SYSTEM

The Founders clearly envisioned that state courts would play a major role in adjudicating and enforcing federal law. The fact that the Constitution did not mandate creating lower federal courts indicates that the Framers understood that state courts would be involved. Moreover, though Congress has always provided lower federal courts, it did not vest them with long lasting general federal-question jurisdiction until 1875. The Supremacy Clause compels the state courts to enforce federal law.

II. STATE-COURT POWER TO ADJUDICATE FEDERAL MATTERS

When Congress creates a right and provides non-exclusive federal jurisdiction to enforce it, courts generally will presume that state and federal courts have concurrent jurisdiction. Occasionally, state courts adjudicate issues that appear to fall within the exclusive jurisdiction of federal courts, as when the exclusive federal matter enters the case by way of defense in a state-court proceeding. Be sure to remember that, with the exception of habeas corpus, the inferior federal courts have no appellate jurisdiction with respect to state-court judgments; federal review of state-court judgments occurs only in the United States Supreme Court. Habeas itself is not an actual appeal; the prisoner commences new litigation in the federal district court. Nomenclature aside, the federal habeas court is reviewing what the state courts did in the prisoner's case.

III. STATE COURTS' OBLIGATION TO ADJUDICATE FEDERAL CLAIMS

When Congress creates a claim and does not mandate exclusive federal jurisdiction, a state court must adjudicate the claim unless the state has a valid excuse not to do so. The valid-excuse doctrine is narrow, but murky, and there are few examples of its application. One is when the state court has limited subject-matter jurisdiction (for example, as to the amount in controversy) and simply could not hear the federal claim even if it were a state claim. Another example is if the state courts would dismiss a state-law claim involving the same situation under the doctrine of *forum non conveniens*. In some circumstances, achieving congressional goals may require state courts to apply federal procedural provisions, such as the requirement of a jury trial in Federal Employers' Liability Act cases. The one thing state courts clearly cannot do is discriminate against federal claims, refusing to adjudicate them while remaining open to parallel claims under state law.

IV. STATE-COURT POWER TO CONTROL FEDERAL OFFICERS

State courts cannot issue writs of habeas corpus against federal officers. *In re Tarble*, 80 U.S. (13 Wall.) 397 (1871) (state court without power to order United States Army officer to release enlisted man). Similarly, state courts cannot issue mandamus to a federal officer. The Supreme Court has not determined whether a state court may enjoin a federal officer. By statute, a federal officer sued in her personal or official capacity for an act under color of office may remove to federal court.

■ CHAPTER XIII: STATE SOVEREIGN IMMUNITY AND THE ELEVENTH AMENDMENT

I. BACKGROUND AND HISTORY OF THE ELEVENTH AMENDMENT

Article III, § 2, which lists the classes of cases falling within the federal judicial power, includes cases "between a State and Citizens of another State." Though some Framers felt that this clause did not envision cases in which a state would be defendant, *Chisholm v. Georgia*, 2 U.S. (2 Dall.) 419 (1793), upheld federal jurisdiction in such a case. The decision led to public uproar and to speedy ratification of the Eleventh Amendment, which removes federal judicial power over cases "commenced or prosecuted against one of the United States by Citizens of another State, or by Citizens of Subjects of any Foreign State." Although the Amendment sounds like it addresses only diversity jurisdiction, the Supreme Court interprets it to bar cases by a citizen against her own state as well—federal-question cases. For generations, the Supreme Court treated the Eleventh Amendment as ensuring that a state could not be held liable in federal court. More recently, however, the court has emphasized a broader notion of sovereign immunity—not only from damages liability, but also from being a defendant in federal courts at all.

II. INTERPRETING THE ELEVENTH AMENDMENT

The Eleventh Amendment's language is narrow, but the Supreme Court has interpreted it broadly. On its face, it only bars suits against a state by citizens of another state or of a foreign country, but the Court now interprets it to bar suits by any individual against a state, irrespective of citizenship or the ground of subject-matter jurisdiction. It *may* also bar suits against Puerto Rico and other territories, though they are not states; the Court at least has recognized a common-law immunity for territorial governments that Congress apparently cannot overcome by statute. It also bars suits by Indian tribes and municipalities. On the other hand, it does not bar suits by the United States against a state. Although it appears not to apply to suits brought against a state in state court, *Alden v. Maine*, 527 U.S. 706 (1999), disallowing a state-court action against a state relied in part on the Eleventh Amendment as illuminating the states' retention of sovereign immunity even in the face of federal legislation if the Court decides the action is not "consistent with the constitutional sovereignty of the state."

Though the Eleventh Amendment sounds jurisdictional, the Supreme Court has sent conflicting signals. If the defense were jurisdictional, a court would have to raise it *sua sponte*, and the state could not waive it. The Court has permitted states to raise the issue at any time, even for the first time on appeal. That makes the defense appear jurisdictional. On the other hand, the Court has not required appellate courts to raise the issue *sua sponte*, and states can waive the defense. So the Amendment's jurisdictional character is not clear, and the Court has hedged, describing it as "sufficiently partak[ing] of the nature of a jurisdictional bar so that it need not be raised in the trial court."

The Court has interpreted "state" broadly. The Eleventh Amendment bars suits in federal court in which a state is the named defendant. Moreover, it bars many cases in which a state is the real party in interest, which requires the court to determine the essential nature and effect of the litigation to determine if it is truly against a state. Thus, a claim against an officer may be one against the state, and thus barred. For many years, the Court considered the state to be the real party in interest if the suit sought recovery from the state treasury. The Court has refined that test, however, and seems now to emphasize avoiding any legal liability for the state, rather than whether the plaintiff seeks to collect from the state treasury. The Court also recently assumed without deciding that Puerto Rico, a territory rather than a state, has a common-law immunity that Congress cannot displace except with a super-strong clear statement in a statute.

III. AVOIDING THE ELEVENTH AMENDMENT

Much of the important case law concerning the Eleventh Amendment addresses methods by which plaintiffs may avoid it. *Ex parte Young*, 209 U.S. 123 (1908), provides an important avenue for plaintiffs challenging state action. Plaintiff sought an injunction prohibiting a state attorney general from enforcing a state law plaintiff alleged was unconstitutional. The injunction would have prevented the state from enforcing the statute. Thus, it seemed to be a case against the state, which the Eleventh Amendment ordinarily bars. The Court allowed relief, but its reasoning seemed strained: because the state officer acted illegally, he lost Eleventh Amendment immunity; the state could not authorize him to violate the Constitution. Since he did not act for the state, the case was against a private individual for Eleventh Amendment purposes, and could proceed. The reasoning is difficult: the state officer's allegedly illegal acts *are not* state action for Eleventh Amendment purposes but *are* state action for purposes of determining whether there was a constitutional-rights violation under the Fourteenth Amendment or some other constitutional provision.

Ex parte Young remains vital. Generally, it applies if: (1) the state officer sued has a duty to enforce the challenged state law, and (2) the state law or action violates federal law, thus offending the Supremacy Clause, unless federal law provides such intricate remedies that the Court infers that Congress did not intend to allow suit under *Ex parte Young*. In addition, the theory is not available if the action would interfere with special state sovereignty interests, such as those implicated by quiet-title actions concerning real property.

Ex parte Young cannot support a claim for damages against the state. It permits only equitable relief—injunction or declaratory judgment—that is prospective. The relief must be forward-looking rather than compensatory. Prospective relief may entail an impact on the state treasury. Some Justices and commentators have criticized this prospective/retrospective distinction, but it remains.

A state may waive Eleventh Amendment protection, but not easily. Because it is a constitutional protection, however, the Court is quite reluctant to infer it. Waiver may result from express provisions of state law or from express consent to suit in federal court. A state's consent to suit in "courts" does not constitute a waiver of Eleventh Amendment immunity to suit in a federal court. A state may waive its Eleventh Amendment immunity by litigation conduct, such as by removing a case from state to federal court.

Sometimes Congress can abrogate the states' Eleventh Amendment protection under the authority of another constitutional provision. The critical question is which constitutional provisions permit it. Congress can override the Eleventh Amendment through legislation passed under § 5 of the Fourteenth Amendment. Though the Supreme Court once allowed congressional abrogation under the Article I's Commerce Clause, it has now, with one exception, apparently limited the legislative power to enforcement of constitutional provisions postdating the Eleventh Amendment. *Seminole Tribe of Florida v. Florida*, 517 U.S. 44 (1996). Congress cannot abrogate Eleventh Amendment protection by legislating under Article I, except for bankruptcy matters. It is not always easy, however, to determine whether Congress has acted under § 5 of the Fourteenth Amendment, and even when it clearly has, the Court has imposed flexible (some might say infinitely malleable) limitations on the abrogation power, fastening on the Fourteenth Amendment's reference to "appropriate legislation."

The Court once allowed Congress to abrogate Eleventh Amendment protection indirectly, on a theory of constructive waiver. The notion was that a state waived its immunity by participating in federal programs after Congress conditioned such participation upon amenability to suit in federal court. *Edelman v. Jordan*, 415 U.S. 651 (1974), rejected that approach.

■ CHAPTER XIV: ACTIONS TO VINDICATE FEDERAL CIVIL RIGHTS

I. PRINCIPAL CIVIL RIGHTS STATUTES

Following ratification of the Thirteenth, Fourteenth, and Fifteenth Amendments, Congress enacted statutes to enforce federal civil rights. Some of these Reconstruction-era statutes are quite specific. In addition, the twentieth-century Congresses passed important civil rights statutes, including the Civil Rights Act of 1964 and the Voting Rights Act of 1965. The main focus of study here, however, is the broad Reconstruction-era statute now codified at 42 U.S.C. § 1983 (and often referred to as "the" Civil Rights Statute), which provides that "every person" acting "under color" of state law who "subjects, or causes to be subjected" a citizen of the United States or a person within the United States to "deprivation of any rights, privileges, or immunity secured by the Constitution and laws" shall be liable in civil suit.

II. LITIGATION UNDER § 1983

Though Congress passed § 1983 shortly after the Civil War, it saw little use until 1961, when the Court decided *Monroe v. Pape*, 365 U.S. 167 (1961), upholding the right to sue municipal police officers who violated plaintiff's Fourth Amendment rights for damages. *Monroe* established two major points. First, a § 1983 plaintiff need not exhaust any state remedies (such as tort suits or administrative claims) before suing in federal court. Second, the police officers' actions were "under color" of state law, as required by § 1983, even though the actions also violated state law and were therefore unauthorized.

As noted, the defendant must act "under color" of state law. *Monroe v. Pape* established that the "under color" requirement looks to whether the defendant acted under some badge of authority to enforce state law, rather than to whether state law authorized the actions. Private actors are subject to suit under § 1983 if they act under color of state law, as, for example, if they engage in joint activity with state actors to deprive the plaintiff of federal rights.

The defendant in a § 1983 case must be a "person." This does not include a state or state officers sued in their official capacities, but it does include officers sued in their personal capacities. The Supreme Court originally said a municipality was not a § 1983 "person," but today it is clear that it is for actions where some municipal policy or custom has violated someone's federal rights. *Monell v. Dept. of Social Servs.*, 436 U.S. 658 (1978). However, a municipality is not liable on a *respondeat-superior* theory, nor is it subject to punitive damages.

Section 1983 creates no substantive rights. Instead, it provides a right of action for vindicating federal "rights, privileges, or immunities." Not all constitutional provisions are enforceable through § 1983. A statute is enforceable under § 1983 only if the statute creates "an unambiguously conferred right" for enforcement. *Gonzaga University v. Doe*, 536 U.S. 273 (2002). The Supreme Court has likened this to the inquiry into whether a statute creates a private right of action.

III. IMMUNITY FOR VIOLATING INDIVIDUALS' CONSTITUTIONAL RIGHTS

Section 1983 says nothing about immunity, but the Supreme Court has consistently recognized that certain individuals may be immune not just from liability, but even from litigation under § 1983. Immunity generally attaches only to suits for damages; a defendant immune from a damages action may not be immune to litigation for equitable relief. Some state actors have absolute immunity, which the Court thinks necessary to permit them to perform their functions with requisite boldness. For example, judges simply cannot be sued for damages under § 1983 for acts taken in their *judicial* (but not an *administrative*) capacity, although they may be liable for attorney's fees under 42 U.S.C. § 1988. Similarly, prosecutors are absolutely immune for damages claims concerning the performance of traditional prosecutorial functions. Legislators enjoy absolute immunity for acts taken within the sphere of legitimate legislative activity.

Other officers, such as governors, mayors, and police officers, enjoy only "qualified" immunity. That is, they are not liable for damages unless they acted contrary to clearly established law of which a reasonable official would have known at the time of the conduct.

IV. DEPRIVATIONS UNDER COLOR OF FEDERAL LAW: *BIVENS* CLAIMS

Section 1983 does not apply to persons acting under color of federal law, and there is no analog statute allowing suit against federal actors. But *Jacobs v. United States*, 290 U.S. 13, 16 (1933), unanimously recognized an action directly under the Fifth

Amendment, saying, "Statutory recognition was not necessary." *Jacobs* does not stand alone. In 1954, the Court unanimously recognized a private right of action in *Bolling v. Sharpe*, 347 U.S. 497 (1954), a companion case to the better known *Brown v. Board of Education*, 347 U.S. 483 (1954). *Bolling* made no reference to a private right of action; it simply held that the plaintiff class could sue for relief under the Fifth Amendment. (Section 1983 obviously did not apply because the District of Columbia is an organ of the federal government. *Id.* at 500.)

Bivens v. Six Unknown Named Agents of Federal Bureau of Narcotics, 403 U.S. 388 (1971), recognized a right of action to seek damages from federal officers for deprivation of Fourth Amendment rights. Some think *Bivens* raises separation-of-powers issues, arguing that it is Congress's role, not the courts', to provide rights of action to enforce constitutional guarantees. A *Bivens* claim lies against individual actors in their personal capacity. The Court also allowed actions under the Fifth (1979) and Eighth (1980) Amendments, but more recently has been chary of going further, inferring in several cases that Congress would disapprove of private actions. Most recently, the Court has appeared to rue those three precedents, not overtly overruling them, but describing recognizing private rights of action in constitutional provisions as " 'disfavored' judicial activity." Generally, a plaintiff asserting a *Bivens* claim need not exhaust administrative remedies. Immunities apply in *Bivens* litigation along the same lines as in § 1983 cases.

Since 1980, the Court has turned its back on judicial recognition of private claims in any constitutional provision, characterizing judicial recognition of private rights of action to enforce rights the Bill of Rights appears to guarantee, characterizing it as "disfavored judicial activity." The final nail in the coffin came in *Egbert v. Boulé*, 596 U.S. 482 (2022), which appears to overrule *sub silentio Jacobs* (1933), *Bolling* (1954), *Bivens* (1971), *Davis v. Passman* (1979), and *Carlson v. Green* (1980).

V. THE CIVIL-RIGHTS REMOVAL STATUTE

The civil-rights removal statute, 28 U.S.C. § 1343, has its roots in Reconstruction. It permits removal of a case from state to federal court, *inter alia*, by a defendant who "is denied or cannot enforce in the courts of such state a right under any law providing for the equal civil rights of citizens of the United States." In this and other provisions, the statute permits removal on a prediction of unconstitutional behavior by a state court, which obviously creates potential for friction between the federal and state court systems. Not surprisingly, the courts interpret the statute narrowly, probably to minimize damage to parity.

■ CHAPTER XV: FEDERAL HABEAS CORPUS

I. BACKGROUND, ORIGINS OF THE WRIT, AND OVERVIEW OF CURRENT STATUTES

The writ of habeas corpus ("the Great Writ") permits a federal court to order someone's release from government custody. Release occurs only if the incarceration violates federal (usually constitutional) law. The writ developed in England and is part of our constitutional heritage; Article I, § 9 provides that the privilege of the writ "shall not be suspended, unless when in cases of rebellion or invasion the public safety may require it." Several provisions of the Judicial Code relate to federal habeas corpus. Congress imposed extensive restrictions on habeas corpus in the Antiterrorism and Effective Death Penalty Act of 1996 (AEDPA), and the Court has restricted it further in the intervening years.

II. HABEAS CORPUS FOR STATE PRISONERS

Title 28 U.S.C. § 2254 governs issuance of the writ of habeas corpus for persons in state custody. Obviously, this use of habeas—by which a federal court reviews the legality of a person's confinement by state authorities—raises profound questions of federalism. There is an exhaustion requirement for state prisoners seeking federal habeas. The petitioner must either have exhausted state-court remedies or demonstrate that no corrective state process is available. Exhaustion requires the state prisoner to present her federal argument to the highest available state court once, either on appeal or collateral attack. The exhaustion requirement means that the federal court reviews the constitutionality of incarceration after the state courts have decided issues of fact. AEDPA makes state fact-finding presumptively correct.

Habeas is a vehicle for reviewing the legality of a state prisoner's conviction and deprivation of liberty. But habeas corpus is not available for every constitutional violation. *Stone v. Powell*, 428 U.S. 465 (1976), held that a federal habeas court cannot review a state prisoner's claim that the state obtained evidence against him in violation of the Fourth Amendment, so that the state trial court should have excluded it. The state court had provided the prisoner an opportunity for full and fair consideration of the claimed illegal seizure. Despite concern that *Stone* would lead to other areas in which a state prisoner could not use federal habeas, the Court has refused to expand it beyond Fourth Amendment cases.

The AEDPA imposes a one-year limitations period (from the conclusion of state direct appeals and collateral attack at the state level) on an application by a state prisoner for federal habeas relief. It also imposes important restrictions on successive applications for habeas relief by state prisoners. Repeat applications are improper without authorization of the court of appeals, and there are clear waiver provisions for claims not appearing in a previous application.

III. "ABORTIVE STATE PROCEEDINGS"—THE PROBLEM OF ADEQUATE AND INDEPENDENT STATE GROUNDS

Some state prisoners seeking federal habeas corpus relief lost in state proceedings because they failed to comply with procedural rules. Such cases involve "abortive state proceedings." The federal habeas court's power to address the merits in such matters has been a difficult issue. Initially, the Supreme Court held that procedural default in state court barred federal habeas review, on much the same basis that the Supreme Court refuses to entertain appeals in cases in which there is an adequate and independent state ground for decision. Later, the Court held that a state prisoner's failure to comply with state procedural requirements did not preclude federal habeas unless the prisoner had deliberately by-passed state judicial remedies. *Fay v. Noia*, 372 U.S. 391 (1963).

The Court has turned away from *Noia*. *Wainwright v. Sykes*, 433 U.S. 72 (1977), held that the state prisoner's failure to raise a contemporaneous objection to admission of a confession at his criminal trial precluded federal habeas review, even though his failure was not a deliberate by-pass of a state judicial remedy. Today a petitioner must establish cause for his failure to object *and* prejudice from the admission of the evidence for a federal court consider the issue in a habeas proceeding.

IV. HABEAS CORPUS FOR FEDERAL PRISONERS

Persons in the custody of the federal government may seek federal habeas corpus relief under 28 U.S.C. § 2241(c)(1). In addition, § 2255 allows a prisoner in federal custody to make a motion to vacate, set aside, or correct her sentence, based upon various grounds, including that the sentence violated the Constitution or a federal statute.

PART ONE

Federal Courts and the Political Branches of the Federal Government

■ ANALYSIS

Chapter I

PROBLEMS OF JUDICIAL REVIEW

■ ANALYSIS

I. Introduction

Judicial review permits the judiciary to declare acts of the executive and legislative branches invalid because they violate the Constitution. Judicial review is necessary to ensure constitutional supremacy, but it creates tension because federal judges are not elected, and thus are not necessarily responsive to the will of the majority. Several doctrines limit the judiciary's ability to engage in judicial review. Article III permits the federal courts to decide "cases" or "controversies," and thereby forbids advisory opinions. In addition, standing, mootness, ripeness, and the political-question doctrine limit the sorts of disputes that the federal judiciary can decide. The proper balance between the need for judicial review and the need for restraint is a subject of ongoing debate.

II. The Institution of Judicial Review

A. Political Insulation of the Federal Judiciary

1. Article III, § 1, provides that federal judges have lifetime tenure and that Congress cannot reduce their pay. The only way to remove a federal judge from office is impeachment and conviction; in the history of the country, Congress has impeached and convicted fewer than ten federal judges.
2. The Constitution accords this extraordinary protection to federal judges to insulate them from political pressure. If federal judges were elected, they might lack the courage to rule in unpopular ways. If Congress could reduce their pay, judges might be reluctant to rule against the federal government. [R35] [R41] [R76]

B. *Marbury v. Madison*

1. *Marbury v. Madison*, 5 U.S. (1 Cranch) 137 (1803), established that the federal judiciary has the constitutional power to declare acts of the other branches of government invalid if they violate the Constitution.
   a. Chief Justice Marshall concluded that the executive branch had violated Marbury's rights by failing to deliver to him his commission as a federal justice of the peace.
   b. Marshall avoided direct conflict with the executive branch, however, by holding that although Marbury had suffered injury and was entitled to a remedy, the Supreme Court was not the proper tribunal to grant it. Article III, § 2, cl. 1, which sets forth the limit of the judicial power of the federal courts dictated this result. *See supra* Ch. VIII, § II.B, at 165 *[R2].*) [R21]
2. Judicial review allows the judiciary to monitor government's functioning. But it creates tension precisely because it permits the unelected branch of the federal government to invalidate the acts of the "political" or "representative" branches.

3. The remainder of this Chapter addresses doctrines that limit judicial power and thus judicial review. As a group, these limitations are the doctrines of justiciability. *See infra* § III, pages 33-56 *[R3]*. [R18]

III. Federal Courts Cannot Issue Advisory Opinions.

A. The Case-or-Controversy Requirement

1. Article III, § 2, extends the federal courts' judicial power to enumerated types of cases and controversies. Thus, the federal courts may not issue opinions simply giving advice to the other branches of the federal government. The judicial power exists only to decide actual disputes; the courts' job is to decide cases, not to make general decrees about the propriety of government action.
   a. Judicial review is possible only if an actual legal dispute presents a question concerning the constitutionality of an act by one of the political branches of government.
   b. No federal court can declare a statute unconstitutional—even if it is plainly so—until litigation properly presents the issue to the court. [R18]
2. The case-or-controversy requirement serves related purposes.
   a. By leaving the political branches to act without prior intrusion by the courts, it promotes separation of powers.
   b. It also helps to ensure that the judiciary acts only when there is a true adversary dispute. The adversary system of litigation then ensures that the issues come before the courts with "concreteness," rather than as hypotheticals. Concreteness facilitates better decision-making.
   c. Like other justiciability doctrines, this requirement also serves as docket control—conserving the federal judiciary's resources by limiting its workload. [R36] [R319] [R326]

B. Applications

1. While Secretary of State in the Washington administration, Thomas Jefferson asked the Justices of the Supreme Court whether the United States could legally undertake certain acts while remaining neutral in a war between France and England. The Justices refused to answer. They cited the roles of the three branches of government and found "strong arguments against the propriety of our extrajudicially deciding the questions."
2. Congress occasionally sets up schemes in which federal courts would have merely advisory functions, violating the case-or-controversy requirement. *See, e.g., C & S Air Lines v. Waterman Corp.*, 333 U.S. 103, 113 (1948) (President could ignore federal courts' review of administrative rulings concerning airline routes; scheme rejected as forcing federal courts to "render an advisory opinion in its most obnoxious form").

3. Suits for declaratory judgments under 28 U.S.C. § 2201 present special problems. Because a declaratory judgment may settle the parties' rights before relevant events occur, it can look advisory, but the Supreme Court has upheld declaratory judgments' constitutionality, "so long as the case retains the essentials of an adversary proceeding, involving a real, not a hypothetical, controversy." *Nashville, C. & St. Louis Ry. v. Wallace*, 288 U.S. 249, 264 (1933). [R37] [R140]

IV. Standing

A. Sources and Purposes of the Standing Requirement

1. A party may only litigate in the federal courts if she has "standing" to bring the suit. Standing's focus, therefore, is whether the plaintiff is an appropriate person to assert the claim—"whether [*this*] litigant is entitled to have the court decide the merits of the dispute or of particular issues." *Warth v. Seldin*, 422 U.S. 490, 498 (1975).

2. Standing requirements have fluctuated over the years, and the Court admits that the concept "has not been defined with complete consistency in all of the various cases decided by this Court." *Valley Forge Christian College v. Americans United for Separation of Church and State*, 454 U.S. 464, 475 (1982). That is a titanic understatement.

3. Nonetheless, standing basically requires that a litigant have some direct, concrete interest in the case's outcome—that the conduct of which the plaintiff complains has caused real injury. Harm is usually obvious in litigation between private parties. The troublesome cases generally involve public-law litigation, or suits by ideological plaintiffs—those who challenge some governmental act because of ideological views. Such cases often give rise to the problem of citizen standing.

4. As do all justiciability doctrines, standing raises questions about the federal courts' proper role. Relaxed standing rules make judicial review more available. Rigorous standing restrictions cause the courts to be more reluctant to review the other branches' actions.

5. There used to be two sources of standing requirements. First, Article III imposes three absolute requirements, which no statute can override. Second, the Supreme Court once recognized additional limitations (that it called "prudential limitations") on standing. The Court, not the Constitution, imposed these restrictions in the interest of judicial administration. Statutes could override prudential limitations, and the Court now recognizes the impropriety of its establishing prudential limitations. That does not mean they have disappeared, however; the Court has simply moved them to other parts of the consideration of whether an action can go forward. In effect, it has renamed and retained them. The Court's most recent comprehensive opinion on standing, *FDA v. Alliance for Hippocratic Medicine*, 602 U.S. 367 (2024), does not mention "prudential." *See infra* § IV.C.1, at 41 *[R4]*.

B. Three Constitutional Requirements for Standing

1. *FDA v. Alliance for Hippocratic Medicine*, 602 U.S. 367 (2024), provides an excellent overview of the Court's standing jurisprudence. The basic question, as then-Judge Scalia phrased it years ago, is "What's it to you?" That question has three sub-parts.

   (1) Injury-in-fact: the plaintiff must have suffered a judicially cognizable injury to person, property, wallet, or the plaintiff's constitutional rights. The injury must either have already occurred or be imminent.

   (2) Causation: the plaintiff must establish that the defendant's action either has given or is about to give rise to plaintiff's injury-in-fact.

   (3) Redressability: the plaintiff must show that judicial relief will set things right. One way to think about redressability is to think of it as remedial causation: judicial relief will undo or at least limit the harm that the defendant caused, prevent continuation of the harm, or compensate the plaintiff for the harm.

2. "Injury-in-fact" is "an invasion of a legally protected interest which is (a) concrete and particularized . . . and (b) actual or imminent, not 'conjectural' or hypothetical" harm. *Lujan v. Defenders of Wildlife*, 504 U.S. 555, 560 (1992).

   a. Demonstrating injury-in-fact is often a problem for ideological plaintiffs challenging government action. The cases are difficult to reconcile and often involve assessment of whether the plaintiff pleaded an injury properly.

   Example: To have standing, prospective tenants attempting to challenge restrictive zoning ordinances have to allege more than that the ordinances had prevented builders from constructing low-income housing. In addition, they must allege facts that demonstrate that, but for the restrictive zoning practices, it is probable that they would have been able to purchase or lease in the area. *Warth v. Seldin*, 422 U.S. 490 (1975).

   b. Injury-in-fact may be "economic or otherwise." *Association of Data Processing Service Organizations, Inc. v. Camp*, 397 U.S. 150, 152 (1970), and so can include non-economic harm to purely aesthetic interests. *United States v. SCRAP*, 412 U.S. 669 (1973), upheld standing in case brought by students who alleged that increased railroad freight rates approved by the government would result in less use of recycled goods which, in turn, would lead to increased use of natural resources, harming their enjoyment of forests and streams in the Washington, D.C. area. On the other hand, *SCRAP* is clearly the high-water mark for aesthetic injury—now characterizable as an outlier; since then, the Supreme Court has been rigorous in requiring allegations of direct injury to the plaintiff.

Example: The Sierra Club sued to challenge a decision by the Secretary of the Interior to allow development of a ski resort in Mineral King Valley in California. It alleged that it had a special interest in conservation and maintenance of parks, game refuges, and forests. The allegations failed to establish injury-in-fact, because there was no allegation that the Sierra Club or its members "use Mineral King for any purpose, much less that they use it in any way that would be significantly affected by the proposed actions of [the developers]." *Sierra Club v. Morton*, 405 U.S. 727, 735 (1972). Congress attempted to overrule *Sierra Club* with 33 U.S.C. § 1365, authorizing citizen suits that allege violations of effluent standards with respect to navigable waters. Two district courts and one circuit court have ruled on its constitutionality, finding that the statute does not violate separation of powers or unduly interfere with executive enforcement of the Clean Water Act. The Supreme Court declined to review.

Example: Plaintiffs, including the National Wildlife Federation (NWF), challenged a government action that permitted increased mining on specific federal lands. Two members of the NWF stated in affidavits that they used land "in the vicinity" of the land on which mining would occur, and that the mining would harm the environment there. The plaintiffs failed to demonstrate injury-in-fact because the "affidavit is ambiguous regarding whether the adversely affected lands are the ones [plaintiffs use]." *Lujan v. National Wildlife Federation*, 497 U.S. 871, 888 (1992). The plaintiffs failed to plead that they used the precise federal land on which mining would occur.

c. Some constitutional violations may injure no specific individual. In such areas, the requirement of injury-in-fact may effectively preclude judicial review, even if the challenged legislation is unconstitutional on the merits.

Example: Former members of the Armed Forces Reserve opposed to United States involvement in Vietnam lacked standing to challenge the membership of congressional representatives in the Reserve as violating the Incompatibility Clause of Article I, § 6, cl. 2, which provides that "no Person holding any Office under the United States shall be a Member of either House during his Continuance in Office." It is highly unlikely that any private plaintiff could claim to have suffered an injury-in-fact in such a situation. As the Court said: "The assumption that if [plaintiffs] have no standing to sue no one would have standing, is not a reason to find standing." *Schlesinger v. Reservists Committee to Stop the War*, 418 U.S. 208, 227 (1974). Thus, only the political branches could resolve the issue.

Example: By statute, the federal executive department may turn over surplus government property to tax-exempt educational institutions free of charge. Citizens dedicated to separation of church and state challenged donation of a former military hospital to a Christian college but failed to allege an injury-in-fact: "Although [they] claim that the Constitution has been violated, they claim nothing else. They fail to identify any personal injury suffered by the plaintiffs *as a consequence* of the alleged constitutional error, other than the psychological consequence presumably produced by observation of conduct with which one disagrees." *Valley Forge Christian College v. Americans United for Separation of Church & State, Inc.*, 454 U.S. 464, 485 (1982).

On the other hand, one who suffers an injury-in-fact does not lose standing just because others also suffer the same harm. Voters challenging a Federal Election Commission decision not to require the American Israel Public Affairs Committee to register as a "political committee" alleged an injury-in-fact. They suffered an "informational injury" because, they asserted, they were denied information that would help them in voting. *Federal Election Commission v. Akins*, 524 U.S. 11, 24 (1998). [R5] [R7] [R11]

d. Violation of a statutory right may constitute injury-in-fact. "Congress may create a statutory right or entitlement the alleged deprivation of which can confer standing to sue even where the plaintiff would have suffered no judicially cognizable injury in the absence of statute." *Warth v. Seldin*, 422 U.S. 490, 514 (1975).

Example: White tenants of an apartment complex alleged that their landlord discriminated by not renting to nonwhites. They alleged that as a result they lost the social and economic benefits of living in an integrated community. The plaintiffs suffered injury-in-fact, because the Civil Rights Act of 1968 had created a right to be free from the effects of racial discrimination. Concurring, Justice White stated that he would have had difficulty finding a case or controversy absent the direct authorization of that Act. *Trafficante v. Metropolitan Life Insurance Co.*, 409 U.S. 205 (1972). [R9]

Example: Under the Endangered Species Act (ESA), "any person may commence a civil suit on his own behalf" to enjoin a violation of ESA. The Act also requires the Secretary of the Interior to promulgate regulations listing endangered species and requires other agencies to ensure that their acts do not jeopardize such species or their habitat. If they do, the agency must consult the Fish and Wildlife Service to find alternatives. The Bureau of Reclamation determined that its Klamath Project threatened protected species of fish and ultimately agreed to maintain higher reservoir levels, which would mean less irrigation water available. Irrigation districts and ranchers who receive water from the Klamath Project sued to challenge the determination of threat and the government action. They demonstrated injury-in-fact under ESA. The Court concluded that under ESA, "standing was expanded to the full extent permitted under Article III." *Bennett v. Spear*, 520 U.S. 154, 165 (1997).

Example: *Lujan v. Defenders of Wildlife*, 504 U.S. 555 (1992), challenged a federal regulation providing that ESA did not apply to federal activities outside the United States. The plaintiffs lacked standing under ESA. "To permit Congress to convert the undifferentiated public interest in executive officers' compliance with the law into an 'individual' right vindicable in the courts is to permit Congress to transfer from the President to the courts the Chief Executive's most important constitutional duty, to take care that the laws be faithfully executed." Thus, Congress can create "statutory standing" only if there is also an Article III injury-in-fact, as there was in *Bennett*. [R8] [R9]

e. *However*, Congress cannot will an injury-in-fact into existence simply by enacting a statute and giving a plaintiff a right to sue for mere violation of the statute. *Spokeo, Inc. v. Robins*, 578 U.S. 330 (2016). Violation of a statutory right, without accompanying real-world injury, does not satisfy Article III.

Example: TransUnion, one of the major credit-reporting agencies, included defamatory information in the credit reports of more than eight thousand individuals. One of the individuals brought a class action, seeking to recover statutory damages under the Fair Credit Reporting Act. The 5-4 Court ruled that only those class members whose credit reports TransUnion had sent to third parties had standing to sue. Even though Congress provided statutory damages for mere inclusion of false information in credit files, the class members whose files TransUnion had not disseminated had not (yet) suffered Article III injury-in-fact. *TransUnion LLC v. Ramirez*, 594 U.S. 413 (2021). [R5] [R7] [R368]

3. In addition to injury-in-fact, the plaintiff must show causation and redressability. Causation requires that the injury-in-fact resulted from the defendant's conduct. Redressability requires that a favorable ruling will remedy (or at least lessen) the harm the plaintiff suffered. In other words, causation traces the causal chain from past to present, while redressability traces the causal chain from present (entry of judgment) to future.

Example: Plaintiffs, low-income persons and their representatives, sued the Secretary of the Treasury to challenge an IRS regulation providing that hospitals can qualify as charitable institutions (to which donations are tax deductible) even though they failed to provide service to indigents except in emergency cases. Plaintiffs alleged an injury-in-fact, because they were denied medical care by such hospitals and thus harmed. But they lacked standing, because there was no necessary connection between the IRS regulation and the harm they suffered. Moreover, even if the plaintiffs won the case, hospitals would not be compelled to provide service to indigents. Instead, they might forego charitable contributions to avoid having to take on that responsibility. *Simon v. Eastern Kentucky Welfare Rights Organization*, 426 U.S. 26 (1976).

Example: In *Allen v. Wright*, 468 U.S. 737 (1984), parents of black public school students sued to challenge the IRS's failure to deny tax-exempt status to private schools that discriminated on the basis of race. They claimed that their children suffered a stigma because the government permitted tax-exempt contributions to discriminatory schools. The Court found that failed to meet the injury-in-fact requirement because it was not sufficiently concrete. The claim that the tax advantages to discriminatory schools harmed the children's ability to have an integrated school by failed to meet the causation requirement. "From the perspective of the IRS, the injury to [plaintiffs] is highly indirect and results from the independent action of some third party not before the court." *Id.* at 757. In short, the children's diminished inability to obtain a desegregated education did not result from the IRS's alleged violation of the law. This was one of the fairly rare cases the Court treated causation and redressability separately, as the Court was willing to assume that the relief requested by the plaintiffs "might have a substantial effect on the desegregation of public schools." *Id.* at 753 n.19. That assumption appears to be in tension with *Simon*.

Example: *Duke Power Co. v. Carolina Environmental Study Group, Inc.*, 438 U.S. 59 (1978), is arguably inconsistent with *Allen*. Plaintiffs, organizations and individuals located near planned nuclear power facilities, sued the power company, challenging the Price-Anderson Act's limitation of private liability in the event of a nuclear accident. Plaintiffs had standing, the Court noting that operating the power plants had immediate harmful effects (such as the increase of thermal pollution of nearby lakes) and caused plaintiffs injury-in-fact, even though no accident had occurred. The Court accepted the lower court finding that only the protections of the Price-Anderson Act allowed building the plants. Once the plants existed, though, the question of whether winning would remedy plaintiffs' injuries remained.

Example: Plaintiffs, students at a public college, attacked the college's "freedom of expression" and "speech code" policies infringed their First Amendment rights. By the time the case reached the Supreme

Court, the college had revised its policies, and plaintiffs were no longer students at the college. Nonetheless, an 8-1 Court held that the students' request for nominal damages was enough to satisfy the redressability requirement and to prevent the case from being moot. *Uzuegbunam v. Preczewski*, 592 U.S. 279 (2021). Chief Justice Roberts, alone in dissent, thought the majority's analysis entirely inconsistent with Article III's justiciability requirements. [R12] [R17]

Example: In *Diamond Alternative Energy, LLC v. Environmental Protection Agency*, 145 S. Ct. 2121 (2025), the Court found the redressability requirement satisfied when fossil-fuel producers challenged EPA's approval of California regulations aimed at increasing purchases of electric vehicles in preference to fossil-fuel vehicles. The Court declined to require plaintiffs to produce affidavits from either economists or automakers detailing likely commercial responses to California's rules. It was sufficient that the plaintiffs could show that it was predictable that automobile manufacturers would produce fewer fossil-fuel vehicles in response to the California regulation, causing plaintiffs injury-in-fact from falling revenues, and that, were the regulation invalidated, the would at least partially remedy the injury-in-fact.

4. The three constitutional standing requirements serve several purposes, mostly in common with other justiciability requirements.

   a. They promote separation of powers by confining the federal courts to the performance of the traditional judicial functions of resolving individual disputes and adjudicating the individuals' rights. The Supreme Court has bluntly said that standing rests "on a single basic idea—the idea of separation of powers." *Allen v. Wright*, 468 U.S. 737, 752 (1984). Standing "is founded in concern about the proper—and properly limited—role of the courts in a democratic society." *Warth v. Seldin*, 422 U.S. 490, 498 (1975).

   b. In recent years, some commentators have criticized the Court for effectively precluding judicial review of government action by restricting standing excessively.

   c. The injury-in-fact requirement helps to ensure that plaintiffs have personal incentives to litigate fully and to present issues concretely rather than as hypotheticals. Courts think that concreteness ensures better decision-making. Some commentators have responded, however, that many institutional litigants possessing solely an ideological interest in the case are just as likely to provide vigorous litigation as many individual litigants.

   d. Standing also serves a docket-control function, avoiding inundation of the federal courts. [R12] [R14] [R19] [R310]

C. Additional Limitations on Standing

1. The Supreme Court had also imposed what it called "prudential" limitations on standing as a matter of judicial administration. The Court identified three: (1) the plaintiff must assert her own interest, not that of a third-party (injury-in-fact); (2) the plaintiff's interest must fall within the "zone of interests" the relevant law protects, and (3) the federal courts will not hear "generalized grievances." Those concepts, while still important in federal litigation, are no longer part of the standing inquiry. *Lexmark Int'l, Inc. v. Static Control Components*, 572 U.S. 118 (2014), unanimously disapproved "prudential" standing requirements as violating separation of powers, referring to the federal courts' "virtually unflagging obligation" to hear cases Congress has committed to them. The Court has split the three concepts that used to be part of the prudential-standing inquiry. The first two—the prohibition of asserting someone else's rights and the zone-of-interests test—the Court has now recognized as relevant only to whether the plaintiff states a claim within the meaning of FED. R. CIV. P. 12(b)(6). The Court also now considers the generalized-grievances requirement to be part of the constitutional case-or-controversy test. Still, it is important to understand how the three factors work. [R4]

2. The prohibition of third-party standing rests on the notion that a person who suffers no *constitutional* deprivation from a statute may not challenge it on the basis that applying it to others might be unconstitutional. *United States v. Raines*, 362 U.S. 17, 21 (1960). Thus, a person may suffer non-remediable injury-in-fact from a government action that violates others' constitutional rights but not her own. Individuals generally lack standing to assert the rights of others.

   a. The rule against third-party standing does not derive from Article III's case-or-controversy requirement. As *Lexmark* recognizes, it goes to whether the plaintiff can state a claim of her own, which makes it sound like an inquiry under FED. R. CIV. P. 12(b)(6).

   b. The traditional third-party standing rule, at least in the context of a constitutional challenge, derived largely from prudential ideas about the judiciary's limited role: courts in a democratic society should not seek out statutes for constitutional perusal until a plaintiff challenges the statute as applied to her.

   c. The prohibition against third-party standing was subject to judicial exception; some courts and commentators referred to it as "*jus tertii*" instead of a prong of standing.

   d. Overbreadth

      (1) The Supreme Court recognized a limited exception to the rule when the constitutional challenge rests on the First Amendment right of free expression. That is the overbreadth doctrine.

(2). The rationale for the overbreadth exception is that free speech rights are of paramount importance; if a law that violates the First Amendment remains in force, persons may be chilled from expressing their views. This chilling effect tends to insulate the law from constitutional challenge because people will not risk violating it.

(3). The Court emphasized that the overbreadth exception is "strong medicine" and rarely appropriate. Thus, the Court would not allow one to whom a law might constitutionally apply to challenge the law unless the overbreadth is "substantial," meaning that the law must be unconstitutional in the large majority of its applications. *New York v. Ferber*, 458 U.S. 747 (1982); *Broadrick v. Oklahoma*, 413 U.S. 601 (1973).

e. The conceptual transfer of the third-party-standing consideration should not affect how it operates, except that a plaintiff who comes within the rule will now suffer dismissal under FED. R. CIV. P. 12(b)(6)—"failure to state a claim upon which relief may be granted"—rather than under FED. R. CIV. P. 12(b)(1)—lack of subject-matter jurisdiction.

3. The second former prudential requirement was that the plaintiff's injury had to fall "arguably within the zone of interest to be protected or regulated by the statute or constitutional guarantee in question." *Association of Data Processing Service Organizations, Inc. v. Camp*, 397 U.S. 150, 153 (1970).

a. This issue almost always arose in cases in which the plaintiff sued under the Administrative Procedure Act to challenge the action of an administrative agency. The plaintiff must be within the group that Congress intended the statute to benefit. *See Clarke v. Securities Industry Association*, 479 U.S. 388, 400 n.16 (1987) (zone-of-interest test "most usefully understood as a gloss" on § 10 of the Administrative Procedure Act, "not a test of universal application").

Example: Section 10 of the Administrative Procedure Act allows judicial review of an agency action by one "aggrieved by agency action within the meaning of the relevant statute." The Bank Service Corporation Act of 1962 forbade banks to engage in any activity other than providing banking services. The Comptroller of the Currency ruled that such corporations could also provide data processing services for other banks and customers. Plaintiff, representing data processing businesses, challenged the administrative ruling. The Supreme Court concluded that the plaintiff had standing. In addition to the Article III requirements for standing, the plaintiff was within the zone of interests Congress intended to protect with the Bank Service Corporation Act of 1962. As a result of *Lexmark*, today's Court would likely characterize the decision as the plaintiff having stated a claim under Rule 12(b)(6).

Example: The Postal Express Statutes provide monopoly status for the United States Postal Service by preventing private competition on certain routes. The Postal Service issued an administrative ruling that exempted international remailing by private couriers, thus giving up its monopoly in that area. Postal workers challenged the ruling because they would likely be harmed by the Postal Service's resulting loss of business. The Supreme Court held that they lacked standing because they were not within the zone of interests the statutes protected. Rather, Congress intended the statutes to benefit the citizenry by providing postal service to all communities. Neither the language of the Postal Express Statutes nor the legislative history supported the plaintiffs' contention that Congress had intended to protect employment with the Postal Service. *Air Courier Conference v. American Postal Workers Union*, 498 U.S. 517 (1991). As a result of *Lexmark*, today's Court would likely conclude that the plaintiff failed to state a claim and would dismiss under FED. R. CIV. P. 12(b)(6).

b. The Supreme Court was inconsistent in applying the zone-of-interests requirement. Sometimes the Court found standing without rigorous application. *See, e.g., Clarke v. Securities Industry Association*, 479 U.S. 388, 399-400 (1987) (creating a presumption that agency action is reviewable; zone-of-interests "test is not meant to be especially demanding; in particular, there need be no indication of congressional purpose to benefit the would-be plaintiff.").

c. The Court conceded that its opinions had not stated a clear rule for applying the restriction. *National Credit Union Administration v. First National Bank & Trust*, 522 U.S. 479, 486 (1998), upheld standing in a five-to-four opinion based upon a less rigorous application of the zone-of-interests test—more like that used in *Clarke* than in *Air Courier Conference*.

4. The third former prudential limitation was that plaintiffs lacked standing "when the asserted harm is a generalized grievance shared in a substantially equal measure by all or a large class of citizens." *Warth v. Seldin*, 422 U.S. 490, 499 (1975). Thus, "even when the plaintiff has alleged redressable injury sufficient to meet the requirements of Article III, the Court has refrained from adjudicating 'abstract questions of wide public significance' which amount to 'generalized grievances,' pervasively shared and most appropriately addressed in the representative branches." *Valley Forge Christian College v. Americans United for Separation of Church & State, Inc.*, 454 U.S. 464, 474-75 (1982) (the president, under a congressional authorization, donating surplus federal land

to a sectarian institution). This requirement makes it difficult to bring suits simply as a citizen concerned with a particular issue.

a. Commentators criticize this limitation as shielding government action that blatantly violates constitutional rights of a large number of people. In application, however, the Supreme Court seems to be saying only that this limitation closes federal courts to the general complaint of a citizen who sues to ensure that the federal government acts in compliance with the law. The Court has made it clear that one who meets the constitutional requirements for standing will not lack standing simply because she shares that harm with many others. *See, e.g., Federal Election Commission v. Akins*, 524 U.S. 11, 24 (1998), *supra* § IV.B.2.c, at 36 *[R5]*. That approach, however, leaves *Valley Forge*'s result untouched.

b. Thus, the rule against generalized grievances is very similar to the rules concerning taxpayer standing. *See infra* § D, at 45 *[R6]*.

c. Examples of cases involving generalized grievances include *Valley Forge Christian College v. Americans United for Separation of Church & State, Inc.*, 454 U.S. 464 (1982), and *Schlesinger v. Reservists Committee to Stop the War*, 418 U.S. 208 (1974). *See supra* § IV.B.2.c at 36-38 *[R7]*.

d. Article III requires the rule against generalized grievances. *Lujan v. Defenders of Wildlife*, 504 U.S. 555, 575-76 (1992), *see supra* § IV.B.2.d, at 38 *[R8]*, rejected standing under the Endangered Species Act, which permits "any person" to commence a suit to enjoin violations of the Act. Because the plaintiffs were asserting merely a generalized grievance rather than cognizable personal harm to themselves, they failed to satisfy Article III standing requirements, and Congress was powerless to confer standing on them.

e. *Elk Grove Unified School Dist. v. Newdow*, 542 U.S. 1 (2003), held, on now-disapproved prudential grounds, that a non-custodial parent did not have standing to challenge the public schools' requirement that his daughter recite the pledge of allegiance. In particular, the parent objected to the inclusion of "under God" in the pledge. Neither the parent who had sole legal custody of the child nor the child objected to the pledge. The Court concluded that it should not determine the issue because of the impact of the decision might have on family relations. *Newdow* looks more like an abstention case than a standing case. [R10]

5. Because these additional limitations were self-imposed, non-constitutional restrictions on the judiciary, Congress could override them. *Bennett v. Spear*, 520 U.S. 154 (1997) and *Trafficante v. Metropolitan Life Insurance Co.*, 409 U.S. 205 (1972), *see supra* § IV.B.2.d, at 37 *[R9]*, exemplify cases in which Congress did just that, limiting the standing inquiry to the three constitutional *minima*. [R4] [R20]

D. Special Problems of Taxpayer Standing

1. One subset of the standing problem concerns the extent to which taxpayers may sue to challenge the constitutionality of governmental spending programs. These cases are similar to the generalized-grievance cases. *See supra* § IV.C.4, at 43-44 *[R10]*.

2. *Frothingham v. Mellon*, 262 U.S. 447 (1923), held that federal taxpayers lacked standing to challenge the constitutionality of federal expenditures. As a practical matter, the Court noted that allowing standing would potentially swamp the federal courts with such challenges. To have standing, the Court held, a party "must be able to show not only that the statute is invalid but that he has sustained or is immediately in danger of sustaining some direct injury as the result of its enforcement, and not merely that he suffers in some indefinite way in common with people generally." *Id.* at 488.

3. Later, however, *Flast v. Cohen*, 392 U.S. 83, 102 (1968), held that federal taxpayers have standing if "they can demonstrate the necessary stake as taxpayers in the outcome of the litigation to satisfy Article III requirements." Such status can exist (a) only in suits challenging statutes enacted pursuant to Congress's power under the Taxing and Spending Clause, Article I, § 8, cl. 1, and (b) only if the taxpayer can establish a "nexus between that status and the precise nature of the constitutional infringement alleged." Since *Flast*, no one has.

   a. *Flast* distinguished *Frothingham* because Frothingham had failed to allege that Congress had breached a *specific limitation* upon its taxing and spending power.

   b. Commentators have long questioned, however, whether the two decisions are distinguishable and whether *Flast*'s two factors rationally relate to standing.

   c. Two concurring Justices in *Flast* expressed the view that taxpayer standing should be allowed only in cases challenging laws under the First Amendment's Establishment Clause.

4. In *Valley Forge Christian College v. Americans United for Separation of Church and State Inc.*, 454 U.S. 464 (1982), the executive branch of the federal government, pursuant to statutory authorization, turned over surplus federal realty to a Christian college. The plaintiffs lacked standing as citizens. *See supra* § IV.B.2.c, at 36-37 *[R11]*. In addition, they lacked standing as federal taxpayers. The Supreme Court held that taxpayer standing is unavailable when the challenge is to a decision by an executive department rather than congressional action. Congressional authorization of the property transfer was not an exercise of authority the Taxing and Spending Clause conferred.

5. Despite these limitations on *federal* taxpayers' standing, the Supreme Court has upheld local (*e.g.*, state or municipal) taxpayers' standing to challenge local expenditures.

a. A municipal taxpayer could challenge the use of public funds to transport students to Catholic schools. *Everson v. Board of Education*, 330 U.S. 1 (1947).

b. On the other hand, state and municipal taxpayers did not have standing in the Supreme Court to challenge a state statute that required a daily Old Testament reading in the public schools. They lacked standing because they were suing over religious differences. *But see infra* § IV.E.2 at 46 *[R12]*. The case was not a "good-faith pocketbook action" involving an economic effect of the state law. *Doremus v. Board of Education*, 342 U.S. 429 (1952) (dismissing an appeal under the version of 28 U.S.C. § 1257 then in effect on case-or-controversy grounds). *Everson*, by contrast, had concerned a direct appropriation or spending of funds because of the challenged activity.

c. The same day as *Doremus*, the Court ruled on the merits of a challenge by local taxpayers and others to a state statute that required firing state school teachers advocating the overthrow of the United States government. Although the local taxpayers, like those in *Doremus*, seemed to lack any economic injury, the Court addressed the merits without even mentioning standing. *Adler v. Board of Education*, 342 U.S. 485 (1952). [R6] [R15]

E. Standing in the Supreme Court to Review State Court Decisions

1. Article III applies to the federal courts, including the Supreme Court. Thus, the Article III standing requirements apply to matters that Court adjudicates, even when they may involve only reviewing state-court decisions involving federal law.

2. Because Article III does not apply to state judiciaries, a state may allow its courts to issue advisory opinions or to resolve cases brought by individuals who would lack Article III standing, as in *Doremus*. [R12]

3. *ASARCO, Inc. v. Kadish*, 490 U.S. 605 (1989), held that the Court had authority to review a decision of the Arizona Supreme Court, though the plaintiffs would have lacked the standing to sue in federal court under Article III. The Arizona judgment was against the defendants, who invoked the Supreme Court's appellate jurisdiction. The negative state court decision harmed the defendants sufficiently to constitute an Article III injury that allowed a federal court to determine the case.

V. Ripeness

A. Sources and Purposes of the Ripeness Requirement

1. Standing concerns whether an appropriate plaintiff has sued; ripeness and mootness (*see infra* § VI, at 49-52 *[R13]*) concern timing. Put roughly, ripeness involves whether the plaintiff has sued "too soon," and mootness involves whether further litigation would be "too late." [R16]

2. The federal courts may not adjudicate when it is speculative whether the plaintiff will actually suffer injury. The courts may not become involved before the dispute has matured sufficiently to require adjudication. That does not mean that the injury must have occurred; it must, however, be impending rather than merely conceivable.

3. To some extent, the requirement flows from Article III's case-or-controversy requirement. Until a dispute ripens, there is no real case or controversy and thus nothing for federal courts to adjudicate. The level of hardship the litigants will suffer if the judiciary does not act affects the ripeness determination.

4. To some extent, the ripeness doctrine also stems from considerations of when other branches of government should resolve issues. "We have noted that ripeness doctrine is drawn both from Article III limitations on judicial power and from prudential reasons for refusing to exercise jurisdiction." *Reno v. Catholic Social Services*, 509 U.S. 43, 58 n.18 (1993).

5. Without doubt, standing and ripeness concerns can overlap. If a plaintiff sued because she thought she might someday be harmed by the defendant, a court might say either that she lacks standing (because she has not suffered an injury-in-fact) or that her claim is not ripe (because any harm is still speculative).

6. Ripeness serves similar functions as standing: (1) honoring separation of powers, (2) promoting better judicial decision-making by providing concrete facts for decision, and (3) docket control. *See supra* § IV.B.4, at 40 *[R14]*.

B. Requirements and Application

1. Ripeness focuses on two points: "the fitness of the issues for judicial decision," and "the hardship to the parties of withholding court consideration." *Abbott Laboratories v. Gardner*, 387 U.S. 136, 149 (1967).

2. The fitness requirement largely concerns whether judicial action is appropriate.

   a. In *California Bankers Association v. Schultz*, 416 U.S. 21 (1974), for example, plaintiffs sought to enjoin enforcement of a federal law imposing bank-reporting requirements that they claimed would violate customers' First Amendment rights. The dispute was not fit for judicial decision, basically because not enough had happened to make clear whether the customers might actually suffer the harm. "[I]n the absence of a concrete fact situation in which competing . . . interests can be weighed, [a court] is simply not in a position to determine whether an effort to compel disclosure of such records would or would not be barred." *Id.* at 56.

   b. Sometimes a pure question of law is fit for immediate review. *See, e.g., Pacific Gas & Electric Co. v. State Energy Resources Conservation & Development Commission*, 461 U.S. 190, 201 (1983) ("The question of preemption is predominantly legal, and although it would be useful to have the benefit of California's interpretation of what constitutes a demonstrated technology or means for the disposal of high-level nuclear waste, resolution of the preemption issue need not await that development.").

3. The hardship factor assesses the extent to which a delay in judicial action will harm the plaintiff. Thus, in some cases, the Court has allowed adjudication even though no harm has yet occurred because delay would likely harm the plaintiff.

Example: The Food and Drug Administration (FDA) required that all prescription medications indicate the generic drug names on labels. Drug companies challenged the regulation as being beyond FDA power. The Supreme Court found the case ripe even though no drug company had been prosecuted for violating the new regulation. The Court noted that violation of the regulation could be punished by civil and criminal penalties, and explained: "If [plaintiffs] wish to comply [with the new regulation] they must change all their labels, advertisements and promotional materials; they must destroy stocks of printed matter; and they must invest heavily in new printing type and new supplies. The alternative to compliance . . . would risk serious criminal and civil penalties. . . ." *Abbott Laboratories v. Gardner*, 387 U.S. 136, 152-53 (1967).

Example: The Court has not always been consistent. A labor union challenged the constitutionality of a federal statute declaring specified political activities of federal employees to be unlawful. The plaintiffs had not violated the law and did not face charges. The Supreme Court held that the case was not ripe, because it was purely speculative whether any harm would result to plaintiffs. *United Public Workers of America v. Mitchell*, 330 U.S. 75 (1947). The problem with the Court's holding, of course, is that the only alternative means to challenge the law would be to risk criminal penalties by violating it and, as an ethical matter, no attorney can advise a client to violate the law. *Abbott Laboratories*, though not citing *Mitchell*, appears at least to call it into question.

Example: Teachers challenged a provision of a New York statute prohibiting employing teachers who advocated overthrowing the government by force and violence. They did not allege that they had engaged in the proscribed conduct or that they had any intention to do so. The Supreme Court decided the case on its merits, without raising the ripeness issue. *Adler v. Board of Education*, 342 U.S. 485 (1952). *See supra* § IV.D.5.c, at 45 *[R15]*. Justice Frankfurter dissented, arguing that the case was not ripe:

> The allegations in the present action fall short of those found insufficient in the *Mitchell* case. These teachers do not allege that they have engaged in proscribed conduct or that they

> have any intention to do so. They do not suggest that they have been, or are, deterred from supporting causes . . . for fear of the [statute].

342 U.S. at 504. [R311]

VI. Mootness

A. Sources, Purposes, and Operation of the Mootness Doctrine

1. Mootness, like ripeness (*see supra* § V.A.1, at 46 *[R16]*) concerns timing. While ripeness asks whether the plaintiff has sued too soon, mootness asks whether circumstances have changed so that there is no longer a live dispute. The inquiry, then, is essentially whether it is too late for judicial action.

2. Cases often become moot. For example, if the parties settle their dispute, if a challenged regulation expires, or if the legislature repeals a challenged statute, the parties' dispute—once live and needing judicial action—is moot. Other cases are not as easy.

Example: Plaintiff challenged the constitutionality of a state law school's admissions process. He won in the trial court, which ordered the school to admit him. By the time the case reached the United States Supreme Court, the plaintiff was nearing completion of his final year, and the school had agreed to permit him to finish. The Supreme Court held that the case was moot, because its decision would no longer affect the plaintiff's interests. *DeFunis v. Odegaard*, 416 U.S. 312 (1974).

Example: Perhaps surprisingly, an 8-1 Court found that a case involving challenges to a school's speech policies did *not* become moot even though by the time the case reached the Supreme Court, the college had changed its policies, and the students had graduated. The former students' request for nominal damages kept the case alive. *Uzuegbunam v. Preczewski*, 592 U.S. 279 (2021). *See supra* at 40 *[R17]*.

3. Mootness derives from Article III's case-or controversy requirement. If the change in circumstances means that the judicial resolution will be meaningless, there is no case or controversy, and the court cannot act because deciding at that point would be advisory. *See supra* § III.A.1, at 33 *[R18]*).

4. As is true throughout justiciability doctrines, there is overlap between mootness and other topics, including standing. The Supreme Court, adopting a famous description by Professor Henry Monaghan, has said that mootness can be seen as the "doctrine of standing set in a time frame: the requisite personal interest that must exist at the commencement of the litigation (standing) must continue throughout its existence (mootness)." *United States Parole Commission v. Geraghty*, 445 U.S. 388, 397 (1980).

5. Mootness serves similar functions to standing and ripeness: (1) protecting separation of powers, (2) promoting better judicial decision-making by providing concrete facts for decision, and (3) docket control. *See supra* § IV.B.4, at 40 *[R19]*.

B. Exceptions to the Operation of Mootness

1. There are three major exceptions to mootness: (1) cases presenting issues "capable of repetition, yet evading review," (2) voluntary cessation, and (3) class actions.

   a. One might view each of these exceptions as avoiding mootness when it is expedient to do so.

   b. The problem is that if mootness doctrine comes from Article III, expediency should not overcome Article III's requirements. Thus, some commentators criticize these exceptions as violating Article III. Others, however, argue that mootness is at least in part a nonconstitutional limitation on judicial power and praise the exceptions as necessary to preserve the proper function of judicial review. In that sense, one might view it as a prudential requirement. The Court has disapproved prudential requirements with respect to standing, *see supra* § IV.C.4 at 41-44 *[R20]*.

2. The capable-of-repetition-but-evading-review exception recognizes that some harms may pass before litigation can remedy them. The exception requires (1) "a reasonable expectation or a 'demonstrated probability' that the same controversy will recur involving the same complaining party," *Murphy v. Hunt*, 455 U.S. 478, 482 (1982), and (2) that the harm complained of is of such short duration that it will become moot before litigation can remedy it. *Southern Pacific Terminal Co. v. Interstate Commerce Commission*, 219 U.S. 498, 514 (1911).

Example: State law denied bail before trial to those accused of violent sex crimes. A defendant challenged the law but lost the criminal case before adjudication of the challenge. The Supreme Court concluded that this particular defendant was unlikely again to be prosecuted and denied bail under the law, so the exception did not apply; the challenge was moot. *Murphy v. Hunt*, 455 U.S. at 483.

Example: Plaintiff, a pregnant woman, challenged the constitutionality of a state law prohibiting abortion. By the time the case reached the Supreme Court, she was no longer pregnant. The Supreme Court adjudicated the case, however, because it fell within this exception. The limited time of pregnancy effectively precludes any similar case from reaching the Supreme Court for review before gestation ends. *Roe v. Wade*, 410 U.S. 113, 125 (1973), *overruled on different issue*, *Dobbs v. Jackson Women's Health Organization*, 597 U.S. 215 (2022).

The Court approached the questions in *Murphy* and *Roe* differently. In *Murphy*, the court focused on whether *that defendant* would again suffer prosecution. In *Roe*, the Court focused on whether *any woman* could get a case adjudicated within the gestation period.

Example: The exception applied to a suit under the Education of the Handicapped Act by an emotionally disturbed 20-year-old expelled from a California public school for violent and disruptive behavior. The Act applies to disabled children between the ages of three and twenty-one. "Although at present he is not faced with any proposed expulsion or suspension proceedings . . . he remains a resident of California and is entitled to a 'free appropriate public education' within that State. . . . Given [the student's] continued eligibility for educational services under [the Act], the nature of his disability, and [defendant's] insistence that all local school districts retain residual authority to exclude disabled children for dangerous conduct, we have little difficulty concluding that there is a 'reasonable expectation' that [the student] would once again suffer the consequences of defendant's allegedly unlawful conduct." *Honig v. Doe*, 484 U.S. 305, 318-20 (1988).

3. The voluntary-cessation exception holds that a case is not moot when the defendant has refrained from the challenged conduct if the defendant (1) is free "to return to his old ways" and (2) there is a strong public interest in resolving the legal issue. *United States v. W.T. Grant Co.*, 345 U.S. 629, 632 (1953).

   a. This exception means that a defendant cannot escape judicial action simply by stopping the challenged behavior while remaining free to resume it later.

   Example: The United States sued several corporations, charging that their interlocking boards of directors violated the antitrust laws. After being sued, the defendants indicated that they had eliminated the interlocking directorships and that they had no intention of resuming them. The Supreme Court held that the case was not moot. The voluntary cessation exception did not apply precisely because the defendant was free "to return to his old ways." Nothing stopped the defendants from reinstituting the practice. *United States v. W.T. Grant Co.*, 345 U.S. at 632.

   b. But the exception will not apply—and the court will dismiss the case as moot—if there is no reasonable expectation that the defendant will resume the challenged activity. *County of Los Angeles v. Davis*, 440 U.S. 625 (1979) (interim injunctive relief ensured that county would not resume discriminatory hiring practices; case dismissed as moot). The Supreme Court held that the party asserting mootness has the burden of showing that it is "absolutely clear" that the behavior will not recur. *Friends of the Earth, Inc. v. Laidlaw Environmental Services*, 528 U.S. 167, 189 (2000).

4. The Supreme Court has been flexible in dealing with mootness in class actions.

    a. If the court certifies a class, the dispute is not moot even when the named representative no longer has an interest in the outcome. *Sosna v. Iowa*, 419 U.S. 393 (1975) (class action challenging residency requirement for divorce, named representative satisfied the requirement during case's pendency). So long as some member of the class has a live controversy, the class action may proceed. In effect, all class members—not just named representatives—are plaintiffs for purposes of mootness.

    b. In *Sosna*, the court certified the class before the representative plaintiff's claim became moot. The Court has explained, however, that "[a]lthough one might argue that *Sosna* contains at least an implication that the critical factor for Art. III purposes is the timing of class certification, other cases, applying a 'relation back' approach, clearly demonstrate that timing is not crucial." *United States Parole Commission v. Geraghty*, 445 U.S. 388, 398 (1980). In *Geraghty*, the district court refused to certify the class and granted summary judgment to the defendants. Geraghty's claim expired during the appeal. The Court held "that an action brought on behalf of a class does not become moot upon expiration of the named plaintiff's substantive claim, even though class certification has been denied. The proposed representative retains a 'personal stake' in obtaining class certification sufficient to assure that Art. III values are not undermined." *Id.* at 404.

    c. Similarly, a named representative may continue to prosecute an appeal of the denial of class certification even if she has settled her individual claims. *Deposit Guaranty National Bank v. Roper*, 445 U.S. 326 (1980). A member of a proposed class may intervene to appeal the denial of class certification. *United Airlines, Inc. v. McDonald*, 432 U.S. 385 (1973). [R13] [R320]

VII. The Political-Question Doctrine

A. Sources and Purposes

1. The political-question doctrine places some issues of constitutional law beyond the federal judiciary's competence. If the Constitution commits a particular matter exclusively to one of the federal political branches, the federal judiciary should decline to adjudicate it.

2. The doctrine shares with other justiciability principles that it undeniably enforces separation of powers. But political question fundamentally differs from the prohibition against advisory opinions, standing, ripeness, and mootness: certain disputes—no matter how live, concrete, and ripe—are simply not judicially cognizable.

3. By declining to adjudicate political questions, courts avoid potentially dangerous confrontations between the judiciary and coordinate federal

branches. That may also funnel decision-making to the branch of government with the greatest expertise on the matter.

4. Because the doctrine concerns separation of powers among the branches of the federal government, it does not apply to clashes between the federal judiciary and branches of state governments. Those are justiciable, assuming the other requirements of justiciability exist. [R314]

5. The political-question doctrine has deep judicial roots. In *Marbury v. Madison*, *see supra* § II.B.1, at 32 *[R21]*, Chief Justice Marshall noted (in dictum) that there are "political act[s], belonging to the executive department alone, for the performance of which entire confidence is placed by our constitution in the supreme executive; and for any misconduct respecting which, the injured individual has no remedy." 5 U.S. (1 Cranch) at 164. Although Marshall spoke of acts of the executive department alone, the doctrine also applies to acts that are Congress's sole responsibility.

6. Although uncertainty plagues each area of justiciability, commentators seem to feel that the lack of meaningful guidance and principle is worse here than in other areas. Moreover, "political question" is misleading. Not all questions dealing with political rights or political issues fall within the doctrine.

7. The argument by some commentators that the doctrine has no place in American government is more important than the ubiquitous criticism of the doctrine's lack of certainty. Invoking the political-question doctrine, they argue, is an abdication of the judiciary's responsibility to interpret the Constitution. The Constitution vests responsibility for its interpretation in the unelected federal judiciary. The Founders intended that function to be performed by the nonpolitical branch. Contrary to that intent, the political-question doctrine funnels the control back to the majoritarian branches.

B. Modern Explication

1. *Baker v. Carr*, 369 U.S. 186 (1962), is the leading explication of the doctrine, holding that a claim that a state's legislative apportionment violated equal protection did not come within the political-question rule and thus was justiciable. The Court listed six factors concerning whether a case presents a political question. The presence of any one factor may trigger application of the doctrine. *Id.* at 217.

   a. A "textual commitment of a matter to another branch of the federal government."

Example: The Republican-Form-of-Government Clause, often called the Guaranty Clause, art. IV, § 4, states "[t]he United States shall guarantee to every State in this Union a Republican form of Government." Claims under this Clause present political questions that federal courts will not adjudicate, in part because by its terms the provision may commit enforcement to another branch of the federal government. *Luther v. Borden*, 48 U.S. (7 How.) 1 (1849) (refusing to determine which competing group constituted the legitimate government of Rhode Island and declaring the issue to be one for Congress).

b. A "lack of judicially discoverable and manageable standards" for resolving the legal issue.

Example: The Guaranty Clause is an example of such a provision.

c. The "impossibility of deciding without an initial policy determination of a kind clearly for nonjudicial discretion. . ."

d. The danger of "expressing lack of the respect due coordinate branches of government . . ."

e. An "unusual need for unquestioning adherence to a political decision already made . . ."

Example: The Court has invoked the political-question doctrine to avoid deciding questions about the validity of the constitutional amendment process.

f. The "potentiality of embarrassment from multifarious pronouncements by various departments on one question."

2. Some commentators see these six factors as embodying three themes: (1) constitutional allocation of the matter to another branch, (2) a functional approach that counsels courts to avoid policy areas in which there are no clear judicial standards, and (3) prudential considerations involving comity, respect for a political decision already made, and avoidance of embarrassment.

C. Categories of Cases in Which the Political-Question Doctrine Applies and Causes Dismissal

1. Guaranty Clause

a. *Luther v. Borden*, 48 U.S. (7 How.) 1 (1849), refused to decide which of two competing factions was the legitimate government of Rhode Island, invoking the political-question doctrine.

b. *Texas v. White*, 74 U.S. (7 Wall.) 700 (1869), held that only Congress has authority to reestablish and recognize governments in the states that had seceded during the Civil War.

2. Foreign Affairs

a. In *Goldwater v. Carter*, 444 U.S. 996 (1979), a group of senators challenged the legality of the President's unilateral notice of termination of the nation's mutual defense treaty with the Republic of China. The Supreme Court summarily vacated the opinion of the court of appeals and ordered the case dismissed.

b. Justice Rehnquist, speaking for four Justices in *Goldwater*, concurred separately, arguing that the case was non-justiciable because the Constitution was silent on how to terminate a treaty, so the political process should determine the issue. He also agreed that the case involved the President's authority to conduct foreign affairs.

c. *Baker v. Carr*, 369 U.S. 186, 211 (1962), noted that issues of foreign affairs frequently "turn on standards that defy judicial application, or involve the exercise of a discretion demonstrably committed to the executive or legislature." In the same breath, however, the Court added that "it is error to suppose that every case or controversy which touches foreign relations lies beyond judicial cognizance." *Id.* [R318]

3. Impeachment

The Constitution vests "sole" power of impeachment in the House of Representatives and "sole" power to try impeachments in the Senate. Thus, federal courts will not intervene in any aspect of impeachment. *Nixon (Walter) v. United States*, 506 U.S. 224 (1993) (refusing to rule on challenge to Senate procedures used to try Judge Walter Nixon).

4. Dates of Duration of Hostilities

In *Commercial Trust Company v. Miller*, 262 U.S. 51 (1923), the issue was whether a congressional proclamation had ended World War I and thus ended the applicability of the Trading with the Enemy Act. The Court concluded: "[T]he power which declared the necessity is the power to declare its cessation, and what the cessation requires. The power is legislative." *Id.* at 67.

5. Regulation of Political Parties

While in a number of cases the Supreme Court has been willing to review the constitutionality of the political parties' actions, *Cousins v. Wigoda*, 419 U.S. 477, 483 (1975), the Court expressly left unresolved the question "whether or to what extent national political parties and their nominating conventions are regulable by, or only by, Congress."

6. Judicial Review of the Training and Weaponry of the National Guard

a. *Gilligan v. Morgan*, 413 U.S. 1 (1973), held that constitutional challenges to the training and weaponry of the Ohio National Guard are non-justiciable.

b. The Court found a conflict with a coordinate branch of the federal government, because Article I, § 8, cl. 16, vests in Congress the power "[t]o provide for organizing, arming, and disciplining the Militia, and for governing such Part of them as may be employed in the Service of the United States, reserving to the States respectively the Appointment of the Officers, and the Authority of training the Militia according to the discipline prescribed by Congress." *Id.* at 6.

D. Areas in Which the Court Has Rejected Applying the Political-Question Doctrine

1. The Constitutionality Under the Equal Protection Clause of State Representational Apportionment

   The Court refused to apply the doctrine in cases like *Baker v. Carr*. *Baker* surprised some commentators by breaking from former practice, under which the Court invoked the doctrine. Justice Frankfurter (author of the leading decision of the former practice) dissented in *Baker*, arguing that apportionment cases were really Guaranty-Clause cases and therefore non-justiciable. 369 U.S. at 289-92.

2. Exclusion of a Member of Congress by One of the Houses of Congress

   In *Powell v. McCormack*, 395 U.S. 486 (1969), a congressman-elect challenged the House of Representatives' s decision not to seat him. Because Article I, § 5 authorizes "each house [to] be the judge of the elections, returns and qualifications of its members," and, "with the concurrence of two thirds, [to] expel a member," there was a strong argument that the legislative branch controlled the issue. Nonetheless, the Court noted that the congressman-elect met the "qualifications" set out by the Constitution and held that his exclusion on other grounds was justiciable. Historically, the Court explained, the quoted provisions had not been intended to provide the houses of Congress such unreviewable authority to expel members.

3. Claims of Executive Privilege

   President Nixon's claim of executive privilege regarding the Watergate tapes did not present a political question. *United States v. Nixon (Richard)*, 418 U.S. 683 (1974). Neither did then-former President Trump's claim. *Trump v. United States*, 603 U.S. 593 (2024). [R3]

Chapter II

CONGRESSIONAL POWER TO REGULATE FEDERAL JURISDICTION

■ ANALYSIS

IV. Congressional Power to Regulate Supreme Court Original Jurisdiction

A. Article III Self-Executing Regarding Some Cases

B. Congressional Role Regarding Supreme Court Original Jurisdiction

V. Congressional Power to Regulate Supreme Court Appellate Jurisdiction

A. The Exceptions Clause

B. *Ex parte McCardle* and the Theory of Broad Congressional Power

C. The Essential-Functions Theory

D. The Limitation-As-to-Fact Theory

VI. Limitations on Congressional Power Deriving from Other Constitutional Provisions

A. Equal Protection

B. Due Process

C. Separation of Powers

VII. Congressional Power to Vest Article III Courts With Non-Article III Powers

A. Characteristics of an Article III Court

B. The Concept of Non-Article III Powers

C. Article III Courts Performing Non-Judicial Functions

D. Article III Courts Entertaining Cases Not Falling Within the Judicial Power of the United States

I. Introduction

The issue is what power Congress has to regulate the federal courts' jurisdiction. The answers depend in part on Article III and perhaps other constitutional provisions. Congressional power over the Supreme Court's jurisdiction differs from its power over the lower federal courts. There is also an important distinction between the Supreme Court's appellate jurisdiction and its original (trial) jurisdiction. In several instances, there is little or no case guidance, but there are significant academic theories. Even when there is case guidance, its ultimate application is unclear. These issues are important because they determine the extent to which Congress can engage in "jurisdiction stripping"—removing certain types of disputes from the federal court docket, perhaps because Congress is displeased with the substantive rulings in specific areas.

II. Distinction Between Congressional Power Over the Jurisdiction of the Supreme Court and of the Lower Federal Courts

A. Article III Provisions About Establishment of the Supreme Court and Lower Federal Courts

1. Article III, § 1, provides that "[t]he judicial Power of the United States shall be vested in one Supreme Court, and in such inferior Courts as the Congress may from time to time ordain and establish."
2. This expressly mandates that there be a Supreme Court. Just as clearly, it vests in Congress the original decision of whether to create any lower (inferior) federal courts. All assumptions about congressional power to control the jurisdiction of the lower federal courts flow from this fact. Common sense suggests that if Congress has the authority to create lower federal courts, it has broad power to regulate their jurisdiction. [R23]
3. Because the Constitution creates the Supreme Court, however, no similar conclusion about congressional power over its jurisdiction is possible. [R28]

B. The Distinction Between the Supreme Court's Original and Appellate Jurisdiction

1. Article III, § 2, cl. 2, provides that "[i]n all Cases affecting Ambassadors, other public Ministers and Consuls, and those in which a State shall be Party, the supreme Court shall have original jurisdiction. In all the other Cases before mentioned [in Article III, § 2, cl. 1], the supreme Court shall have appellate Jurisdiction, both as to Law and Fact, with such Exceptions, and under such Regulations as the Congress shall make." Original jurisdiction means that the Supreme Court has trial jurisdiction. Such cases are rare, but when they arise, Article III's language is clearly mandatory: the Supreme Court can try the case. It is less clear *how* the Court is to try the case.

2. Article III, § 2, cl. 1, lists nine types of cases within the judicial power of the federal courts and vests two types in the Supreme Court for trial, though the Court's original jurisdiction is not always exclusive; Congress's jurisdictional grants to the inferior courts may include cases within the Supreme Court's original jurisdiction, subject to the Eleventh Amendment's restrictions. *See generally infra* Ch. XIII, 283-299 *[R22]*. The vast majority of the Supreme Court's workload is appellate. Article III, § 2, cl. 2, provides in all "other" cases—presumably the other seven types of cases the federal judiciary can hear—the Supreme Court has appellate jurisdiction, as to law and fact, "with such Exceptions, and under such Regulations as the Congress shall make." This provision, the Exceptions Clause, clearly vests some power in Congress to tailor the Court's appellate jurisdiction.

3. Congress can explicitly remove lower-court jurisdiction with statutory language. It can also do so by implication, as it did in Thunder Basin Coal Co. v Reich, 510 U.S. 200 (1994), with the federal Mine Act's detailed enforcement mechanism topped by review in the Court of Appeals. However, *Axon Enterprise, Inc. v. FTC*, 598 U.S. 175 (2023), held that the congressional enforcement scheme ousted jurisdiction with respect to challenges of individual enforcement actions but not to a challenge to the agency's the constitutional legitimacy. [R124] [R314]

C. Relevance of Other Constitutional Provisions

In addition to considering Article III's language, those who debate congressional power over federal-court jurisdiction also point to other provisions of the Constitution that might limit the legislature's power. In particular, the Due Process Clause of the Fifth Amendment, the equal-protection component the Court has read into that Clause, and the largely implicit constitutional doctrine of separation of powers may prove relevant. [R34]

III. Congressional Power to Regulate Lower Federal Court Jurisdiction

A. The Traditional Theory of Broad Congressional Power

1. By its terms, Article III vests in Congress the original decision of whether to establish lower federal courts. *See supra* § II.A.1 & 2, at 59 *[R23]*. According to generally accepted historical analysis, the Framers reached an impasse. One group believed that the Constitution should mandate lower federal courts, while the other believed the Constitution should prohibit lower federal courts and that state courts should be the only trial courts to adjudicate federal law, with appellate supervision by the Supreme Court. The Madisonian Compromise resolved the deadlock: the delegates left to Congress the question of whether there should be lower federal courts. [R32]

2. Although the Judiciary Act of 1789 immediately established lower federal courts, the first historical assumption has been—and in large measure continues to be—that Congress did not have to do so. Consequently,

the second historical assumption has been that if Congress did create lower federal courts, it could abolish them. And if Congress may abolish lower federal courts, the long-held assumption has been that Congress may instead choose the less radical step of limiting their jurisdiction. In other words, the "greater" power (to abolish lower federal courts altogether) includes the "lesser" power (to curb their jurisdiction without abolishing them).

3. This principle—that the greater includes the lesser—underlies the Supreme Court's long-held conclusion that Congress has very broad power to limit the lower federal courts' jurisdiction. *See, e.g., Lockerty v. Phillips*, 319 U.S. 182 (1943); *Sheldon v. Sill*, 49 U.S. (8 How.) 441 (1850).

4. Because the Framers vested discretion to create lower federal courts in Congress, they apparently assumed that Congress could choose instead to rely on state courts as the primary adjudicators of federal law and enforcers of federal rights. The Supremacy Clause, art. VI, cl. 2, establishes the state courts' obligation to obey and enforce federal law as "the supreme law of the land . . . any Thing in the Constitution or laws of any state to the contrary notwithstanding." [R33]

5. Although Congress created lower federal courts in 1789, not until 1875 did it enact a long lasting general grant of federal-question jurisdiction, and it has the power to withdraw that grant. Until 1875, Congress largely relied on the state judiciaries for original adjudication of federal-question cases; most of the federal trial courts' cases sounded in diversity. *See infra* Ch. IV, § III.A, at 97-98 *[R24]*. [R212]

[R29] [R144]

B. Alternative Constructions of Article III

1. The traditional theory that Congress has plenary power to regulate the lower federal courts' jurisdiction has dominated, but it is not the only theory. Other major notions concerning congressional control of lower court jurisdiction include: (a) Justice Joseph Story's mandatory theory, (b) the changing-circumstances theory, and (c) the two-tier theory.

2. In the early 19th century, Justice Story argued that Congress lacked any authority to regulate lower federal court jurisdiction. Dictum in *Martin v. Hunter's Lessee*, 14 U.S. (1 Wheat.) 304, 328-31 (1816), noted that Article III, § 1, states that the federal judicial power "*shall* be vested" in the Supreme Court and the lower federal courts that Congress may establish. He construed "shall" to require that all federal judicial power be exercised *somewhere in the federal judiciary*. Because the Supreme Court only has appellate jurisdiction in many areas, Story reasoned that if no lower federal court existed there would be no original forum from which an appeal could run to the Supreme Court.

    a. Thus, Story opined, Congress was under a duty (1) to create *some* lower federal courts and (2) to vest in them the full judicial power—all types of cases listed in Article III, § 2, cl. 1 (except, of course, the two types over which the Supreme Court has original jurisdiction). "If, then, it is the duty of Congress to vest the judicial power of the United States, it is a duty to vest the whole judicial power. The language, if imperative as to one part, is imperative as to all." *Id.* at 330.

b. Although Congress has always provided lower federal courts, it never has vested the entire judicial power in them. Chapters IV and V discuss statutory limitations on federal-question and diversity jurisdiction, respectively, that make it obvious that Congress did not vest the whole constitutional grant of those two bases of jurisdiction.

c. Noting this, Story concluded that while the Constitution was mandatory on these points, it was not self-executing. Thus, if Congress failed to vest the whole of the judicial power in the lower courts, nothing could be done about it. *See White v. Fenner*, 29 Fed. Cas. 1015 (Cir. Ct. D.R.I. 1818) (Story, J., sitting as circuit judge).

d. Story's theory also ignores the possibility of state-court availability to determine questions of federal law, subject to Supreme Court review. Had Congress created no lower federal courts, state courts would have heard the various types of cases within the Supreme Court's appellate jurisdiction.

e. Some modern commentators have supported Story's theory, arguing that the Framers felt that state courts would fail to hear cases involving federal issues. On the whole, however, Story's theory has not fared well. The typical Supreme Court view long has been: "Congress is not bound, and it would, perhaps, be inexpedient, to enlarge the jurisdiction of the federal courts, to every subject, in every form, which the constitution might warrant." *Turner v. The President, Directors, and Co. of the Bank of North America*, 4 U.S. (4 Dall.) 8, 10 (1799).

f. One interesting case is consistent with Story's theory. Indeed, the language of the opinion is broader than the theory. In *Eisenstrager v. Forrestal*, 174 F.2d 961 (D.C. Cir. 1947), a prisoner of the American military in Germany sought habeas corpus relief from the federal court for the District of Columbia. The relevant venue statutes, however, required that federal habeas be sought only from a court in the district where the prisoner was. Obviously, there was no district court in Germany. No state court can grant habeas relief to one in federal custody. *See infra* Ch. XII.V.A, at 280-281*[R25]*. The Supreme Court lacked original jurisdiction, so there appeared to be no court that could entertain the petition. The District of Columbia Circuit exercised jurisdiction over the case, holding that Congress has a duty to confer all of the judicial power on some *federal* court. The court held that the Constitution compelled exercising jurisdiction. Thus, the court went beyond

Story, concluding that the Constitution was self-executing in this regard. The court also noted that lack of jurisdiction would effectively allow the government to suspend the writ of habeas corpus, in violation of art. I, § 9, cl. 2.

3. Several modern commentators argue the changing-circumstances theory. They assert that changing circumstances today render the Framers' original plan unworkable. In 1787, the Framers could rely on the availability of the Supreme Court to unify federal law and to police state courts. Today, the modern workload of the Supreme Court and sheer number of cases in various trial courts make this assumption untenable. The courts have not ruled on this theory, and it seems unlikely that it would win widespread acceptance.

4. Several modern commentators have also espoused a two-tier theory regarding congressional power to control lower court jurisdiction. Justice Story initially raised this idea as an alternative to his mandatory theory. Proponents argue that some federal court—either a lower court or the Supreme Court—must be available to adjudicate cases arising under federal law, cases affecting ambassadors, and admiralty cases. These three categories deserve special treatment because they are the only categories of cases listed in art. III, § 2, cl. 1, preceded by "all." Thus, all cases falling within these three heads of jurisdiction must be tried by some federal court. Little, if any, historical evidence demonstrates that the Framers considered such a structure.

C. Recent Congressional Regulation of Lower Federal Court Jurisdiction

1. Congress passed the Antiterrorism and Effective Death Penalty Act (AEDPA) and the Illegal Immigration Reform and Immigrant Responsibility Act (IIRIRA) in 1996. The latter amended the Immigration and Nationality Act in significant ways and purported to restrict federal courts' power to review certain immigration and deportation orders.

2. One part of the 1996 legislation limits judicial review of deportation to three issues: (a) the decision to commence proceedings, (b) adjudication of cases, and (c) execution of the deportation orders. The Acts clearly provide that this applies even to deportation proceedings pending when the statutes became effective. When some immigrants sued to challenge deportation proceedings against them and contended that the government engaged in selective enforcement, targeting them because they were members of politically unpopular groups, *Reno v. American-Arab Anti-Discrimination Committee*, 525 U.S. 471, 486 (1999), upheld the restriction on jurisdiction and ordered the case dismissed for lack of jurisdiction. The courts were powerless because the plaintiffs did not raise one of the three issues within the limited grant of judicial review.

   a. The Court concluded that "protecting the Executive's discretion from the courts . . . can fairly be said to be the theme of the legislation."

b. A circuit court, discussing one of the Acts, noted that it removed jurisdiction to review "not only a decision in an individual case *whether* to commence, but also *when* to commence," removal. Thus, the court lacked jurisdiction to review the petitioner's claim that the INS was under an obligation to commence deportation proceedings immediately upon learning that she was in the United States illegally. *Jimenez-Angeles v. Ashcroft*, 291 F.3d 594, 599 (9th Cir. 2002). [R31]

D. An Important Omission of Jurisdiction

It is critical to understand that the inferior federal courts lack subject-matter jurisdiction to review, either *de facto* or *de jure*, the judgments of state courts. The only exception is habeas corpus, *see generally infra* Ch. XV, at 331-346 *[R26]*, and even there, although Congress has conferred jurisdiction on the inferior federal courts to hear habeas cases involving persons in state custody, it has not referred to such cases as appeals. But it is not always easy to decide whether a federal plaintiff is seeking review of a state-court judgment or of something else, even when there is a preceding state-court judgment. The *Rooker-Feldman* doctrine addresses such problems. *See infra* Ch. XII § III.C, at 273-275 *[R27]*.

IV. Congressional Power to Regulate Supreme Court Original Jurisdiction

A. Article III Self-Executing Regarding Some Cases

1. Article III, § 1, requires that the Supreme Court exist. *See supra* § II.A, at 59 *[R28]*. Thus, unlike the situation with the lower federal courts, Congress has no power to abolish the Supreme Court. *See supra* § III.A, at 60-61 *[R29]*.

2. Article III, § 2, cl. 2, provides that in two types of cases—(a) those "affecting Ambassadors, other public Ministers and Consuls," and (b) those "in which a State shall be a party"—the Supreme Court "shall have original Jurisdiction."

3. This provision is self-executing. That is, the Constitution vests the Supreme Court with this trial jurisdiction, with no need for Congress to act.

   a. In *Chisholm v. Georgia*, 2 U.S. (2 Dall.) 419 (1793), a citizen of South Carolina sued the state of Georgia. The Court concluded that Article III's language clearly vested original jurisdiction in it. One justice dissented, arguing that in the absence of a statute, the Court should apply the common-law rule precluding actions against a sovereign.

   b. *Chisholm* inspired the Eleventh Amendment, which generally removes federal jurisdiction in actions by individuals against states. *See generally infra* Ch. XIII, 283-299 *[R30]*.

B. Congressional Role Regarding Supreme Court Original Jurisdiction

1. Because the original jurisdiction of the Supreme Court with regard to two classes of cases is self-executing, all seem to agree that Congress cannot restrict it. Congress has never expressly tried to do so. *See Wisconsin v. Pelican Insurance Company of New Orleans*, 127 U.S. 265, 300 (1888).
2. *South Carolina v. Katzenbach*, 383 U.S. 301, 357 n.1 (1966) (Black, J., dissenting), suggested that a provision of the Voting Rights Act of 1965 would be unconstitutional if it were interpreted to limit the Supreme Court's original jurisdiction in actions by the United States against a state. The Court did not interpret the Act that way.
3. Article III does not make the Supreme Court's original jurisdiction exclusive. Accordingly, Congress can grant original jurisdiction over these types of cases to a lower federal court. *United States v. California*, 297 U.S. 175 (1936).
4. *Marbury v. Madison* held unconstitutional Congress's effort to expand the Court's original jurisdiction by vesting jurisdiction to issue mandamus to federal officers. It concluded that issuing mandamus was a function of original, not appellate jurisdiction. Chief Justice Marshall noted that Article III prescribes only two classes of cases as falling within the original jurisdiction of the Supreme Court and that *Marbury* fell within neither. Because Article III provides that in all other cases the Supreme Court "shall have appellate Jurisdiction," the effort to vest original jurisdiction in the Court was unconstitutional. Marshall said: "If congress remains at liberty to give this court appellate jurisdiction, where the constitution has declared their jurisdiction shall be original; and original jurisdiction where the constitution has declared it shall be appellate; the distribution of jurisdiction, made in the constitution, is form without substance." *Id.* at 174.
5. The Supreme Court has discretion to refuse to hear a case invoking its original jurisdiction (even if its jurisdiction is exclusive, *see Texas v. California*, 141 S. Ct. 1469 (2021)) and is reluctant to try cases between states and private litigants when another forum is available. *See Ohio v. Wyandotte Chemicals Corp.*, 401 U.S. 493 (1971) (claim based on common-law nuisance theory better tried in another court, with the possibility of Supreme Court review).

V. Congressional Power to Regulate Supreme Court Appellate Jurisdiction

A. The Exceptions Clause

1. After delineating the Supreme Court's original jurisdiction, art. III, § 2, cl. 2, provides in "all the other Cases [within the judicial power of the United States], the supreme Court shall have appellate jurisdiction, both as to Law and Fact, with such Exceptions, and under such Regulations as the Congress shall make."
2. Clearly, the Exceptions Clause vests some power in Congress to tailor the appellate jurisdiction of the Supreme Court. [R129] [R315]

B. *Ex parte McCardle* and the Theory of Broad Congressional Power

1. *Ex parte McCardle*, 74 U.S. (7 Wall.) 506 (1868), involved an extraordinary set of facts. McCardle was incarcerated in Mississippi under Reconstruction statutes. After the federal trial court denied his petition for habeas corpus, he appealed to the Supreme Court. A recent statute had created that appellate jurisdiction. McCardle argued that he was entitled to habeas corpus because the Reconstruction statutes authorizing his detention were unconstitutional. After oral argument, members of Congress, fearful that the Court would invalidate the challenged parts of the Reconstruction legislation, repealed the statute that had vested appellate jurisdiction in the Court.
   a. The Court refused to reach the merits, and held that Congress's repeal of appellate jurisdiction was effective. The repealer was a legitimate exercise of the legislative power under the Exceptions Clause. The fact that the case was pending on appeal when Congress acted was irrelevant.
   b. The repeal of appellate jurisdiction is an archetypal example of jurisdiction stripping. Congress took action precisely because it feared how the Court would rule on the merits of the challenge to the Reconstruction statutes.
2. *McCardle* contains broad language implying nearly unfettered congressional authority under the Exceptions Clause. Indeed, through the years, many people have, in the words of Professor Henry Hart, read *McCardle* "for all it's worth"—a signal that Congress has essentially plenary power over the Supreme Court's appellate jurisdiction.
3. More recently, however, many have argued against reading *McCardle* so expansively. They point out that just one year after *McCardle*, the Supreme Court held that it had the authority to issue original writs of habeas corpus. *Ex parte Yerger*, 75 U.S. (8 Wall.) 85 (1869). Thus, although Congress removed the Court's appellate jurisdiction to review habeas cases, another statute allowed the Court to issue original writs. Therefore, commentators argue, *McCardle* may stand for the proposition that Congress can remove Supreme Court appellate jurisdiction if Supreme Court adjudication is available by other means.
4. Section III.C, *see supra* at 63-64 *[R31]*, notes the important 1996 legislation—AEDPA and IIRIRA. One part of AEDPA prohibits a state prisoner from filing successive petitions for habeas corpus unless the United States Court of Appeals approves the additional petition. The Act also precludes Supreme Court review of a Court of Appeals decision concerning a state prisoner's petition for a successive habeas petition. The Supreme Court unanimously upheld the restriction on its jurisdiction, but emphasized that the legislation did not completely preclude Supreme Court review of the denial of permission to file successive petitions, because the Court retains the authority to entertain original petitions for habeas corpus relief. *Felker v. Turpin*, 518 U.S. 651 (1996). [R323]

C. The Essential-Functions Theory

1. Several commentators have argued that Congress may not make exceptions to the Supreme Court's appellate jurisdiction that will destroy the Court's essential role in the constitutional plan. They propose that providing a uniform interpretation of federal law and policing state court interpretation and enforcement of federal law are essential functions. They note that the congressional restriction *McCardle* upheld did not prevent the Supreme Court from hearing habeas corpus cases as original matters. Thus, the *McCardle* statute did not totally block access to the Supreme Court in a case involving supremacy.

2. There is neither a linguistic nor a firm historical basis supporting this theory, but its advocates find it implicit in the constitutional structure. The courts have never spoken on the theory.

D. The Limitation-As-to-Fact Theory

1. Several commentators have focused on the phrase immediately preceding the Exceptions Clause. Article III, § 2, cl. 2, states that the Supreme Court shall have appellate jurisdiction, "both as to Law and Fact, with such Exceptions, and under such Regulations as the Congress shall make." These commentators argue that the Founders intended to limit Congress's authority under the Exceptions Clause to the power to limit Supreme Court review of factual determinations.

2. Although there is historical evidence that the Framers were concerned about Supreme Court review of lower-court findings of fact, the Clause's language simply does not lend itself to such a limited interpretation. In addition, the broader grant of the Supreme Court's appellate jurisdiction in the Judiciary Act of 1789 is a strong indication that the Framers did not intend such a narrow scope of appellate review. Finally, *McCardle* at least implicitly rejected this theory, since the statute did not confine its limitation of the Court's appellate jurisdiction to review of factual findings.

VI. Limitations on Congressional Power Deriving from Other Constitutional Provisions

A. Equal Protection

1. Although the Fifth Amendment contains no express equal protection provision, the Supreme Court has construed that Amendment's Due Process Clause to include such a requirement. *Bolling v. Sharpe*, 347 U.S. 497 (1954) (a companion case to *Brown v. Board of Education*). Thus, it is clear that Congress cannot employ its Article III power, for example, to prohibit racial or religious groups from gaining access to the federal courts.

2. In fact, some commentators argue that the equal-protection component extends further, preventing Congress from limiting access to the federal courts for specific fundamental rights, because such a limitation would

discriminate on the basis of a fundamental right. No case has tested this theory. [R313]

B. Due Process

1. The Supreme Court has held that the Due Process Clause requires that the government take neither liberty nor property absent some form of hearing before an independent adjudicator. Several cases suggest that due process may require an independent judicial forum, although the courts have not fully defined the status and contours of this requirement. *See, e.g., Bartlett v. Bowen*, 816 F.2d 695 (D.C. Cir. 1987); *Battaglia v. General Motors Corp.*, 169 F.2d 254 (2d Cir. 1948).

2. It is unlikely, however, that this requirement imposes significant limits on Congress's authority to regulate the lower federal courts' jurisdiction or the Supreme Court's appellate jurisdiction. As to the former, while due process may prevent Congress from denying access to any judicial forum for the adjudication of a constitutional right (*see Bartlett* and *Battaglia*), traditionally Congress has been able to satisfy the due process requirement by allowing *state* courts to serve as the ultimate protectors of federal constitutional rights. Congress can do this because—as the Madisonian Compromise and the Supremacy Clause reflect—state courts have the power and the obligation to vindicate federal rights. *See supra* § III.A.1 & 4, at 60 *[R32]*, 61 *[R33]*.

3. Limiting the Supreme Court's appellate jurisdiction does not violate due process, because the Court has never construed due process to require any appellate review. [R324]

C. Separation of Powers

1. While Congress may well retain broad power to limit the federal courts' jurisdiction, the inferred constitutional doctrine of separation of powers confines that power. This limitation arises even if one accepts the proposition that the Exceptions Clause would permit Congress to remove the Supreme Court's appellate jurisdiction altogether.

2. *United States v. Klein*, 80 US. (13 Wall.) 128 (1871), involved a Civil War statute that permitted persons whose property the government had seized to recover it or its monetary value if they could show that they had not aided the rebellion. The Supreme Court held in 1869 that a presidential pardon constituted proof for purposes of this statute that someone *had not* aided the rebellion. *United States v. Padelford*, 76 U.S. (9 Wall.) 531 (1869). In reaction to numerous presidential pardons, Congress then passed a statute providing that such a pardon was proof that the person *had* aided the enemy and that once a pardon was proved, "the jurisdiction of the court shall cease" and the case for recovery of property would be dismissed.

   a. The Court held the statute unconstitutional. "What is this [law] but to prescribe a rule for the decision of a cause in a particular way?" the Court asked. "We must think that Congress has inadvertently passed the limit which separates the legislative power from the judicial power." *Klein*, 80 U.S. at 146, 147.

b. Commentators have long debated *Klein*'s holding. Some interpret *Klein* broadly to mean that Congress cannot restrict jurisdiction to direct a particular substantive outcome. Others argue for a narrower reading. These commentators note that the statute in *Klein* was an unconstitutional interference with the President's pardon power under Article II, § 2, and that it arguably effected a denial of property without just compensation, violating of due process. Thus, they see *Klein* as holding only that Congress cannot limit jurisdiction by with statute that violates other provisions of the Constitution.

c. In 1980, the Supreme Court described *Klein* as having held the statute unconstitutional in two respects: "it prescribed a rule of decision in a case pending before the courts, and did so in a manner that required the courts to decide a controversy in the Government's favor." *United States v. Sioux Nation of Indians*, 448 U.S. 371, 404 (1980). *Sioux Nation* supports a broad reading of *Klein*, because it does not require that the congressional act itself be unconstitutional. In the narrower interpretation, noted *supra* ¶ b, *Klein* would apply only if the statute violates some other constitutional provision, such as the President's pardon power.

3. The Supreme Court revisited *Klein* in 1992. The case involved an appropriations statute that required the Bureau of Land Management to offer certain land for sale and to restrict timber harvesting on other land. The Act took note of two cases and set out Congress's determination that if the specific land involved in those two suits were managed according to substantive provisions of the Act, that would constitute "adequate consideration for the purpose of meeting the statutory requirements that are the basis for [the two pending cases]." The Supreme Court upheld the law. *Robertson v. Seattle Audubon Society*, 503 U.S. 429 (1992).

   The Ninth Circuit had held that *Klein* rendered the statute unconstitutional, but the Supreme Court reversed that decision and distinguished *Klein*. *Klein* applies when Congress dictates to the courts a substantive decision under an extant law. By contrast, *Robertson* involved enacting a new substantive law, so *Klein* did not govern. Some commentators have found the Court's effort to distinguish the two fact patterns unconvincing.

4. More recently, in a different context the Court indicated that separation of powers limits congressional power in this general area. After the Supreme Court had held that plaintiffs had to bring certain securities fraud cases within a specific (relatively short) period (*Lampf, Pleva, Lipkind, Prupis & Petigrow v. Gilbertson*, 501 U.S. 350 (1991)), Congress

amended the law to allow cases already dismissed to reactivate on plaintiff's motion if they antedated the Supreme Court decision and would have been timely under the law as it then existed. The Court held that the statute violated separation of powers and thus was unconstitutional. *Plaut v. Spendthrift Farm, Inc.*, 514 U.S. 211 (1995).

a. The statute was unconstitutional because it robbed the judiciary of its power to "render dispositive judgments." The statute would have permitted a party to resuscitate a case after the federal judiciary had finally dismissed it. In effect, the statute attempted to undo final, unappealable judgments.

b. Although the statute did not involve a congressional effort to remove federal jurisdiction, it clearly indicates that separation-of-powers principles limit congressional power to dictate substantive results in federal litigation.

5. Section III.C, *supra* at 60, *[R34]* discusses two important 1996 statutes—the AEDPA and IIRIRA. Before those Acts, a statute expressly gave the Attorney General discretion to waive deportation of resident aliens convicted of specific crimes. AEDPA and IIRIRA repealed that provision. Before the repeal, a resident alien pleaded guilty to a crime that made him deportable. By the time the government commenced deportation proceedings, however, Congress had passed the two Acts. The government claimed (1) that the Attorney General no longer had authority to waive deportation because the repeal contained in the two Acts was retroactive, and (2) that the jurisdiction-stripping provisions of both Acts precluded any judicial review of the legal question of whether the Attorney General retained discretion to waive deportation. *Immigration and Naturalization Service v. St. Cyr*, 533 U.S. 289 (2001), rejected both contentions.

a. The Court held that the restrictions on jurisdiction did not repeal habeas corpus jurisdiction. Thus, the resident alien was entitled to raise the legal question of the Attorney General's discretion to waive deportation in a habeas corpus proceeding. In other words, the restrictions on jurisdiction applied to judicial review of deportation orders but not to block habeas review on the question of whether the repeal of the Attorney General's discretion was retroactive.

b. The strong presumption in favor of judicial review of administrative action and the requirement of a clear legislative statement of intent to repeal habeas corpus jurisdiction supported the conclusion that habeas review remained available.

c. Construing the Acts "entirely [to] preclude review of a pure question of law by any court would give rise to substantial constitutional questions, . . ." specifically under the Suspension Clause, art. I, § 9, cl. 2: "the privilege of the Writ of Habeas Corpus shall not be suspended, unless when in Cases of Rebellion or Invasion the public Safety may require it." According to the Court, "a serious Suspension Clause issue would be presented if we were to accept the INS's submission that the 1996 statutes have withdrawn that power from federal judges and provided no adequate substitute for its exercise." The Court avoided that constitutional question by concluding that Congress had not repealed habeas corpus jurisdiction.

d. On the merits, the Court held that the repeal of the Attorney General's discretionary power to waive deportation did not apply retroactively.

e. Congress subsequently (8 U.S.C. § 1252 (2005)) withdrew authorization for habeas review of such cases under 28 U.S.C. § 2241 but restored jurisdiction for the courts of appeals to review "constitutional claims or questions of law. . . ." [R316]

VII. Congressional Power to Vest Article III Courts With Non-Article III Powers

A. Characteristics of an Article III Court

1. Article III courts are the federal courts whose judges possess the life tenure and salary protections provided in Article III, § 1. *See supra* Ch. I, § II.A, at 32 *[R35]*.
2. The federal district courts, courts of appeals, and the Supreme Court are Article III courts.

B. The Concept of Non-Article III Powers

1. Traditionally, the Article III courts hear cases falling within the categories in Article III, § 2, cl. 1, which lists the cases to which the Constitution extends the federal "judicial power."
2. Occasionally, however, Congress has attempted to expand the "business" of Article III courts to include a broader array of responsibilities. It has done so in two ways. First, it has allowed some Article III courts to entertain disputes that not within the judicial power of Article III, § 2, cl. 1. Second, it has required some Article III courts to engage in tasks other than adjudicating disputes.
3. In lieu of vesting Article III courts with such non-Article III powers, Congress can establish non-Article III courts. Chapter III discusses such courts (which Chief Justice Marshall termed "legislative courts") including whether non-Article III courts may hear Article III matters. This section considers whether Article III courts may exercise non-Article III powers.

C. Article III Courts Performing Non-Judicial Functions

1. Article III extends the federal judicial power only to "cases" or "controversies." *See supra* Ch. I, § III.A, at 33 *[R36]*. Starting in the 1920s, Con-

gress vested the United States District Court for the District of Columbia and the Court of Appeals for the District of Columbia with responsibilities beyond adjudicating cases or controversies. For instance, Congress required them required to assume some administrative and even some legislative functions concerning setting utility rates in the District of Columbia.

a. The Supreme Court held that these courts were created under Congress's power to legislate regarding the District of Columbia under Article I, § 8. Thus, they could perform, in addition to adjudication, the various non-judicial functions Congress gave them. The Supreme Court, however, being an Article III tribunal, cannot entertain appeals from matters that are non-judicial. *Keller v. Potomac Electric Power Co.*, 261 U.S. 428 (1923). *See also Federal Radio Commission v. General Electric Co.*, 281 U.S. 464 (1930) (reaching same conclusions regarding review of FRC orders).

b. In dictum, the Court later declared that the District of Columbia courts were not Article III courts. *Ex parte Bakelite Corporation*, 279 U.S. 438 (1929).

c. Next, the Court held that they were "hybrid" courts. They were Article III courts when they adjudicated cases or controversies under Article III, but were non-Article III courts when they performed non-judicial tasks. *O'Donoghue v. United States*, 289 U.S. 516 (1933).

d. The District Court for the District of Columbia upheld a statute requiring it to appoint school board members for the District. It relied on the "hybrid" theory to do so. *Hobson v. Hansen*, 265 F. Supp. 902 (D.D.C. 1967). (Congress amended the statute to take this responsibility from the judiciary by providing for an elected school board.)

2. Congress ended the hybrid nature of those federal courts in 1970 by establishing a set of local courts, which clearly are not Article III courts. These tribunals function as state courts do in the states, and, because Article III does not limit them, clearly can perform non-judicial tasks. Thus, there is no longer doubt that the United States District Court for the District of Columbia and the United States Court of Appeals for the District of Columbia are Article III courts.

3. Similarly, the Court of Claims and the Court of Customs and Patent Appeals presented difficult issues. These courts performed non-Article III functions, including issuing what essentially were advisory opinions, which an Article III court simply cannot do. *See supra* Ch. I, § III, at 33-34 *[R37]*.

a. *Ex parte Bakelite Corporation*, 279 U.S. 438 (1929), held that the Court of Customs Appeals was not an Article III court. Four years later, the Court reached the same conclusion regarding the Court of Claims and Patent Appeals. *Williams v. United States*, 289 U.S. 553 (1933).

b. In 1953 and 1956, Congress passed statutes declaring these two courts to be Article III courts.

c. Finally, *Glidden Company v. Zdanok*, 370 U.S. 530 (1962), held that they were Article III courts. The Justices split badly on the question of why this is so, however, and there is no definitive explanation for the holding. The Court instructed these bodies to avoid performing non-Article III functions, and they complied. Congress overruled *Zdanok* by declaring the Court of Claims to be an Non-Article III court. 28 U.S.C. § 171. [R42] [R44]

4. Congress largely alleviated the difficulties, however, by removing the advisory function from the Court of Claims and giving it only to the chief commissioner of that court. In addition, it removed judicial involvement until after the President had acted in certain matters, thereby deleting another aspect of the advisory nature of the Court's function.

5. Today, the Court of Claims and the Court of Customs and Patent Appeals no longer exist. Congress merged them into the United States Court of Appeals for the Federal Circuit, plainly an Article III court. In this reorganization, Congress vested the Court of Claims' trial functions and other matters in what is now the United States Court of Federal Claims, which is not an Article III court. The Customs Court is now the Court of International Claims and is an Article III court.

6. The Supreme Court has on occasion upheld congressional direction to Article III judges to perform functions other than the adjudication of cases or controversies.

   a. *Morrison v. Olson*, 487 U.S. 654 (1988), upheld using a specially created Article III court to perform certain administrative tasks as part of creating and implementing the system for appointing and overseeing an independent counsel appointed to investigate and prosecute high ranking government officials. Under Article II, Congress can vest the appointment of some officers in an Article III court. The power to appoint carries with it power to supervise.

   b. The Court reasoned that those functions of an Article III court are not inherently executive, and were "directly analogous to functions that federal judges perform in other contexts. . . ." Moreover, the Court found that courts' power to terminate the independent counsel did not unduly interfere with executive discretion.

   c. *Mistretta v. United States*, 488 U.S. 361 (1989), upheld the statutory requirement that several Article III judges sit on the United States Sentencing Commission, which Congress created to promulgate binding sentencing guidelines. The Court reasoned that breaches of separation of powers were invalid only when they "either accrete to a single branch powers more appropriately diffused among separate branches or . . . undermine the authority and independence of one or another coordinate branch."

d. The Court further noted that the judiciary had long performed the function of determining sentences in the course of specific adjudications. It also relied on the fact that no specific court had the power to promulgate sentencing guidelines. Rather, the statute directed that individual Article III judges were be members of the Commission. The Court cited the long tradition of Supreme Court Justices' service in non-judicial capacities, and noted that "[t]he text of the Constitution contains no prohibition against the service of active federal judges on independent commissions such as that established by the Act."

7. Thus it seems clear that Congress can (but rarely does) require Article III judges to perform some administrative tasks.

D. Article III Courts Entertaining Cases Not Falling Within the Judicial Power of the United States

1. From the earliest days, the Supreme Court has made it clear that Article III courts cannot adjudicate disputes that do not fall within the Article III judicial power. *Marbury v. Madison* rejected Congress's effort to permit the Supreme Court to issue a writ of mandamus, because such original jurisdiction did not fall within Article III. *Hodgson v. Bowerbank*, 9 U.S. (5 Cranch) 303 (1809), struck a legislative grant of jurisdiction over cases in which an alien was a party because it would have permitted suit by an alien against an alien; the judicial power Article III defines does not reach such cases. *See infra* Ch. V, § II.A.3, at 117 *[R38]*.

2. A majority rejected the notion that Congress could grant jurisdiction to an Article III court in excess of Article III in the famous case of *National Mutual Insurance Co. v. Tidewater Transfer Co.*, 337 U.S. 582 (1949). *See also infra* Ch. V, § III.A.7, at 118 *[R39]*. The Court upheld legislation vesting the Article III federal courts with diversity jurisdiction over suits between citizens of a state and those of the District of Columbia. The statute provided that citizens of the District of Columbia were citizens of a State for diversity purposes. The statute was inconsistent with an old Supreme Court holding that the District was not a State for diversity purposes. *Hepburn & Dundas v. Ellzey*, 6 U.S. (2 Cranch) 445 (1804).

a. Although a majority of the Supreme Court upheld the statute, it did so on the basis of two theories, neither of which commanded a majority. Thus, there is no single rationale for the holding.

b. Justice Jackson's opinion (in which two other Justices joined) is of most interest. It concluded that Congress has the authority to vest the federal courts with jurisdiction over non-Article III cases using its legislative powers under Article I.

c. Six Justices, however, rejected this potentially wide-reaching theory, expressing concern about federalism and separation-of-powers factors.

d. Two of those six Justices concurred, however, in upholding the jurisdictional statute, on the ground that the District should properly be deemed a "state" for diversity purposes; they would have overruled the old Supreme Court authority to the contrary. [R325]

3. Thus it seems clear that Congress cannot expand the jurisdiction of the federal courts to adjudicate beyond the judicial power in Article III, § 2, cl. 1. [R40]

Chapter III

NON-ARTICLE III COURTS

■ ANALYSIS

I. Introduction

Chapter II, § VII, *see supra* at 71 *[R40]*, considered whether Article III courts can exercise non-Article III powers: either non-judicial functions or adjudicating cases not falling within the federal courts' judicial power. This Chapter addresses the converse situation—whether non-Article III courts can perform judicial tasks falling within Article III. It is helpful to distinguish between non-Article III courts, on one hand, and officers or bodies that act as adjuncts to Article III courts on the other. Non-Article III courts (such as the territorial courts, military courts, the local courts in the District of Columbia, and the tax court) act as independent adjudicatory bodies; they enter final judgments, subject ultimately to appellate review in the Supreme Court. Adjuncts to Article III courts (such as administrative agencies, bankruptcy courts, and magistrate judges) adjudicate various matters, but a lower Article III court reviews their decisions. Both situations involve the problem of vesting Article III business in non-Article III decision-makers.

Non-Article III courts come in two flavors: Article I courts and Article IV courts. Military courts and the local courts of the District of Columbia (as distinguished from the United States District Court for the District of Columbia and the United States Court of Appeals for the District of Columbia) are examples of Article I courts. Territorial courts are Article IV courts. Chief Justice John Marshall coined the term "legislative courts" in 1828. That term, however, may misleadingly suggest that such courts can enact laws.

II. Article III Courts and Non-Article III Courts

A. Article III Provides Protection for Article III Judges and Defines Judicial Power.

1. Article III, § 1, declares the "judicial Power of the United States shall be vested in one supreme Court, and in such inferior Courts as the Congress may from time to time ordain and establish." It then provides that Article III judges shall serve during good behavior (which means they have lifetime tenure, subject to removal only by impeachment) and that Congress cannot reduce their compensation. These conditions provide Article III judges with great job security, insulating them from retaliation by the political branches and the populace. They are free to rule in ways that may be unpopular. *See supra* Ch. I, § II.A, at 32 *[R41]*.
2. Article III, § 2, then defines the "judicial power of the United States" by listing those sorts of cases or controversies that can fall within federal subject-matter jurisdiction.
3. These provisions seem to make it clear that only Article III courts can exercise the "judicial power of the United States"—as defined in Article III, § 2, because only Article III judges enjoy the constitutional protections from outside influence.

B. Articles I and IV Permit Congress to Create Non-Article III Courts

1. Article I lists Congress's enumerated powers. Pursuant to those powers and the Necessary-and-Proper Clause, Congress has the authority to create courts not bound by the restrictions of Article III. Article IV, § 3, cl. 2 authorizes Congress to govern territories of the United States, and Congress has long created territorial courts as a part of that function. These tribunals have been called "non-Article III courts," "Article I courts," "Article IV courts," or "legislative courts." This volume will use the term "non-Article III courts" throughout.
   a. The Supreme Court could have held that Congress cannot create courts other than pursuant to Article III but reached the contrary conclusion. *American Ins. Co. v. Canter*, 26 U.S. (1 Pet.) 511 (1828) (upholding Congress's power to create territorial courts).
   b. Because non-Article III courts do not exist under Article III, none of the Article III case-or-controversy limitations apply to them. For example, they can issue advisory opinions.
   c. More important, because Congress creates such courts under Articles I and IV, not Article III, Article III's guarantees of lifetime tenure and freedom from salary reduction do not protect non-Article III judges. [R43]
2. The territorial courts, military courts, the tax court, and local courts for the District of Columbia are examples of non-Article III courts.
3. Originally, the Supreme Court held that the Court of Claims and the Court of Customs and Patent Appeals were non-Article III courts. The Court overturned that in 1962, concluding that both were Article III courts. *See supra* Ch. II, § VII.C.3, *supra* at 72-73 *[R42]*. Subsequently, Congress replaced those courts with the United States Court of Appeals for the Federal Circuit and a trial forum known as the United States Court of Federal Claims. They are Article III courts.

III. Constitutional Limits on Congressional Power to Vest Non-Article III Courts with Authority to Decide Article III Matters

A. Importance of the Issue

1. While no one today denies Congress's power to create non-Article III courts, *see supra* § II.B.1, there is a serious question about whether those courts can entertain matters falling within the "judicial power of the United States," which Article III, § 2, defines.
2. If Congress can permit non-Article III courts to hear cases within Article III, then judges who lack the Article III protections of lifetime tenure and salary guaranty may decide Article III cases. That would eviscerate a central goal of Article III—that only judges protected from political

retaliation adjudicate Article III cases. If Congress diverts cases from Article III courts to Non-Article III courts, it places such cases before judges whose pay and tenure it controls.

3. This concern might suggest that non-Article III courts cannot hear Article III cases. Though the Supreme Court once seemed to embrace this position, it has since departed from it.

B. Early Uncertainty About Whether Non-Article III Courts May Adjudicate Article III Matters

1. *American Ins. Co. v. Canter,* 26 U.S. (1 Pet.) 511 (1828), was the first important case concerning non-Article III courts. It arose in Florida, then a territory. Congress had created two superior courts in the territory; the judges served a limited term. The territorial legislature created inferior courts, one of which was a salvage court. That court entered a judgment for Canter, which the insurance company later challenged in a separate action in an Article III court. The question was whether the salvage court's judgment was valid. The Supreme Court held that it was.

   a. The insurance company argued that the salvage-court judgment was void because the case fell within admiralty jurisdiction, and thus required an Article III court.

   b. The Supreme Court noted that neither the salvage court nor the superior court was an Article III court, because neither court's judges enjoyed the protections of Article III judges.

   c. The Court agreed that neither court could entertain admiralty cases, which fall within the Article III judicial power. Non-Article III courts "are not constitutional Courts, in which the judicial power conferred by the Constitution . . . can be deposited. They are incapable of receiving it." *Canter*, 26 U.S. (1 Pet.) at 546.

   d. But the Court held that the case the salvage court heard was not an admiralty case, and thus did not fall within the Article III judicial power. Rather, the salvage-court jurisdiction "is conferred by Congress, in the execution of those general powers which that body possesses over the territories of the United States." *Id.*

2. *Canter* established at least three things: (a) Congress has the authority to create non-Article III courts; (b) the territorial courts are non-Article III, not Article III, courts; and (c) non-Article III courts are "incapable of receiving" Article III judicial power.

3. The notion that non-Article III courts are "incapable of receiving" Article III judicial power was problematic even then.

   a. Before *Canter*, the Supreme Court had held that it had appellate jurisdiction to review territorial-court judgments. *Durousseau v. United States*, 10 U.S. (6 Cranch) 307 (1810).

b. Supreme Court appellate jurisdiction, however, extends only to cases within the judicial power of Article III. *See infra* Ch. VIII, § II.A.1, at 164 *[R43]*.

c. It is inconsistent to say, on one hand, that territorial courts do not hear Article III cases yet, on the other, that the Supreme Court has appellate jurisdiction over their cases.

d. The Supreme Court has never addressed this inconsistency; territorial courts are to this day non-Article III courts.

e. A territorial judge may not sit by designation on the United States Court of Appeals because only Article III judges may do so. *Nguyen v. United States*, 539 U.S. 69 (2003).

4. The Supreme Court early characterized military courts as non-Article III tribunals: "Congress has the power to provide for the trial and punishment of military and naval offenses in the manner then and now practiced by civilized nations. . . . [T]he power to do so is given without any connection between it and the 3d article of the Constitution." *Dynes v. Hoover*, 61 U.S. (20 How.) 65, 79 (1858).

a. Military courts can deprive military personnel of personal liberties.

b. The judges in military courts are military officers, and, thus are not independent of the authority prosecuting the defendant.

5. The Supreme Court has never recognized any constitutional problem with having non-Article III military courts enter orders depriving military personnel of their liberty.

a. The Court has noted practical considerations: "[E]xigencies of military discipline require the existence of a special system of military courts in which not all of the specific procedural protections deemed essential in Art. III trials need apply." *O'Callahan v. Parker*, 395 U.S. 258, 261 (1969).

b. Some commentators question why the need for military discipline should preclude having an independent adjudicator in military cases.

c. Others have argued that the Framers intended military courts to be independent of Article III requirements, but the Court has never expressly embraced this argument.

6. Chapter II, § VII.C.3, *see supra* at 72 *[R44]*, discussed *Ex parte Bakelite Corp.*, 279 U.S. 438 (1929), and *Williams v. United States*, 289 U.S. 553 (1933), in which the Supreme Court held, respectively, that the Court of Customs and Patent Appeals and the Court of Claims were non-Article III courts. But the Court later ruled inconsistently with respect to both cases, and Congress has since restructured and renamed those courts, which today are Article III courts.

7. Nonetheless, the two opinions remain noteworthy for their treatment of whether Non-Article III courts may entertain Article III cases.

   a. *Bakelite* seemed to assume that Non-Article III courts could hear Article III cases except possibly "inherently judicial" matters, a term the Court did not define.

   b. *Williams*, however, indicated that an Non-Article III court simply cannot adjudicate Article III matters.

8. *Glidden Co. v. Zdanok*, 370 U.S. 530 (1962), overruled both, holding that the courts were Article III courts. In the plurality opinion, Justice Harlan expressly rejected the *Williams* notion that Non-Article III courts may not hear Article III cases.

   a. *Glidden* made it clear that Congress can give Article III business to non-Article III courts, but it failed to delineate how much.

   b. In addition, *Glidden* left open the possibility that *Bakelite* suggested: that there are "inherently judicial" matters that non-Article III courts cannot adjudicate.

9. In *Palmore v. United States*, 411 U.S. 389 (1973), the local District of Columbia Superior Court, an non-Article III court, had convicted the defendant of a felony. The Supreme Court agreed that court had the authority to deprive a defendant of personal liberty. The holding is unclear but seems premised on the unique relationship between Congress and the District of Columbia under Art. I, § 8, cl. 17.

10. In addition to upholding the local-court ruling, *Palmore* cited three situations in which Congress had properly vested non-Article III courts with Article III power: (1) territorial courts, (2) military courts, and (3) state courts (by making some grants of federal-court jurisdiction concurrent). *Palmore*, of course, adds the District of Columbia local courts to that list.

    a. Of these, note that state-court judges are immune from political retaliation by a branch of the federal government. While state-court judges certainly lack Article III tenure protection, neither Congress nor the executive branch of the federal government may reduce their pay or remove them from office. That is not so with territorial and military courts.

    b. Thus, at least in separation-of-powers terms, it is easier to justify vesting Article III matters in state courts than in non-Article III courts. Judges of the latter two are subject to oversight by the political branches of the federal government. [R317]

C. Modern Evolution: The "Inherently Judicial" Doctrine and Adjudication of Constitutional Facts

1. In recent years, the Supreme Court has indicated that there are two areas in which Congress may not place adjudicative power in non-Article III courts: (1) "inherently judicial" cases involving private rights and

(2) determination of constitutional facts—facts that form the underlying basis for the claim that a governmental act is unconstitutional.

2. *Northern Pipeline Construction Co. v. Marathon Pipe Line Co.*, 458 U.S. 50 (1982) (*Marathon*), struck down part of the 1978 Bankruptcy Reform Act. Specifically, it held that the judges of the bankruptcy courts (non-Article III judges) could not hear state-law claims involving the bankrupt. In his plurality opinion, Justice Brennan distinguished between cases involving "public rights" and those involving "private rights."

   a. Public rights cases are those that arise "between the Government and persons subject to its authority in connection with the performance of the constitutional functions of the executive or legislative departments." *Crowell v. Benson*, 285 U.S. 22, 50 (1932).

   b. Private-rights cases are disputes between private litigants.

   c. Public-rights cases are not "inherently judicial" and thus do not require Article III judges. *SEC v. Jarkesy*, 603 U.S. 109 (2024), held that an SEC action seeking civil penalties for securities fraud was analogous to a common-law fraud action and therefore required an Article III court. At the same time, the Court acknowledged its public-rights doctrine's lack of precision, passing up a chance to clarify it.

   d. Private-rights cases are "inherently judicial," and thus Article III judges must determine them, and because the Bankruptcy Reform Act of 1978 allowed non-Article III courts to determine private rights disputes—state claims between private litigants—it violated Article III. The Court has since modified this general statement, however, ruling that entitlement to an Article III court is a personal right that the parties may waive by consenting to Bankruptcy Court adjudication of claims that would otherwise require Article III courts. *Wellness Int'l Network, Ltd. v. Sharif*, 575 U.S. 665 (2015). [R50]

3. Congress responded to *Marathon* by substantially revamping bankruptcy jurisdiction. It converted bankruptcy courts into "adjuncts" of the federal district courts. *See infra* § IV.C, at 87 *[R45]*.

4. The notion that public-rights cases (cases involving the federal government) are not "inherently judicial" rests on sovereign immunity. Because Congress must waive the federal government's sovereign immunity to allow suit, Congress may take the lesser step of permitting suit against the government only in an non-Article III court.

   a. Commentators have criticized the public-rights/private-rights dichotomy. Most note that it deprives litigants of the protection of an Article III decision-maker in the types of cases in which having an independent judge may be most important.

   b. Many public-rights disputes—such as an individual's claim that the government wrongfully withheld a statutory benefit—seem to call for adjudication by a judge with the political insulation Article III grants. Yet, according to this doctrine, non-Article III courts can hear such cases.

c. On the other hand, many private-rights disputes—such as *Marathon*—involve state-law claims between private citizens. It is difficult to see why such politically insulated judges must decide those disputes. Yet, according to the public-rights/private-rights dichotomy, they must.

d. Justice White's *Marathon* dissent argued for a balancing process that would weigh the interest in salary and tenure protections against the government's interest in flexibility.

5. More recent Supreme Court decisions, while not overruling *Marathon*, suggest a move toward such a balancing test.

a. For example, *Thomas v. Union Carbide Agricultural Products Co.*, 473 U.S. 568 (1985), upheld a constitutional challenge to a federal statute providing binding arbitration with only limited judicial review as the mechanism for resolving disputes among participants in a congressional scheme for pesticide registration.

b. *Thomas* rejected the *Marathon*'s notion that the public-rights/private-rights dichotomy always "provides a bright line test for determining the requirements of Article III." The Court cited Justice White's balancing test as the basis for deciding what issues only Article III courts can hear.

c. The Supreme Court held that the dispute in *Thomas* involved a public right, even though the federal government was not a party. The right involved was "so closely integrated into a public regulatory scheme as to be a matter appropriate for agency resolution." That conclusion extended *Marathon*'s definition of public rights.

d. *Commodity Futures Trading Commission v. Schor*, 478 U.S. 833 (1986), upheld an administrative regulation that allowed the Commodity Futures Trading Commission to adjudicate a counterclaim arising out of the same transaction as the complaint before the Commission, even though the counterclaim involved a state-created private right. Though the Court probably could have rationalized the decision in terms of *Marathon*'s recognition of the legitimate use of non-Article III adjuncts, *see infra* § IV.A, at 85 *[R46]*, it instead relied heavily on Justice White's balancing analysis.

6. In addition to holding that Article III courts must determine private-rights cases, *Marathon* recognized that independent tribunals must determine cases involving constitutional rights. *Crowell v. Benson*, 285 U.S. 22 (1932), is the leading case. The Court held that Congress cannot constitutionally remove from the judiciary the final authority to find, *de novo*, constitutional facts.

a. Under *Crowell*, courts independent of the political branches of the federal government, whether Article III courts or state courts (whose judges' salary and tenure are not subject to federal regulation), must decide such constitutional issues.

b. The Court was not entirely clear about the basis for its decision. In part, it was separation of powers, but the opinion appeared also to include a due-process element.

c. Justice Brandeis dissented, asserting that because Congress could entirely close the federal courts and instead have state courts make these findings, it could also provide that non-judicial administrative agencies make final determinations of them. He concluded that the only time judicial review of factual findings was necessary was when personal liberty was at stake, because due process required such review. [R321]

7. The Court later modified *Crowell* to this extent: when judicial review is necessary, it need not be *de novo*. Judicial review of a non-judicial body's fact-finding need not entail a hearing; the court may simply review the record the non-judicial body created. *St. Joseph Stock Yards Co. v. United States*, 298 U.S. 38 (1936).

8. Many commentators have attacked *Crowell*; some even assert that its doctrine is dead. The Court has never overruled it, however, and more recent cases clearly indicate that it survives, at least in cases involving personal liberty.

Example: In a prosecution for obscenity, a court must retain the final authority to determine whether books or films are legally obscene. The question is one of constitutional fact. *Jacobellis v. Ohio*, 378 U.S. 184 (1964). [R47] [R48] [R49]

IV. Adjudication by Adjuncts to Article III Courts

A. Background: The Adjunct Theory

1. Non-Article III courts operate independently of the lower Article III federal courts. They enter final judgments, subject ultimately to appellate review by the Supreme Court.

2. In addition to non-Article III courts, several other non-Article III federal bodies and officers adjudicate disputes. The most important of these are administrative agencies, bankruptcy courts, and magistrate judges.

3. Non-Article III decision-makers cannot perform certain "inherently judicial" functions. *See supra* § III.C, at 82-85 *[R47]*. Notwithstanding that limitation, administrative agencies, bankruptcy courts, and magistrate judges may adjudicate regarding inherently judicial matters, if an Article III court can substantially review their decisions.

4. This is constitutional because the non-Article III decision-maker does not function independently; it is merely an "adjunct" to an Article III

court. Because the Article III court makes the final decision, the judicial power remains in that court. [R46]

B. Administrative Agencies

1. The political branches of the federal government, both executive and legislative, have created myriad administrative agencies, which have varying authority over matters legislation addresses. Typically, an agency has both rulemaking and adjudicatory authority.

   a. The Security and Exchange Commission's promulgation of Rule 10b-5 under the Securities Exchange Act of 1934 is an example of rulemaking authority. Rule 10b-5 has become the principal federal tool for addressing insider trading in securities.

   b. Agencies adjudicate a wide variety of issues. For example, the Social Security Administration, through administrative law judges, makes findings about whether eligible employees have been injured and, if so, what the appropriate compensation is. The Department of Veterans Affairs renders decisions concerning veterans' benefits, including reimbursement for medical expenses. The Immigration and Naturalization Service adjudicates applications for permanent resident alien status; and the Customs Service assesses forfeitures and penalties.

2. *Crowell v. Benson* held that administrative findings of constitutional facts must be reviewable by an Article III court. *See supra* § III.C, at 82-85 *[R48]*. The Court readily recognized "the utility and convenience of administrative agencies for the investigation and finding of facts," but noted that Congress cannot vest in agencies the power to make all determinations "with finality. . . . That would be to sap the judicial power . . . and to establish a government of a bureaucratic character alien to our system." 285 U.S. at 57.

   a. In *Crowell*, the Federal Employees' Compensation Commission made an award in favor of an employee and against Benson. The Commission found that the employee suffered injury while working for Benson upon the navigable waters of the United States.

   b. The Supreme Court viewed *Crowell* as a private-rights, in which a non-Article III body cannot enter a final adjudication. *See supra* § III.C, at 82-85 *[R49]*.

   c. The Court also noted, however, that Article III judges often delegate fact-finding to others, such as special masters, whose findings stand if the court finds that the evidence supports them. Similarly, Congress can delegate fact-finding to an administrative agency, subject to judicial review. Congress thus "relieve[s] the courts of a most serious burden [of hearing thousands of cases in the first instance] while preserving their complete authority to insure the proper application of the law." 285 U.S. at 54.

d. *Crowell* also held that a court must determine "constitutional" facts. Such facts underlie a constitutional claim but also encompass jurisdictional facts. For example, in *Crowell*, Benson claimed that the injury did not occur upon navigable waters. Because the legislation under which the employee made his claim would not apply unless it had, the issue included a jurisdictional fact. Thus, a court had to determine not only whether a compensation order was in accordance with law but also "the fact . . . which underlies the operation of the statute." *Crowell*, 285 U.S. at 62. [R299] [R304] [R322]

3. Although Congress has adopted different schemes from time to time, the typical provision permits a party to an administrative hearing to file a petition for review in the Court of Appeals for the Circuit where that party resides or in the Court of Appeals for the District of Columbia Circuit—Article III courts.

   a. The reviewing court gives no deference to the agency's interpretation of law; it is the court's province to determine matters of law finally.

   b. The reviewing court defers to agency findings of fact only if the record supports them. Whether the evidence supports the agency's findings is an issue of law.

C. Bankruptcy Courts

1. In *Marathon*, *see supra* § III.C.2, at 83 *[R50]*, the Court invalidated portions of the 1978 Bankruptcy Reform Act. The Act was unconstitutional to the extent it permitted non-Article III judges to determine private-rights disputes. Article I bodies or officers cannot adjudicate such disputes.

2. In 1984, Congress responded to *Marathon* by revamping the bankruptcy courts. Bankruptcy judges are Article I officers and serve as adjuncts to the federal district court, an Article III court.

3. Bankruptcy judges' jurisdiction embraces only core bankruptcy issues. The district court retains jurisdiction over plenary matters. [R45]

D. Magistrate Judges

1. In 1968, Congress created the office of federal magistrate, now known as magistrate judge. These judges serve a term of years and clearly are not Article III judges.

2. The increase in complex federal litigation motivated Congress, which intended magistrate judges to assist federal district judges.

3. Title 28 U.S.C. § 636 defines magistrate judges' authority and requires that the district judge—an Article III judge—make the ultimate decision. The district judge may refer various matters to a magistrate judge.

a. Without consent of the parties, the district judge may refer "non-dispositive" pretrial matters to a magistrate judge. The magistrate's orders on such matters are reviewable on the record by the district judge for "clear error."

b. Without consent of the parties, the district judge may refer "dispositive" pretrial matters, such as motions for summary judgment, to the magistrate judge. The magistrate enters findings and recommendations, which the district judge reviews *de novo*.

c. The parties may consent to trial before the magistrate judge. They thereby waive the right to have an Article III judge try the case; the court of appeals can review the magistrate judge's final determination.

d. *Roell v. Withrow*, 538 U.S. 580 (2003), held that the court may infer consent from the parties' conduct.

Review Questions (Part I; Chapters I-III)

True or False Questions

1. **T or F** A private individual hears that the parents of a deformed infant, conspiring with the doctors of a county hospital, are not feeding the infant properly. The individual sues in federal court to protect the infant's federal civil rights. The private individual has standing to bring the suit.

2. **T or F** A state indicts one of two individuals distributing political leaflets at a shopping center and threatens the second individual with prosecution if she continues to distribute the materials. The second individual sues in federal court, seeking a declaratory judgment that her future prosecution would violate her constitutional rights and seeking an injunction against prosecution. The second individual's case is not ripe for adjudication.

3. **T or F** Black citizens sue in federal court, challenging the constitutionality of the operation of a major political party's primary in their state on the grounds that it excludes Black citizens from participation. The defendants contend that the federal court may not adjudicate the dispute because of the political-question doctrine. The federal court determines that the political-question doctrine does not preclude it from adjudicating the suit. The federal court is correct.

4. **T or F** Because Congress retains power under Article III to regulate the lower federal courts' jurisdiction, it may prohibit certain racial and religious groups from gaining access to those courts.

5. **T or F** Because Article III mandates the Supreme Court's existence but not that of lower federal courts, Congress possesses no power to control Supreme-Court Jurisdiction.

6. **T or F** Though Congress retains power to regulate federal courts' jurisdiction, it cannot order those courts to convict an individual without allowing the courts to inquire into the constitutionality of the law under which the prosecution has been brought.

7. **T or F** In light of the Supreme Court's decision in *Northern Pipeline Construction Co. v. Marathon Pipe Line Co.*—which invalidated portions of the 1978 Bankruptcy Reform Act to the extent that the Act permitted non-Article III judges to determine disputes involving private rights—it logically follows that federal administrative agencies are unconstitutional.

8. **T or F** A soldier about to be transferred to duty in the Middle East sues in federal court, claiming that the military involvement in the Middle East is unconstitutional because it does not follow a congressional declaration of war. She seeks an injunction against her transfer. The federal court may refuse to hear the suit because of the political-question doctrine.

9. **T or F** Under accepted principles of standing, an organization with a special interest in an area of social concern may bring an action to challenge governmental interference in that particular area.

10. **T or F** The degree of public interest in having a particular legal issue resolved can influence application of the mootness doctrine.

11. **T or F** Though Congress can circumvent the Article III courts by creating non-Article III courts, an Article III court must finally resolve issues of constitutional interpretation.

12. **T or F** *Ex parte McCardle* definitively upholds plenary congressional authority to limit the Supreme Court's appellate jurisdiction.

13. **T or F** Congressional exclusion of Supreme-Court appellate jurisdiction in constitutional cases would violate the Fifth Amendment's Due Process Clause.

14. **T or F** Congress may require Article III federal courts to adjudicate cases falling outside the scope of the Article III, § 2, judicial power.

15. **T or F** Congress may not require Article III federal courts to issue advisory opinions.

Essay Question

You are a legal assistant to a United States Senator who is unhappy with the Supreme Court's decision holding prayer in public schools unconstitutional. He would like to learn your views on the constitutionality of legislation he is considering proposing:

(1) A statute requiring the federal courts to hold that prayer in public schools is constitutional.

(2) A statute prohibiting any federal court from adjudicating cases concerning the constitutionality of prayer in the public schools.

(3) A statute prohibiting any court, state or federal, from adjudicating cases concerning the constitutionality of prayer in the public schools.

(4) A statute similar to proposal 3, except that in addition the law would create a new federal non-Article III court finally to adjudicate all such cases in lieu of existing federal or state courts.

Prepare a memorandum in response to the Senator's request.

PART TWO

The Structure of Federal Jurisdiction

■ ANALYSIS

Chapter IV

FEDERAL-QUESTION JURISDICTION

■ ANALYSIS

I. Introduction

Federal-question jurisdiction (sometimes called arising-under jurisdiction) is a staple of the federal court docket. Unlike diversity jurisdiction, *see generally infra* Ch. V, § I, at 112 *[R51]*, there is no controversy about whether the federal courts should have federal-question jurisdiction; everyone seems to agree that determining cases that arise under federal law is an appropriate task for the federal judiciary. Although there are many specialized federal statutes granting jurisdiction for narrow categories of cases, the focus here is on the general federal-question jurisdiction statute, 28 U.S.C. § 1331, which grants jurisdiction over cases arising under any federal law and has no amount-in-controversy requirement. (Until 1980 it did, tracking the amount in the diversity statute, 28 U.S.C. § 1332.) Understand at the outset that there are two arising-under clauses, one in Article III and the other in § 1331. They do *not* have the same scope.

II. Constitutional and Policy Bases for Federal-Question Jurisdiction

A. The Constitutional Grant of Judicial Power

1. Article III, § 2, cl. 1, extends the federal judicial power of the federal courts to nine types of cases or controversies.
2. One type is cases "arising under this Constitution, the Laws of the United States, and treaties made, or which shall be made, under their authority." [R57]
3. *Osborn v. Bank of the United States*, 22 U.S. (9 Wheat.) 738 (1824), gave this Arising-Under Clause an extremely broad construction.
   a. Chief Justice Marshall's opinion held that when any issue of federal law "might form an ingredient" in the case, the case "arise[s] under" federal law for purposes of Article III. This also allows a federal court to decide all issues of *state* law involved, even if the federal issue never actually appears in the case—as long as a federal issue *might* enter the dispute.

Example: P, a resident of a state outside the original thirteen colonies, sues D, asserting that D has trespassed upon P's land. Although D does not raise the issue, the question of whether P actually owns the land could be part of the case. Moreover, because the federal government originally owned the land and transferred it to individual owners over a century ago, the chain of title questions could trace back to original federal ownership. Because a federal issue could conceivably enter the case (no matter how unlikely or farfetched), the case "arises under" federal law and falls within the Article III definition of federal-question jurisdiction. Note, though, that it does not come within 28 U.S.C. § 1331.

b. Though the Court has never overruled *Osborn*, some modern Justices have criticized its broad language.

c. *Verlinden B.V. v. Central Bank of Nigeria*, 461 U.S. 480 (1983), shows that the Article III arising-under clause continues to receive a broad construction. However, the Court expressly declined to reconsider *Osborn*'s current status. *American National Red Cross v. Solicitor General*, 505 U.S. 247 (1992), by five to four, appeared to confirm *Osborn*. *Lightfoot v. Cendant Mortgage Corp.*, 580 U.S. 82 (2017), offered the Court another opportunity to reconsider *Osborn*, but the unanimous Court did not, instead focusing on the statutory sue-and-be-sued clauses that have haunted the Court since the early nineteenth century. *See infra* § III.D, at 107 *[R52]*.

4. Some commentators suggest the Court never intended *Osborn* to be so broad, despite its language. Rather, they argue, it should apply only to cases involving a federal instrumentality (such as the Bank of the United States), because there is an especially strong federal interest in such cases, even if the dispute involves only state law. Chief Justice Marshall's opinion, however, appears broader than this narrow construction.

5. A broad interpretation of the constitutional grant of federal-question jurisdiction does not settle all federal-question-jurisdiction issues. Congress, granting jurisdiction to federal courts through jurisdictional statutes, has (and has exercised) the option to vest less than full constitutional jurisdiction.

a. Narrow interpretation of the constitutional grant would be difficult to overcome even if desirable; it would require resort to the deliberately cumbersome constitutional-amendment process. On the other hand, Congress always has the power to overcome undesirable interpretation of a jurisdictional statute by amending the statute.

b. However, Article III arising-under jurisdiction with the virtually unlimited scope *Osborn* suggested effectively makes Article III no limit at all on Congress's ability to displace state judicial authority in cases containing any federal issue, but Congress has been self-limiting.

c. The statutory grant of federal-question jurisdiction is far narrower than the constitutional grant. *See infra* § III, at 97-107 *[R53]*. Thus, while the constitutional grant determines how far Congress *could go* in vesting federal-question jurisdiction in the federal courts, statutes show how far Congress actually has gone. [R61] [R327]

B. Protective Jurisdiction

1. "Protective jurisdiction" describes two theories to justify vesting authority in the federal courts under Article III's "arising under" provision to hear cases involving solely issues of state law. Both theories threaten the assumption of parity of federal and state courts to decide questions of federal law. *See infra* Ch. XII, § II.C, at 269-270 *[R54]*.

2. Congress has never attempted to vest such authority in the federal courts, so there has been no test of the theories' validity. Justice Frankfurter's dissent in *Textile Workers Union v. Lincoln Mills*, 353 U.S. 448, 476 (1957), severely criticized both.

3. *Mesa v. California*, 489 U.S. 121 (1989), declined to recognize protective jurisdiction in a case involving removal of a state prosecution of a federal officer when there was no substantive federal-law issue.

4. The Greater-Includes-the-Lesser Theory.

   a. One version of protective jurisdiction, associated with Professor Herbert Wechsler, suggests that if Congress possesses constitutional authority to legislate substantively in an area, it can take the lesser step of choosing not to enact substantive law but simply vesting jurisdiction in the federal courts to apply relevant state law.

   b. The theory is subject to criticism because it is not necessarily true that the jurisdictional grant is a "lesser" step than substantive legislation; the two may be conceptually distinct.

   c. Wechsler's theory also ignores that one reason for federal-question jurisdiction is the expertise of federal judges in matters of federal law. In cases involving only state law (many diversity and alienage cases), that justification is absent.

5. The Articulated-and-Active-Federal-Policy Theory.

   a. The other version of protective jurisdiction, which Professor Paul Mishkin developed, suggests that when Congress already has an active and articulated policy in a substantive area, it may protect its program from undermining in state court adjudication by allowing the federal courts to adjudicate even pure state-law issues in areas related to the federal program. This approach also implicitly clashes with parity. *See infra* Ch. XII, § II.C, at 269-270 *[R55]*.

   b. As an illustration, Professor Mishkin pointed to the cases upholding provisions of the bankruptcy law vesting jurisdiction in the federal courts to adjudicate non-diverse suits under state law when the bankrupt is a party. He also viewed *Osborn* as an illustration of his approach.

C. Policy Underpinnings for Federal-Question Jurisdiction

1. The policy bases for the grant of federal-question jurisdiction are clear and universally accepted.
2. Federal judges presumably develop expertise in interpreting federal law and may be more attuned to policies underlying federal law. But this idea also implicates parity. *See infra* Ch. XII, § II.C, at 269-270 *[R56]*.
3. There also seems to be no dispute, even considering overloaded dockets, that federal-question jurisdiction is salutary. Adjudicating federal issues, and protecting federal rights and policy is arguably the federal courts' primary function.
4. Remember, however, that Congress's extending federal-question jurisdiction does not automatically exclude state jurisdiction. State and federal courts have concurrent jurisdiction over cases arising under federal law unless Congress specifies exclusive jurisdiction. State courts may hear federal-question cases even if there are no state-law issues, counter-intuitive as that may be. [R58]

III. The Statutory Grant of Federal-Question Jurisdiction

A. The General Federal-Question Statute

1. The general federal-question statute is 28 U.S.C. § 1331. It provides that "[t]he district courts shall have original jurisdiction of all civil actions arising under the Constitution, laws, or treaties of the United States." The operative language of this statutory grant—"arising under [federal law]"—is almost identical to the Article III, § 2, cl. 1, grant of judicial power. *See supra* II.A.2, at 94 *[R57]*.
2. Despite the well-established policy underpinnings for federal-question jurisdiction, *see supra* § II.C, at 97 *[R58]*, Congress did not enact a long-lasting general federal-question statute until 1875. Before then there were numerous limited grants of federal-question jurisdiction over specified types of disputes, but, except for a very short-lived attempt by the outgoing Federalists to expand jurisdiction in advance of the Jefferson administration, there was no general statute such as § 1331.
3. In 1875, the president *pro tempore* of the Senate declared in two short sentences that Congress intended the federal-question bill to have the same scope as the Article III provision, but there is *no* other legislative history.
4. The courts have always interpreted the statutory language far more narrowly than the constitutional language. Without stronger evidence, courts will not assume that Congress wished to burden the federal courts with many cases having merely a tangential relationship to federal interests, even if Article III would permit it.

5. "Arising under" includes not only claims that arise under the Constitution, federal statutes, and treaties, but also those arising under federal common law.

6. Many jurisdictional statutes other than § 1331 remain on the books as specific exercises of "arising under" jurisdiction. One is 28 U.S.C. § 1338(a), which provides the federal courts with jurisdiction over cases arising under acts of Congress relating to patents, plant variety protection, copyrights, and trademarks.

7. Section 1338(a) expressly grants *exclusive* federal jurisdiction except as to trademarks; only federal courts may hear the cases falling within that grant. State courts have no subject-matter jurisdiction over such cases. Although some argue that the grant of exclusive jurisdiction should counsel a narrow interpretation of § 1338, on the whole the Court has given both exclusive and non-exclusive jurisdictional statutes identical breadth. *See, e.g., Holmes Group v. Vornado Air Circulation*, 535 U.S. 826 (2002) ("arising under" in § 1338 meaning the same thing as in § 1331). [R351]

8. While some specific federal-question statutes provide exclusive jurisdiction, it is critical to remember that § 1331 does not. Thus, federal or state courts may hear cases that arise under federal law and that do not fall within one of the narrow class of cases for which federal jurisdiction is exclusive.

   a. This recognizes state courts' duty under the Supremacy Clause to follow federal law and indicates faith in the state courts' willingness to do so.

   b. Concurrent jurisdiction of the federal and state courts also serves a docket-control function and helps limit the federal courts' caseload—at the expense of state-court dockets, of course.

   c. Just as federal courts determine cases arising under state law in diversity cases, *see generally infra* Ch. V, at 111-131 *[R59]*, so concurrent jurisdiction of federal-question cases allows state courts to gain expertise in federal law. This may tend to keep both sets of courts from becoming overly specialized. [R24] [R71] [R215]

B. Scope of the Statutory Grant: The Well-Pleaded-Complaint Rule

1. The well-pleaded-complaint rule allows a federal court to consider only a plaintiff's well-pleaded complaint in assessing whether the case arises under federal law. A well-pleaded complaint sets forth only a claim, without adding extraneous issues such as responses to defenses the defendant might raise.

2. Applying the well-pleaded-complaint rule, the court looks only to the plaintiff's *claim* and ignores other things the plaintiff may allege. The question is whether the claim itself arises under federal law.

3. The term "well-pleaded complaint" means that the plaintiff may not anticipate and respond to defenses that the defendant might raise. There is another way to analyze complaints to take anticipation into account. Ask whether deleting allegations of federal law from complaint would cause the complaint to succumb to a Rule 12(b)(6) motion. If so, the federal allegations are necessary—well pleaded. If not, then the claim is not a federal-question claim.

Example: The Mottleys had passes on Railroad, renewable annually for the rest of their lives, as a result of a settlement following injuries in a train crash in 1871. In exchange for the right to receive the passes, the Mottleys agreed not to sue on their negligence claim. Thirty-five years later, Congress passed a law outlawing free transportation, after which Railroad declined to send the Mottleys their annual passes. The Mottleys sued Railroad for specific performance of their lifetime-pass agreements, alleging in their complaint that Railroad would rely on the new statute but that the statute did not apply to them or, if it did, that it was unconstitutional. There were no disputes of fact. [R62]

There was no federal-question jurisdiction. The Mottleys' claim was for breach of contract—that Railroad breached its agreement to send them annual passes in exchange for their agreement not to sue on their negligence claims. There was nothing federal about their claim under the settlement contract. The federal elements that did appear in the complaint were not necessary to allow the Mottleys to state their claim. Instead, they were part of an anticipated defense and the Mottleys' response to it. Because the federal elements were not part of the claim, the Supreme Court ignored them in determining whether the case arose under federal law. There being nothing federal about the claim, the federal courts lacked federal-question jurisdiction. *Louisville & Nashville Railroad v. Mottley*, 211 U.S. 149 (1908). [R224]

4. Some commentators defend the well-pleaded-complaint rule as allowing courts to determine from the face of the complaint whether the case qualifies for federal-question jurisdiction. Thus, it avoids having to await the defendant's response to see whether there really is a federal issue in the case.

5. Others attack the rule, however, as excluding from the federal courts cases that will turn on the interpretation of federal law—including some that will turn exclusively on such an interpretation.

Example: In *Mottley*, the actual litigation focused on two issues: (1) whether the 1906 federal statute applied to the Mottleys and (2) if so, whether it was constitutional. Both are federal issues, yet the case could not be in a federal trial court because the plaintiffs' *claim itself*—breach of contract—did not arise under federal law.

6. Obviously, because the well-pleaded-complaint rule limits a court to considering only the bare bones of the plaintiff's claim (irrespective of what surplusage the plaintiff may include), it also precludes a court from considering any defenses that the defendant actually asserts in the answer. 75 the well-pleaded *complaint*.

7. Accordingly, a court may not consider defenses or counterclaims to determine whether a case arises under federal law. "Admittedly, our prior cases have only required us to address whether a federal defense, rather than a federal counterclaim, can establish 'arising under' jurisdiction. Nonetheless, those cases were decided on the principle that federal jurisdiction generally exists 'only when a federal question is presented on the face of the plaintiff's properly pleaded complaint.' . . . It follows that a counterclaim—which appears as part of the defendant's answer . . . cannot serve as a basis for 'arising under' jurisdiction." *Holmes Group v. Vornado Air Circulation*, 535 U.S. 826, 831 (2002).

   a. The Court thus refused to distinguish between a defendant raising federal defenses and a defendant asserting a claim under federal law.

   b. Arguably, the Court erred by not making such a distinction. The counterclaiming defendant acts as a plaintiff, asserting a claim for affirmative relief that does arise under federal law. In a state-court action, if the counterclaim is compulsory under a state procedural rule similar to FED. R. CIV. P. 13(a), that appears to deprive the defendant of the federal forum to which it otherwise might be entitled.

      If the plaintiff sues in a federal court, FED. R. CIV. P. 13(a) requires the defendant to assert any transactionally related counterclaim. If the plaintiff's claim really is *not* federal, then the court will dismiss, leaving the defendant free to invoke federal-question jurisdiction as a plaintiff (and the former plaintiff free to plead his original claim as a compulsory counterclaim, invoking the court's supplemental jurisdiction). *See infra* Ch. VI, at 133-149 *[R60]*).

8. The well-pleaded-complaint rule shows how statutory "arising under" is narrower that constitutional "arising under." Constitutional arising-under embraces a case if any issue of federal law might conceivably enter the case at any time. *See supra* § II.A, at 94-95 *[R61]*. Obviously, *Mottley* satisfied that standard, since Railroad defended by arguing that the federal statute prevented it from honoring the Mottleys' contractual right and that the statute did not violate the Constitution. (There were no other contested issues.) But because Article III does not *vest* jurisdiction in any inferior federal court, the Mottleys had to satisfy § 1331's predecessor and fell victim to the Court's narrow interpretation of the statute.

9. Applying the well-pleaded-complaint rule is especially difficult when the plaintiff seeks declaratory relief.

a. A declaratory judgment is a judicial decree of the respective rights and obligations of the parties. In federal court, this remedy may be available under the Declaratory Judgment Act, 28 U.S.C. §§ 2201-2202. Problems arise because the person seeking the declaratory judgment may not be the party who could have sued for *coercive* relief— relief that requires the defendant to do something (*e.g.* pay money damages or perform some act under a mandatory injunction) or to cease or refrain from doing something under a prohibitive injunction.

Example: Think of *Mottley*. The Mottleys and Railroad are parties to a contract. The Mottleys claim that Railroad refuses to perform and has breached the contract. They intend to sue Railroad for damages. Before the Mottleys sue, however, Railroad sues the Mottleys, seeking a declaratory judgment that there is no breach because the statute makes performance impossible.

b. The Supreme Court has assumed that Congress did not intend the Declaratory Judgment Act to expand federal jurisdiction—that is, that the Act does not allow into the federal courts cases that would not qualify for federal-question jurisdiction if framed as coercive actions. So one cannot argue that the declaratory-judgment action arises under federal law unless, had the plaintiff instead sought damages or injunctive relief, the claim would have qualified for federal-question jurisdiction. A plaintiff cannot circumvent the well-pleaded-complaint rule by using the declaratory-judgment device.

c. If, without the declaratory-judgment device, the plaintiff could have brought a coercive action that would satisfy the well-pleaded-complaint rule, then the declaratory judgment action qualifies for federal-question jurisdiction. *See Skelly Oil Co. v. Phillips Petroleum Co.*, 339 U.S. 667 (1950).

Example: This Example refers to the facts of *Mottley* in ¶ 3, *supra* at 99 *[R62]*. Railroad sues the Mottleys, seeking a declaratory judgment that (1) the federal law prohibiting railroads from giving free transportation applies to the Mottleys' annual renewable passes, and (2) the federal law is constitutional. The case does not qualify for federal-question jurisdiction; neither party has a federal case for coercive relief on these facts. The Mottleys' complaint does not arise under federal law, and Railroad has no coercive action whatever. (In *Mottley*, Railroad could not have sought declaratory judgment; there was no federal declaratory-judgment act until 1917.)

Example: Patent Holder (PH) asserts that Manufacturer (M) is infringing her patent. M sues for a declaratory judgment that (1) PH's patent is invalid, and (2) even if PH's patent is valid, M's device does not infringe it. This case qualifies for federal-question jurisdiction, because PH could sue for coercive relief (damages or an injunction against further infringement), and *that* well pleaded complaint would arise under federal law. PH's complaint would allege that the patent is valid and that M is infringing it. *E. Edelmann Co. v. Triple-A Specialty Co.*, 88 F.2d 852 (7th Cir. 1937).

d. *Franchise Tax Board v. Construction Laborers Vacation Trust*, 463 U.S. 1 (1983), held that these principles, developed for suits brought under the federal Declaratory Judgment Act, apply equally to suits in the federal courts under state declaratory judgment acts, whether they get there originally or by removal. *See infra* Ch. VII, at 151-161 *[R63]*. But *Franchise Tax*, although citing *E. Edelmann* with approval, did not apply it even though the Trust defendant had a possible coercive claim that was exclusively federal, just as the patent action in *E. Edelmann* was.

10. Notwithstanding the well-pleaded-complaint rule, there are substantive areas in which federal law is so all-encompassing that it takes over the entire field. In these very rare situations, there is no longer state law; federal claims have displaced state claims. Accordingly, when a plaintiff asserts what she thinks is a state-law claim in state court, the defendant may be able to remove to federal court because federal law has "federalized" the state claim. For fuller discussion, *see infra* Ch. VII, § II.D, at 153-154 *[R64]*. *See also Metropolitan Life Insurance Co. v. Taylor*, 481 U.S. 58 (1987) ("[o]ne corollary of the well-pleaded-complaint rule . . . is that Congress may so clearly pre-empt a particular area, that any civil complaint raising this select group of claims is necessarily federal in character."). [R344]

C. Scope of the Statutory Grant: The Substantiality Consideration

1. In addition to the well-pleaded-complaint rule, the Supreme Court has imposed another requirement under the federal-question statute. It is more difficult to label than the well-pleaded-complaint rule, but concerns whether the issue of federal law is sufficiently important—*i.e.*, whether the federal matter is "substantial."

2. Through the years, the Supreme Court has adopted different tests for this aspect of federal-question jurisdiction. The decisions have not been consistent, and the present state of the law is not clear. The major cases are: (a) *American Well Works Co. v. Layne & Bowler Co.*, 241 U.S. 257 (1916), (b) *Smith v. Kansas City Title & Trust Co.*, 255 U.S. 180 (1921), (c) *Moore v. Chesapeake & O. Ry. Co.*, 291 U.S. 205 (1934), (d) *Merrell Dow Pharmaceuticals, Inc. v. Thompson*, 478 U.S. 804 (1986), (e) *Grable & Sons Metal Products, Inc. v. Darue Engineering & Mfg.*, 545 U.S. 308 (2005), and (f) *Gunn v. Minton*, 568 U.S. 251 (2013). Some commentators

view *Smith* and *Moore* as irreconcilable; others think careful application of the well-pleaded-complaint rule explains the results in both.

3. *American Well Works* sets forth the cause-of-action test for determining whether a claim arises under federal law. Justice Holmes, for the majority, concluded that "[a] suit arises under the law that creates the cause of action." If state law creates the cause of action, the case is not a federal-question case within the meaning of § 1331. This is so even if the substance of the litigation will substantially (or entirely, as in *Mottley*) concern issues of federal law. It is not entirely clear that Holmes's articulation was necessary; applying the *Mottley* rule would have reached the same result. There is language in the opinion that sounds like an oblique reference to *Mottley*, but Justice Holmes did not cite it, and no Justice filed a concurrence suggesting that basis for disposition.

   a. One might criticize the test as placing form over substance, to the detriment of policy: if the bulk of the case will ultimately turn on matters of federal law, the need for the expertise of the federal courts is as great as when the cause of action is itself federal.

   b. Subsequent developments expanded statutory federal-question jurisdiction, but at the very least, *American Well Works* remains accurate as a statement of cases that generally *do* arise under federal law: if federal law creates the cause of action, as a general rule there is federal-question jurisdiction. The converse, however, is often not true. Even if federal law does not create the cause of action, there may nonetheless be federal-question jurisdiction.

   c. On the other hand, in rare cases where federal law creates the cause of action, but Congress also directs that the applicable law's content is state law, *see infra* Ch. XI, § VI.B.1, at 246-246 *[R65]*, such cases may not fall within the federal-question statute. *See Shoshone Mining Co. v. Rutter*, 177 U.S. 505 (1900).

4. *Smith v. Kansas City Title & Trust Co.*, 255 U.S. 180 (1921), revisited the statutory definition of arising under, holding that a case arises under federal law if the plaintiff's complaint establishes that her "right to relief depends upon the construction or application of the Constitution or laws of the United States." *Id.* at 199.

   a. This test looks not simply at the law that created the cause of action, but also at whether any issues in the well-pleaded complaint requires adjudicating federal law. It is an outcome-determinative test.

   b. Smith, a shareholder, sued to enjoin the state-chartered corporation from investing in bonds issued under a federal statute that he thought was unconstitutional. State law prohibited state-chartered companies from investing in illegal bonds. Thus, state law created plaintiff's shareholder-derivative claim, but the complaint had to allege the invalidity (unconstitutionality) of the bonds to state a claim for relief. The case arose under federal law.

c. In *Moore*, the plaintiff sued his employer on a state negligence claim, also alleging (though it was surplusage) that the employer violated the Federal Safety Appliance Act. Under that statute, if the plaintiff could show that the employer violated "any law enacted for the safety of employees," the employer could not assert a contributory negligence defense. Although it seems that the litigation, as in *Smith*, would focus on federal law—whether the employer violated the federal act—the Court held that the case did not arise under federal law. The Federal Safety Appliance Act would not have entered the case until the employer raised contributory negligence as a defense, so the *Mottley* rule explains the result, although the Court did not cite *Mottley*.

d. Only much later, in *Merrell Dow*, *see infra* § VI.C.6, at 104-105 *[R66]*, did the Court try to reconcile *Smith* and *Moore*. It failed, though they are reconcilable; the well-pleaded-complaint rule explains both.

5. *Gully v. First National Bank*, 299 U.S. 109, 112-13 (1936) (citations omitted), summed up the post-*Smith* state of federal-question jurisdiction.

> To bring a case within the statute, a right or immunity created by the Constitution or laws of the United States must be an element, and an essential one, of the plaintiff's cause of action. . . . [Echoing *Mottley*'s approach.] The right or immunity must be such that it will be supported if the Constitution or laws of the United States are given one construction or effect, and defeated if they receive another. . . . [Echoing *Smith*'s approach.] A genuine and present controversy, not merely a possible or conjectural one, must exist with reference thereto [rejecting *Osborn*'s broad approach to Article III arising under, in favor of a narrower approach to statutory federal-question jurisdiction] . . . and the controversy must be disclosed upon the face of the complaint, unaided by the answer or by the petition for removal. [*Mottley* again.]

Justice Cardozo later discussed substantiality, making clear that the federal issue had to be a substantial part of the plaintiff's case, not merely some remote antecedent in federal law that indirectly contributed to the dispute. (Otherwise, for example, all real-property disputes involving land outside the original thirteen colonies would become federal-question cases because title to western lands originally came through the federal government. *Shoshone Mining Co. v. Rutter*, 177 U.S. 505 (1900), rejected that approach.) Fifty years elapsed before the Court changed the *Gully* approach. [R96]

6. The *Merrell Dow* plaintiffs alleged multiple claims against a drug manufacturer, including negligence *per se*. That claim (a state-tort claim) rested on the defendant's alleged violation of the Federal Food, Drug, and Cosmetic Act (FDCA) by misbranding pharmaceuticals. The parties

agreed that FDCA did not explicitly create a private right to sue for violations. If it had, jurisdiction would have been clear under the *American Well Works* test. The *Merrell Dow* Court proceeded on the assumption it should not recognize a federal private right of action either. If the FDCA had outlawed certain activity, such as misbranding drugs, and had also provided that anyone harmed by a violation of the Act had the right to sue to recover for injuries, then federal law would have created the cause of action, which would have arisen under the federal law. But, FDCA did not create such a right to sue.

a. The five-to-four Court ruled that incorporating the federal statutory standard in the state-law negligence-*per-se* claim did not make the action a federal-question case under § 1331.

b. The absence of a private right of action in FDCA influenced the majority. The majority assumed that Congress had *decided* not to create a cause of action and concluded that the courts are "not free to supplement that decision in a way that makes it meaningless." *Id.* at 814, n.12.

c. Although this standard appears inconsistent with *Smith*, *Merrell Dow* explicitly distinguished *Smith* because of "the differences in the nature of the federal issues at stake. In *Smith* . . . the issue was the constitutionality of an important federal statute. . . ."

d. *Merrell Dow* thus seemed to adopt a nebulous "substantiality" standard that, in cases where the cause of action is itself not federal, reserves federal-question jurisdiction for state claims presenting "important" federal issues. The Court did not focus on the fact that *Smith* involved a constitutional question whereas *Merrell Dow* did not, so for these purposes, that is apparently a distinction without a difference.

   The majority relied on a sentence from *Gully* that, read in isolation, might appear to support the Court's new idea: " 'What is needed is something of that common-sense accommodation of judgment to kaleidoscopic situations which characterizes the law in its treatment of causation . . . a selective process which picks the substantial causes out of the web and lays the other ones aside.' " But when Justice Cardozo used the phrase "substantial causes," he was referring to substantial causes *of the dispute* (a typical causation question), rejecting *Osborn*'s background-question approach. He was not speaking of some more ethereal concept of the abstract importance of the federal question to the government.

e. The dissenting Justices criticized the majority's reliance on the importance of the federal interest as infinitely malleable. Many commentators agree. The dissent argued that *Smith* and *Moore* are simply irreconcilable, and that the Court should have overruled *Moore*. *But see supra* § III.C.4.c, at 104 *[R67]*.

7. *Merrell Dow* caused confusion. Some concluded that it had simply reinstated Holmes's law-that-creates-the-cause-of-action test, though the opinion did not say that. Others saw it as altering the substantiality criterion. In *Smith*, substantiality meant "outcome-determinative." *Gully* added "and not too remote." *Merrell Dow* left a strong impression that substantiality referred to something *outside* of the case rather than to the importance of federal law to the plaintiff's case. After *Merrell Dow*, statutory federal-question jurisdiction meant (1) a well-pleaded complaint, (2) with an outcome-determinative federal issue as part of the plaintiff's claim, (3) that is not too remote from the actual dispute, and (4) that is "substantial." The majority did not offer any guidance on how to distinguish a well-pleaded, outcome-determinative, non-remote, substantial federal issue from a well-pleaded, outcome-determinative, non-remote, insubstantial federal issue.

8. *Grable & Sons Metal Products, Inc. v. Darue Engineering & Mfg.*, 545 U.S. 308 (2005), revisited substantiality. IRS sold Grable's property at a tax-delinquency sale; Darue purchased it. Grable brought a quiet-title action against Darue, arguing that IRS's service of the notice of the sale by certified mail was inconsistent with the governing statute (which created no private right of action). The unanimous Court found that the federal issue was substantial, noting three factors: (1) the essentiality to the government of efficient collection of taxes, (2) the government's need for federal judicial expertise in tax matters (not to mention the home-court advantage), and (3) the unlikelihood of there being many cases in this mold, leaving undisturbed the division of judicial labor between the federal and state judiciaries that the Court assumed (without evidence) Congress intended.

9. *Gunn v. Minton*, 568 U.S. 251 (2013), is substantiality's latest chapter. Minton sued his former attorneys in state court for malpractice (a state-tort claim) in handling a patent-infringement suit (an exclusively federal claim). Losing at trial, Minton argued on appeal that the federal courts had exclusive jurisdiction over his malpractice action because it arose from a patent. The state's highest court agreed. The Supreme Court unanimously disagreed and offered a four-part test. There is federal-question jurisdiction over a state-law claim containing a well-pleaded, outcome-determinative federal issue that is "(1) necessarily raised, (2) actually disputed, (3) substantial, and (4) capable of resolution in federal court without disrupting the federal-state balance approved by Congress." Only the first two elements are reasonably clear. [R1] [R96]

10. Even if a claim arises under federal law, jurisdiction fails if the claim is "frivolous" or "insubstantial." *Hagans v. Lavine*, 415 U.S. 528, 536-37 (1974). This requirement goes to the claim's legal substance, not its monetary value. Thus, it requires some assessment of the merits. For example, a lawyer's claim that the federal law that authorizes the Patent and Trademark Office to regulate conduct of attorneys appearing before it preempted discipline by a state bar association was so frivolous that it

did not properly invoke federal-question jurisdiction. *Kroll v. Finnerty*, 242 F.3d 1359 (Fed. Cir. 2001).

11. *Tanzin v. Tanvir*, 592 U.S. 43 (2020), added a general *caveat* to *Merrell Dow* analysis, when the unanimous eight-Justice Court (newly appointed Justice Barrett not participating) recognized that interpreting legislative material, the critical thing is "the phrase's plain meaning at the time of enactment." In *Merrell Dow*, the phrase was "arising under," and it entered the jurisdiction statute in 1875, not in 1938 when Congress enacted the Food, Drug, and Cosmetic Act.

D. The Especially Vexing Problem of Statutory Sue-and-Be-Sued Clauses

Sue-and-be-sued clauses have now troubled the Court for more than two centuries. Part of the problem stems from Congress's entire inconsistency in the verbal formulas it uses in such clauses. The variations are subtle, but much turns on them. Congress has not settled on one expression for when it intends to confer jurisdiction and a second for when it does not. The question confronting the Court has always been whether the clauses are simple grants of capacity to an entity or whether they are grants of jurisdiction to the federal courts. From the first case, *Bank of the United States v. Deveaux*, 9 U.S. (5 Cranch) 61 (1809), to the most recent, *Lightfoot v. Cendant Mortgage Corp.*, 580 U.S. 82 (2017), the Court has ruled on six of these clauses, no two using precisely the same language. Three times it found jurisdiction; three times it did not. The following chart attempts to organize the data. [R53] [R328]

2. Parsing the Language

Case (Date)	Statute	Jurisd?	Mentions	
			Federal Courts?	State Courts?
Deveaux (1809)	"to sue and be sued, plead and be impleaded, answer and be answered, defend and be defended, in courts of record, or any other place whatsoever"	No	No	No
Osborn (1824)	"to sue and be sued, plead and be impleaded, answer and be answered, defend and be defended, *in all State Courts having competent jurisdiction*, and in any Circuit Court of the United States" [Emphasis added]	Yes	Yes	Yes (qualified: see italicized phrase)
Texas & Pac. R. Co. v. Rigsby (1916)	"to sue and be sued, plead and be impleaded, defend and be defended, in all courts of law and equity within the United States"	Not discussed	No	No
D'Oench, Duhme (1942)	"To sue and be sued, complain and defend, in any court of law or equity, State or Federal"	Yes	Yes	Yes
American Red Cross (1992)	"To sue and be sued, complain and defend, in any court of law or equity, State or Federal"	Yes	Yes	Yes
Lightfoot (2016)	"to sue and to be sued, and to complain and to defend, *in any court of competent jurisdiction*, State or Federal" [Emphasis added]	No	Yes (qualified)	Yes (qualified: see italicized phrase)

What can one learn from the comparison? The *Deveaux* and *Osborn* statutes are easy to distinguish, because the latter statute qualifies itself with respect to state court, which Congress recognizes might not have subject-matter jurisdiction. By the same token, Congress appears to have assumed that the federal circuit courts (then the primary trial courts rather than the appellate courts of today) did have subject-matter jurisdiction, and it is wise to keep in mind that language usage was different in the early nineteenth century from what it is now. In any event,

Chief Justice Marshall's *Osborn* Court made the inference that Congress thus intended to vest jurisdiction in the circuit courts.

One may then be tempted to say that if the statute mentions federal courts specifically, it confers subject-matter jurisdiction, but that conclusion is too hasty, because the *Lightfoot* statute does mention the federal courts but does not confer jurisdiction. Of course, Congress qualified the grant by specifying that only courts of competent jurisdiction (federal or state) could hear cases under the statute, which connotes that Congress did not think the statute granted jurisdiction to any court.

Accordingly, the lesson appears to be that the Court construes only an unqualified specific mention the federal courts (*Osborn*, *D'Oench*, and *American Red Cross*) to be a grant of subject-matter jurisdiction, does not construe a mention of courts in general ("courts of record" in *Deveaux*, and does not construe a qualified specific mention of federal courts (*Lightfoot*) to be a grant. As for *Rigsby*, there is no mention of jurisdiction; the Court inferred that the relevant statute allowed Rigsby to sue.

(The foregoing explanation attempts to reconcile the Court's decisions linguistically. Be sure to distinguish that analysis from the more important question of whether the decisions are logically satisfying.) [R52] [R53] [R119] [R328]

Chapter V

DIVERSITY AND ALIENAGE JURISDICTION

■ ANALYSIS

I. Introduction

Diversity (more cumbersomely known as diversity-of-citizenship) and alienage cases are two more types of disputes that federal courts may hear. They have been part of congressional grants of jurisdiction since the Judiciary Act of 1789. Diversity cases are between citizens of different states of the United States. Alienage cases are between a citizen of a state of the United States and a citizen or subject of a foreign country—really just a specialized type of diversity. Either type must also satisfy a jurisdictional-amount requirement, currently by having an amount in controversy *exceeding* $75,000. Alienage jurisdiction accounts for little of the federal docket and has never been controversial. Diversity jurisdiction accounts for about twenty percent of the federal trial court docket and has always been controversial. The debate about the wisdom of having federal courts decide cases that substantive state law controls, as in diversity, has never abated. [R51]

II. Constitutional, Statutory, and Policy Bases

A. The Constitutional Grants of Judicial Power

1. Article III, § 2, cl. 1, extends the judicial power of the federal courts to nine types of cases or controversies.
2. That basis of judicial power includes controversies "between Citizens of different States." That is the constitutional authority for diversity jurisdiction.
3. Another constitutional basis of judicial power includes controversies "between a State, or the Citizens thereof, and foreign States, Citizens or Subjects." Note the breadth of this phrase. It extends, for example, to cases between one of the states of the United States and a foreign country. Alienage jurisdiction, as courts call it, involves only disputes between a citizen of a state of the United States and a foreign citizen or subject.
    a. The words "citizen or subject" were employed to reflect the possibility that the foreigner might be deemed one or the other in her home country, depending upon the type of government that country has. Thus, people who reside in territories of a foreign country might not have all the rights of a citizen of the foreign country but fall within the phrase "citizen or subject." The thrust is whether the person is a foreign national. *JPMorgan Chase v. Traffic Stream (BVI) Infrastructure*, 536 U.S. 88, 98-100 (2002) (British Virgin Island (BVI) corporation is subject of the United Kingdom notwithstanding BVI's status as merely a territory of the United Kingdom). [R73]
    b. Instead of using the cumbersome phrase "foreign citizen or subject," courts routinely refer to such persons as "aliens."
    c. Note that alienage jurisdiction does not exist simply because an alien is a party. The litigation must be between an alien on one

hand, and a citizen of one of the States of the United States on the other.

d. Congress once attempted to vest jurisdiction in the federal courts whenever an alien was a party, but the Supreme Court found that unconstitutional, *Hodgson v. Bowerbank*, 9 U.S. (5 Cranch) 303 (1809), because it would have permitted jurisdiction over a case between aliens, and Article III does not include such a case within the judicial power, with one exception under which a permanent resident alien has a state citizenship for diversity purposes only. [R33] [R67] [R69] *See infra* § II.B.5, at 114 *[R68]*. [R75]

4. Most of the constitutional bases of judicial power are not self-executing. The fact that a type of case appears in Article III, § 2, cl. 1, does not mean that federal courts automatically can entertain such cases. Note that the Constitution actually *vests* jurisdiction (a named court "shall have jurisdiction") only in one court: the Supreme Court. There was uncertainty during the constitutional period about whether Congress would create any inferior federal courts (*see* Art. III, § 1), so it would have made little sense for the Constitution to vest then-non-existent courts with jurisdiction.

   The inferior federal courts can hear disputes only if Congress grants jurisdiction over them. Thus, for the inferior federal courts to exercise jurisdiction over a dispute, there must be both (a) a constitutional grant of the judicial power and (b) a statutory grant of the subject-matter jurisdiction over that kind of dispute. Section B, *infra*, reviews current statutory grants of diversity and alienage jurisdiction.

5. Note that Article III does not impose an amount-in-controversy requirement. Such restrictions on jurisdiction, applicable in diversity and alienage (and, until 1980, federal-question) cases come from statutes. [R125]

B. The Statutory Grants

1. In 28 U.S.C. § 1332(a), Congress granted the federal courts subject-matter jurisdiction over diversity and alienage cases. Throughout the jurisdictional statutes (not so for the Constitution), when "state" is capitalized, it refers to one of the United States. Otherwise, it refers to another nation. This volume follows that convention when quoting the statutes.

2. In both diversity and alienage cases, the amount in controversy must "exceed[ ] the sum or value of $75,000, exclusive of interest and costs." *See infra* § IV, at 124-129 *[R69]*.

3. Assuming the amount in controversy exists, § 1332(a)(1) grants jurisdiction over cases "between Citizens of different States." This is the diversity-jurisdiction grant. Congress employed the identical phrase as the Article III grant of judicial power. *See supra* § A.2, at 117 *[R70]*. As with federal-question jurisdiction, *see supra* Ch. IV, § III.A, at 97-98 *[R71]*, however, the Court has interpreted the constitutional and statutory grants to mean different things. *See infra* § III.A, at 116-119 *[R72]*. [R82]

4. Assuming the amount in controversy exists, § 1332(a)(2) grants jurisdiction over cases "between citizens of a State and citizens or subjects of a foreign state." This is alienage jurisdiction. *See supra* § II.A.3, at 112 *[R73]*.

   a. As with the constitutional grant, most courts refer to "citizens or subjects of a foreign state" simply as "aliens." *See id.*

   b. The statutory grant is now consistent with the Constitution in this respect: it does not grant jurisdiction simply because an alien is a party. The litigation must involve an alien on one hand and a citizen of one of the states of the United States on the other. [R347]

5. The last sentence of § 1332(a), which Congress added in 1988, provides that "an alien admitted to the United States for permanent residence shall be deemed a citizen of the State in which such alien is domiciled."

   a. An alien is a citizen or subject of a foreign country. This provision does not apply to all aliens, only to those who have permanent-resident status in the United States.

   b. This provision ascribes to a permanent resident alien the citizenship of the "State" in which she is domiciled. (Capitalized "State" always refers to one of the United States.)

   c. There is a question about this provision's validity. The Supreme Court has held that a human being is a citizen of a State *only* if she is (a) a citizen of the United States and (b) domiciled in a State. *Sun Printing & Publishing Association v. Edwards*, 194 U.S. 377, 383 (1904). By definition, the permanent-resident alien cannot satisfy the first requirement. Section III.B.6, *see infra* at 121 *[R74]*, shows that this statute can result in federal litigation by an alien against an alien. There is no constitutional authority for such jurisdiction. *See supra* § A.3, at 112-113 *[R75]*. [R68] [R83] [R84] [R85]

C. Policy Underpinnings

1. The Founders apparently engaged in surprisingly little discussion of the justifications for diversity jurisdiction.

2. The traditional justification of diversity jurisdiction is to provide a federal forum to avoid possible prejudice that an out-of-state litigant might suffer—or at least fear—in a state court.

3. A federal district court might be less inclined than a state court to engage in discrimination against an out-of-state litigant for two reasons.

   a. First, federal judges serve lifetime appointments, and no one can reduce their pay, so they need not fear political reprisal even if they rule against the local interest. *See supra* Ch. I, § II.A, at 32 *[R76]*. By contrast, a state-court judge may be an elected official whose job security depends on voter approval.

b. The federal district court draws its jury from the entire federal district Congress has defined, which may include numerous counties. A state court draws its jury from a smaller geographic area, usually a single county. The federal jury might harbor less local bias than a group drawn from a more localized area.

4. In all likelihood, the Founders provided diversity jurisdiction to allay fears of commercial interests that might invest in various states. It seems clear that diversity jurisdiction helped foster economic expansion to the southern and western United States. By alleviating fears of local bias, the availability of a federal forum made it more attractive to invest in distant states.

5. Many commentators argue, however, that diversity jurisdiction is no longer necessary. Specifically, in light of modern communication facilities and transportation systems, they argue, fear of local bias is minimal. In an era of overcrowded courts, diversity jurisdiction is an unneeded drain of limited federal judicial resources.

6. Defenders of diversity jurisdiction respond that fear of regional bias is still a problem. Moreover, they note that diversity jurisdiction gives the federal bench additional opportunity to decide traditional common-law disputes, and thus to avoid becoming specialized tribunals dealing exclusively with federal common law, statutes, and constitutional provisions. (Supplemental jurisdiction creates similar opportunities, and it is quite common for state-law issues to arise in what clearly are federal-question cases.) In addition, defenders praise the symbiosis that may evolve when federal courts must interpret state substantive law; federal input may benefit development of state law.

7. If fear of local bias animates diversity jurisdiction, then perhaps the statutory grant of diversity jurisdiction should require that at least one litigant be a citizen of the forum, but it does not. Thus, a citizen of Oklahoma can sue a citizen of Nevada in a federal court in Maine, where presumably neither litigant would benefit or suffer from local bias.

8. Unlike diversity jurisdiction, alienage jurisdiction has never been controversial. It has widespread support as an appropriate investment of federal judicial resources serving two major purposes. *See JPMorgan Chase v. Traffic Stram (BVI) Infrastructure*, 536 U.S. 88, 93-97 (2002).

   a. It provides aliens involved in litigation with American citizens a forum with judges free from political influence, thereby lessening fears of unfair treatment of aliens.

   b. It thus signals foreign countries that litigation involving their citizens or subjects is sufficiently important to deserve determination by the national judiciary.

III. Determining Whether the Case Involves Appropriate Litigants

Throughout this section, assume that the amount in controversy (*see infra* § IV, at 124-129 *[R77]*) exists. A case must satisfy both it and the requirements discussed here to qualify for diversity or alienage jurisdiction.

A. The Complete-Diversity Rule

1. *Strawbridge v. Curtiss*, 7 U.S. (3 Cranch) 267 (1806), held that the diversity statute extends only to cases of "complete" diversity. Complete diversity means that every plaintiff must be a citizen of a different state from *every* defendant; if the same State citizenship appears on both sides of the "*v.*," diversity jurisdiction fails.

   a. Thus, under *Strawbridge*, diversity jurisdiction does not extend to cases involving mere "minimal diversity"—those in which at least one plaintiff is a citizen of a different State from at least one defendant. Diagramming cases with the parties' citizenships can be helpful.

Example: A, a citizen of New York, and B, a citizen of Illinois, sue C, a citizen of Iowa, and D, a citizen of Oregon in federal district court.

A	&	B	*v.*	C	&	D
(NY)		**(IL)**		**(IA)**		**(OR)**

This case satisfies the complete-diversity rule, because both plaintiffs are citizens of different States from both defendants.

Example: A, a citizen of New York, and B, a citizen Illinois, sue E, a citizen of Illinois.

A	&	B	*v.*	E
(NY)		**(IL)**		**(IL)**

This case demonstrates "minimal" diversity, because at least one plaintiff is diverse from at least one defendant, but it does not qualify for diversity jurisdiction, because it does not satisfy the complete-diversity rule. IL appears on both sides of *versus*. One plaintiff (B) is a co-citizen with one defendant (E), so the case does not satisfy *Strawbridge*. The case could proceed in federal court only if B (the non-diverse plaintiff) were dropped from the suit (or, obviously, if there were some other basis of subject-matter jurisdiction, such as federal question).

   b. The complete-diversity rule does not require that every litigant be of diverse citizenship from every other *litigant*. It requires only that every *plaintiff* be of diverse citizenship from every *defendant*.

Example: F and G, both citizens of California, sue H and J, both citizens of Arizona.

F	**&**	**G**	***v.***	**H**	**&**	**J**
(CA)		**(CA)**		**(AZ)**		**(AZ)**

This case satisfies the complete-diversity rule. Even though the plaintiffs are co-citizens and the defendants are co-citizens, no plaintiff is a citizen of the same state as any defendant. [R98]

2. Note that the basis of jurisdiction is diversity of *citizenship*, not residence. Although some courts use the terms interchangeably, keep them distinct. Residence is relevant to venue, which you studied in Civil Procedure. Citizenship is relevant here. Although a litigant's residence and citizenship may be the same, do not mix the terms. If the plaintiff files a suit claiming diversity jurisdiction but alleges the parties' residence (not citizenship), the court should dismiss unless the plaintiff amends. [R64] [R70]

3. For over a century and one-half, it was not clear whether the *Strawbridge* complete-diversity rule, which was an interpretation of the diversity statute, would also apply to Article III. If the complete-diversity rule rests on the constitutional language "between citizens of different States," then Congress could not create jurisdiction based upon minimal diversity. But *Strawbridge* simply interpreted the diversity statute, having no reason to address the constitutional question. If the Constitution does not require complete diversity, Congress may grant jurisdiction based upon minimal diversity. [R38]

4. *State Farm Fire & Casualty Co. v. Tashire*, 386 U.S. 523 (1967), held that *Strawbridge*'s complete-diversity requirement does not apply to Article III's diversity language. Therefore, the Court upheld the Federal Interpleader Act, 28 U.S.C. §§ 1335, 1397, 2361, which extends diversity jurisdiction to some cases where there is only minimal diversity. [R332]

   a. Thus, diversity jurisdiction under § 1332(a)(1) includes the complete-diversity rule. But Article III does not have that requirement; mere minimal diversity satisfies it, notwithstanding that the constitutional and statutory provisions have precisely the same operative language. *See supra* § II.B.3, at 113 *[R78]*. This recalls the situation in federal-question jurisdiction; the statutory and constitutional provisions, though using identical operative language, mean different things.

   b. Although Congress clearly could abolish the complete-diversity requirement in § 1332(a)(1), it has not done so and no one expects that.

5. There is some debate about the rationale for the complete-diversity requirement. Some suggest that the presence of co-citizens on both sides

of the litigation neutralizes the effect of local bias, and thus obviates the need for a neutral federal forum. But this may not always be true.

Example: K, a citizen of Alabama, and L, a citizen of Massachusetts, sue M, a citizen of Massachusetts in an Alabama state court.

K	**&**	**L**	***v.***	**M**
(AL)		**(MA)**		**(MA)**

This case presents the possibility of local bias. The fear is that the Alabama plaintiff will have a home-town advantage over Massachusetts defendant (even though there is a Massachusetts co-plaintiff). Yet the Massachusetts defendant is stuck in the Alabama state court. This case does not qualify for diversity jurisdiction because it violates the complete-diversity rule, and it is not removable. *See infra* Ch. VII § II.D.1, at 153 *[R79]*.

6. There is no question that the complete-diversity rule has a docket control effect, limiting the number of diversity cases. If jurisdiction could exist with only minimal diversity, the increased caseload might inundate the federal courts.

7. Section 1332(d) makes the District of Columbia, Puerto Rico, and American territories "States" for diversity purposes. Many commentators questioned this provision's constitutionality because those jurisdictions are not States. Indeed, the Supreme Court early held that a citizen of the District of Columbia was not a citizen of a "State" for purposes of diversity jurisdiction. *Hepburn & Dundas v. Ellzey*, 6 U.S. (2 Cranch) 445 (1804). The Court eventually upheld the provision's constitutionality. *National Mutual Insurance Co. v. Tidewater Transfer Co.*, 337 U.S. 582 (1949). The case is curious; although its holding is clear, no majority of Justices adopted a single theory justifying it. [R39]

8. The supplemental jurisdiction statute, 28 U.S.C. § 1367, operates to make the complete-diversity rule inapplicable in some cases. *See infra* Ch. VI, § IV.F.2, at 148-149 *[R80]*.

9. In alienage cases, courts apply a version of the complete-diversity rule.

Example: N, a citizen of France, sues O, a citizen of Florida, in federal court.

N	***v.***	**O**
(FR)		**(FL)**

This case gets alienage jurisdiction, because it is between a citizen of a state of the United States and an alien. It does not matter whether the alien is the plaintiff or the defendant; the case would also get alienage jurisdiction if O had sued N.

Example: P, a citizen of Spain, sues Q, a citizen of Australia.

P	***v.***	**Q**
(SP)		**(AU)**

This case does not get alienage jurisdiction, because the case is not (as Article III and § 1332(a)(2) both require) between a citizen of a State of the United States and an alien.

Example: R, a citizen of Italy, sues S, a citizen of Colorado, and T, a citizen of Venezuela.

R	*v.*	**S**	**&**	**T**
(IT)		**(CO)**	**&**	**(VE)**

Most courts addressing this case hold that there is no alienage jurisdiction, because of the presence of aliens on both sides of the litigation. Thus, they adopt a form of a complete-diversity rule in alienage cases, looking not to individual nationalities but rather treating almost all aliens as co-citizens for diversity purposes, despite the fact that *Strawbridge* did not involve alienage. *But see infra* § III.B.3.f, at 120-121 *[R81].* [R72] [R343]

B. Human Beings' Citizenship

1. Diversity jurisdiction looks to the litigants' citizenship (not residence). *See supra* § II.B.3, at 113 *[R82].* This section addresses the definition of the citizenship for human beings.
2. If the litigant is a citizen of the United States, she is a citizen of the State of her domicile.
3. One's domicile is usually referred to as one's permanent home—the place where an individual resides and has no fixed intention to relocate. There are several important points to consider in assessing domicile.
   a. An individual may have only one domicile at a time; it is impossible to have more than one domicile simultaneously. Thus, it is impossible for a human being to be a citizen for diversity purposes of more than one State at a time.
   b. One's initial domicile arises at birth and is usually the parents' domicile. An individual may change her domicile by establishing two things. Although courts differ in stating the requirements, they are: (1) presence in the new place and (2) the subjective intent to make that state one's home for the indefinite future (the place from which there is no present intention to relocate). Thus, there are physical and mental components to changing one's domicile. Both must exist simultaneously or the person retains her former domicile, no matter how long she may have been absent from it and even if she never intends to return.

Example: Olivia's birth and home were in Oregon. After high school, she went to Massachusetts to attend college. After that, she went directly to New York to attend law school. After that, she went directly to Virginia to attend medical school. She has not set foot in Oregon in eleven years. She does not know where she wants to live permanently, although she is sure she will not go back to Oregon. Her domicile is still Oregon, because although she has resided in other states, she has never formed the subjective intent to make any of them her domicile. Thus, her citizenship for diversity jurisdiction is Oregon.

Example: Mel is a citizen of Minnesota. He forms the intent to make Florida his permanent home. On the drive to Florida, he is involved in an auto wreck in Tennessee. His domicile is still Minnesota. Even though he has left Minnesota and formed the intent to make Florida his domicile, he has not been present in Florida. Thus, his citizenship for diversity jurisdiction remains Minnesota until he arrives in Florida.

c. One's domicile is not necessarily the same as one's residence. Olivia was a non-resident of Oregon for eleven consecutive years. Nonetheless, she remained a domiciliary (and thus a citizen) of Oregon, even though she was sequentially a *resident* of Massachusetts, New York, and Virginia (and clearly is never going to stop going to school).

d. In contested cases, the court determines domicile. No single factor determines intent. The court considers all relevant evidence, focusing on the person's *indicia* of permanence (such as driver's license and voting registration), not just statements of intent.

e. Never refer to "diversity of domicile"; there is no such thing. It is always "diversity of citizenship."

f. Note that one need not be a United States citizen to have a domicile in a State. Thus, permanent-resident aliens have a United States domicile, even though they are not (and may never become) United States citizens. *See supra* § II.B.5, at 114 *[R83]*. By the same token, a United States citizen may be domiciled in another country without being a citizen or subject of its government. *See infra* § III.B.5, at 120-121 *[R84]*. [R75] [R81]

4. The court assesses diversity when the action begins, at filing. Thus, a subsequent change is irrelevant. If a Missouri citizen sues an Ohio citizen, and becomes a citizen of Ohio while the case is pending, there still is diversity jurisdiction. Similarly, a pre-suit change in citizenship is irrelevant. If that a citizen of Missouri has a claim against another citizen of Missouri in federal court and changes her domicile to Kansas before suing, she can use diversity jurisdiction.

5. A citizen of the United States who is a domiciliary of a foreign country has no State citizenship and is also not an alien. He cannot be a party in a diversity case.

Example: U, a United States citizen but a French domiciliary, sues V, a citizen of Kentucky, in federal court.

U	*v.*	**V**
( )		**(KY)**

This case does not get diversity jurisdiction because it is not "between citizens of different States." U is not a citizen of any State because she is not domiciled in any State. Neither is she a French citizen (and thus an alien) merely because of her French domicile. Only France can confer French citizenship. [R81] [R84]

6. A litigant not a citizen of the United States is an alien. If an alien is legally a permanent United States resident, however, § 1332(a) treats her as a citizen of the State of her domicile. This provision is problematic because it ascribes State citizenship to people who are not citizens of the United States. *See supra* § II.B.5, at 114 *[R85]*. Arguably, that expands the jurisdiction of the federal courts beyond Article III.

Example: W, a citizen of Japan is a North Carolina domiciliary legally permanently residing in the United States. W sues X, a citizen of Canada, in federal court.

W	*v.*	**X**
(NC)		**(CA)**

Under § 1332, W is a citizen of North Carolina. If that is so, then this case invokes alienage jurisdiction, because it is between a citizen of a state (W) and an alien (X). In fact, however, this is a case by an alien against an alien. (This is the answer to the riddle of "when is an alien not an alien?" "When the alien is lawfully domiciled in one of the United States and gets involved in the right kind of lawsuit.") Article III does not extend the judicial power to such a case. *See* § II.A.3, above. So far, courts have managed to avoid confronting this issue. [R74] [R126] [R348] [R349]

C. Corporations' Citizenship(s)

1. In *Bank of the United States v. Deveaux*, 9 U.S. (5 Cranch) 61 (1809), Chief Justice Marshall stated that a corporation is an "invisible, intangible, and artificial being" and therefore retains the citizenship of *each* of its shareholders. Corporations, unlike individuals, can have more than one domicile. In light of the complete-diversity requirement, *Deveaux* significantly reduced potential diversity cases involving corporations if a corporation's shareholders were citizens of numerous States.

2. *Louisville, Cincinnati & Charleston Railroad Co. v. Letson*, 43 U.S. (2 How.) 497 (1844), overruled *Deveaux*. The Court held that a corporation is a citizen for diversity purposes only in the State of incorporation. The Court created a conclusive presumption that all shareholders were citizens of the State of incorporation.

3. In 1958, Congress finally defined corporate citizenship by adding a provision (now 28 U.S.C. § 1332(c)(1)). "[A] corporation shall be deemed a citizen of any State by which it has been incorporated and of the State where it has its principal place of business. . . ." Under this statute, the corporation is an entity, not an aggregate of the people who own or manage it.

a. The language "any State by which it has been incorporated" implies that there may be more than one such State. While it is possible that a corporation will incorporate in more than one State, today, as a practical matter, multiple incorporation is virtually nonexistent. As a nearly universal rule, then, there will be only one State of incorporation.

b. Just as clearly, the language "the State where it has its principal place of business" makes it clear that there is only one such State. Every corporation has one principal place of business. And no corporation can have more than one principal place of business simultaneously. The principal place of business need not be the State of incorporation.

c. Thus, a corporation—unlike a human being—may be a citizen of more than one State. If a Delaware corporation has its principal place of business in Kansas, it is a citizen of *both* Delaware and Kansas for diversity purposes. Note that this makes it twice as difficult to get diversity jurisdiction. [R86]

4. It is easy to determine the State of incorporation, which charters the corporation.

5. Determining a corporation's principal place of business, however, used to be difficult. It was an *ad hoc* decision, based upon the facts, and several theories developed. In 2010, however, *Hertz Corp. v. Friend*, 559 U.S. 77 (2010), adopted the nerve-center test, which almost always will be corporate headquarters: "the place of actual direction, control, and coordination . . . " of corporate affairs. For diversity purposes, it does not matter whether the corporation produces any goods or provides any services in the State of its headquarters. Only if the place the corporation designates as its headquarters is clearly a sham will the courts undertake a factual determination. The headquarters is often *not* in the chartering State (not least because so many corporations have Delaware charters that there would not be room in the state for all those headquarters). [R333]

D. Non-Incorporated Associations' Citizenships

1. Many businesses, such as partnerships, labor unions, and insurance associations are not corporations. The law regards such associations as aggregations of their members, not as entities. This view contrasts with corporations, which are entities separate from their shareholders, directors, and officers. *See supra* § III.C.3, at 121-122 *[R86]*.

2. Jurisdictional theory also adopts this "aggregate" approach for unincorporated associations. *Chapman v. Barney*, 129 U.S. 677 (1889), held that a unincorporated association's citizenship for diversity purposes was that of each of its members. The Court has consistently adhered to this view. Although the view is judge-made (like the complete-diversity rule), it is now part of the definition of "citizen" in § 1332(a)(1).

3. This rule decreases the availability of diversity jurisdiction, by increasing the likelihood that litigation will not satisfy the complete-diversity rule.

Example: Big Law Firm is a partnership with partners who are citizens of California, Arizona, Texas, New York, New Jersey, Virginia, Maryland, and Illinois. For diversity purposes, it is a citizen of all eight States. Thus, no case involving it as a litigant qualifies for diversity jurisdiction if any party on the opposing side is a citizen of any of those eight States.

4. There was long a question about how to treat limited partnerships—whether the court should assess only the citizenship of the general partners or include limited partners as well. *Carden v. Arkoma Associates*, 494 U.S. 185 (1990), resolved the debate, holding that the focus was the citizenship of all partners—general and limited.

5. The "business trust," long a staple of Massachusetts law, is different from other unincorporated businesses. *Navarro Savings Association v. Lee*, 446 U.S. 458 (1980), held that individual trustees of a business trust may invoke diversity jurisdiction on the basis of their own citizenship, regardless of the trust beneficiaries' citizenship. Business trusts bear certain similarities to associations, but the Court noted that in some ways they also resemble corporations. If the trustees are active and the real parties in interest, their citizenship controls. [R334]

E. Citizenship in Cases by or Against Representatives

1. Litigation by or against minors ("infants"), incompetents, and decedents usually involves a representative as a party. Minors and incompetents lack legal capacity, and a parent or a fiduciary, such as a guardian, guardian *ad litem*, or conservator, must represent their interests in litigation. Decedents' estates' interests, obviously, require fiduciary representation—executors or administrators.

2. In suits involving decedents, minors, and incompetents, § 1332(c)(2) provides that "the legal representative of the estate of a decedent shall be deemed to be a citizen only of the same State as the decedent, and the legal representative of an infant or incompetent shall be deemed to be a citizen only of the same State as the infant or incompetent." Thus, only the citizenship of the person *represented* (not the citizenship of the representative) is relevant in assessing whether there is diversity.

Example: Executor, a citizen of Nevada acting on behalf of the estate of Decedent, formerly a citizen of Utah, sues Defendant, a citizen of Nevada. Diversity jurisdiction exists, because Executor's citizenship is irrelevant. Under § 1332(c)(2), only Decedent's citizenship, and not Executor's, "counts." Thus, the case is by a Utah citizen against a Nevada citizen.

3. Section 1332(c)(2) does not apply to class action litigation. *Supreme Tribe of Ben-Hur v. Cauble*, 255 U.S. 356 (1921), originally laid down the

rule for class actions, holding that the citizenship of the class was only the citizenship of the class representatives. In other words, the citizenships of unnamed class members were irrelevant.

Example: P, suing as representative of a class, is a citizen of Florida. Class members are citizens of Georgia, Alabama, Mississippi, and South Carolina. The defendants are citizens of Georgia and South Carolina. The case qualifies for diversity jurisdiction. Under *Ben-Hur*, the class's citizenship is the representative P's citizenship: Florida; the other class members' citizenships are irrelevant. For jurisdictional purposes, this case is between a Florida citizen and citizens of Georgia and South Carolina.

In 2005, Congress amended 28 U.S.C. § 1332, adding the Class Action Fairness Act ("CAFA") as new subsection (d), which, in cases where the amount in controversy exceeds five million dollars, requires only minimal diversity: (1) any member of the plaintiff class having a different State citizenship from any defendant, or (2) any party (plaintiff or defendant) is foreign (including foreign governments) and any opposing party is a citizen of some State. Congress acted to try to limit class-action plaintiffs (their attorneys, really) from bringing large class actions in "magnet jurisdictions"—state courts known to be hospitable to class actions seeking damages under FED. R. CIV. P. 23(B)(3). [R87] [R89] [R120]

IV. Determining Whether the Required Amount in Controversy Exists

Throughout this section, assume that the case satisfies the diversity or alienage requirements (*see supra* § III, at 116-124 *[R87]*). A case must satisfy one of those and the requirements in this section to qualify for diversity or alienage jurisdiction.

A. The Amount-in-Controversy Requirement and Its Rationale

1. For any case invoking jurisdiction under § 1332—diversity or alienage jurisdiction—the amount in controversy must "exceed[ ] the sum or value of $75,000, exclusive of interest and costs." Note that the claim must *exceed* $75,000, so a claim for $75,000.00 does *not* qualify for diversity or alienage jurisdiction, whereas a claim for $75,000.01 would. (And you thought pennies had lost their value!)

2. The purpose of a jurisdictional minimum is clear: the federal courts have limited time and resources, so Congress limits what would otherwise be insurmountable judicial burdens. Imposing a jurisdictional floor reflects Congress's judgment that cases not "worth" the specified amount simply do not justify expending federal judicial time and effort.

3. Congress amends the amount in controversy requirement periodically. The current requirement dates from 1997. From 1989 until then, the floor was an amount in excess of $50,000 and before that, for thirty

years, in excess of $10,000. It originally was in excess of $500. [R340] [R346]

B. Assessing the Amount in Controversy

1. *St. Paul Mercury Indemnity Co. v. Red Cab Co.*, 303 U.S. 283 (1938), held that "the sum claimed by the plaintiff controls if the claim is apparently made in good faith. It must appear to a legal certainty that the claim is really for less than the jurisdictional amount to justify dismissal."

   a. This decision created the legal-certainty test for jurisdictional amount: before the court may dismiss a case for failure to meet the amount in controversy requirement, it must appear as a matter of law that the plaintiff cannot recover more than $75,000.

   b. This rule does not mean that the plaintiff has the burden to demonstrate that she will "certainly" recover more than $75,000; the burden is on the defendant to show to a legal certainty that the plaintiff *cannot* recover that much.

   Example: Plaintiff brings a diversity suit for damages suffered allegedly due to defendant's negligence in a serious auto accident, alleging that damages exceed $75,000. At the outset, it is impossible to know whether plaintiff's damages exceed $75,000. The court cannot dismiss the claim for lack of jurisdiction, despite this uncertainty, because it is not clear to a legal certainty that plaintiff's damages do not exceed $75,000. [R110]

2. The clearest cases for dismissal, of course, are those rare instances in which the plaintiff demands $75,000 or less. Also clear are cases in which either the applicable substantive state law or a private arrangement between the parties imposes a ceiling on damages that does not exceed $75,000.

Example: Plaintiff sues Hotel for negligence in providing security; she alleges that $100,000 worth of valuables were stolen from her room. A state statute limits innkeepers' liability to $25,000. The court will dismiss the case for failure to meet the amount-in-controversy requirement; given the statute, it is clear to a legal certainty that Plaintiff cannot recover more than $75,000.

3. Absent a liquidated-damages clause or a state-law ceiling, courts only occasionally invoke the *St. Paul* test to deny jurisdiction. Doing so is proper only if the court concludes that it would vacate a jury award in excess of $75,000 as unreasonable on the basis of the available evidence and then order a new trial under FED. R. CIV. P. 59(a). Then it is clear to a legal certainty that the jurisdictional amount is lacking. Such cases are rare, however, and involve claims that on their face seem shockingly exaggerated.

Example: In a suit for negligence arising out of an auto accident, where plaintiff suffered a sprained wrist and her junker automobile was totaled, and where there was no other claim, such as loss of employment compensation or punitive damages, the federal court would probably dismiss for lack of jurisdiction. The court would set aside any jury award exceeding $75,000 as capricious. *See Nelson v. Keefer*, 451 F.2d 289 (3rd Cir. 1971).

4. *St. Paul Mercury* also indicated that plaintiff must claim an amount in excess of the jurisdictional minimum in good faith. This statement raises confusion over whether good faith and legal certainty refer to distinct conditions for meeting the jurisdictional minimum or whether they are simply different articulations of the same test.

   a. While certain courts and commentators have expressed the view that "good faith" merely represents a means of finding "legal certainty," the two might concern different questions at least as an abstract matter.

   Example: Plaintiff sues for injuries, including pain and suffering, caused by Defendant's negligence. The amount claimed far exceeds $75,000. Plaintiff and her lawyer say to friends that in reality they do not expect to recover anywhere near $75,000. Under a "good faith" test, the court might dismiss Plaintiff's complaint. But if Plaintiff and her lawyer are merely being pessimistic about the claim, under the legal-certainty test the claim should survive.

   b. Ultimately, the motivation for the jurisdictional-amount requirement—keeping small cases out of federal court—suggests an *objective* legal-certainty test is preferable to a *subjective* good-faith test.

   c. Of course, demonstrating that the plaintiff does not believe the claim to be worth more than $75,000 could be powerful evidence in making the objective legal-certainty finding, so the two criteria may tend to merge.

5. The plaintiff's actual recovery in the litigation is irrelevant to jurisdiction. Thus, if a plaintiff sues for $100,000 and wins only $10,000, the court does not lose jurisdiction. Jurisdiction attaches at the outset, with the good faith allegation that the claim exceeds $75,000. Because the court did not dismiss under the legal-certainty test, jurisdiction existed. *But*,

   a. Ordinarily, the prevailing party recovers costs from the other side. (In the United States, "costs" does not include attorney's fees; those are recoverable only if a statute, *see, e.g.*, 42 U.S.C. § 1988, authorizes recovery.)

b. However, if the plaintiff recovers less than $75,000.01, § 1332(b) allows the court to deny her recovery of her costs and even to impose liability for the defendant's costs. [R339]

C. Aggregating Claims

1. Under long-accepted principles, a single plaintiff may aggregate the amounts of all of her separate claims against a single defendant, regardless of whether those claims arise out of the same transaction or occurrence.

Example: A sues B in federal court in a diversity suit, joining a breach-of-contract claim for $40,000 with a wholly unrelated tort claim for $55,000. Although neither of claim alone satisfies the amount-in-controversy requirement, because this case involves only one plaintiff and one defendant, the court adds the claims' values. Thus, the amount in controversy is $95,000, and the case satisfies the amount-in-controversy requirement.

2. By contrast, multiple plaintiffs cannot aggregate their claims against a single defendant, and a single plaintiff cannot aggregate claims against multiple defendants. However, if the claims are joint rather than several, the amount in controversy is the total value of the joint claims asserted. Although "joint" and "several" are abstract concepts that the courts have never adequately distinguished and that have caused substantial confusion, there are some clear cases.

Example: Four joint tortfeasors injured plaintiff. She sues all four in a single action, claiming damages of $80,000. The case satisfies the amount-in-controversy requirement. This is clearly a joint claim, so the court will look to the total value of the claim—$80,000—which, of course, exceeds $75,000. Recall that joint tortfeasors are jointly and severally liable in many states.

Example: Plaintiff is the obligee in a contract with two obligors. A dispute arises, and Plaintiff sues the obligors, seeking $100,000 damages. The case meets the amount-in-controversy requirement. There is only one contract and therefore only a single claim. Do not mislead yourself by thinking that Plaintiff is actually aggregating two claims, each of $50,000, against the obligors.

3. The Supreme Court has ruled that the supplemental jurisdiction statute, 28 U.S.C. § 1367, has overruled the non-aggregation principle in certain cases, permitting joinder of multiple plaintiffs, so long as one has a claim exceeding $75,000. *See infra* Ch. VI, § IV.F, at 148-149 *[R88]*.

4. For a long time, there were questions about how to determine the amount in controversy in a class action.

   a. *Snyder v. Harris*, 394 U.S. 332 (1969), held that plaintiff class members cannot aggregate their claims to meet the amount in controversy requirement. In *Snyder*, no class member's claim met the requirement, so the case could not invoke diversity jurisdiction.

b. *Zahn v. International Paper Co.*, 414 U.S. 291 (1973), held that the claim of *each* member of the plaintiff class—not just the named representatives' claims—must meet the amount in controversy requirement (except in the rare situation in which the rights asserted are joint). Although the named representative's claim met the amount in controversy requirement, some class members' claims did not. Those class members could not be part of the class.

c. *Zahn* was an unfortunate decision, and many commentators criticized it. There are two major criticisms of *Zahn*.

(1) First, the holding of the case was completely inconsistent with the manner of determining *citizenship* in a class action. For citizenship purposes, *Ben-Hur* held in 1921 that only the named representative (not all class members) need be diverse from the opposing party. *See supra* § III.E.3, at 123-124 *[R89]*.

(2) Second, the majority failed to consider the operation of supplemental (then called "ancillary") jurisdiction for the claims of class members.

d. *Zahn* undermined the class-action device, which in part allows numerous small claims to be joined in one suit when it would be inefficient or impractical for class members to sue separately and inefficient for courts to have to try each case separately.

5. The Court has now recognized that the supplemental jurisdiction statute, 28 U.S.C. § 1367, overruled *Zahn* by explicitly permitting class members to invoke supplemental jurisdiction. *Exxon Mobil Corp. v. Allapattah Services, Inc.*, 545 U.S. 546 (2005). *See infra* Ch. VI, § IV.F.2, at 148-149 *[R90]*. [R99] [R113] [R350]

D. Claims for Equitable Relief

1. In most cases, plaintiffs seek damages, which are easy to quantify. When the plaintiff seeks equitable relief—injunction, declaratory judgment, rescission, or reformation—the court must determine whether the claim exceeds $75,000 if the defendant seeks dismissal under Rule 12(b)(1).

2. The courts have employed two tests to assess equitable claims' value. The plaintiff's-viewpoint test asks whether the defendant's act has caused plaintiff more than $75,000 of harm. The defendant's-viewpoint test asks whether it will cost the defendant more than $75,000 to effect the relief. The choice of test may yield quite different conclusions.

Example: Plaintiff sues to enjoin Defendant's operation of a power plant, alleging nuisance. The harm to Plaintiff is air pollution, largely immeasurable. If the court enters the injunction, however, Defendant would have to shut down its plant for a substantial time each day.

Under the plaintiff's-viewpoint test, the amount is insufficient. Under the defendant's-viewpoint test, however, the amount in controversy might well be sufficient. Certainly it would be difficult to rule as a matter of legal certainty that the relief could not cost defendant in excess of $75,000.

3. The defendant's-viewpoint test is consistent with the main purpose of the amount-in-controversy requirement—keeping trivial cases out of the federal judicial system. If either party stands to be affected by more than $75,000, the case is not trivial. Some courts exercise diversity jurisdiction if the amount in controversy exists from either viewpoint. *See, e.g., Smith v. Washington*, 593 F.2d 1097 (D.C. Cir. 1978).

4. Federal docket control argues in favor of the plaintiff's-viewpoint test. Using it probably results in fewer diversity cases. On the other hand, that just means that the cases end up in state-court systems, themselves with crowded dockets. [R69] [R77] [R118]

V. Exceptions to Diversity and Alienage Jurisdiction

A. Judge-Made Exceptions for Domestic-Relations and Probate Cases

1. The federal courts refuse to exercise diversity or alienage jurisdiction in two areas—domestic relations and probate—even if the requirements for jurisdiction exist.

2. Although judges do not speak of them in these terms, these judge-made exceptions are forms of abstention. *See generally infra*, Ch. IX, § III.B.2 at 191 *[R91]*. There is an interesting argument that courts should not be able simply to refuse to hear particular kinds of cases. It is Congress's responsibility and prerogative to determine the federal courts' jurisdiction (within Article III), so refusal to adjudicate arguably violates separation-of-powers. Perhaps, but these exceptions are well established.

3. The domestic-relations exception derives from a dissenting opinion in *Barber v. Barber*, 62 U.S. (21 How.) 582, 603-05 (1859) (Daniel, J., dissenting). *Ankenbrandt v. Richards*, 504 U.S. 689 (1992), answered questions about the scope of the exception. *Ankenbrandt* is the leading modern statement of the exception, although its statement is dictum because, on the facts, the exception did not apply).

   a. The federal courts will not hear cases "involving the issuance of a divorce, alimony, or child custody decree." *Id.* at 704.

   b. Thus, the exception is rather narrow. It does not apply, for example, to intra-family torts or other disputes between family members that do not involve "issuance of a divorce, alimony, or child custody decree."

4. History and policy explain the domestic relations exception.

   a. The original Judiciary Act granted jurisdiction to federal courts over cases "at common law or in equity." Historically, ecclesiastical courts heard domestic relations cases, which were neither law nor equity, so the statutory grant of federal jurisdiction did not include such disputes. The fact that more recent jurisdictional statutes do not use the phrase "at common law or in equity" is irrelevant. Any change to require federal courts to hear domestic-relations cases will have to come from Congress. *Ankenbrandt*, 504 U.S. at 700.

   b. As a matter of policy, state courts have developed expertise in domestic-relations cases and there is a considerable local interest in how the courts handle issues relating to marriage and child custody.

5. The federal courts will not probate a will or administer an estate. This exception's scope is not clear; the Supreme Court has not discussed it recently.

   a. The mere fact that an executor or administrator is a party to a diversity case does not preclude jurisdiction.

   b. The court may, for example, decide a case brought against an executor to assert a claim, but not if the court is asked to take control of the estate or to interfere with state-court probate proceedings. *See Markham v. Allen*, 326 U.S. 490 (1946).

6. The probate exception undoubtedly rests on similar policy bases as those supporting the domestic-relations exception. Judge Richard Posner also notes that judicial economy is a relevant policy factor:

   > When a person dies, his will has to be admitted to probate somewhere, or if he dies intestate the control of his property has to be vested in some court initially, and it is hard to imagine in either case how the initial jurisdiction over the decedent's estate could be elsewhere than in a state court. Only as the probate proceeding unfolds will the prerequisites of diversity jurisdiction-the diverse citizenship of the contestants and the minimum required amount in controversy-appear. If the probate proceeding thus must begin in state court, the interest in judicial economy argues for keeping it there until it is concluded.

   Dragan v. Miller, 679 F.2d 712, 714 (7th Cir. 1982).

B. Statutory Prohibition of Collusive Joinder to Create Jurisdiction

1. Title 28 U.S.C. § 1359, provides: "A district court shall not have jurisdiction of a civil action in which any party, by assignment or otherwise, has been improperly or collusively made or joined to invoke the jurisdiction of such court."

2. Today, this statute applies mostly with regard to assignments of claims to create diversity jurisdiction. *Kramer v. Caribbean Mills, Inc.*, 394 U.S. 823 (1969), is the leading case. A would-be plaintiff, realizing that there was no diversity between him and the would-be defendant, assigned his claim to someone diverse from the defendant. The assignee agreed to return ninety-five percent of any recovery to the assignor. The Supreme Court held that § 1359 applied, because assignor and assignee colluded to create diversity.

    a. The Court looked to all relevant facts in assessing whether the statute applied. The assignee had no previous connection with the underlying business deal, so the Court concluded that he was a mere collection agent for the assignor and applied the statute.

    b. Not all assignments of claims run afoul of § 1359. Courts assess all relevant factors, including any legitimate business reason for the assignment, any interest retained by the assignor, and the subjective intent of the parties.

    c. Section 1359 does not invalidate the assignment. Rather, if the statute applies, the court ignores the assignment, and decides jurisdiction based upon the assignor's citizenship. The result in *Kramer*, of course, was to find that there was no subject-matter jurisdiction, because the assignor was not diverse from the defendant, so the Court dismissed. [R59]

Chapter VI

SUPPLEMENTAL JURISDICTION

■ ANALYSIS

I. Introduction

Every single claim in a federal court—without exception—needs a subject-matter ticket of admission. That applies to plaintiff's claims, counter- and cross-claims, claims by intervenors, claims by or against parties whom the court brings into the action under FED. R. CIV. P. 19, and third-party practice. You are familiar with some of those tickets: 28 U.S.C. §§ 1331-1334, 1337-1338, 1343-1346 for example. These are the "stand-alone" tickets of admission. If a claim properly invokes diversity or federal-question jurisdiction, obviously a federal court can hear it. Sometimes a claim does not have a stand-alone ticket, but a federal court may nonetheless hear the claim if it has what the airlines call a "companion ticket" or "companion certificate"—a reduced-fare ticket that accompanies a stand-alone ticket for travel on the same itinerary. Title 28 U.S.C. § 1367—supplemental jurisdiction—is the companion ticket of federal jurisdiction. Supplemental jurisdiction exists only when the claim asserted bears a sufficiently close factual relationship with a claim that has a stand-alone ticket of admission (*e.g.*, federal-question or diversity). The Supreme Court has long upheld the constitutionality of supplemental jurisdiction. Although the courts developed the doctrine, Congress codified it in 1990 with a few changes from the judge-made doctrine. [R329]

II. Policy Issues

Supplemental jurisdiction permits a federal court to hear claims that have no stand-alone, subject-matter ticket of admission. In other words, it allows the court to hear non-federal, non-diverse claims. Supplemental jurisdiction is proper *only* if the supplemental claim has an appropriate relationship to the claim that is properly in federal court. *See infra* § IV.B, at 141-143 *[R92]*.

Example 1: P, a citizen of Arizona, asserts a $100,000 tort claim against D, a citizen of California, for damages suffered in an automobile crash between the two. The claim obviously invokes diversity jurisdiction and can go to federal court. Assume D has a compulsory counterclaim under Rule 13(a) in tort against P (one that arises from the same accident), but D's claim is for only $45,000. That tort claim sounds in state law, so there is no federal-question jurisdiction. It also does not qualify for diversity jurisdiction because it does not meet the amount-in-controversy requirement of § 1332; it does not exceed $75,000. However, because the claim is transactionally related to P's claim, which qualifies for diversity jurisdiction, the federal court can exercise supplemental jurisdiction over D's compulsory counterclaim. (By definition, the court would not have jurisdiction over a permissive counterclaim (Rule 13(b), because it is transactionally unrelated to the complaint.)

Example 2: P asserts a federal-question claim against D and a state-law claim against D that arises from the same transaction as the federal-question claim. P and D are co-citizens. The federal-question claim satisfies § 1331 and is properly in federal court, and § 1331 is a stand-alone ticket of admission. The state-law claim has no stand-alone ticket. There is no federal-question jurisdiction, and because P and D are co-citizens, no diversity jurisdiction either. However, because the state-law claim arises from the same operative facts as the federal-question claim, a federal court has supplemental jurisdiction.

Supplemental jurisdiction fosters litigation efficiency, because it allows the court to determine all transactionally related claims in a single case. In Example 1, it would be wasteful to try P's claim against D in federal court and yet try D's claim against P in state court. In Example 2, it would be wasteful if P's federal-question claim were in federal court but her state-law claim had to go to state court. In both of the modified examples, there would be enormous overlap of evidence in the proceedings, consuming roughly twice as much judicial and litigant time (and expense).

Note, however, that the plaintiff could try to ensure that both claims in both of the examples were litigated in a single forum by filing the case in *state* court. In Example 1, filing the case in a California state court would guarantee the state forum; the defendant, a citizen of California, could not remove. Filing in some other state court would allow the defendant to remove to federal court. *See infra* Ch. VII, § III.D, at 156-158 *[R93]*. In Example 2, however, filing in a state court would deprive P of a federal forum for her federal claim (a tactical decision P is entitled to make) unless the defendant removed the case to federal court. In part for this reason, there has always been broader acceptance of supplemental jurisdiction in federal-question cases than in diversity cases.

Untrammeled use of supplemental jurisdiction in diversity cases could eviscerate the complete-diversity rule. *See infra* § IV.C, at 143-146 *[R94]*. Thus courts and Congress have struggled with § 1367(b) to limit supplemental jurisdiction in diversity cases.

Some commentators criticize supplemental jurisdiction because it relieves state courts from discharging their responsibility to adjudicate matters of state law and prevents improvements of state-court ability to interpret federal law by keeping some federal claims out of the state courts. The opposite, however, seems just as compelling: unduly *limiting* supplemental jurisdiction precludes *federal* courts from exercising their primary responsibility to interpret, develop, and apply federal law and limits federal courts' familiarity with state law that they must deal with in diversity and many federal-question cases.

III. Historical Development of Supplemental Jurisdiction

A. Definitional Issues: "Pendent," "Ancillary," "Pendent-Party," and "Supplemental"

1. Historically, courts talked of such jurisdiction using three terms: "pendent," "ancillary," and "pendent-party" jurisdiction. Pendent jurisdiction generally operated over state claims asserted by plaintiffs in federal-question cases. Ancillary jurisdiction generally operated over claims asserted by a party other than the plaintiff and was usually available in either diversity or federal-question cases. Pendent-party jurisdiction involved "addition of a party which is implicated in the litigation only with respect to the pendent state law claim and not also with respect to any claim as to which there is an independent basis of federal jurisdiction."

Moor v. Alameda County, 411 U.S. 693, 713 (1973). *Moor* declined to decide pendent-party jurisdiction's legitimacy, and the Court, although acknowledging the concept, declined to apply it until ruling that § 1367 authorized it. *See Exxon Mobil Corp. v. Allapattah Services, Inc.*, 545 U.S. 546 (2005).

2. Some scholars suggested that there was no principled difference between pendent and ancillary jurisdiction and thus that a generic term—supplemental jurisdiction—should refer to both.

3. Congress accepted that suggestion and codified supplemental jurisdiction in 1990, *see* 28 U.S.C. § 1367, using the unitary phrase "supplemental jurisdiction." Nonetheless, many courts still refer to "pendent" and "ancillary" jurisdiction, and you need to be familiar with those terms because they are what you will see in cases antedating § 1367.

B. Until 1990, Case Law, Not Legislation, Developed the Doctrine

1. Supplemental jurisdiction stems from *Osborn v. Bank of the United States*, 22 U.S. (9 Wheat.) 738, 822-23 (1824).

   a. Chief Justice John Marshall said "[t]here is scarcely any case, every part of which depends on the constitution, laws, or treaties of the United States." Thus, he concluded, "when a question to which the judicial power of the Union is extended by the constitution, forms an ingredient of the original cause, it is in the power of Congress to give the [federal] Circuit Courts [which then were trial courts] jurisdiction of that cause, although other questions of fact or law may be involved in it."

   b. In other words, federal judicial power extends to cases as a whole under Article III, § 2. A case includes all related claims, facts, and issues, not merely those falling independently within the federal judicial power. ***Caution*****:** That was Chief Justice Marshall's justification for federal courts hearing non-federal *issues*—when they are part of a single constitutional case. It still is necessary to examine every *claim* in *every* case individually to ensure that it has a jurisdictional ticket of admission.

2. *Freeman v. Howe*, 65 U.S. (24 How.) 450 (1860), held that a federal court had authority in a diversity case to adjudicate the rights of non-diverse parties with interests in the disposition of property within the federal court's control. The Court did not subsequently limit the doctrine to *in rem* or *quasi in rem* cases.

3. *Moore v. New York Cotton Exchange*, 270 U.S. 593 (1926), allowed a defendant in a federal antitrust suit to assert a state-law counterclaim, even though the adverse parties were not diverse. The counterclaim came within the federal court's (then) ancillary jurisdiction because it arose from the same transaction or occurrence as plaintiff's federal-question claim.

4. *Hurn v. Oursler*, 289 U.S. 238 (1933), showed that pendent jurisdiction was available only where the federal and state claims are part of the same cause of action.

   a. "Cause of action" is by no means self-defining. *Hurn* found a state unfair-competition claim arising out of an uncopyrighted version of the same play that gave rise to plaintiff's federal copyright claim to be part of the same cause of action, because "[plaintiff] alleges the violation of a single right, namely, the right to protection of the copyrighted play" and because "the claims of infringement and unfair competition so precisely rest upon identical facts as to be little more than the equivalent of different epithets to characterize the same groups of circumstances."

   b. However, the Court found different causes of action when the plaintiff sought to append an additional state claim for defendant's copying from a *modified* but uncopyrighted version of the same play.

   c. Though the opinion was unclear, courts generally interpreted *Hurn* to require total factual identity of state and federal claims.

   d. As the Court phrased it,

      > The distinction to be observed is between a case where two distinct grounds in support of a single cause of action are alleged, one only of which presents a federal question, and a case where two separate and distinct causes of action are alleged, one only of which is federal in character. In the former, where the federal question averred is not plainly wanting in substance, the federal court, even though the federal ground be not established, may nevertheless retain and dispose of the case upon the nonfederal ground; in the latter it may not do so upon the nonfederal cause of action.

      Some have kindly characterized the Court's distinction as "difficult of application."

5. *United Mine Workers v. Gibbs*, 383 U.S. 715 (1966), is the Court's leading discussion of the constitutionality of what today we call supplemental jurisdiction. A Tennessee plaintiff asserted a federal-question claim against a Tennessee defendant and appended a state-law claim that arose from the same dispute. Although the federal claim invoked federal-question jurisdiction, there was no stand-alone jurisdictional ticket for the state-law claim. The Court permitted federal court to hear both claims, however, because they satisfied the test *Gibbs* articulated.

   a. *Gibbs* replaced *Hurn*'s murky cause-of-action approach with a pragmatic, fact-based inquiry. A federal court can hear supplemental claims meeting provided:

      > The state and federal claims must derive from a common nucleus of operative fact. But if, considered without regard to

> their federal or state character, a plaintiff's claims are such that he would ordinarily be expected to try them all in one judicial proceeding, then, assuming substantiality of the federal issues, there is power in federal courts to hear the whole.

Gibbs, 383 U.S. at 725.

b. There is no doubt that *Gibbs* extended then-pendent jurisdiction beyond the narrow factual identity *Hurn* required. Courts interpreted *Gibbs* to permit pendent jurisdiction for any claims arising from the same transaction or occurrence as the stand-alone claim (thus comprising a single constitutional case) if the plaintiff would expect to try them in a single proceeding.

c. Elaborating on when a plaintiff would ordinarily expect to try multiple claims together, *Gibbs* held there was pendent jurisdiction over claims that involve "a common nucleus of operative fact" sufficiently to constitute one constitutional case (as when they arise from the same transaction or occurrence).

d. *Gibbs* also recognized discretionary factors that might counsel a court to decline to exercise supplemental jurisdiction: (1) dismissal of the federal claims before trial, (2) state claims and issues substantially predominating over federal claims (the tail-wagging-the-dog phenomenon), (3) state claims not closely tied to questions of federal policy, and (4) trying the claims together sufficiently likely to lead to jury confusion that the federal court, even if it retained all the claims, would sever them under FED. R. CIV. P. 42(b) and try them separately. However, 28 U.S.C. § 1367(c) appears to contract the discretionary-dismissal power courts had under *Gibbs*. *See infra* § IV.D.2 at 147 *[R95]*. [R108] [R109]

e. *Gibbs* recognized that the plaintiff's federal-question claim had to be a substantial part of the case. In this regard, the Court was merely reiterating a requirement for invoking federal-question jurisdiction in any case. *See supra* Ch. IV, § III.C.5, at 104 *[R96]*. *Gibbs* preceded *Merrell Dow*, so the Court had not yet added the substantiality criterion that exists today. *See generally supra* Ch. IV, § III.C.6-9, at 104-106 *[R97]*. [R100] [R102] [R103] [R112]

6. Supplemental jurisdiction allows a federal court to decide claims (and to rule on issues) not ordinarily within the federal "judicial power" in Article III, § 2. For example, it can permit federal courts to determine state-law claims despite lack of diversity. This is what Chief Justice Marshall adverted to in *Osborn*. At least with respect to issues, that should surprise no one; the Constitution and Congress confer jurisdiction over cases, not issues. Nonetheless, there was long suspicion that supplemental jurisdiction over state-law claims might be unconstitutional.

7. The cases above, however, clearly establish supplemental jurisdiction's constitutionality. They recognize that while a single claim may invoke federal subject-matter jurisdiction (for instance, either federal-question

or diversity (subject to the complete-diversity rule, *see supra* Ch. V, § III.A.I, at 116-117 *[R98]*) and the rules of aggregation, *see supra* Ch. V, § IV.C, at 127-128 *[R99]*), the federal court may decide other claims when they are part of the same "case or controversy" as the claim having stand-alone subject-matter jurisdiction. Federal courts have jurisdiction over the entire case, including those non-federal, non-diverse aspects that satisfy § 1367.

8. However, a serious question remained: whether supplemental jurisdiction required a statutory grant by Congress.

   a. In *Hurn* and *Gibbs*, the Supreme Court seemed simply to assume that federal courts have authority to exercise supplemental jurisdiction, notwithstanding Congress's silence. There was at that time no general statutory grant of supplemental jurisdiction, but jurisdictional statutes spoke of "civil actions," not "claims."

   b. Some scholars opined that the federal courts' creating supplemental jurisdiction violated separation of powers. The bases of federal judicial power in Article III, § 2 generally are not self-executing but instead require a statutory grant. Critics argued that the courts' recognizing supplemental jurisdiction usurped a legislative function.

   c. *Finley v. United States*, 490 U.S. 545 (1989), questioned supplemental jurisdiction's legitimacy in the absence of a statute.

C. *Finley* Led to Passage of the Supplemental Jurisdiction Statute in 1990

1. *Finley v. United States*, 490 U.S. 545 (1989), involved pendent-party jurisdiction, in which the additional claim is by or against a party other than the one involved in the claim that has stand-alone subject-matter jurisdiction.

Example: P, a citizen of California, brings a Federal Tort Claims Act suit against D-1, the United States. P also asserts a state-law claim against D-2, a citizen of California. The claims arise from a single airplane crash and thus share a common nucleus of operative fact. The claim against D-2 invokes neither federal-question nor diversity jurisdiction and runs against a different defendant from the one against whom the jurisdiction-invoking claim runs.

P	*v.*	**D-1**	**&**	**D-2**
(CA)		**(US)**	**&**	**(CA)**

2. On these facts, *Finley* rejected supplemental jurisdiction by a five-to-four vote even though the Court recognized that the state-law claim against D-2 satisfied the constitutional test for pendent jurisdiction because it arose from the same transaction as the federal-question claim; thus, the claim satisfied *Gibbs*. *See supra* § III.B.5, at 137-138 *[R100]*.

3. Justice Scalia based the holding on the absence of a congressional grant of pendent or pendent-party jurisdiction. Because no statute authorized such jurisdiction, the power to exercise it "lies dormant." *Finley*, 490 U.S. at 548.

4. *Finley* was consistent with *Aldinger v. Howard*, 427 U.S. 1 (1976), an earlier pendent-party case. There, P asserted a federal civil rights claim under 42 U.S.C. § 1983 against a state officer, and appended a state-law claim against a non-diverse municipality. Though the claim against the second defendant satisfied *Gibbs*, the Court rejected jurisdiction.

   a. *Aldinger* rested on then-existing law that municipalities were not "persons" and thus could not be § 1983 defendants. *See infra* Ch. XIV, § III.D.3, at 308 *[R101]*. The Court reasoned that permitting suit against a municipality under a state-law tort claim was inconsistent with that understanding. Thus, the Court saw § 1983 as a statutory impediment to exercising pendent-party jurisdiction even though § 1983 is not a jurisdictional statute.

   b. Two years after *Aldinger*, the Court changed its view, holding that municipalities are "persons" under § 1983. *Monell v. Department of Social Services of the City of New York*, 436 U.S. 658 (1978). *See infra* Ch. XIV, § III.D.3, at 308 *[R102]*. *Aldinger* lost its force as precedent.

   c. *Aldinger* left open the possibility that the pendent-party jurisdiction was legitimate in cases involving exclusive federal-question jurisdiction, *Aldinger*, 427 U.S. at 18, but *Finley* rejected pendent-party jurisdiction in just such a situation.

   d. *Aldinger*'s reasoning differed from *Finley*'s. The *Aldinger* Court assumed that pendent or pendent-party jurisdiction was appropriate unless Congress precluded it by statute. *Finley* indulged the opposite: jurisdiction was inappropriate unless Congress permitted it by statute.

5. Commentators criticized *Finley*'s reasoning and result.

   a. The theory—that there was no pendent, ancillary, or pendent-party jurisdiction without a congressional grant for it—was inconsistent with the Court's approach in every other pendent- and ancillary-jurisdiction case. Those cases seemed to assume that the federal courts had authority to exercise additional jurisdiction when a case, such as *Gibbs*, satisfied the appropriate test.

   b. The result was most unfortunate for the plaintiff and inefficient for the judicial system. Because the Federal Tort Claims Act specifies exclusive federal jurisdiction, such claims must be in federal court. Without federal jurisdiction over the state-law claim, the plaintiff had to litigate in two judicial systems concerning potential liability for a single airplane crash.

c. *Finley*'s broad language about the necessity of a statutory grant of jurisdiction created uncertainty about whether all forms of additional jurisdiction—even, for example, *Gibbs*'s simple fact pattern—might be suspect.

6. In response to *Finley*, Congress passed the supplemental jurisdiction statute, 28 U.S.C. § 1367, which became effective for actions filed on or after December 1, 1990. The stated purposes of the statute are (1) to overrule *Finley*, thus to permitting pendent-party jurisdiction in federal-question cases, and (2) to codify pre-*Finley* practice. The statute has succeeded in some respects, but it has also caused considerable confusion and controversy. [R104]

IV. The Supplemental-Jurisdiction Statute

A. Overview

1. The supplemental jurisdiction statute has five subsections: § 1367(a) grants supplemental jurisdiction; § 1367(b) limits that grant, but only in pure diversity cases; § 1367(c) lists discretionary factors that allow a court to refuse to exercise supplemental jurisdiction; § 1367(d) provides tolling the statutes of limitations for supplemental claims the federal court dismisses, and § 1367(e) specifies that "State" in the statute includes the District of Columbia, Puerto Rico, and "any territory or possession of the United States," thus tracking the diversity statute, 28 U.S.C. § 1332(e).

2. Congress drafted and passed the statute in haste, and it has been the target of considerable criticism. The statute overruled *Finley* but created enormous uncertainty in other areas, particularly in the operation of § 1367(b).

3. The statute refers to federal jurisdiction to hear non-federal, non-diversity claims as "supplemental jurisdiction." Under previous case law, there were the three closely related concepts—pendent, ancillary, and pendent-party jurisdiction—now subsumed under supplemental jurisdiction, although some courts continue to speak of pendent and ancillary jurisdiction.

B. The Grant of Supplemental Jurisdiction in § 1367(a)

1. Section 1367(a) grants supplemental jurisdiction to the full extent of Article III. It provides that in a civil case invoking the original jurisdiction of the federal courts, the "courts shall have supplemental jurisdiction over all other claims that are so related to claims in the action . . . that they form part of the same case or controversy under Article III. . . ." This grant clearly codifies that part of *Gibbs* and includes all claims that share a common nucleus of operative fact with a stand-alone, jurisdiction-invoking claim. *See supra* § III.B.5, at 137-138 *[R103]*.

2. In addition, the last sentence of § 1367(a) provides that the grant "shall include claims that involve the joinder or intervention of additional parties." That overrules *Finley* (and *Aldinger*). *See supra* § III.C, at 139-141 *[R104]*.

3. Nothing in § 1367(a) limits it to federal-question cases involving exclusive federal jurisdiction.

Example: P, a citizen of California, files an ordinary federal-question claim against D-1 and a transactionally related state-law claim against D-2. P and D-2 are co-citizens. The claim against D-2 qualifies for neither federal-question jurisdiction (because it is sounds in state law) nor diversity jurisdiction (because P and D-2 are not diverse).

P	*v.*	**D-1**	**&**	**D-2**
(CO)		**(WY)**	**&**	**(CO)**

Section 1367(a) grants supplemental jurisdiction over the claim, however; it satisfies the relatedness test originally in *Gibbs*. The fact that the claim involves a different defendant from the federal-question defendant is irrelevant, as is the fact that the federal-question jurisdiction is not exclusive.

4. Nothing in § 1367(a) limits it to cases of federal-question jurisdiction. Thus, the grant in § 1367(a), read in isolation, applies in diversity cases as well. Without some limitation, such a result would have eviscerated *Strawbridge v. Curtiss*'s and § 1332's complete-diversity rule. *See infra* § IV.C, at 143-146 *[R105]*.

Example: P, a citizen of California, files a state-law claim of $100,000, against D-1, a citizen of Arizona, and a transactionally related state-law claim against D-2, a citizen of California.

P	*v.*	**D-1**	**&**	**D-2**
(CA)		**(AZ)**	**&**	**(CA)**

The case violates the complete-diversity rule because P and D-2 are co-citizens. Nonetheless, § 1367(a) *appears* to grant supplemental jurisdiction over the claim against D-2 because the claim satisfies *Gibbs*'s relatedness test. Because nothing in § 1367(a) limits it to federal-question cases, supplemental jurisdiction seems be available. *However*, § 1367(b) restricts that grant in this fact pattern and thus preserves the complete-diversity rule. This is a case "of which the district courts have original jurisdiction founded solely on section 1332 of this title, . ." and so § 1367(b) excludes jurisdiction over the state claim.

5. Section§ 1367(a) does not override the Eleventh Amendment's prohibition of individuals' suing states in the federal courts. Thus, if a state has not lost its immunity under that Amendment (by waiver or congressional action, *see infra* Ch. XIII, § IV, at 290-299 *[R106]*, § 1367(a) does

not force it to defend a supplemental-jurisdiction claim. *Raygor v. Regents of the University of Minnesota*, 534 U.S. 533 (2002). [R92] [R107] [330]

C. Section 1367(b): Restrictions on Supplemental Jurisdiction

1. Congress restricted supplemental jurisdiction in diversity cases to prevent erosion of the complete-diversity rule and head off a new flood of federal cases.
2. Section 1367(b) restricts supplemental jurisdiction from § 1367(a), but only when original jurisdiction rests "solely" on § 1332. Thus, the § 1367(b) restrictions apply in diversity-only cases, not in federal-question or mixed federal-question/diversity cases.
3. The restrictions in § 1367(b) apply only to specific claims:
   a. claims asserted "by plaintiffs against persons made parties under Rule 14, 19, 20, or 24 of the Federal Rules of Civil Procedure";
   b. claims asserted "by persons proposed to be joined as plaintiffs under Rule 19 of such rules"; and
   c. claims by persons "seeking to intervene as plaintiffs under Rule 24 of such rules."
4. Note that these claims over which supplemental jurisdiction does not exist in diversity cases are all plaintiffs' claims, not those of defendants or other parties.

Example 1: P, a citizen of New York, asserts a $100,000 state-law claim against D, a citizen of Pennsylvania. The claim obviously invokes diversity jurisdiction. D asserts a compulsory counterclaim against P. The claim is for $45,000.

P *v.* **D** **($100,000)**
($45,000)
(NY) **(PA)**

The counterclaim qualifies for neither federal-question jurisdiction (because it sounds in state law) nor diversity jurisdiction (because the amount in controversy is insufficient). The counterclaim qualifies for supplemental jurisdiction, however, under § 1367(a), because it arises from the same transaction or occurrence as the underlying claim. Even though plaintiff's is a pure diversity case, § 1367(b) does not limit the grant of supplemental jurisdiction here. Section 1367(b) removes supplemental jurisdiction only from claims *by plaintiffs*, prospective plaintiffs, or plaintiff intervenors; this claim is by a defendant

Example 2: Same facts as the Example 1, except that D's claim against P is a permissive counterclaim (not from the same transaction or occurrence as P's claim).

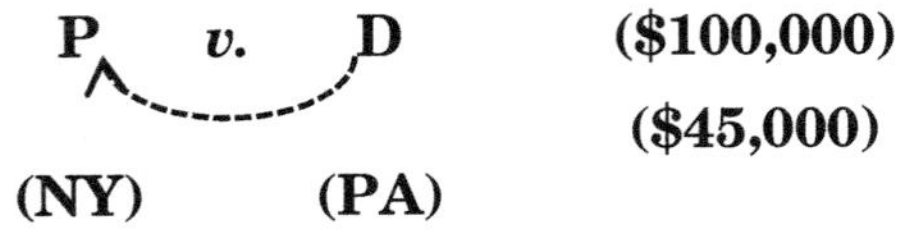

This claim does not get supplemental jurisdiction because it does not arise from the same transaction or occurrence as the jurisdiction-invoking claim. Thus, § 1367(a) does not grant supplemental jurisdiction at all, and there is no need to assess § 1367(b).

5. Prohibiting supplemental jurisdiction in a diversity case over a claim by a plaintiff against a person made a party under Rule 14 comes from *Owen Equipment & Erection Co. v. Kroger*, 437 U.S. 365 (1978), which explained that allowing supplemental jurisdiction over a state-law claim by a plaintiff against a third-party defendant would undermine the complete-diversity rule.

Example 1: P, a citizen of Illinois, asserts a $100,000 state-law claim against D, a citizen of New Jersey. The claim invokes diversity jurisdiction. Now D impleads a third-party defendant (3PΔ), seeking indemnity on the underlying claim. (Rule 14 permits such joinder of a new party as procedurally proper, but always remember that *no* Federal Rule of Civil Procedure ever grants, refuses, or in any way modifies subject-matter jurisdiction). But 3PΔ is a citizen of New Jersey. Thus, the claim by D against 3PΔ does not invoke diversity, and it does not invoke federal-question jurisdiction because the indemnity claim arises under state law.

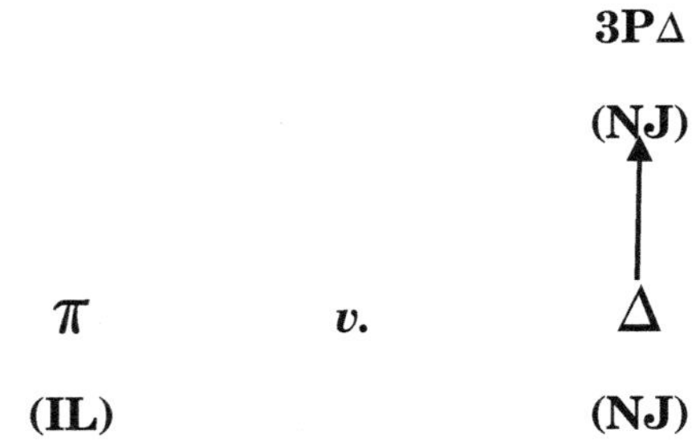

Nonetheless, the court can exercise supplemental jurisdiction over that claim by D against 3PΔ. Why? First, it invokes supplemental jurisdiction under § 1367(a) because it involves the same nucleus of operative facts as the underlying claim by P against D. Second, although § 1367(b) is relevant (because this is a diversity case), it does not remove the grant of supplemental jurisdiction. Why not? Because D's claim against 3PΔ is not a claim *by a plaintiff*, and thus does not fall within § 1367(b)'s list of prohibited claims.

Example 2: P, a citizen of Illinois, asserts a $100,000 state-law tort claim against D, a citizen of New Jersey. The claim invokes diversity jurisdiction. Now D impleads 3PΔ, a citizen of Illinois, for indemnity on the underlying claim. This claim invokes diversity jurisdiction, because it is by a citizen of New Jersey against a citizen of Illinois, and exceeds $75,000. Now assume that P asserts an upsloping claim in the same case against 3PΔ (Rule 14(a) allows that as a matter of pleading, but remember that no Federal Rule of Civil Procedure either confers or takes away federal subject-matter jurisdiction.)

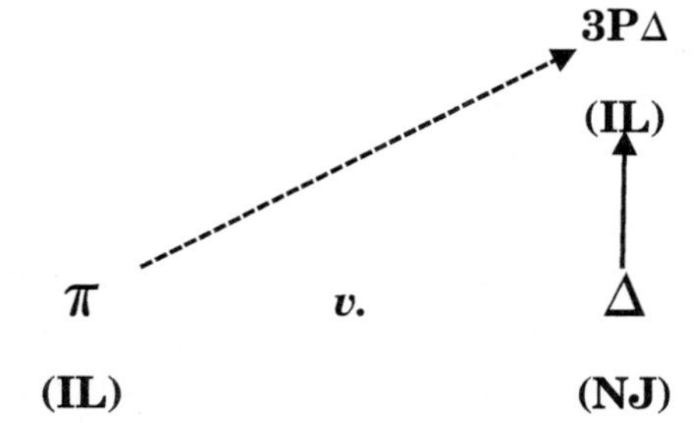

There is no diversity jurisdiction over that (upsloping) claim, because P and 3PΔ are co-citizens, and no federal-question jurisdiction, because these are state-law claims. Section 1367(a), read in isolation, grants supplemental jurisdiction because the claim is transactionally related to the underlying dispute (Rule 14(a) requires that). But § 1367(b) removes that grant, because this is a claim, asserted in a diversity case, *by a plaintiff* "against a person[ ] made a party under Rule 14. . . ."

Example 3: P, a citizen of Illinois, asserts a $100,000 state-law tort claim against D, a citizen of New Jersey. The claim invokes diversity jurisdiction. Now D impleads 3PΔ, a citizen of Illinois, for indemnity on plaintiff's claim. This claim invokes diversity jurisdiction, because it is by a citizen of New Jersey against a citizen of Illinois, and exceeds $75,000. (These are the facts of Example 2.)

Now assume that 3PΔ asserts a transactionally related tort claim in the same case against P, as Rule 14(a)(2)(D) permits.

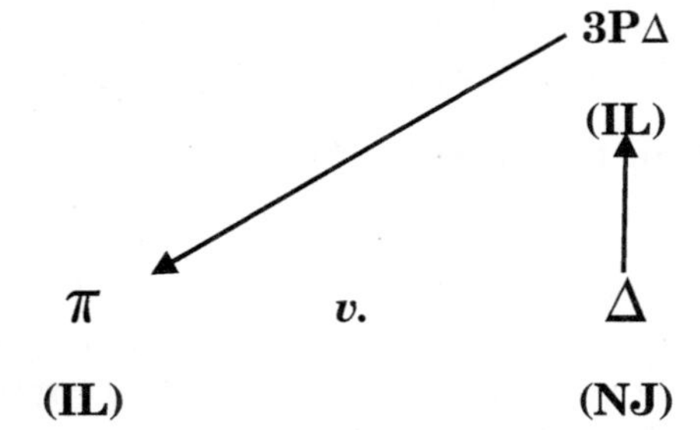

3PΔ's (downsloping) claim qualifies for supplemental jurisdiction. Section 1367(b) does not exclude it because it is (a) not a claim by a *plaintiff* and (b) does not run *against* a party joined under Rule 14.

However, that does not mean that P may now file an upsloping state claim against 3PΔ.

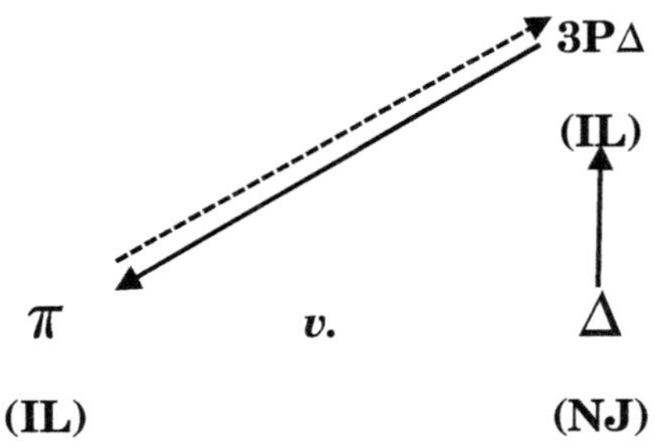

That *would be* a claim by a plaintiff against a party joined under Rule 14, and § 1367(b) withholds supplemental jurisdiction from such a claim. Note that P's claim against 3PΔ is still a Rule 14 claim; it does not magically become a Rule 13(a) compulsory counterclaim merely because 3PΔ asserted the downsloping Rule 14 claim against P.

This apparent imbalance of procedural possibilities gives P an incentive to bring the action in a state court, joining 3PΔ as a party-defendant. The lack of diversity then does not matter, and the case is not removable because of the complete-diversity rule.

6. Prohibiting supplemental jurisdiction in a diversity case over claims by a plaintiff against "persons made a party under Rule . . . 20 . . ." was also necessary to protect the complete-diversity rule. Rule 20 permits joinder of multiple initial parties in a civil case. Without this part of § 1367(b), there would be supplemental jurisdiction over a transactionally related claim by the plaintiff against a non-diverse defendant.

7. The prohibition over claims involving necessary parties under Rule 19 comports with pre-*Finley* practice.

8. However, the prohibition over claims involving intervenors is inconsistent with pre-*Finley* practice. Before § 1367, federal courts had long recognized supplemental jurisdiction over claims by or against intervenors of right under Rule 24(a). [R94] [R105] [R331]

D. Discretionary Refusal to Exercise Supplemental Jurisdiction: § 1367(c)

1. *Gibbs* distinguished a court's having power to exercise supplemental jurisdiction from having to exercise it. Section 1367(a) codifies the *Gibbs*'s power aspect and extends to claims sharing a common nucleus of operative fact with a claim that invokes federal subject-matter jurisdiction. *See supra* § IV.B, at 141-143 *[R107]*.

   a. *Gibbs* recognized, though, that a federal court should not necessarily exercise supplemental jurisdiction whenever it is available.

b. *Gibbs* announced four discretionary factors, *see supra* § III.B.5.d, at 138 *[R108]*, suggesting that a court may decline supplemental jurisdiction when (1) the district court dismisses the federal-question claim (if any) before trial; (2) if state-law issues "predominate" in the case; (3) the state claims are not closely linked to federal policy, or (4) if the multiplicity of claims is likely to confuse the jury.

2. Section 1367(c) codifies only some of the *Gibbs* discretionary factors. *See supra* § III.B.5.d, at 138 *[R109]*. Commentators have criticized the statute for not adhering more faithfully to *Gibbs*. Nonetheless, the statute provides that a court "may decline to exercise supplemental jurisdiction":

   a. if the supplemental claim raises "a novel or complex issue" of state law;

   b. if the supplemental claim "predominates over the claim or claims over which the district court has original jurisdiction";

   c. if the district court "has dismissed all claims over which it has original jurisdiction"; or

   d. if, "in exceptional circumstances, there are other compelling reasons for declining jurisdiction."

   Two circuits have ruled that § 1367(c) is indeed narrower than *Gibbs* and that declining jurisdiction under § 1367(c)(4) is permissible only for reasons at least equal in weight to the first three subsections and in truly exceptional circumstances. The Ninth Circuit also ruled that dismissing under § 1367(c)(4) requires the district court to state its precise reasons for doing so.

   Note that Congress's grant of discretion under this section supersedes, for supplemental-jurisdiction purposes, the legal-certainty approach of *St. Paul Mercury Indemnity Co. v. Red Cab Co.*, 303 U.S. 283 (1938). *See supra* at Ch. V, § IV.B.1, at 125 *[R110]*. [R95]

E. The Tolling Provision of § 1367(d)

1. Section 1367(d) provides that the statute of limitations for any supplemental claim under § 1367(a) "and for any other claim in the same action that is voluntarily dismissed at the same time as or after the dismissal" of a supplemental claim "shall be tolled while the claim is pending and for a period of 30 days after it is dismissed . . ." unless state law provides a longer toll.

2. *Jinks v. Richland County, S.C.*, 538 U.S. 456 (2003), upheld the tolling provision against a constitutional challenge.

   a. Plaintiff sued the county in federal court, asserting a claim under 42 U.S.C. § 1983. He also asserted state-law claims under supplemental jurisdiction. The district court dismissed the § 1983 claim on the merits and exercised its discretion under § 1367(c)(3) to decline supplemental jurisdiction over the state-law claims. Plaintiff then sued on the state-law claims in state court.

b. The South Carolina Supreme Court held that § 1367(d) was unconstitutional because it interfered with state "sovereign authority to establish the extent to which its political subdivisions are subject to suit."

c. The Supreme Court unanimously reversed and upheld the tolling provision as "necessary and proper for carrying into execution Congress's power" to establish the lower federal courts and assure that they fairly exercise the judicial power of the United States. 538 U.S. at 462.

3. The Court has held, however, that the tolling provision cannot extend the period in which a nonconsenting state may be sued in state court for claims dismissed on Eleventh Amendment grounds. *Raygor v. Regents of the University of Minnesota*, 534 U.S. 533 (2002). *See generally infra* Ch. XIII, at 283-299 *[R111]*. Thus, the plaintiff who elects to try to sue the state in federal court risks having a time-barred claim in state court if the federal court dismisses because of the Eleventh Amendment.

F. Some Problems in Applying § 1367

1. Congress drafted § 1367 in haste, without sufficient consultation. As a result, the statute creates confusion in some areas and unfortunate and possibly unintended changes from pre-*Finley* practice in others.

2. The most contentious issue was whether § 1367 changed prior practice concerning the amount-in-controversy requirement for a diversity class action.

a. Before § 1367, the Supreme Court ruled that each member of a diversity class must meet the amount-in-controversy requirement. *Zahn v. International Paper Co.*, 414 U.S. 291 (1974).

b. Under § 1367(a), however, if the class representative's claim exceeds $75,000, and she is diverse from the defendant, a court has supplemental jurisdiction over claims by all class members, assuming their claims meet the *Gibbs* test (*see supra* § III.B.5, at 137-138 *[R112]*), even if their claims do not exceed $75,000.

c. Nothing in § 1367(b) refers to class actions, so that subsection does not appear to remove the grant of supplemental jurisdiction in class actions. Unnamed class members, after all, join the action under Rule 23, not Rule 20.

d. One sentence in § 1367's legislative history purported to indicate that Congress did not intend to overrule *Zahn*'s requirement that each member of the class assert a claim exceeding $75,000.

e. The Courts of Appeals had split badly on the issue, but *Exxon Mobil Corporation v. Allapattah Services, Inc.*, ruled five-to-four that

§ 1367 had overruled *Zahn*. *See supra* Ch. V, IV.C.5, at 128 *[R113]*. [R341]

f. The Class Action Fairness Act of 2005, the relevant portions of which appear at 28 U.S.C. § 1332(d), resolves some of these problems by permitting class actions with minimal diversity and permitting aggregating the claims of class members, provided that the aggregation exceeds five million dollars. [R80] [R90]

3. Pre-*Finley* practice permitted diversity class actions if the class representative's citizenship was diverse from each defendant's. The unnamed class members' citizenships were irrelevant. *Supreme Tribe of Ben-Hur v. Cauble*, 255 U.S. 356 (1921).

a. *Ben-Hur* thus recognized then-pendent jurisdiction over the claims by the non-diverse class members.

b. Nothing in § 1367 purports to change *Ben-Hur*.

4. The statute did change supplemental jurisdiction over claims involving intervenors of right, prohibiting, in § 1367(b)'s reference to FED. R. CIV. P. 24, what previously was permissible. That makes efficient joinder in diversity cases more difficult.

5. Read literally, § 1367(b) does not allow supplemental jurisdiction in diversity cases over claims by plaintiffs asserted in a defensive capacity. For example, an impleader claim by a plaintiff against whom the defendant has counterclaimed seems to run afoul of the provision that there be no supplemental jurisdiction over claims by plaintiffs against persons made parties under Rule 14.

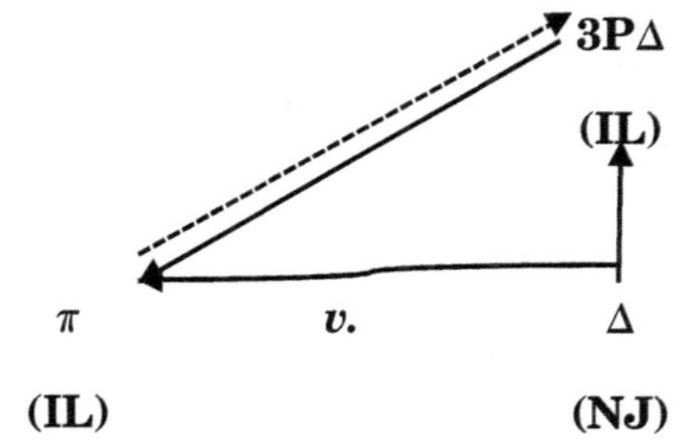

[R60] [R88]

Chapter VII

REMOVAL: A METHOD OF INVOKING JURISDICTION

■ ANALYSIS

I. Introduction

When there are several proper courts, the plaintiff gets the first choice of where the litigation will occur. Sometimes, however, the defendant may override the plaintiff's choice of forum. Removal allows the defendant to move a state-court case to the federal court for the district where the state court sits. Removal is not an *appeal* from state to federal court; it is a *transfer* from a state trial court to a federal district court. As a general rule subject to limited exceptions, a case is removable only if it qualifies for federal subject-matter jurisdiction—that is, if the plaintiff could properly have brought the action in federal court in the first place.

Note that removal is *not* a form of subject-matter jurisdiction. It is a procedural device for invoking federal jurisdiction that Congress has vested in a federal court in some other statute, such as 28 U.S.C. §§ 1330-1345.

II. General Principles of Removal

A. Removal Contrasted with Remand

1. *Removal* operates in one direction only: it permits transfer of a case filed in state court to a federal court. It never operates in reverse; there is no such thing as "removing" a case from federal to state court.
2. If the federal court finds that removal was improper, either procedurally or because the federal court lacks subject-matter jurisdiction, the federal court will *remand* the case to state court. Remand, like removal, operates in one direction only; it's just that the direction is opposite to removal.
3. Thus, the combination of original jurisdiction statutes and removal statutes provides a right to both parties to have a federal court decide an appropriate case.
   a. If the plaintiff selects the federal forum and the case meets the requirements of subject-matter jurisdiction, the defendant has no power to veto plaintiff's choice and have the case sent to the state court.
   b. On the other hand, if the plaintiff sues in state court, and the case meets the removal requirements, the defendant may remove the case to federal court. Unless removal was improper, the plaintiff has no power to shift the case back to state court.

B. Removal Is Ordinarily Available Only to Defendants

1. The general removal statute, 28 U.S.C. § 1441(a), allows removal by "*the* defendant or defendants," (***N.B.*** not "*a* defendant") making it clear that all defendants served in the case in state court must join in removal. *Chicago, R.I. & P. Ry. Co. v. Martin*, 178 U.S. 245 (1900). If any defendant refuses to join, the case is not removable, *see infra* § III.D, at 156-158 *[R114]*, unless the case satisfies the requirements of 28 U.S.C. § 1441(c). [***Style note***: To avoid the cumbersome notation "defendant(s),"

all further references to removal mean removal by all defendants unless otherwise specifically noted.]

2. The statute specifying removal procedure, 28 U.S.C. § 1446, refers to "[*a*] defendant or defendants desiring to remove." Perhaps to avoid any possible ambiguity from the two sections' different wording, § 1446(b)(2)(A) explicitly echoes § 1441's requirement that *all* defendants join in removal.

3. Congress has, however, enacted an exception to this rule. Pursuant to 28 U.S.C. § 1454(a), cases in which any party asserts a claim involving violation of a patent, copyright, or plant variety protection are removable by any party. Thus, where the defendant in a state-court action files such a claim as a counterclaim, either party may remove. [R117]

4. Otherwise, even when a defendant asserts a garden-variety federal-question counterclaim, the plaintiff may not remove, *Shamrock Oil & Gas Corp. v. Sheets*, 313 U.S. 100 (1941).

5. If the case is removable at the outset and the defendant fails to remove it, a later-added defendant cannot remove the case. *Noble v. Bradford Marine, Inc.*, 789 F. Supp. 395 (S.D. Fla. 1992). This is consistent with the rule that all defendants must agree to removal. If the original defendant did not remove, then the court infers she does not agree to removal. Moreover, as a practical matter, it would be cumbersome to allow removal after the later addition of a defendant, because removal would waste the state court's efforts.

C. General Venue Provisions Do Not Apply in Removal Cases

1. The general venue statute for federal civil actions, 28 U.S.C. § 1391, allows the plaintiff to lay venue in any district in which all defendants reside or in which a substantial part of the events forming the basis of the claim arose. But this statute applies only to cases the plaintiff files in federal court; thus, it does not apply in cases removed from state court. 28 U.S.C. § 1390(c).

2. Venue is proper in only one district in all removed cases: the federal district "embracing" the place in which the state action was pending. 28 U.S.C. § 1441(a).

D. Generally, a Case Is Removable Only if the Federal Court Has Subject-Matter Jurisdiction

1. 28 U.S.C. § 1441(a) allows removal of a civil action "of which the district courts of the United States have original jurisdiction." Thus, as a starting point, the defendant may remove the case only if the case has some stand-alone ticket of federal subject-matter jurisdiction, such as diversity or federal question. But note that 28 U.S.C. § 1454, *supra* § II.B.3, is an exception to this general rule, because removal may rest upon defendant's assertion in a counterclaim of a patent, copyright, or plant-variety-protection violation. [R79]

2. Other provisions in the removal statutes, however, modify the general rule. *See infra* § III.C, at 155 *[R116]*.

3. Ordinarily, a federal court will determine whether it has subject-matter jurisdiction before addressing any other issue, but *Ruhrgas AG v. Marathon Oil Co.*, 526 U.S. 574 (1999), rejected an "unyielding jurisdictional hierarchy." If the subject-matter jurisdiction issue is difficult but the court clearly lacks personal jurisdiction, the court does not abuse its discretion by dismissing for lack of personal jurisdiction (FED. R. CIV. P. 12)(b)(2)) without addressing subject-matter jurisdiction (FED. R. CIV. P. 12(b)(1). [R59] [R64]

E. A Case Is Removable Even if the State Court Lacked Subject-Matter Jurisdiction

1. For many years, a federal court's jurisdiction on removal was "derivative" of the state court's subject-matter jurisdiction. (It was a bit like the rule of property law that a grantor cannot transfer better title than she has.) Thus, if the state court had no subject-matter jurisdiction over a case (*e.g.* a case within the federal courts' exclusive subject-matter jurisdiction), the case was not removable. If the defendant removed, the federal court would have to remand because the state court never had jurisdiction. Then, the state court would have to dismiss, and the plaintiff would have to refile in federal court.

2. This problem no longer exists, however, because 28 U.S.C. § 1441(f) ended that bizarre and time-wasting dance, providing that a state court's lack of subject-matter jurisdiction is no bar to federal jurisdiction on removal.

III. Grants of Removal

A. Statutes Govern Removal

1. The right to remove a case from state to federal court is statutory only. There is no constitutional provision for removal.

2. The Supreme Court has consistently upheld removal against constitutional attacks. *See, e.g., Ames v. Kansas ex rel. Johnston*, 111 U.S. 449 (1884).

3. The Court construes removal statutes strictly, however, to avoid untoward deprivation of state court jurisdiction. *See, e.g., Shamrock Oil & Gas Corp. v. Sheets*, 313 U.S. 100, 108-09 (1941) (no removal by plaintiffs even if the defendants file counterclaims that qualify for federal subject-matter jurisdiction, subject to the § 1454 exception for intellectual property cases, *see supra* § II.B.3, at 153 *[R117]*). As in all cases, the party invoking federal jurisdiction (the defendant in removal situations, the appellant or petitioner seeking federal appellate review) has the burden of establishing that federal jurisdiction exists.

B. The General Provision for Removal of Diversity and Federal-Question Cases

1. Title 28 U.S.C. § 1441(a) authorizes most removal, permitting the defendants to remove a civil action "of which the district courts . . . have original jurisdiction." This grant clearly encompasses diversity and federal-question cases.

2. The requirements for diversity and federal-question jurisdiction apply in removal cases as well.

   a. Removal of a diversity case requires that it satisfies the complete-diversity rule and amount-in-controversy requirement. *See supra* Ch. V, §§ III, IV, at 116-129 *[R118]*.

   b. For federal-question jurisdiction, the case must meet the well-pleaded-complaint rule and "substantiality" requirements. *See supra* Ch. IV, § III, at 97-109 *[R119]*.

   c. Thus, defendant cannot make a state-law case removable simply by asserting a federal defense. Under the well-pleaded-complaint rule, the case invokes federal-question jurisdiction only if the plaintiff's claim (not a defense or counterclaim) arises under federal law.

   d. Resolving a split among courts of appeals, the Supreme Court held that the All Writs Act, 28 U.S.C. § 1651, does not support removal, because it does not confer a basis of federal subject-matter jurisdiction. *Syngenta Crop Protection, Inc. v. Henson*, 537 U.S. 28 (2002).

3. There are important statutory limitations, however, on the defendant's ability to remove a case on the basis of diversity or federal-question jurisdiction. [R342]

C. Special Considerations Regarding Removal of Federal-Question Cases

1. 28 U.S.C. § 1441(a) allows removal of civil actions "[e]xcept as otherwise expressly provided by Act of Congress."

2. Thus, Congress can prevent removal even of cases that would otherwise arise under federal law and qualify for federal-question jurisdiction under 28 U.S.C. § 1331. It has done so in several particulars in 28 U.S.C. § 1445.

Example: For example, a case brought under the Federal Employers' Liability Act (FELA), which authorizes railroad employee negligence suits against employers, is not removable. *See* 28 U.S.C. § 1445(a). Congress chose to provide the plaintiff with an unchallengeable option to sue either in state or federal court.

3. In addition, statutes in other parts of the United States Code may prohibit removal.

Example: Title 15 U.S.C. § 77v(a) both vests district-court jurisdiction in actions under the Securities Act of 1933 and prohibits removal of such actions from "any State court of competent jurisdiction."

4. The well-pleaded-complaint rule, a general limitation on federal-question jurisdiction, precludes removal based upon a federal defense. Thus, many courts conclude that the plaintiff is the "master of her claim" and can avoid removal by asserting only state law causes of action and eschewing any applicable federal-question claims.

5. *Federated Department Stores, Inc. v. Moitie*, 452 U.S. 394 (1981), however, held that a state plaintiff cannot employ "artful pleading" to avoid removal.

   a. In that case, the plaintiff's state-court complaint purported to raise only state-law claims, though they tracked closely a separate federal action under the federal antitrust laws.

   b. In a footnote, the Court indicated that the court of appeals had correctly affirmed the district court's conclusion that removal was proper because the claims presented were "federal in nature."

6. *Moitie* even hinted that the existence of a defense of federal preclusion could be a basis for removal. *Rivet v. Regions Bank of Louisiana*, 522 U.S. 470 (1998), rejected this interpretation of *Moitie* in favor of the "fundamental" rule "that a defendant cannot remove on the basis of a federal defense." *Id.* at 478.

7. There are situations, however, in which federal law so completely occupies a substantive area of law that state law cannot exist. Such cases are removable even though the plaintiff purports to assert only a state law claim. The Supreme Court has endorsed this principle under § 301 of the Taft-Hartley Act, 29 U.S.C. § 185, *see Avco Corp. v. Aero Lodge No. 735*, 390 U.S. 557 (1968), and ERISA, 29 U.S.C. § 1132(a)(1)(B); *see Metropolitan Life Ins. Co. v. Taylor*, 481 U.S. 58 (1987). In effect, federal preemption "federalizes" previously existing state claims.

Example: Plaintiff sues in state court to enforce rights under a labor collective bargaining agreement. Federal law so dominates the area in such labor cases that federal law has supplanted state law entirely. Thus, federal law does not simply provide a defense to a state law contract action, but forms the basis for all rights under the labor contract. The defendant can remove. [R116] [R217]

D. Special Considerations Regarding Removal of Diversity Cases Not Containing Federal-Question Claims by Plaintiff

1. Congress has imposed restrictions on the defendant's ability to remove a diversity case.
2. Under 28 U.S.C. § 1441(b), the defendant can remove a diversity case "only if none of the parties in interest properly joined and served as defendants is a citizen of the State in which such action is brought." Because of this restriction, some cases in which the plaintiff could invoke diversity jurisdiction if she sued in federal court are nonetheless not removable.

Example: Plaintiff, a citizen of Arizona, sues Defendant, a citizen of Colorado, on a state-law claim in a state court in Colorado. The claim satisfies the amount-in-controversy requirement for diversity jurisdiction.

π	*v.*	Δ
(AZ)		**(CO)**

Although Plaintiff could have sued in federal court under § 1332, the case is not removable from the defendant's "home court." [R195] [R345]

3. This rule is consistent with diversity jurisdiction's accepted purpose of avoiding prejudice against out-of-state citizens. Because the defendant is a citizen of the forum state, she need not fear local bias in the state courts.
4. The result is equally clear, but more difficult to justify, in the case of two defendants, only one of whom is a citizen of the forum.

Example: Same facts as in the preceding Example, except there are two defendants, D-1, a citizen of Colorado, and D-2, a citizen of Texas. Again, plaintiff sues in state court in Colorado.

π	*v.*	Δ_1	**&**	Δ_2
(AZ)		**(CO)**	*v.*	**(TX)**

The defendants cannot remove, because § 1441(b) precludes removal of a diversity case if *any* defendant is a citizen of the forum, as D-1 is here. The result here seems inconsistent with the underlying rationale for diversity, however, because D-2, a non-local defendant, might fear local bias in the Colorado courts. She could worry that the state court in Colorado would be more likely to impose liability on her than on her Colorado co-defendant.

5. Ordinarily, there must be federal subject-matter jurisdiction both when plaintiff files in state court and when defendant removes. Nonetheless, courts have permitted removal of a case that became removable through the plaintiff's voluntary dismissal in state court of a party that thwarted removal, by co-citizenship or refusal to remove.

Example: Plaintiff, a citizen of New York, sues D-1, a citizen of Georgia, and D-2, a citizen of New York, in a state court. The claim satisfies the amount-in-controversy requirement for diversity jurisdiction.

π	*v.*	Δ_1	&	Δ_2
(NY)		**(GA)**		**(NY)**

The case is not removable because it does not satisfy the complete-diversity rule. *See* supra Ch. V § III, at 116-124 *[R120]*. If Plaintiff voluntarily dismisses the claim against D-2,

π	*v.*	Δ_1	&	Δ_2
(NY)		**(GA)**		(NY)

the case becomes removable, because it now satisfies the complete-diversity rule (a citizen of New York against a citizen of Georgia). In this instance (where plaintiff voluntarily dismisses the claim against the defendant who defeats removal), courts allow the remaining defendant to remove.

6. Unfortunately, 28 U.S.C. § 1446(b) provides that a diversity case is not removable "more than one year after commencement of the action." This provision opens the door to gamesmanship by plaintiffs.

Example: Same facts as the preceding Example, but plaintiff waits one year and one day after filing the case in state court before dismissing the claim against D-2. Even though all the requirements of diversity jurisdiction now exist, the remaining defendant cannot remove.

7. Neither the one-year limitation in ¶ 6 nor the in-state-defendant rule in ¶ 2 applies in federal-question cases. They apply only in pure diversity cases. [R93] [R114]

E. Specialized Grants of Removal

1. 28 U.S.C. § 1441(c) is a difficult provision of limited utility. It provides that when a federal-question accompanies a "separate and independent" claim that is not removable, the defendant can remove the entire case. The federal court must then sever and remand the state claim that, by hypothesis, does not share a common nucleus of operative fact with the federal claim. The federal court has no subject-matter jurisdiction to hear the state claim.

   a. There is a special rule for this type of case: only defendants on the *federal* claim need to agree to removal.

   b. Courts have had enormous difficulty determining what constitutes a "separate and independent" federal-question claim. Historically, they have read the requirement very narrowly, meaning that the statute is rarely useful.

   c. *American Fire & Cas. Ins. Co. v. Finn*, 341 U.S. 6 (1951), is best-known case applying a narrow interpretation. It involved an earlier version of the statute that allowed removal of separate and independent diversity claims. The narrow interpretation may be less appropriate in federal-question cases, but there is very little authority applying the statute as it now exists.

2. 28 U.S.C. § 1442 allows removal of either civil actions or criminal prosecutions in a state court against the United States, any federal agency, or any federal employee for an act taken under color of federal office. This is federal-entity/officer removal.

   a. Originally, Congress limited federal-officer removal to actions against revenue officers. In 1948, Congress expanded the provision to include all federal officers.

   b. *Tennessee v. Davis*, 100 U.S. 257 (1879), upheld the constitutionality of federal-officer removal even though the state court proceeding rested entirely on state law. Because federal-officer removal does not rely upon federal-question jurisdiction under 28 U.S.C. § 1331, the well-pleaded-complaint rule does not apply. The possible assertion of a federal defense and the federal government's interest in insulating its programs from attack in state courts support federal-officer removal under Article III, § 2.

   c. *Mesa v. California*, 489 U.S. 121 (1989), followed other cases, interpreting § 1442(a)(1)'s language "for or relating to any act under color of such office or on account of any right, title or authority claimed under any Act of Congress for the apprehension or punishment of criminals or the collection of the revenue" as requiring a federal defense to activate federal-officer removal. The Court suggested that eliminating that requirement for federal-officer removal would raise serious constitutional questions. [R122]

3. 28 U.S.C. § 1443 provides removal in civil rights cases. *See infra* Ch. XIV, § VI, at 324-330 *[R121]*.

IV. Procedures for Removal and Remand

A. Defendant Files the Notice of Removal in Federal Court

1. Under 28 U.S.C. § 1446(a), a defendant desiring to remove a case files a "notice of removal," subject to Rule 11, in the federal court. The notice must contain "a short and plain statement of the grounds for removal, together with a copy of all process, pleadings, and orders served upon [the defendant] in such action." Note the similarity of the first requirement to Rule 8(a)(1). That is because the party who invokes federal jurisdiction at any level, whether plaintiff, defendant, appellant or petitioner, must demonstrate its existence.

2. Promptly after filing the notice of removal, the defendant must give written notice to all adverse parties and must file a copy of the notice with the state-court clerk. That filing "shall effect removal and the State court shall proceed no further unless and until the case is remanded." 28 U.S.C. § 1446(d). (Until the 1948 recodification of what is now § 1446, a

removal petition went to the state court, which could refuse removal and retain the case.) [R291] [R294] [R295]

3. Today, the defendant neither makes a motion nor requests either court's permission to remove. She simply effects removal under the statute. If removal is improper, the federal court remands.

B. Timing of Removal

1. In a civil case, the defendant must remove within thirty days after her receipt, "through service or otherwise," of a copy of the initial pleading or within thirty days "after the service of summons upon the defendant if such initial pleading has then been filed in court and is not required to be served on the defendant, whichever period is shorter."

   a. This provision recognizes that states have different methods of notifying a defendant of the suit. In most states, the defendant receives service of a summons and a copy of the complaint. In some, however, the plaintiff files the original complaint then serves the defendant only with a summons. The statute intends to give the defendant at least thirty days from formal service in which to file her notice of removal.

   b. *Murphy Bros. v. Michetti Pipe Stringing, Inc.*, 526 U.S. 344 (1999), interpreted "through service or otherwise" to mean either the date of formal service of the summons and complaint or, in states allowing the plaintiff to serve only a summons, the date on which the filed complaint becomes available to the defendant. Informal delivery of the complaint does not begin the thirty-day period. In *Murphy Bros.*, plaintiff faxed a "courtesy copy" of the complaint to the defendant but did not serve the summons until two weeks later. The Court held that the thirty days ran from the service of summons, not from the receipt of the fax.

2. If a civil case is not removable at the outset, the defendant must file the notice of removal within thirty days of receipt of the document that makes the case removable.

3. The notice of removal in a criminal case must be filed within thirty days after state-court arraignment, or at any time prior to trial, whichever is earlier. For good cause shown, the federal court may grant permission to file the notice later.

C. Remand

1. If the plaintiff thinks the defendant removed the case improperly, the plaintiff can move to remand to state court. She might do so either because the federal court lacks subject-matter jurisdiction or because of a procedural defect in the defendant's removal.

2. If the motion to remand is based upon "any defect other than lack of subject-matter jurisdiction," it must come not later than thirty days after the defendant filed the notice of removal. 28 U.S.C. § 1447(c). Defects

in removal other than lack of subject-matter jurisdiction are not jurisdictional and are therefore waivable.

Example: Defendant files a notice of removal in federal court but fails to attach all documents served upon her in the state court proceeding. This is a defect unrelated to subject-matter jurisdiction. Plaintiff must move to remand for that reason within thirty days of defendant's filing. Failure to do so waives the defect.

3. Remember that lack of subject-matter jurisdiction is never waivable, so any party—even the party who invoked federal jurisdiction—or the court *sua sponte* may raise the issue at any time. If there is no subject-matter jurisdiction, the federal court must remand to the state court from which the case came. 28 U.S.C. § 1447(c).
4. If, after removal, the plaintiff seeks to join additional defendants whose joinder will destroy diversity jurisdiction, the federal court may either deny the joinder, or permit joinder and remand the case. 28 U.S.C. § 1447(e).
5. An order remanding the case to state court is not reviewable by appeal or otherwise. 28 U.S.C. § 1447(d). There is an exception for remand of a civil-rights case removed under 28 U.S.C. § 1343. *See supra* § III.E.2, at 159 *[R122]*; *see infra* Ch. XIV, § VI, at 324-330 *[R123]*.

V. The Civil-Rights Removal Statute: 28 U.S.C. § 1343

There is a special statute allowing removal in some civil and criminal cases. It has only to do with enforcing civil rights. An order remanding the case *is* appealable. *See infra* Ch. XIV, § VI, at 324. [R63] [R216] [R289]

Chapter VIII

SUPREME-COURT JURISDICTION

■ ANALYSIS

I. Introduction

The Supreme Court is the part of the federal judiciary most visible to the general public. Few people know of the district courts and the courts of appeals, but everyone has some sense of the Supreme Court's work and importance. This Chapter reviews the types of cases the Supreme Court entertains and how they get there. It is no surprise, of course, that the Supreme Court has appellate jurisdiction over cases decided by the federal courts of appeals. It is perhaps surprising that the Court can review decisions of state courts; this obviously implicates federalism concerns. As we will see, though, such review is available only on questions of federal law, in keeping with the Court's role as the ultimate arbiter of federal law and enforcer of the Supremacy Clause. Most surprising, perhaps, are the provisions for Supreme Court original jurisdiction, a narrow class of cases in which the Supreme Court serves as the trial court. There are important (and sometimes arcane) rules and restrictions for each of these types of jurisdiction.

II. Constitutional and Statutory Structure

A. Article III Distinguishes Original from Appellate Jurisdiction

1. Article III, § 2, cl. 1, lists all types of cases the "judicial power" of federal courts reaches, nine types of cases that, as a constitutional matter, federal courts can hear. *See supra* Ch. II, § II.B, at 59-60 *[R124]*. Theoretically, no federal court, including the Supreme Court can hear any case—either originally or on appeal—that is not within that enumeration. *But see supra* Ch. V, § II.A.5, at 113 *[R125]*; Ch. V, § III.B.6, at 121 *[R126]*. [R43]

2. Article III, § 2, cl. 2, then provides that the Supreme Court "shall have original Jurisdiction" over cases "[1] affecting Ambassadors, other public Ministers and Consuls, and [2] those in which a State shall be Party." The clause continues, "in all other cases before mentioned," meaning all other cases falling within the federal judicial power, the Supreme Court "shall have appellate Jurisdiction. . . ." [R133] [R135]

3. Original jurisdiction is trial jurisdiction. Thus, in cases "affecting Ambassadors, other public Ministers and Consuls" and in cases "in which a State shall be a Party" the Supreme Court can actually try the case, but such cases are rare. *See infra* § III.C, at 168 *[R127]*.

4. Appellate jurisdiction means the Supreme Court reviewing the decision of another court, either a lower federal court or a state court, usually (but not always) the state's highest court. Those cases constitute the overwhelming bulk of the Court's docket. *See infra* § IV, at 168-181 *[R128]*.

B. Relationship Between Original and Appellate Jurisdiction

1. In *Marbury v. Madison*, 5 U.S. (1 Cranch) 137 (1803), [R2] Chief Justice Marshall wrote that the divisions between the Court's original and appellate jurisdictions are rigid. He treated the Supreme Court's original jurisdiction as exclusive. No court other than the Supreme Court could have original jurisdiction over cases affecting ambassadors and cases with a state party, and the Supreme Court thus could not have appellate jurisdiction over such cases.

2. The Court has since rejected Marshall's view. Today, these rules are clear:

   a. The Court's original jurisdiction extends only to the two types of cases listed in the original-jurisdiction clause, but original jurisdiction over those cases is not exclusive. Congress may vest original jurisdiction over those two types of cases in a lower federal court, such as the federal district court.

   b. When a lower federal court decides such a case, the Supreme Court has appellate jurisdiction.

Example: The state of Illinois sued the city of Milwaukee to stop pollution of Lake Michigan. The case fell within the Court's original jurisdiction, because a state was a party. Nonetheless, Congress had also vested original jurisdiction in the federal district courts by statute (28 U.S.C. § 1251(b)(3)). The Supreme Court chose to allow the district court to exercise original jurisdiction under § 1331, denying Illinois's motion for leave to file the complaint in the Supreme Court. *Illinois v. City of Milwaukee (I)*, 406 U.S. 91 (1972) (*Milwaukee* I). The Supreme Court thereafter exercised appellate jurisdiction.

3. The Court's original jurisdiction is self-executing; no congressional grant is necessary. *Kentucky v. Dennison*, 65 U.S. (24 How.) 66 (1860).

4. Nonetheless, Congress enacted a jurisdictional statute, 28 U.S.C. § 1251, dealing with the types of cases within the Court's original jurisdiction. The statute does not treat all cases in which a state is a party in the same way. It handles cases solely between states differently from other cases in which a state is a party.

   a. Section 1251(a) makes the Court's original jurisdiction over controversies "between two or more states" *exclusive*. A lower federal court cannot hear such cases.

   b. Section 1251(b) makes the Supreme Court's original jurisdiction nonexclusive with respect to: (1) actions or proceedings to which ambassadors, other public ministers, consuls, or vice consuls of foreign states are parties; (2) controversies between the United States and a State; and (3) actions or proceedings by a State against the citizens of another State or against aliens. Such cases *may* proceed in the Supreme Court or in a federal district court.

It is crucial to remember, however, that neither Article III nor § 1251(b) *vests* jurisdiction in any lower federal court. There is no federal subject-matter jurisdiction in a district court simply because a state or an ambassador is a party. The case in a district court still must fall within one of the Article III grants of judicial power such as federal-question jurisdiction or diversity. *Duhne v. New Jersey*, 251 U.S. 311 (1920). This does not appear to be true if the Supreme Court does exercise jurisdiction over one of the cases § 1251(b) mentions, because Article III *does vest* jurisdiction in that Court. [R130] [R131] [R134]

5. Although Congress has no power to limit the Supreme Court's original jurisdiction (§ 1251(b), merely allowing the district courts to have concurrent original jurisdiction), it has considerable authority to regulate and limit the Court's appellate jurisdiction. Article III, § 2, cl. 2, expressly gives the Court appellate jurisdiction "with such exceptions, and under such regulations as the Congress shall make." *See supra* Ch. II, § V.A, at 65 *[R129]*. The Constitution gives Congress no such power regarding the Court's original jurisdiction. [R2] [R335]

III. Original Jurisdiction

A. Cases Between Two or More States

1. The Constitution grants original jurisdiction to the Supreme Court is "those in which a State shall be a Party." Congress subdivided such cases, making the Court's original jurisdiction is exclusive when the "between two or more States," 28 U.S.C. § 1251(a), and otherwise allowing district courts to exercise concurrent original jurisdiction. *See supra* § II.B.4, at 165-166 *[R130]*.

2. For purposes of this statute, political subdivisions, such as cities and counties, are not states. Thus, a case brought by a state against a city in another state is not "between two or more States" and does not fall within the Court's exclusive original jurisdiction. *Illinois v. City of Milwaukee (I)*, 406 U.S. 91 (1972).

3. Jurisdiction over cases between two or more states is important in interstate disputes over boundaries, water rights, and in rare cases when more than one state claims a right to tax an estate or fund. *See, e.g., California v. Texas*, 457 U.S. 164 (1982) (*per curiam*) (estate of Howard Hughes).

4. Such cases usually seek an equitable remedy, such as a declaration of a border or an injunction stopping a state from doing something. *See, e.g., Pennsylvania v. West Virginia*, 262 U.S. 553 (1923) (attempting to enjoin West Virginia's distribution of natural gas that would diminish the supply available for Pennsylvanians). Far more rarely, a state will sue to

recover money from another state. *See Virginia v. West Virginia*, 246 U.S. 565 (1918) (awarding Virginia a judgment of $12 million).

5. The Court often refers matters in such cases to special masters so it is not tied up with lengthy trial proceedings. *See Maryland v. Louisiana*, 451 U.S. 725, 734 (1981) ("[A]s is usual, we appointed a Special Master to facilitate handling of the suit.").

6. Occasionally, the Supreme Court refuses leave to file an original proceeding before it, as it did in *Milwaukee I*. *See infra* § III.B. Refusal creates no great problem in areas of original jurisdiction that are not exclusive to the Court.

    a. For cases involving a dispute between two or more states, however, refusal to allow the case to proceed is quite troublesome. The Court's original jurisdiction is exclusive; there is no other court that can entertain the case.

    b. Nonetheless, the Court refuses to hear some cases. *Texas v. California*, 141 S. Ct. 1469 (2021); *Arizona v. New Mexico*, 425 U.S. 794 (1976) (*per curiam*) (reasoning that a state-court action already pending involving the same questions (but other parties) would provide adequate adjudication); *Louisiana v. Mississippi*, 488 U.S. 990 (1988); *California v. West Virginia*, 454 U.S. 1027 (1981) (the latter two without explanation). Other cases, even if the Court does exercise jurisdiction, make clear that the Court sees itself as having discretion to decline. *See, e.g., California v. Texas*, 457 U.S. 164 (1982) (*per curiam*); *Maryland v. Louisiana*, 451 U.S. 725 (1981). When that happens, there is no forum—federal or state—available to the states.

B. Other Cases with a State As a Party

1. Section 1251(b) lists types of cases with state parties where the Court's original jurisdiction is not exclusive. *See supra* § II.B.4.b, at 165-166 *[R131]*. Two types of cases come under this part of the statute:

    a. "between the United States and a State," and

    b. "by a State against the citizens of another State or against aliens."

2. Because the Court's original jurisdiction over these cases is not exclusive, plaintiffs may bring them in federal district court. The cases must, qualify for federal subject-matter jurisdiction, such as federal-question jurisdiction. The fact that such cases can be in a district court usually leads the Supreme Court to decline to exercise original jurisdiction. District courts are far more able to exercise original jurisdiction, and the appellate docket keeps the Supreme Court busy.

3. The Supreme Court may refuse to exercise its original jurisdiction on other grounds as well. In *Ohio v. Wyandotte Chemicals Corp.*, 401 U.S. 493 (1971), a state sued citizens of another state and aliens, seeking abatement of a nuisance created by the defendants' allegedly dumping

mercury into rivers that empty into Lake Erie. The Court recognized that the case fell within its original jurisdiction and that there also was subject-matter jurisdiction because the claim arose under federal law. Nonetheless, the Court exercised its discretion to refuse to exercise original jurisdiction, noting that the case presented complex scientific issues more readily tried to a district court.

4. The Court exercises "original jurisdiction sparingly and [is] particularly reluctant to take jurisdiction of a suit where the plaintiff has another adequate forum in which to settle his claim." *United States v. Nevada*, 412 U.S. 534 (1973) (*per curiam*).

5. The Eleventh Amendment, *see generally infra* Ch. XIII, at 283-299 *[R132]*, in most cases now prevents federal adjudication of cases against a state by a citizen of another state. The Supreme Court's original jurisdiction does not extend to such cases. [R336]

C. Cases Involving Ambassadors, Public Ministers, etc.

1. The Constitution provides original Supreme-Court Jurisdiction over cases otherwise within the judicial power "in all Cases affecting Ambassadors, other public Ministers and Consuls," *see supra* § II.A.2, at 164 *[R133]*, but Congress has made original jurisdiction in such cases nonexclusive. *See supra* § II.B.4.b, at 165-166 *[R134]*.

2. The Supreme Court very rarely exercises that original jurisdiction. One reason may be that ambassadors and public ministers (but not consuls) have diplomatic immunity from suit. And, because the Court's original jurisdiction is not exclusive in such cases, denying attempts to invoke it merely sends the plaintiff to federal district court rather than denying adjudication entirely. [R127]

IV. Appellate Jurisdiction

A. Statutes for Appellate Jurisdiction

1. 28 U.S.C. § 1257 allows the Court to exercise appellate jurisdiction by writ of certiorari over final decisions of "the highest court of a State in which a decision could be had" (not always the state's highest court) in any of the following situations: (1) where there is a constitutional challenge to a federal law or treaty, (2) where there is a supremacy challenge to state law as violating the Constitution or other federal law, and (3) where the petitioner claims any title, right, privilege, or immunity under the Constitution, treaties, or laws of the United States. [R136]

2. Title 28 U.S.C. § 1254(1) gives the Court appellate jurisdiction by certiorari to review *any* decision of a federal court of appeals, without the limitations that apply to reviewing state-court decisions. Thus, the Court has the power to review pure diversity cases involving no federal at all, counterintuitive as that may seem.

3. The Court grants a writ of certiorari only if at least four Justices vote to do so. The Court denies the writ in the overwhelming majority of cases.
4. Until 1988, the Court had appellate jurisdiction either by appeal or certiorari. The Supreme Court's appeal jurisdiction was mandatory (review "as of right"), while its certiorari jurisdiction was discretionary.
   a. The requirement that the Court adjudicate cases on appeal created significant caseload burdens.
   b. The Court found ways work around the burdens. The Court having jurisdiction by appeal did not guarantee the appellant a plenary hearing. Sometimes the Court would dismiss the appeal "for want of a substantial federal question." On other occasions, it would summarily affirm, reverse, or vacate and remand for further consideration. In practice, chances of getting a plenary hearing were little better by appeal than by certiorari. ***However***, decisions in appeals cases were decisions on the merits, and while they certainly have less precedential weight than the Court's full decisions, they are nonetheless authoritative. Denials of certiorari have no precedential weight at all; they merely reflect that there were not four Justices who wanted to hear the case.
   c. In response, and in recognition of the burdens the Court faced, Congress amended §§ 1254, 1257 to their present form in 1998, abolishing mandatory appellate jurisdiction in those sections and leaving the decision to review a case to the Court's discretion.
5. Note, however, that the Court retains "appeal" jurisdiction under 28 U.S.C. § 1253 in the review of decisions of special three-judge district courts. Such cases are quite rare, and force the Court to rule without the guidance of an opinion from the court of appeals. The trend in the past half century has been to reduce the number of cases that qualify for three-judge district courts. Occasionally, though, Congress passes a law and requires a special three-judge district court to hear a challenge to the law. (Of course, the dispute must be justiciable and qualify for subject-matter jurisdiction.) The law may expressly provide that the case is appealable directly to the Supreme Court, bypassing the court of appeals. The Bipartisan Campaign Reform Act of 2002, part of which the Court invalidated in *Citizens United v. FEC*, 558 U.S. 310 (2010), followed this model.

B. Review of State-Court Decisions: Background

1. The Constitution does not explicitly provide Supreme Court appellate jurisdiction over state-court decisions. On the other hand, after specifying the Court's original jurisdiction, art. III, § 2, allows appellate jurisdiction in all other cases falling within the federal judicial power, subject to the Exceptions Clause. *See supra* § II.A.2 at 164 *[R135]*. It is a hallmark of American federalism that the supreme court of one government has the power to review decisions of the judiciary of another government.

2. Thus, if the case being reviewed falls within the federal judicial power that art. III, § 2, cl. 1, delineates, the Supreme Court has the constitutional power to exercise appellate jurisdiction.

3. Congress has always provided legislation allowing the Supreme Court to review state-court decisions, but with restrictions. Today, 28 U.S.C. § 1257 contains those restrictions. *See supra* § IV.A.1, at 168 *[R136]*.

4. First, the decision must be "rendered by the highest court of a State in which a decision could be had." *See infra* § IV.C, at 170-171 *[R137]*.

5. Second, the state-court decision must be a final judgment[ ] or decree[ ]. *But see infra* § IV.D, at 171-174 *[R138]*, because "final judgment" is as protean a term as any to be found in the law.

6. Third, the decision of the state court must either (1) "draw[ ] in question" the validity of a treaty or federal statute (*i.e.* a supremacy challenge), (2) "draw[ ] in question" the validity of a state statute as being contrary to federal law (*i.e.* also a supremacy challenge), or (3) set up any title, right, privilege, or immunity claimed under federal law or of any commission held under federal law.

   a. A case within any of the three areas is within the constitutional grant of federal-question jurisdiction, assuming the federal question is sufficiently substantial. *See Zucht v. King*, 260 U.S. 174 (1922). Thus, the Supreme Court has subject-matter jurisdiction without regard to amount in controversy or party citizenship.

   b. Until 1914, Congress only allowed the Court to review state-court cases that *rejected* supremacy challenges or ruled *against* the "title, right, privilege, or immunity" the party seeking review asserted. For other cases, where the decision below favored federal law, Congress may have felt less need for Supreme Court review because the state court vindicated federal law.

   c. Nonetheless, Congress extended the appellate jurisdiction in 1914 to permit the Supreme Court to review any state-court case falling within the three reviewable categories, irrespective of whether the decision below was for or against the supremacy assertion or claim of federal right. Accordingly, the Court now may review state-court opinions striking a state law as contrary to federal law.

7. The Supreme Court has also recognized an important limitation on its power to review state-court decisions, known as the adequate-and-independent-state-ground rule. *See infra* § IV.E, at 174-179 *[R139]*.

C. Review of State-Court Decisions: "Highest State Court . . ."

1. Section 1257 permits appellate review only of decisions by "the highest court of a State *in which a decision could be had*." (Emphasis added.)
2. In many (probably most) cases, the highest state court in which review could be had will be the state's highest court, but not always. In *Thompson v. City of Louisville*, 362 U.S. 199 (1960), the Supreme Court reviewed a case that the Louisville, Kentucky, police court decided. The case involved so little that no Kentucky court had appellate jurisdiction. Thus, the police court was "the highest state court in which a decision could be had."
3. In many states, the fact that state appellate review is jurisdictionally possible does not mean it will occur. Many states' appellate courts have discretionary appellate jurisdiction. To qualify for review in the United States Supreme Court, the litigant must seek all possible appellate review in the state system. *Costarelli v. Massachusetts*, 421 U.S. 193 (1975). Denial of discretionary state appellate review allows the appellant to seek Supreme Court review under § 1257. [R137]

D. Review of State-Court Decisions: The Final-Judgment Rule

1. Section 1257 allows the Supreme Court to review only final judgments or decrees from the state court.
2. The final-judgment rule serves two purposes:
   a. *Efficiency*, by avoiding piecemeal adjudication and taking advantage of the fact that a state-court decision on the merits favorable to the would-be appellant may moot numerous potential grounds for appeal.
   b. *Protection of federalism*, by avoiding Supreme Court friction with state courts, which might result from Supreme Court review of state cases with which the state judicial system has not finished.
3. "Final judgment," however, is less well defined than one might suspect. The Supreme Court has often taken a practical view of cases and has allowed review of four categories of interlocutory state decisions, eschewing reading § 1257's finality requirement literally. (As you read through the categories, bear in mind that when the Court defined them, § 1257 still allowed review by appeal—that is, review as of right rather than discretionary review. Under today's § 1257, which has eliminated review as of right in cases coming from the state courts, the Court still *has* jurisdiction to review these cases but may deny certiorari.)
   a. Category 1 includes "cases in which there are further proceedings—even entire trials—yet to occur in the state courts but where for one reason or another the federal issue is conclusive or the outcome of further proceedings preordained." *Cox Broadcasting Corp.*

v. Cohn, 420 U.S. 469, 479 (1975). *Mills v. Alabama*, 384 U.S. 214 (1966), is the Court's example of this category. Mills demurred to a criminal complaint on First Amendment grounds, and the state's trial court sustained the demurrer. The Alabama Supreme Court reversed and remanded for trial. Mills had no defense on the facts and no other legal defense and so could not prevail at trial. The United States Supreme Court reviewed the case without waiting for trial, on the theory that the Alabama Supreme Court's decision on the First Amendment question was final within the meaning of § 1257 and would require U.S. Supreme Court review after the conviction certain to follow the trial. The Court thus avoided "a completely unnecessary waste of time and energy in judicial systems already troubled by delays due to congested dockets." 384 U.S. at 217-18.

b. Category 2 is exactly like Category 1 *except* that "the federal issue, finally decided by the highest court in the State, will survive and require decision regardless of the outcome of future state-court proceedings." *Cox*, 420 U.S. at 480. The Court's example of a Category-2 case is *Radio Station WOW, Inc. v. Johnson*, 326 U.S. 120 (1945). The state's highest court had ordered a transfer of property that WOW claimed impermissibly interfered with its FCC license. All that remained in the state court was an accounting of profits. The Court reviewed, reasoning that the state court had finally adjudicated the federal issue (as in Category 1) and that the state-court accounting to come "could not remotely give rise to a federal question . . . that may later come here." The uncertainty about the details of the final outcome of the accounting distinguished *WOW* from a Category-1 case; the two orders were distinct, and therefore in effect constituted multiple litigation.

Together, Categories 1 and 2 amount to the Justices saying, "You can see us now, or you can see us later." They opt for now.

c. Categories 1 and 2 both involve cases where the federal issue will survive and require review irrespective of what the state courts subsequently do with the cases. Category 3 is strikingly different. It includes cases

> where the federal claim has been finally decided, with further proceedings on the merits in the state courts to come, but in which later review of the federal issue can***not*** be had, whatever the ultimate outcome of the case. Thus, in these cases, if the party seeking interim review ultimately prevails on the merits, the federal issue will be mooted; if he were to lose on the merits, however, the governing state law would not permit him again to present his federal claims for review.

Cox, 420 U.S. at 481 (emphasis added). *California v. Stewart*, 384 U.S. 436 (1966), a companion case to the better known *Miranda v. Arizona*, 384 U.S. 436 (1966), exemplifies Category 3. The California Supreme Court, apparently prescient about *Miranda*, overturned Stewart's conviction and directed a new trial without the disputed confession. The U.S. Supreme Court granted the prosecution's petition for certiorari. Had it not reviewed at that point, one of two things could have happened in further state-court proceedings: (1) the new trial might result in conviction, but Stewart would not be entitled to federal review because the trial was without the tainted confession, or (2) the new trial might result in acquittal. Acquittals are not appealable, so the prosecution would be unable to obtain United States Supreme Court review of the California Supreme Court's holding that the Fifth and Fourteenth Amendments forbade use of the confession.

If Categories 1 and 2 are the "now or later" categories, Category 3 is the "now or never" category.

d. Category 4, as then-Justice Rehnquist's vigorous solo dissent sardonically noted, requires reading in its entirety.

> [T]here are those situations where the federal issue has been finally decided in the state courts with further proceedings pending in which the party seeking review here might prevail on the merits on nonfederal grounds, thus rendering unnecessary review of the federal issue by this Court, and where reversal of the state court on the federal issue would be preclusive of any further litigation on the relevant cause of action rather than merely controlling the nature and character of, or determining the admissibility of evidence in, the state proceedings still to come. In these circumstances, if a refusal immediately to review the state court decision might seriously erode federal policy, the Court has entertained and decided the federal issue, which itself has been finally determined by the state courts for purposes of the state litigation.

Cox Broadcasting Corporation v. Cohn, 420 U.S. 469, 482-83 (1975). Cohn had sued Cox Broadcasting for having published a news story containing the name of Cohn's daughter, the deceased victim of a violent sex crime. A Georgia statute forbade publication, not of the crime or the trial, but only of the victim's identity. Cox's reporter had found the identity in public records of the criminal case. The trial court rejected Cox's First Amendment argument against the statute and granted Cohn summary judgment on the issue of liability. The Georgia Supreme Court, although finding that Cohn had no right of action under the Georgia statute and vacating the summary judgment, nonetheless found that he did state a cognizable common-law claim for invasion of privacy. It ultimately ruled that the statute did not violate the First

Amendment and remanded for trial. The United States Supreme Court found jurisdiction and reviewed the case on the merits.

Category 4 is more difficult to characterize because it lacks the certainty of the other three categories. The federal issue *might* survive and require review by appeal (if Cox lost on the merits), but survival is not guaranteed as it is in Categories 1 and 2. On the other hand, the federal issue *might not* survive, precluding review as in Category 3. The U.S. Supreme Court reasoned that delaying (and perhaps never) deciding so important a constitutional "*might* seriously erode federal [First Amendment] policy." (Emphasis added.)

To sum up, Categories 1 and 2 are the "now or later" categories. Category 3 is the "now or never" category. And Category 4? That seems to be the Court's formulation of "a bird in the hand is worth two in the bush."

Justice Rehnquist's dissent rested on two bases. First, he argued that there was no "final" decision in *Cox*, as § 1257 requires. Second, he criticized the majority for ignoring the Court's long-standing reluctance to reach out to decide constitutional issues that it might avoid.

4. Categories 3 and 4 represent considerably more than a construction of finality. In each, it is undeniable that further state-court proceedings may make review of the federal issue entirely unnecessary. By some commentators note that by expanding the meaning of "final" the Court may be undermining the final-judgment rule's purposes and risking an unnecessary clash with a state court. For all Category 3 cases and for those Category 4 cases in which the federal issue would not have survived, the Court's adjudication takes on a bit of the stain of an advisory opinion because it adjudicates a federal issue that either cannot (Category 3) or might not (Category 4) have any effect on disposition of the case.

5. The Supreme Court thus claims great discretion in determining whether the state-court judgment is final within the meaning of § 1257. One ordinarily expects the Court to avoid unnecessarily deciding constitutional questions and disputes with state courts. Still, there are cases in which the Court has refused to strain to invoke any of the four *Cox* factors, *see, e.g., Florida v. Thomas*, 532 U.S. 774 (2001), so the Court appears to hold itself in check to some extent. [R138] [R338]

E. Review of State Court Decisions: The Adequate-and-Independent-State-Ground Doctrine

1. The Supreme Court lacks authority to review state court decisions interpreting state law. *See Murdock v. City of Memphis*, 87 U.S. (20 Wall.) 590 (1875). It is not clear that the Constitution requires this rule, but it is well established as doctrine and practice.

2. *Murdock* established a corollary to this principle: the Court lacks authority to review federal issues contained in state-court decisions when

the decisions rest on adequate and independent state-law grounds. Note, therefore, that if there is an adequate and independent state ground, it insulates the case from Supreme Court review. In recent years, this has happened more frequently as some states have interpreted state constitutional provisions that echo some amendments—prominently the Fourth Amendment—to provide greater protection against state government overreaching than does the federal constitution.

3. The Court has divided this doctrine into two sub-categories:

   a. Substantive state law grounds: when the state court decision rests upon both federal and non-federal grounds, the Supreme Court will not review if the non-federal ground, standing alone, would support the judgment.

   b. Procedural state law grounds: when the state court refuses to adjudicate a federal issue because the litigant has failed to comply with a legitimate state procedural rule, the Supreme Court will ordinarily not review the federal claim.

4. The *substantive* branch seems to rest on the advisory-opinion rationale of Article III's case-or-controversy requirement; no federal court may issue an advisory opinion (one that does not resolve an actual case or controversy, *i.e.* has no effect on the disposition of the case). *Herb v. Pitcairn*, 324 U.S. 117 (1945). *See supra* Ch. I, § III, at 33-34 *[R140]*. If substantive state grounds support the state-court judgment, then no matter how the Supreme Court resolves the federal issue, it will have no effect on the outcome. One might also justify this branch of the doctrine by the prudential principle that the Court should avoid unnecessary pronouncements of federal law (especially constitutional law), particularly when doing so might result in friction with state courts or state substantive policies.

Example: Fox Films distributed movies to theater owners under a standardized agreement that included an arbitration clause. The United States Supreme Court found that the arbitration clause violated federal antitrust law. When a dispute later arose between Fox and a different theater owner, Fox sued to recover under the contract to recover damages, arguing that the contract *without* the arbitration clause was consistent with federal antitrust law. The state supreme court ruled that the clause was not severable and gave judgment to the defendant. The Supreme Court took the case on certiorari, but dismissed the writ "for want of jurisdiction," because the question of severability was not a question of federal law. (In this pre-*Erie* era, the Court characterized the issue as "general law"; today the Court would recognize it as state common law. *See infra* Ch. XI, § V.B.3.b, at 242 *[R141]*) Thus, there was an adequate and independent non-federal ground supporting the state court's judgment, making it unnecessary (and improper) for the Supreme Court to decide the hypothetical question of whether the contract without the arbitration clause would violate federal antitrust law. Regardless of what the Court might have said about that issue, the result of the case would not have changed. *See Fox Film Corporation v. Muller*, 296 U.S. 207 (1935).

5. The advisory-opinion rationale, however, does not support the *procedural* branch of the doctrine. Instead, this branch rests on Supreme Court's desire to avoid undermining uniform, predictable, defensible state procedures. This aim would suffer were the Court to allow litigants to circumvent legitimate state procedures by raising federal issues without having complied with state procedural rules.

6. The Supreme Court is not bound, however, by an inadequate state substantive or procedural rule. It is less likely to find inadequacy in a state substantive finding than in a state procedural rule. However, in s series of cases, the Arizona Supreme Court persisted in ignoring a long established ruling that due process entitled a defendant in a capital case to have the jury informed that if the court sentenced the defendant to life imprisonment, it would be without possibility of parole. *See infra* the text paragraph following the example below.

7. The Court has recognized categories of procedural rules that are inadequate to bar appellate review.

   a. *Arbitrary state rules*. If a state rule "lacks fair or substantial support" or it is arbitrary, the Court deems it to be nothing more than an attempt to insulate the state court holding from federal review and will disregard it.

Example: Defendant moved to quash a murder indictment arguing that the state systematically excluded African-Americans from grand jury service. The state supreme court refused to consider the motion because it was "prolix," though the motion took up only two pages in the printed record. The Supreme Court found the state ground to be inadequate, reviewed, and reversed. *Rogers v. Alabama*, 192 U.S. 226 (1904).

That practice includes a state's courts obvious bad-faith attempt to avoid applying U.S. Supreme Court precedent. Arizona's Supreme Court persisted in ignoring a long established ruling (*Simmons v. South Carolina*, 512 U.S. 154 (1994)),that due process entitled a defendant in a capital case to have the jury informed that if the court sentenced the defendant to life imprisonment, it would be without possibility of parole. In 2016, a *per curiam* Court summarily reversed the Arizona Supreme Court, holding that its refusal to apply *Simmons* was fundamental error. In *Cruz v. Arizona*, the Arizona Supreme Court again refused to apply *Simmons*, stating that the 2016 decision was not a "significant change in the law" under an Arizona procedural statute, making the statute an adequate and independent state ground. Said the U.S. Supreme Court, "It is not."

b. *Novel state rules*. When the state court applies a state rule that is inconsistent with prior state practice, the Supreme Court may find the rule inadequate to bar review.

c. *Discretionary rules*. The Supreme Court closely scrutinizes state procedural rules that apply solely at the state court's discretion. The rationale is that state courts may employ discretionary rules solely to insulate the state decision from federal review, not because the state otherwise has a legitimate procedural interest that the rules serve.

Example: Plaintiff asserted a federal right against racial discrimination. The state appellate court denied the appeal because opposing counsel had not received reasonable notice and a copy of the transcript, as required by state rule, treating the rule as jurisdictional. But the state court had not consistently treated the notice requirement as a denial of its power to adjudicate, so the Court found the state rule "discretionary [rather] than jurisdictional" and adjudicated the federal issue. *Sullivan v. Little Hunting Park, Inc.*, 396 U.S. 229 (1969).

8. *Henry v. Mississippi*, 379 U.S. 443 (1965), appeared to expand the scope of the exceptions to the doctrine's procedural aspect significantly and thus to expand the opportunity for the Court to review state decisions, but its ultimate impact remains unclear.

a. The state supreme court upheld the defendant's conviction on a minor charge, holding that he waived his objection to introduction of illegally seized evidence by failing to object contemporaneously, as state law required. The Supreme Court exercised jurisdiction and remanded the case for a hearing on whether defense counsel deliberately waived the Fourth Amendment objection.

b. Regarding adequate state ground, the Court said: "procedural defaults in state proceedings do not prevent vindication of . . . federal rights unless the State's insistence on compliance with its procedural rule serves a legitimate state interest." 379 U.S. at 447.

c. The Court almost immediately declared that the rule served a legitimate state interest by giving the trial court the opportunity to conduct the trial without the tainted evidence. This made it sound like the Court would consider the rule's legitimacy "on its face." But the very next sentence said, "*In every case* we must inquire whether the enforcement of a procedural forfeiture serves such a state interest." That made it sound like an as-applied consideration. Then Court opined that Henry's motion for directed verdict at the close of the state's evidence "may have . . . served" this purpose equally well. Commentators criticize this position as unduly interfering in the state's choice of procedural rules and for improperly equating the two procedural practices' utility.

d. The implication that the contemporaneous-objection rule, though quite common and well known to any trial attorney, might not be an adequate state ground in a particular case was controversial, because it appeared to give the Court more leeway to ignore a state rule perfectly legitimate on its face.

e. The remand to determine whether the failure to object was as a result of defense counsel's negligence or conscious choice demonstrated that a waiver doctrine might temper the Court's potentially broad exception to the adequate-independent-state-ground doctrine that is procedural.

9. The Supreme Court has rarely relied upon *Henry*. Decisions have not been entirely consistent; most observers conclude that *Henry* has not diluted the adequate-and-independent-state-ground doctrine much.

   a. *Camp v. Arkansas*, 404 U.S. 69 (1971), relied upon *Henry* to reverse a conviction summarily after the state court had refused to consider an issue because the defense counsel had made no contemporaneous objection. The Court concluded that the "alleged procedural default does not bar consideration of his constitutional claim in the circumstances of this case." *Id.*

   b. But *Wainwright v. Sykes*, 433 U.S. 72 (1977), a federal habeas corpus case, expressed significant doubt about the *Henry* assertion that a directed verdict motion was an adequate substitute for the contemporaneous-objection rule, pointing out the contemporaneous-objection-rule's utility. It did not overrule *Henry*, though, and did not directly concern the state-ground doctrine as it applies to Supreme Court review of state-court decisions.

10. The Court has occasionally encounters difficulty determining whether a state decision rests on state or federal law when it refers to both. If the decision rests on federal law, then the adequate-and-independent-state-ground doctrine is irrelevant, and the Supreme Court may hear the case. At one time, the Court remanded such cases to the state court for clarification of the basis for the holding. *Minnesota v. National Tea Co.*, 309 U.S. 551 (1940). But *Michigan v. Long*, 463 U.S. 1032 (1983), changed course, holding that when the basis for a state court's opinion is ambiguous, "when the adequacy and independence of any possible state law ground is not clear from the face of the opinion," the Court will presume that the state court decided the case on the basis of federal law. This presumption permits the Supreme Court to take the case, and applies irrespective of whether the articulated state law basis for decision is substantive or procedural.

    a. *Long* does not prevent a state court from relying on state, rather than federal, law. Rather, it establishes a plain-statement rule; if the state court wishes to rule on the basis of state law, it must make that basis explicit.

b. Even so, the Court still occasionally vacates a judgment and remands for further proceedings to clarify the decision's grounds. It did so in *Bush v. Palm Beach County Canvassing Bd.*, 531 U.S. 70, 78 (2000), vacating the Florida Supreme Court's decision that directed manual recounts of the votes in the 2000 presidential election in specified counties. The Court cited *National Tea*.

c. The Court has never prescribed a verbal formula by which a state court can indicate its reliance on state law. Some state courts take no chances. *See, e.g., Rocky Mountain Oil and Gas Association v. State Board of Equalization*, 749 P.2d 221, 233 n.10 (Wyo. 1987): "The decision of this court is based on an adequate and independent state ground and any reference to federal law is for illustrative purposes only and in no way compels the result obtained." It is almost as if the state court is saying, "You want a clear statement? Here comes your clear statement!")

d. Note that if the state court clearly rested its decision on federal constitutional grounds, the mere possibility that state law *might have provided* an alternate basis is irrelevant, and the Supreme Court will review the federal constitutional issues. *Oregon v. Guzek*, 546 U.S. 517 (2006).

e. Occasionally, state court decisions indicate that the state court construes state constitutional provisions identically with federal constitutional provisions. Then the Court considers the decision to rest on federal law and can thus decide to hear the case. *See, e.g., Pennsylvania v. Muniz*, 496 U.S. 582 (1990).

Example: State law taxed proceeds from slot machines at 20% if the machines were on riverboats, but at 36% if the machines were at race tracks. Plaintiffs challenged the provision under the federal and state constitutions. The state supreme court held that the law violated both state and federal equal-protection provisions, applying the same analysis to each. The Court treated the decision as resting on federal constitutional grounds and thus exercised jurisdiction. *Fitzgerald v. Racing Assn. of Central Iowa*, 539 U.S. 103, 106 (2003). [R139] [R305] [R306] [R307] [R308] [R337]

F. Review of State Court Decisions: Findings of Fact

1. Traditionally, the Supreme Court denies authority to review state court factual findings.

2. On the other hand, the Court has recognized its duty to make an independent examination of the record when a litigant alleges constitutional deprivations.

3. If the Court concludes that the state-court findings in such cases lack supporting evidence in the record or if factual findings are inseparable

from the state court's conclusion of law about the federal right, it will make an independent judgment about the facts.

Example 1: The state court held that the state criminal syndicalism act did not violate the Due Process Clause as applied, finding that the defendant was a member of an organization that taught and advocated violent overthrow of the government. The Supreme Court found that there was no evidence to support the state court's conclusion about the organization's aims, and reversed. *Fiske v. Kansas*, 274 U.S. 380 (1927).

Example 2: Choctaw Tribe members received land allotments under a federal statute that declared the lands not taxable for a certain period. A later Congress removed the exemption before expiration of the period, and the state assessed taxes on the property. When the owners resisted, the state threatened to seize and sell their property (and did in some cases) to satisfy the assessments. Some Tribe members sued, and the United States Supreme Court held that the exemptions were vested property rights that made the later Congress's attempted repeal unconstitutional under the Fifth Amendment's Due Process Clause. While those actions were pending, other owners had paid under protest to prevent seizure and sale. Then they challenged the assessments. The state supreme court refused relief, ruling that they had paid the taxes voluntarily. The United States Supreme Court reviewed the case and reversed, noting "that the finding or decision that the taxes were paid voluntarily was without any fair or substantial support [in the record]." *Ward v. Board of County Commissioners*, 253 U.S. 17 (1920). [225]

G. Review of Decisions of the United States Courts of Appeals

1. The Constitution expressly grants the Court appellate jurisdiction in all cases invoking federal subject-matter jurisdiction over which the Court does not have original jurisdiction. Congress has granted appellate review in very broad terms. Title 28 U.S.C. § 1254(1) provides Supreme Court review by writ of certiorari "upon the petition of any party to any civil or criminal case, before or after rendition of judgment or decree."

2. This statutory grant is appropriate. Supreme Court review of decisions by the federal courts implicates no federalism concerns. Cases from those federal courts necessarily involve at least a colorable claim of federal subject-matter jurisdiction.

3. Unlike § 1257, § 1254(1) has no final-judgment requirement, explicitly allowing review "before or after rendition of judgment or decree." Thus, the Supreme Court may review interlocutory rulings. Indeed, the Court may grant a writ of certiorari any time after a case reaches the court of appeals. This permits the Court to bypass the court of appeals, but the practice is quite rare, and the Court follows it only when there is a question of great importance and time is of the essence. Ordinarily, the Court waits until the court of appeals has entered a final judgment. *Air Line*

Pilots Association, International v. UAL Corp., 897 F.2d 1394, 1397 (7th Cir. 1990).

4. Under 28 U.S.C. § 1254(2), the court of appeals may certify to the Supreme Court "any question of law in any civil or criminal case as to which instructions are desired, and upon such certification the Supreme Court may give binding instructions or require the entire record to be sent up for decision of the entire matter in controversy." This provision, rarely invoked, permits the court of appeals to request a ruling from the Supreme Court on difficult and discrete questions of law. Although the statute is not explicit, the Supreme Court's jurisdiction over such questions is discretionary. *See, e.g., National Labor Relations Bd. v. White Swan Co.*, 313 U.S. 23 (1941). [R128] [R213]

Chapter IX

CONGRESSIONAL AND JUDICIAL RESTRICTIONS ON EXERCISING FEDERAL JURISDICTION

■ ANALYSIS

IV. Injunctions of Federal Judicial Proceedings

A. By a Federal Court

B. By a State Court

I. Introduction

The fact that a statute says that a federal court has jurisdiction over a case does not necessarily mean that the court can or will exercise it. Exceptions come in two areas. First, several specialized statutes prohibit the federal courts from taking certain kinds of actions in cases over which they clearly have jurisdiction. Three statutes demand attention: The Anti-Injunction Act, the Johnson Act of 1934, and the Tax Injunction Act of 1937. None of these laws withdraws jurisdiction; all of them tell the federal courts that they cannot issue injunctions in three particular situations. They remove a remedy. Like most other topics in Federal Courts, little is cut and dried; there are nuances. That is the picture on the legislative side.

On the judicial side, something different is going on. Under the general label of abstention, the Supreme Court has created five types of cases in which the federal courts must consider abstaining. Abstention is not a withdrawal of jurisdiction; it is, instead, a judicial refusal to exercise the jurisdiction Congress has clearly given. (Never forget that all of the abstention doctrines are federal common law and could alternatively be part of Chapter IX, but since they are specialized refusals to exercise jurisdiction, they also fit here, after the overview of federal jurisdiction.)

Abstention raises a critical separation-of-powers question. Is a congressional grant of jurisdiction an offer that can be refused? Since 1941, in a variety of contexts, the Supreme Court's answer has been "yes" while it has also recognized what Justice Brennan, ironically while announcing a new abstention doctrine for the Court, called "the virtually unflagging obligation of the federal courts to exercise the jurisdiction given them." As you will see, there are circumstances in which the obligation flags.

II. Congressional Restrictions

A. The Anti-Injunction Act, 28 U.S.C. § 2283

This statute focuses on when a federal court can and cannot enjoin parties in a federal action from litigating in a state court, The Anti-Injunction Act sharply limits a federal court's power. The statute's default position is to prohibit such injunctions, subject to three narrow exceptions.

1. The Statute

   a. The Anti-Injunction Act provides, "A court of the United States may not grant an injunction to stay proceedings in a State court except as expressly authorized by Act of Congress, or where necessary in aid of its jurisdiction, or to protect or effectuate its judgments."

   b. Obviously, the statute's default position is that a federal court may not enjoin pending state-court proceedings. There are three unnumbered exceptions to the default "don't":

      (1) The expressly-authorized exception;

      (2) The in-aid-of-jurisdiction exception; and

      (3) The relitigation exception.

c. Remember to consider Anti-Injunction Act's prohibition in conjunction with non-statutory comity restrictions the Supreme Court has imposed on federal courts' injunctive power. See *infra* § III.G.3.c.(4), at 211-211 *[R142]*, and § III.G.6.b(4)(b) at 218-218 *[R143]*. [R177]

2. History and Background

   a. The original version of the Anti-Injunction Act was § 5 of the Judiciary Act of 1793. For most of its history, the Act was absolute in its prohibition on federal-court power to enjoin pending state proceedings. However, over the years, the courts recognized various common-law exceptions.

   The most significant common-law exception concerned jurisdiction over property—a "*res.*" It is old law that in *in-rem* and *quasi-in-rem* cases, and other cases (such as interpleader) in which a court attaches property that is either the basis of the dispute or a basis of jurisdiction, the court in possession of the property may enjoin parties from litigating in another forum. Thus, federal courts that had seized property recognized an exception to the Anti-Injunction Act to permit them to enjoin subsequently filed state cases.

   Congress enacted the current version of the Act in 1948. The primary motivation for the current version was to overrule *Toucey v. New York Life Insurance Co.*, 314 U.S. 118 (1941), which held that there was no common-law exception for cases in which a party sought to relitigate in state court a case or factual question that a federal court had previously decided in a completed proceeding. [R150]

   b. There has been much debate over the motivations behind the 1793 Act. Perhaps Congress intended the Act to curb federal courts' equity jurisdiction, reflecting law's general preference for relief at law rather than in equity. Over time, however, the Act has come to be an important centerpiece in federalism, "to prevent needless friction between federal and state courts." *Oklahoma Packing Co. v. Oklahoma Gas & Electric Co.*, 309 U.S. 4, 9 (1940).

      (1) The Act certainly reflects the Framers' original understanding that the state courts were fully competent to interpret and enforce federal law. (Parity smiles.) *See supra* Ch. II, § III.A, at 60-61 *[R144]*.

      (2) Federal judicial review of state-court interpretations of federal law happens, habeas corpus excepted, *see infra* Ch. XII, § III.C, at 273 *[R145]*, only on direct review by the United States Supreme Court, rather than through the disruptive device of a lower federal court injunction affecting state proceedings.

(3) Parity of state and federal courts for determining federal questions is a matter for congressional judgment, and Congress has provided specified exceptions to the otherwise absolute ban on federal courts' enjoining state court actions.

c. Though the statute seems clearly to allow only three exceptions to the default no-injunctions rule, *Leiter Minerals, Inc. v. United States*, 352 U.S. 220 (1957), appeared to create one more exception.

(1) The Court held that the Act's prohibition does not apply to a case the United States brings, even though the Act makes no such provision. NLRB v. Nash-Finch Co., 404 U.S. 138 (1971), expanded that ruling to include suits by federal agencies.

(2) The Court characterized § 2283 as "an ambiguous statute" and refused to construe it to limit the federal government's entitlement to seek injunctions against state-court proceedings.

(3) Thus, when the United States seeks an injunction against state court proceedings, the Anti-Injunction Act is no barrier.

(4) *Leiter* led some courts to conclude that they could find other exceptions to the operation of the statute.

d. *Atlantic Coast Line R.R. v. Brotherhood of Locomotive Engineers*, 398 U.S. 281 (1970), ended such speculation. The Court made it clear that adding exceptions to the basic operation of the statute is a legislative, not a judicial, function. Congress may create new exceptions, but the federal courts cannot. No opinion mentioned *Leiter* or *Nash-Finch*.

e. Even when an exception applies, the party seeking an injunction does not automatically get it. It is still necessary to satisfy the typical requirements for the injunction: (1) irreparable harm is likely without an injunction, and (2) the party has no adequate remedy at law.

f. Note also that when an exception applies so that injunction is appropriate, the injunction issues *against the litigants, not against the state court*. If the federal court enjoins a litigant from proceeding in state court, violating the injunction is a contempt, which can include incarceration until the litigant agrees to abide by the injunction. (**Style note:** to avoid repetition of the cumbersome language of "enjoining a litigant from proceeding in state court," we will simply talk about "enjoining state proceedings" as a shorthand, with the understanding that the federal court actually enjoins the litigants.)

g. The Act prohibits federal injunctions of state-court proceedings. Thus, it does not apply if no state case has begun because there is no proceeding to enjoin. Accordingly, a federal injunction stopping the parties from filing a state court case in the first instance does not implicate the Anti-Injunction Act. *Dombrowski v. Pfister*, 380 U.S. 479 (1965).

3. The Scope of the Statutory Exceptions: Expressly Authorized

a. The Constitution does not limit the judicial power with respect to enjoining proceedings in other courts. Congress, having passed the Anti-Injunction Act, may withdraw the statute's bar.

b. "Expressly" does not require that Congress refer to § 2283 *in haec verba*. Statutory language allowing a federal court injunction against state-court proceedings is sufficient. Statutory language allowing a federal court injunction against "any proceeding," without mentioning state courts, is probably sufficient.

c. The Supreme Court has also recognized an "express" authorization by Congress in the absence of any statutory reference to federal court authority to issue an injunction. *Mitchum v. Foster*, 407 U.S. 225 (1972), held that the Civil Rights Act of 1871, 42 U.S.C. § 1983, is an expressly authorized exception to the Anti-Injunction Act, even though § 1983 is silent about whether a federal court can enjoin state-court proceedings.

(1) *Mitchum*'s test for determining whether a silent federal statute is an expressly authorized exception is "whether an Act of Congress, clearly creating a federal right or remedy enforceable in a federal court of equity, could be given its intended scope only by the stay of a state court proceeding."

(2) The Court found § 1983 met the test, because (1) it specifically authorizes equitable relief, and (2) legislative history established that Congress passed the Act largely because of mistrust of state-court ability or willingness to protect federal constitutional rights. *See infra* Ch. XV, § II, at 332 *[R146]*. (So much for parity, at least during and shortly after Reconstruction.) Professor Redish noted, "In what may be one of the most bizarre contortions of Supreme Court analysis, the *Mitchum* Court found section 1983 to be an 'implied' express exception (an oxymoron if ever there was one). . . ." [R169]

d. *Vendo Co. v. Lektro-Vend Corp.*, 433 U.S. 623 (1977), had difficulty applying *Mitchum*. The defendant in a state-court fiduciary-duty case, against which the court entered a substantial judgment, sought a federal injunction against collection. It argued that the judgment violated § 16 of the Clayton Act by having an anti-competitive purpose. The district court granted the injunction.

(1) By five to four, the Supreme Court concluded that the court should not have issued the injunction, but Justices were so badly split on the reasoning that the case may not be helpful in applying *Mitchum*.

(2) Three Justices concluded that *Vendo* failed the *Mitchum* test: the Clayton Act does allow equitable relief, but the legislative history did not sufficiently indicate that Congress believed the laws could have their intended scope only by means of stays of state court-proceedings.

(3) The other majority Justices concluded that the Clayton Act is an exception to the Anti-Injunction Act only in very narrow circumstances, such as when a litigant uses state proceedings to assert baseless claims for an anticompetitive effect. They concluded that *Vendo* was not such a case.

(4) The four dissenters agreed that the Clayton Act is an exception to the Anti-Injunction Act and found the injunction proper.

4. The Scope of the Statutory Exceptions: In Aid of Jurisdiction

a. The Act prohibits a federal court from enjoining state-court proceedings "except . . . where necessary in aid of its jurisdiction."

b. The clearest case in which the exception applies is when the federal court has taken possession of property that is either the subject of the litigation or a basis for jurisdiction—a *res* case. Cases had recognized this exception before the 1948 version of § 2283, which specifically included it.

(1) When an action is *in rem* and the federal court is in possession of property, "the exercise by the state court of jurisdiction over the same *res* necessarily impairs, and may defeat, the jurisdiction of the federal court already attached." *Kline v. Burke Construction Co.*, 260 U.S. 226, 230 (1922). Thus, an injunction against the state-court proceedings is appropriate to allow the federal court to maintain authority over the property.

(2) The converse is also true: if a state court "has first attached, the federal court is precluded from exercising its jurisdiction over the same *res* to defeat or impair the state court's jurisdiction." *Id.* at 230. [R181] This is the only circumstance in which a state court may enjoin federal-court proceedings. *See infra* § II.D.2.b at 193 *[R148]*. [R151]

c. According to the Reviser's Note to the 1948 revision, Congress intended this exception also to authorize federal injunction of state proceedings following removal. This is consistent with the command of 28 U.S.C. § 1446(d) that when the state-court clerk receives the notice of removal, that "effect[s] the removal and the

State court shall proceed no further unless and until the case is remanded."

d. Scholars have argued that courts should read this exception more broadly, to permit a federal court to enjoin state-court proceedings outside the attachment-of-property situation. The rule, however, is that parallel *in personam* proceedings proceed without injunctive interference, notwithstanding the waste such duplicative litigation causes. *See infra* § III.H.2.b, at 223 *[R149]* (noting abstention generally not available simply to avoid duplicative litigation). [R186]

e. Some courts have expanded the exception to *in personam* cases, at least in limited circumstances where state court proceedings would clearly interfere with the federal court's adjudicating the case.

   (1) When an insurance company seeks a federal declaratory judgment that a policy is invalid because of fraud, some courts have enjoined the insured from pursuing state-court litigation to recover under the policy.

   (2) Some courts overseeing school-system desegregation have enjoined state-court litigation that would interfere.

   (3) Some courts overseeing complex litigation, such as class actions or multidistrict litigation, have enjoined state-court litigation that would interfere. [R369]

5. The Scope of the Statutory Exceptions: Relitigation

   a. The Act prohibits a federal court from enjoining state court proceedings "except . . . to protect or effectuate its judgments."

   b. Congress passed the present version of the Act partly to overrule *Toucey*'s holding that allowed state-court relitigation of matters a federal judgment had already determined. *See supra* § II.A.2.a, at 186 *[R150]*.

   c. *Chick Kam Choo v. Exxon Corp.*, 486 U.S. 140, 147 (1988), explained that the relitigation exception rests on "the well-recognized concepts of res judicata and collateral estoppel."

      (1) Res judicata and collateral estoppel (also known, respectively, as claim and issue preclusion) flow only from valid final judgments on the merits (though *please note that* collateral estoppel requires only a final judgment on the merits of the *issue* as to which a party seeks preclusion, not the entire case), resulting in entry of an appealable order. Thus, a federal court may enjoin state-court relitigation of the subject matter of federal final judgments and interlocutory rulings that are appealable as of right.

(2) Curiously, *Chick Kam Choo* also said that "an essential prerequisite for applying the relitigation exception is that the claims or issues that the federal injunction insulates from litigation in state proceedings actually have been decided by the federal court." 486 U.S. at 148. This seems to indicate that issue preclusion, *not* claim preclusion, falls within this exception (because issue preclusion only requires that the *issue* on which a party seeks preclusion have actually been litigated and determined). If that is what the Court intended, it is inconsistent with the ordinary rule of claim preclusion: it affects not only claims that the first action did litigate but also claims so transactionally related to them that the parties should have litigated. It may be best not to read the Court's language literally.

(3) Nonetheless, some courts have adopted this narrow interpretation of the third exception to the Anti-Injunction Act.

d. *Parsons Steel, Inc. v. First Alabama Bank*, 474 U.S. 518 (1986), held that a litigant who unsuccessfully argued claim preclusion in a *state* court (based on an earlier federal-court judgment) may not thereafter seek federal relief under the relitigation exception. The proper course is for the litigant to appeal within the state-court system and, if necessary, to seek review from the United States Supreme Court by certiorari. The Court was unanimous. [R160]

B. The Johnson Act of 1934

1. Now codified at 28 U.S.C. § 1342, this statute prohibits a district court in diversity cases from enjoining, suspending, or restraining the operation of, or compliance with, a public utility rate that a state or local administrative agency set, *provided* (1) the utility order does not interfere with interstate commerce, (2) reasonable notice and hearing preceded issuance, and (3) a "plain, speedy and efficient remedy" is available in the state courts.

2. Courts interpret and apply the plain-speedy-and-efficient requirement in the same manner as under the Tax Injunction Act. *See infra* Ch. IX. II.C.3 at 192. [R91]

C. The Tax Injunction Act of 1937

1. This Act, now at 28 U.S.C. § 1341, provides that "[t]he district courts shall not enjoin, suspend or restrain the assessment, levy or collection of any tax under State law where a plain, speedy and efficient remedy may be had in the courts of such State."

2. This "reflects a congressional concern to confine federal intervention in state government. . . ." *Arkansas v. Farm Credit Services of Central Arkansas*, 520 U.S. 821, 826-27 (1997). While states always have an interest in the integrity of their own processes, the interest is particularly great when tax revenue is involved.

3. Thus, there can be no federal interference with state tax collection if state law provides a "plain, speedy and efficient remedy. . . ."

   a. The phrase, "plain, speedy and efficient" addresses only *procedural* criteria. If state procedure allows the taxpayer to seek a refund in an ordinary judicial proceeding, it satisfies those criteria. *Rosewell v. LaSalle National Bank*, 450 U.S. 503 (1981), rejected the taxpayer's argument that state law's failure to mandate payment of interest on any refunded tax amount rendered the state remedy inefficient. The Court pointed out that the taxpayer could raise the Fourteenth Amendment property claim in the state refund proceeding.

   b. Allowing the taxpayer to raise a defense in an action to collect the tax is a "plain, speedy and efficient remedy" under the Act. *Kohn v. Central Distributing Co.*, 306 U.S. 531 (1939).

   c. Requiring the taxpayer to pay the tax and then sue for a refund also satisfies the Act.

   d. On the other hand, if state procedure requires multiple suits involving the taxpayer, there is no "plain, speedy and efficient remedy" and federal courts may grant relief. *Georgia R.R. & Banking Co. v. Redwine*, 342 U.S. 299 (1952).

4. Although the Act's words limit only the federal courts' authority to "enjoin, suspend, or restrain" assessment or collection of state taxes, the Act "also prohibits a district court from issuing a declaratory judgment holding state tax laws unconstitutional," *California v. Grace Brethren Church*, 457 U.S. 393, 408 (1982), the Court noting that the declaratory judgment "procedure may in every practical sense operate to suspend collection of the state taxes until the litigation is ended. . . ." [R162]

5. The Court has also recognized non-statutory comity limits on the power of federal courts to interfere with state taxing systems. Comity precludes a taxpayer from suing in federal court under 42 U.S.C. § 1983 for damages for allegedly unconstitutional administration of a state tax system. *Fair Assessment in Real Estate Association, Inc. v. McNary*, 454 U.S. 100 (1981).

6. Title 26 U.S.C. § 7421 parallels the Tax Injunction Act in forbidding injunctions against collecting federal taxes. However, *CIC Services, LLC v. IRS*, 593 U.S. 209 (2021), allowed an action contesting an IRS reporting requirement (that might ultimately have led to a tax levy).

D. Injunctions of Federal Judicial Proceedings

1. By a Federal Court

   a. The Anti-Injunction Act sharply limits federal courts' power to enjoin *state-court* proceedings. It does not apply to federal injunctions of federal-court proceedings.

b. A federal court enjoining another federal action does not implicate federalism, nor does it affront state courts.

c. Thus, a federal court has discretion to determine whether to enjoin litigants from proceeding in a parallel *in personam* federal case. Alternatively, a federal court may stay its own proceedings to allow parallel litigation to proceed. Either avoids duplicative federal litigation.

d. *Kerotest Manufacturing Co. v. C-O-Two Fire Equipment Co.*, 342 U.S. 180 (1952), acknowledged a federal court's broad discretion to stay its own proceedings but did not definitively address its power to enjoin another federal court's proceedings. The lower federal courts generally speak of equitable considerations of wise judicial administration in determining whether to enjoin parties from engaging in parallel federal litigation or to stay litigation in favor of a parallel federal case.

(1) In general, federal courts follow the first-filed rule, which provides that the court in which the first of related cases was filed should proceed. That court may enjoin the parties from proceeding in parallel federal litigation

(2) Generally, courts in which later duplicative cases are pending stay their own proceedings to allow the first-filed action to proceed to judgment, making an injunction unnecessary.

(3) The first-filed rule is merely a default rule, however, and circumstances may make it appropriate for a later-filed case to proceed, with that court enjoining parties from litigating parallel federal cases. *See, e.g., Semmes Motors, Inc. v. Ford Motor Co.*, 429 F.2d 1197 (2d Cir. 1970).

e. A federal court that has attached property, either as the subject of litigation or as a basis for *in rem* or *quasi-in-rem* jurisdiction may enjoin litigants from proceeding in another federal court (or state) concerning that property.

2. By a State Court

a. As a general rule, state courts cannot enjoin *in personam* proceedings in a federal court. *Donovan v. City of Dallas*, 377 U.S. 408 (1964).

b. However, a state court may enjoin a federal proceeding when the state court's jurisdiction rests on already attached property and federal litigation would therefore interfere with the state court's jurisdiction. *See supra* § II.A.4.b(2), at 189 *[R151]*. [R148] [R168]

III. Judicial Restrictions: Abstention

A. Introduction

There are judge-made doctrines allowing a federal court to refuse to exercise subject-matter jurisdiction that it clearly has. Despite a strong argument that it is improper for federal courts to decline to adjudicate when they have subject-matter jurisdiction, the abstention doctrines are a long-standing part of the federal judicial landscape. The courts use most of them rarely, but abstention under *Younger v. Harris*, 401 U.S. 37 (1971), *see infra* § III.G, at 207-220 *[R152]*, is quite common. The federal courts predominantly invoke abstention out of considerations of federalism and to defer to state courts and other decision-making bodies when federal court involvement might be disruptive or seem disrespectful of state efforts. Each abstention doctrine has different requirements, however, and slightly different justifications. Procedures vary as well. All abstention doctrines are controversial, and one might view their overzealous employment as abdicating part of the federal courts' constitutional function.

B. Sources of the Abstention Doctrines

1. "Abstention" is a generic label for several distinct but related doctrines under which a federal court in a case that properly invokes federal subject-matter jurisdiction will either decline to exercise it or postpone decision, deferring to state proceedings.
2. The abstention doctrines, however, are entirely judge-made. Make no mistake: the abstention doctrines are all federal common law.
3. Some scholars criticize abstention as a separation-of-powers violation. Congress vests subject-matter jurisdiction in the inferior federal courts. The Constitution nowhere gives the inferior federal courts power to determine which cases they will hear. Chief Justice John Marshall, speaking of the federal judiciary, said: "We have no more right to decline the exercise of jurisdiction which is given, than to usurp that which is not given. The one of the other would be treason to the Constitution." *Cohens v. Virginia*, 19 U.S. (6 Wheat.) 264, 404 (1821). [R211] [R185]
4. In Chief Justice Marshall's terms, the federal courts commit treason every day; abstention is an accepted practice.
   a. Remember, though, that abstention other than *Younger* abstention is exceptional.
   b. Mere difficulty in ascertaining the meaning of state law does not itself "afford a sufficient ground for a federal court to decline to exercise its jurisdiction to decide a case which is properly brought to it for decision." *Meredith v. City of Winter Haven*, 320 U.S. 228, 235 (1943). After all, federal courts routinely must apply state substantive law in diversity cases. Allowing them to abstain simply because of difficult questions of state law would erode diversity jurisdiction. [R159]

C. Comparative Aspects of the Different Forms of Abstention

1. There are five major abstention doctrines. Most go by the name of the case that introduced them. Thus, courts and lawyers speak of *Pullman* abstention, *Thibodaux* abstention, *Burford* abstention, and *Colorado River* abstention. However, *In re Sawyer*, 124 U.S. 200 (1888), introduced what now is *Younger* abstention; *Younger v. Harris*, 401 U.S. 37 (1971), revitalized the doctrine.
2. It is a mistake to think that the five types of abstention are hermetically sealed from one another. A case may fall within more than one type of abstention, and courts are not always clear about which abstention doctrine they invoke. It is quite common for the Court to discuss multiple abstention doctrines within a single opinion, so one must be careful to identify which doctrine the Court is applying.
3. With each type of abstention, it is important to understand the Supreme Court's justification for permitting a federal court to refuse to exercise subject-matter jurisdiction. Abstention may reflect (1) desire to avoid a constitutional ruling, (2) the need to have state courts determine difficult questions of state law, (3) desire to avoid overlapping litigation, (4) respect for state regulatory mechanisms, or (5) a combination of such justifications.
4. With each type of abstention, note whether the federal court dismisses the case or simply stays it, the latter leaving the possibility of the parties returning to federal court after a final state-court decision.
5. Finally, be sure to note whether each type of abstention applies in federal-question cases, diversity cases, or both.

D. *Pullman* Abstention

1. The Case
    a. *Railroad Commission of Texas v. Pullman Co.*, 312 U.S. 496 (1941), concerned an order entered by the Texas Railroad Commission (TRC), overseer of railroad operations and Texas's oil and gas industry. *See infra* § III.E, at 201-205 *[R153]*. The TRC ordered that "no sleeping car shall be operated on any line of railroad in the State of Texas . . . unless such cars are continuously in the charge of an employee . . . having the rank and position of Pullman Conductor."
        (1) Only trains on heavily-traveled routes had conductors. Trains serving lesser-traveled routes, with no conductors aboard, had porters in charge of sleeping cars.
        (2) Conductors were white. Porters were black. Thus the TRC order (and presumably its intent) was to prohibit blacks from being in charge of sleeping cars. This order thus kept black persons from having the responsibility of (and, presumably, receiving the pay for) being in charge of sleeping cars.

(3) The Pullman Company challenged the order as violating equal protection and due process. Porters also challenged the order, on grounds of racial discrimination. There was, however, a serious issue as to whether the TRC had statutory authority to make the order at all.

(4) The Supreme Court, noting that the Texas statute permitting the TRC to enter such orders was "far from clear," ordered the federal court to abstain to allow the parties to go to the state courts for a definitive interpretation of the statute.

(a) If the Texas courts determined that the TRC lacked authority to enter the order, they would strike the order, and the federal court would never have to reach the federal constitutional issues the parties raised.

(b) On the other hand, if the Texas courts upheld the order, the federal court could address the federal constitutional issues, which then would be ripe.

(c) Thus, *Pullman* abstention counsels the federal court to *stay* proceedings pending state-court determination. It does not require dismissal. *See infra* § III.D.4, at 199-201 *[R154]*, for *Pullman* abstention procedure.

2. Rationale and Requirements for *Pullman* Abstention

a. The major justifications for *Pullman* abstention are (1) avoiding constitutional adjudication that may be unnecessary to resolve the case, and (2) avoiding needless friction with state policies that might result from the federal court misunderstanding the relevant state law.

b. Some justify all abstention doctrines as limiting the federal docket. This is doubtful for two reasons. First, since courts rarely invoke most abstention doctrines, they have minimal effect on the docket. Second, when the case involves important federal issues, abstention implicitly exalts docket control through court-created doctrines over explicit congressional grants of subject-matter jurisdiction. Query whether Congress—a majoritarian branch of government—or the courts—a designedly counter-majoritarian branch—should make that policy choice. In more modern terms, is a congressional grant of jurisdiction merely an offer that the federal courts can refuse? Third, when a federal district court remanded a properly removed action for stated reasons having no connection with those that 28 U.S.C. § 1447(c) states, the Court overturned the remand and sharply rebuked both the district judge and the circuit court that had refused to review the remand order. *See Thermatron Products, Inc. v. Hermansdorfer*, 423 U.S. 336 (1976). *Thermatron* at least supplies some basis for arguing that judge-made abstention doctrines violate separation of powers by ignoring applicable jurisdiction statutes.

c. *Pullman* abstention is appropriate only when (1) there is a federal constitutional challenge (2) to an ambiguous or uncertain state law, (3) clarification of which might avoid the need to resolve the constitutional issue or significantly change the nature of the issue. *See infra* § d, e. Justice Frankfurter's opinion for the Court also mentioned "avoiding needless friction with state policies," "scrupulous regard for the rightful independence of state governments," and "furthering the harmonious relation between state and federal authority," but those three considerations are goals of or justifications for *Pullman* abstention rather than being criteria.

d. By "ambiguous" or "uncertain," courts mean that the state law is subject to at least two interpretations, one of which would obviate the need to address the federal constitutional challenge or materially change the nature of the challenge.

Example: In *Pullman*, if state law did not permit the TRC to enter the challenged order, the federal constitutional issues would be moot; the state court would strike the order under state law.

e. "Ambiguous" or "uncertain" also came to include cases where state-court clarification of the uncertain question of state law might significantly modify any remaining constitutional question. *See Harman v. Forssenius*, 380 U.S. 528, 534 (1965).

Example: A state statute sharply limited polluting discharges into state waters. Plaintiffs raised an assortment of constitutional challenges—interference with interstate commerce, due-process vagueness, equal protection and supremacy (because of the Federal Water Pollution Control Act) among them—seeking declaratory and injunctive relief from the statute's potential application to them. *Lake Carriers' Association v. MacMullan*, 406 U.S. 498, 512 (1972), ruled abstention appropriate because the state courts might interpret the state law in several ways, depending on the interaction between state law and forthcoming federal regulations under the federal statute. "[W]e are satisfied that authoritative resolution of the ambiguities in the Michigan law is sufficiently likely to avoid *or significantly modify the federal questions* appellants raise to warrant abstention. . . ." (Emphasis added.)

f. The mere fact that state courts have not yet interpreted a state law does not render it "ambiguous" or "uncertain." It is always conceivable that a state court might construe state law to avoid a federal constitutional problem, but "the relevant inquiry is not whether there is a bare, though unlikely, possibility that state courts might render adjudication of the federal question unnecessary." *Hawaii Housing Authority v. Midkiff*, 467 U.S. 229, 237 (1984) (refusing *Pullman* abstention; statutory language, though state courts had not yet interpreted it, unambiguously raised federal constitutional issues).

g. Similarly, a unconstitutional-vagueness challenge to a state law does not automatically avoid *Pullman* abstention, *provided* that a single construction of the state law may clear up the vagueness problem. On the other hand, if numerous interpretations by state courts will be necessary for clarification, abstention is inappropriate.

***Example*:** State employees challenged an oath the state required as a condition of employment. The oath provided, in pertinent part, that employees "by precept and example promote respect for the flag and the institutions of the United States of America and the State of Washington, reverence for law and order and undivided allegiance to the government of the United States." The Court held that the oath and other requirements of state law that the oath required employees to know were so vague that

> the uncertain issue of state law does not turn upon a choice between one or several alternative meanings of a state statute. The challenged oath is not open to one or a few interpretations, but to an indefinite number. . . . It is fictional to believe that anything less than extensive adjudications, under the impact of a variety of factual situations, would bring the oath within the bounds of permissible constitutional certainty. Abstention does not require this.

Baggett v. Bullitt, 377 U.S. 360, 377-78 (1964).

h. There is some difficulty if a state law is clear and implicates a federal constitutional problem, but might also violate a *state constitutional* provision.

(1) Generally, if the state provision merely mirrors the federal (*e.g.*, with a clause substantially like the Due Process Clause), abstention is not appropriate. *Wisconsin v. Constantineau*, 400 U.S. 433 (1971).

(2) On the other hand, a specialized state constitutional provision that may obviate the federal constitutional challenge may make abstention appropriate. *Reetz v. Bozanich*, 397 U.S. 82 (1970) (upholding abstention to permit state-court consideration of whether specialized state constitutional provisions relating specifically to fishing invalidated state law, which would moot plaintiffs' federal equal-protection challenge).

i. Of course, a federal court could always simply interpret the unclear state law, but that would not be a definitive precedent, although it would certainly dispose of the case. In such a situation, the federal courts consider it wise to defer to a state-court interpretation of state law. Doing so avoids potential federal interference with important state functions. *Harman v. Forssenius*, 380 U.S. 528, 534 (1965).

j. In *Pullman* abstention, the federal court stays the case rather than dismissing it. *See infra* § 4, at 199-201 *[R156]*, for discussion of the complex *Pullman*-abstention procedure involving state and federal courts. [R158]

3. Costs of *Pullman* Abstention

a. *Pullman* abstention imposes high costs on the administration of justice.

(1) The doctrine usually results in significant delays resolving federal constitutional claims. In one case, the abstention process took three years from when the Court ordered abstention (*Bellotti v. Baird I*, 428 U.S. 132 (1976)), to final resolution of the constitutional questions (*Bellotti v. Baird II*, 443 U.S. 622 (1979)).

(2) *Pullman* abstention requires the participation of federal and state court systems, with concomitant waste of resources in duplicative proceedings. *See infra* § 4, at 199-201 *[R157]*.

b. To avoid such harms, the Court has held that abstention is less appropriate when there is great need to resolve the federal constitutional claims. This is especially true in cases challenging state statutes that may chill the exercise of the First Amendment right of free expression.

4. Procedural Aspects of *Pullman* Abstention

a. The *England* Doctrine: Procedure in *Pullman* Abstention

(1) *Pullman* abstention involves litigation in both state and federal courts; the federal court stays its proceeding to allow state-court litigation of state issues. *See supra* § III.D.2, at 196-199 *[R158]*. *England v. Louisiana State Board of Medical Examiners*, 375 U.S. 411 (1964), is the leading discussion of *Pullman*-abstention procedure.

(2) Chiropractic graduates sued a state medical licensing board that refused to license them under the state law for medical licensure. They sued in federal court, arguing that the state law was unconstitutional as applied. The trial court invoked *Pullman* abstention; it was unclear whether the state law applied to chiropractors. It stayed the federal action pending state-court litigation on the state law's applicability.

(3) The Supreme Court made clear that once the state court resolved the state-law issue, the plaintiff had the option to return to federal court for the adjudication of remaining federal constitutional issues.

(4) The Court held that when the plaintiff presents the state issue to the state court, however, she must also *notify* the state court of the constitutional issue, even though she retains the option to return to federal court.

(a) The reason is that the state court needs the opportunity to narrow the construction of the ambiguous statute to avoid constitutional infirmity.

(b) There is an important difference between *notifying* the state court that there is a federal constitutional issue and *relying* on that issue in the state court. If the plaintiff argues the federal constitutional issue, and the state court decides it, issue preclusion should prevent the plaintiff from returning to the abstaining federal court.

(c) To avoid this problem, the Supreme Court requires that waiver of the option to return to federal court be explicit.

(d) Of course, appeal in the state-court system may protract litigation. When state appeals have run their course, and the state courts have definitively determined the state-law issues, the plaintiff may return to federal court to litigate the federal issues.

(5) Many criticize *England* procedure for causing enormous delay. Nevertheless, the Court stands by the doctrine.

(6) Occasionally, restrictions on state-court jurisdiction necessitate dismissal of the federal action, although such dismissal should be without prejudice so the plaintiff can refile it after the state litigation is complete. *See, e.g., Harris County Commissioners Court v. Moore*, 420 U.S. 77 (1975) (dismissal without prejudice appropriate because Texas courts, not permitted to issue advisory opinions, would not permit litigation on the state-law issues if federal action was pending).

b. Certification to State Court

(1) Certification can avoid abstention's waste and delay, and a federal court may employ it if the state authorizes certification from federal courts. At this writing, 49 states and the District of Columbia have certification procedures. Some allow certification only by federal appellate courts; others permit certification from district courts.

(2) Certification (sometimes under a state statute and other times pursuant to a state-court rule), allows the federal court to refer unsettled state-law questions directly to the state's highest court, avoiding the necessity of proceeding through the entire state judicial system.

(3) If certification is available, it is highly advisable for a federal court to resort to it in the presence of an unclear issue of state law. *See Lehman Brothers v. Schein*, 416 U.S. 386 (1974). *McKesson v. Doe*, 592 U.S. 1 (2020), took the Fifth Circuit to task for not certifying. The Supreme Court acknowledged that certification is discretionary but nonetheless reversed and remanded with instructions to certify. The Court did not explicitly find that the Fifth Circuit had abused its discretion, but there is no other apparent way to explain the decision.

(4) But mere availability of certification does not automatically trigger resort to it. It is just as inappropriate, for example, to certify a question where there is no uncertain question of state law as it would be to invoke *Pullman* abstention; the state law must by truly unclear. "A federal court may not properly ask a state court if it would care in effect to rewrite a statute." *City of Houston v. Hill*, 482 U.S. 451, 471 (1987).

(5) The relationship between abstention and certification may be confusing. In *Arizonans for Official English v. Arizona*, 520 U.S. 43 (1997), two lower federal courts held an Arizona ballot initiative (that would have made English the state's official language) unconstitutional. The Supreme Court held that the decisions were premature, noting the state law was unclear and state courts had not interpreted it. The Court suggested that the lower courts should have certified the unsettled question of state law to the Arizona Supreme Court. Some language in the Court's opinion, however, suggests that *Pullman* abstention may be more difficult to obtain than certification, because abstention requires "unique circumstances" while certification does not. Certification's availability may also limit using *Pullman* abstention. [R154] [R156] [R157] [R358]

E. *Burford* Abstention

1. The Case

a. *Burford v. Sun Oil Co.*, 319 U.S. 315 (1943), created a second type of abstention. Like *Pullman*, *Burford* also involved a challenge to a Texas Railroad Commission (TRC) order. TRC had considerable authority over allocation of oil and gas drilling rights and entered an order granting Burford the right to drill for oil in specific areas.

(1) Sun Oil challenged the order, invoking diversity jurisdiction and federal-question jurisdiction by raising a federal constitutional challenge to the order as violating its rights.

(2) Texas had a complex regulatory scheme for such orders and judicial review of them. TRC had jurisdiction to make initial determinations, and only a specific state court could review. (The Texas legislature was clear about avoiding numerous state courts of coordinate jurisdiction reviewing TRC orders because that would threaten uniformity of adjudication, so it vested review in a single state trial court.)

b. The Supreme Court held that the district court should have abstained by dismissing (not staying, as in *Pullman*). Federal judicial review would threaten the Texas regulatory scheme and cause the very confusion the Texas single-court requirement sought to avoid. Federal courts had to honor Texas's decision to channel judicial review of TRC orders into a particular state court.

c. Courts sometimes call *Burford* abstention "administrative abstention" because it defers to state administrative regulation of specific topics.

Example: A state regulatory commission refused to permit Railroad to discontinue certain train routes. The state regulatory scheme permitted Railroad to appeal the order to a particular state court. Instead, Railroad sued in federal court. The Supreme Court held that the federal court should have dismissed: "As adequate state court review of an administrative order based upon predominantly local factors is available to appellee, intervention of a federal court is not necessary for protection of federal rights." *Alabama Public Service Commission v. Southern R. Co.*, 341 U.S. 341, 349 (1951).

2. Rationale and Requirements of *Burford* Abstention

a. *Burford* abstention is appropriate only when a federal court decision might "disrupt[ ] . . . state efforts to establish a coherent policy with respect to a matter of substantial public concern." *Colorado River Water Conservation District v. United States*, 424 U.S. 800, 814 (1976).

b. Thus, for *Burford* abstention to be appropriate, the state must have established some systemic mechanism for handling an important issue (such as allocation of oil-drilling rights in Texas), and federal-court involvement must threaten to interfere with that mechanism. Such state systems feature expertise in the substantive area, and state decision-makers will have appropriate sympathy with underlying state policy.

c. *Burford* abstention is not appropriate simply because a federal judgment might overturn the state policy itself. Constitutional challenges to state law routinely involve this. Only when a federal proceeding would disrupt a complex, state-established regulatory scheme for dealing with an important local issue is *Burford* abstention permissible.

Example: A state statute provides that anyone under a legal obligation to support children of whom the person does not have custody may not remarry without court permission. Plaintiff challenges the statute in federal court on equal-protection grounds. *Burford* abstention is not proper. The case does not involve complex issues of state law in which federal interference might disrupt coherent state policy. The policy itself is the subject of the challenge. *Zablocki v. Redhail*, 434 U.S. 374 (1978).

d. Although the *Burford* majority mentioned federal courts having to interpret state law, *Burford* abstention, (unlike *Pullman*) does not require uncertain state law. *Burford*'s point is that a federal court decision will involve federal courts in areas where states have sophisticated mechanisms for resolution of disputes in complex regulatory areas. Two sets of courts adjudicating such disputes might result in the courts acting at cross-purposes, even if unwittingly.

e. *Burford* itself involved, at least in part, a federal constitutional challenge to a state administrative decision.

(1) By relegating decision-making to the state system, *Burford* abstention funnels federal constitutional issues to the state courts. Their decision is reviewable only by the United States Supreme Court. Because that Court's review is discretionary, there is little chance that a federal court will address the federal issues.

(2) Some scholars have argued that this makes abstention less appropriate in cases involving constitutional challenges. While it may be appropriate to have state courts deal with the intricacies of complex state administrative schemes, these scholars argue that the federal courts should not abdicate their responsibility to determine federal constitutional issues.

(3) The Supreme Court's more recent efforts in this area have not discussed the fact that *Burford* involved a federal constitutional issue. The Court has discussed *Burford* abstention (while not necessarily applying it) as applicable in cases not involving constitutional challenges.

f. The mere existence of a state mechanism for dealing with important local issues does not guarantee *Burford* abstention. The court must look carefully at the claim to determine whether federal resolution will enmesh the court in a complex area for which the state has established dispute resolution and review mechanisms. Thus, *New Orleans Public Service, Inc. v. Council of New*

Orleans, 491 U.S. 350 (1989) (*NOPSI*), rejected *Burford* abstention despite the existence of a state regulatory body.

(1) A utility company incurred costs participating in nuclear power plant venture. It sought reimbursement. The state rate-making authority determined that the utility company should not receive full reimbursement because it had been negligent in some respects.

(2) The company sued in federal court, seeking an injunction and a declaration that the rate-making authority lacked power to decide because federal law pre-empted the issue.

(3) Rejecting *Burford* abstention, the Court noted:

> The present case does not involve a state law claim, nor even an assertion that the federal claims are "in any way entangled in a skein of state law that must be untangled before the federal case can proceed. . . ."
>
> . . .
>
> While *Burford* is concerned with protecting complex state administrative processes from undue federal interference, it does not require abstention whenever there exists such a process, or even in all cases where there is a "potential for conflict" with state regulatory law or policy.

(4) Applying those principles, *NOPSI* found that "[u]nlike a claim that a state agency has misapplied its lawful authority or has failed to take into consideration or properly weigh relevant state-law factors, federal adjudication of this sort of pre-emption claim would not disrupt the State's attempt to ensure uniformity in the treatment of an 'essentially local problem.' "

(5) *NOPSI* is thus helpful in defining *Burford* as appropriate (1) when there are "difficult questions of state law bearing on policy problems of substantial public import whose importance transcends the result of the case at bar" or (2) when "the exercise of federal review of the question . . . would be disruptive of state efforts to establish a coherent policy with respect to a matter of substantial public concern." 491 U.S. at 361. [R184]

g. *Burford* directed dismissal rather than merely staying the case (as in *Pullman* abstention).

(1) Dismissal seems appropriate; the parties will not return to federal court to litigate federal issues, as in *Pullman* abstention. Rather, the state judicial system will resolve all of the dispute, subject, of course, to Supreme Court review. [R361]

(2) Nonetheless, *Quackenbush v. Allstate Ins. Co.*, 517 U.S. 706 (1996), indicated that sometimes a court invoking *Burford* abstention should stay the federal action rather than dismiss. *Quackenbush* was a damages action, and the Court ruled that while it was proper under *Burford* to dismiss actions seeking only equitable relief, it was not proper in actions for damages. [R153]

F. *Thibodaux* Abstention

1. The *Thibodaux* and *Frank Mashuda* Cases

a. *Louisiana Power & Light Co. v. City of Thibodaux*, 360 U.S. 25 (1959), gave rise to another abstention doctrine. The basis and scope of *Thibodaux* abstention have always been confusing, in part because of inconsistencies between *Thibodaux* and *County of Allegheny v. Frank Mashuda Co.*, 360 U.S. 185 (1959), which the Court decided the same day. Both involved eminent-domain condemnation of land.

b. In *Thibodaux*, the city brought a state-court condemnation action to seize Owner's land. Owner removed to federal court on the basis of diversity jurisdiction. The state condemnation law under which the city proceeded was old, and state courts had not construed it; there was some question of whether the statute allowed condemnation on the facts.

(1) The district court abstained, staying proceedings to permit state courts to construe the statute.

(2) A six-to-three Supreme Court upheld abstention, emphasizing the "special nature of eminent domain" proceedings, "intimately involved with sovereign prerogative." 360 U.S. at 28.

c. In *Frank Mashuda*, the landowner sued in federal court, invoking diversity jurisdiction. The claim was for ouster and challenged the taking's validity. Unlike *Thibodaux*, state law on condemnation was clear.

(1) The trial judge abstained on the basis that hearing the case would interfere with the administration of local affairs.

(2) A five-to-four Court held that abstention was improper and ordered the district court to adjudicate.

(3) The Court said that eminent domain "is no more mystically involved with 'sovereign prerogative' than [a series of other matters in which abstention is improper]." And "the fact that a case concerns a State's powers of eminent domain no more justifies abstention than the fact that it involves any other issue related to sovereignty." 360 U.S. at 192.

d. The Court's positions on whether eminent domain embodies a "sovereign prerogative" are irreconcilable. The *Thibodaux* dissent is largely indistinguishable from the majority opinion in *Frank Mashuda*. Portions are verbatim.

e. Some commentators have argued that because state law was unclear in *Thibodaux* but clear in *Frank Mashuda*, the cases are reconcilable. Thus, in the latter case, the district court merely had to resolve disputes of fact rather than engaging in a difficult exercise of state statutory interpretation. That sounds plausible on first hearing, but it does not at all address the Court's contradictory statements about eminent domain and sovereign prerogative.

f. But *Quackenbush v. Allstate Insurance Co.*, 517 U.S. 706, 720 (1996), distinguished the two cases because the *Thibodaux* district court had merely stayed the federal case, whereas the *Frank Mashuda* district court had dismissed.

2. Rationale and Requirements of *Thibodaux* Abstention

a. Unlike *Pullman* abstention, *Thibodaux* abstention does not seek to avoid determining a federal constitutional question. *Thibodaux* presented no federal question. It did not involve a constitutional challenge to condemnation.

b. *Thibodaux*'s rationale appears to be the nature of eminent domain as involving an important sovereign prerogative. The problem with that, of course, is that *Frank Mashuda* declared that eminent domain did *not* involve an important sovereign prerogative.

c. Perhaps *Thibodaux* abstention is appropriate only when the case involves eminent domain *and* state law on condemnation is unclear. Then abstention permits the state court to determine the state-law issue, rather than the federal court guessing at the law's meaning.

(1) If so, the federal court should stay proceedings while the litigants go to state court for the state-law determination. In *Thibodaux*, the Court upheld such a stay, the procedure being reminiscent of *Pullman* abstention but for the absence of a federal constitutional issue.

(2) But since there was no federal challenge to the condemnation law, arguably a stay made no sense. If there were a federal constitutional issue, *Pullman* abstention would be appropriate, and the parties could return to federal court to resolve federal constitutional matters after state-court interpretation of state law. In *Thibodaux*, however, there was no federal issue for decision, and thus no need on that score for the litigants to return to federal court. On the other hand,

perhaps the *Thibodaux* Court was being sensitive to the concerns underlying diversity jurisdiction, particularly because the non-citizen owner was the defendant in state court.

(3) If *Thibodaux* abstention is appropriate in part because state law is unclear, it comes dangerously close to permitting abstention on that basis in diversity cases generally. The Court has routinely rejected the idea, however, that a federal court can abstain in a diversity case to avoid having to determine difficult issues of state law. *See supra* § III.B.4.b, at 194 *[R159]*.

(4) Thus, *Thibodaux* abstention must rest in part upon some notion that eminent domain indeed involves a special prerogative of local sovereignty, *Frank Mashuda* notwithstanding. [R360]

G. *Younger* Abstention: "Our Federalism"

1. Introduction

"Our Federalism" is a federal common-law doctrine that serves a function similar to the Anti-Injunction Act's. *See supra* Ch. IX, § II.A at 185-191 *[R160]*. It requires federal courts to abstain from issuing equitable relief that interferes with a state proceeding. Originally, the doctrine prohibited federal courts from ever enjoining ongoing state criminal proceedings, and forbade enjoining threatened state criminal proceedings unless the party seeking the injunction (1) had no adequate remedy at law and (2) could show great, immediate, and irreparable harm if the federal court did not act. *Fenner v. Boykin*, 271 U.S. 240 (1926). Later, *Younger v. Harris*, 401 U.S. 37 (1971), modified the doctrine to allow injunctions of pending state criminal proceedings, but only if the two *Fenner* criteria were present. Since then, the Court has had to determine whether this doctrine of deference should apply as well to (1) claims for federal declaratory relief, (2) claims concerning future state proceedings, and (3) claims involving non-judicial state actions. The doctrine is controversial. Some hail it as an appropriate accommodation and deference to the states. Others decry it as an abdication of the federal judiciary's responsibility to adjudicate federal-law, particularly constitutional-law, issues.

2. Background

a. "Our Federalism": Concept and Contours

(1) *Younger v. Harris*, 401 U.S. 37 (1971), most famously espoused "Our Federalism," a federal common-law doctrine the Supreme Court developed. It imposes significant restrictions on federal courts' power to interfere with state proceedings. In its classic form, the doctrine prohibits federal courts from enjoining (1) pending (2) state (3) criminal proceedings.

State criminal defendants ordinarily must raise their constitutional challenges while defending the state prosecution. *See infra* § III.G.3.c(3), at 210 *[R161]*.

(2) Some commentators argue that "Our Federalism" simply embodies the well-known rule of equity jurisprudence that equity will not act if there is an adequate remedy at law. On this view, "Our Federalism" counsels the federal court not to issue an injunction because the party seeking it has an adequate remedy at law: the right to raise the federal constitutional defense in the state criminal proceedings. [R171]

(3) Although the doctrine originated in cases to enjoin state prosecutions, *Samuels v. Mackell*, 401 U.S. 66 (1971), applied it to bar *declaratory relief* affecting ongoing state criminal judicial proceedings.

    (a) *Samuels* reasoned that a declaratory judgment can interfere with a state criminal prosecution in the same way as an injunction, because the federal decision may have issue-preclusive effect in the state proceedings. Under the Declaratory Judgment Act, 28 U.S.C. §§ 2201-2202, a declaratory judgment can also be the basis for a subsequent injunction. If this reasoning sounds similar to *Grace Brethren Church*, *see supra* 192 *[R162]*, that's because it is.

    (b) The Court left open the possibility that it might recognize exceptions, but gave no indication what they might be. [R175]

(4) Traditionally, "Our Federalism" limits federal judicial interference with pending state judicial proceedings, originally only criminal proceedings. *See infra* § G.6.a(1), at 216 *[R163]*. One important question is whether it prevents federal involvement even there is no state proceeding. *See infra* § G.6.a, at 216 *[R164]*.

(5) Originally, the doctrine limited federal judicial interference with state criminal matters. Subsequently, the Court expanded it to cover what the Court termed "quasi-criminal" matters. Then the Court applied it in limited civil contexts and to state administrative and executive action. *See infra* §§ G.6.b(2) and G.7, at 217-217 *[R165]*, 218-220 *[R166]*, respectively.

(6) There are important exceptions to the doctrine. *See infra* § G.4, at 212-212 *[R167]*. [R170]

b. Relationship to the Anti-Injunction Act

(1) Usually, the Anti-Injunction Act, 28 U.S.C. § 2283, prohibits federal-court interference with state judicial proceedings. *See supra* § II at 185-193 *[R168]*.

(2) *Mitchum v. Foster*, 407 U.S. 225 (1972), however, held that federal civil rights suits under 42 U.S.C. § 1983 are an expressly authorized exception to the Anti-Injunction Act. *See supra* § II.A.3.c, at 188 *[R169]*. Thus, *Younger* abstention is necessary in civil rights actions to limit the federal judiciary's power to interfere with state-court cases. [R368]

(3) The year before *Mitchum*, *Younger v. Harris*, 401 U.S. 37 (1971), the seminal case in the development of "Our Federalism," refused to consider whether the Anti-Injunction Act applied to § 1983 suits seeking to enjoin state judicial proceedings. Perhaps the Court anticipated *Mitchum*, but in any case, the Court ignored § 2283, though the federal courts generally cannot do so. [R370]

3. Historical Development

a. A series of decisions from the 1920s through the 1940s developed the principle that a federal court could not enjoin even a threatened state prosecution except in the most extraordinary circumstances. *See, e.g.*, *Douglas v. City of Jeannette*, 319 U.S. 157 (1943); *Fenner v. Boykin*, 271 U.S. 240 (1926).

b. *Dombrowski*

(1) *Dombrowski v. Pfister*, 380 U.S. 479 (1965), authorized a federal injunction of threatened state prosecutions of civil rights workers in Louisiana. The plaintiffs alleged that the prosecution was not for the purpose gaining a valid conviction, but was part of systematic harassment against First Amendment free expression.

(2) The Court recognized that ordinarily the right to raise a constitutional defense during the state prosecution is adequate protection of federal constitutional rights.

(a) On the facts, however, that was not true. The pattern of repeated prosecutions had a "chilling effect" on free speech, cowing the persons seeking the federal injunction.

(b) The plaintiffs also alleged that the threat of prosecutions and the prosecutions themselves were in bad faith.

(3) Many perceived *Dombrowski* as opening the federal courthouse doors to cases seeking to protect federal constitutional rights, at least with regard to threatened, as opposed to

pending, state criminal prosecutions. *Younger v. Harris* dashed hopes that the Court would interpret *Dombrowski* broadly. [R366]

c. *Younger v. Harris* and the Modern Concept of "Our Federalism"

(1) *Younger v. Harris* is the cornerstone of the modern concept of "Our Federalism." *See supra* § III.G.2.a, at 207-208 *[R170]*. California indicted Harris, a member of the Progressive Labor Party, for distributing leaflets allegedly violating the California Criminal Syndicalism Act. He sued in federal court, seeking to enjoin prosecution on the ground that the statute violated his First Amendment rights.

(2) The Supreme Court refused to allow the injunction.

(a) The Court relied heavily on decisions from the 1920s through 1940s.

(b) It distinguished *Dombrowski* on the grounds that Harris alleged no bad faith or harassment.

(c) It concluded that "the possible unconstitutionality of a statute 'on its face' [as Harris alleged] does not in itself justify an injunction against good-faith attempts to enforce it. . . ." 401 U.S. at 54.

(d) The Court described its deference to the state court prosecution in terms of "equity," "comity," and "federalism."

(3) The reliance on "equity" refers to the traditional equitable principle that an equity court will not enjoin a criminal prosecution or otherwise act when there is an adequate remedy at law. *See supra* § III.G.2.a(2), at 208 *[R171]*.

(a) The Court declared that being able to raise the constitutional argument as a defense is an adequate remedy at law.

(b) The Court disregarded the long-established principle that adequacy of remedy for purposes of federal equitable jurisdiction referred exclusively to remedies available within the *federal*-court system.

(c) The Court also rejected the argument that the possible chilling effect caused by the delay in adjudication of First Amendment rights renders the availability of a criminal defense an inadequate remedy. More generally, the Court seems no longer to regard "chilling effect" as having any significant persuasive value. [R161]

(4) "Comity" and "federalism" reflect "a proper respect for state functions."

(a) As *Younger* abstention has developed, it turns out that the deference is to both state *judiciaries* and to state *substantive* policies, such as those state criminal law reflects.

(b) According to *Younger*, allowing a federal court to enjoin a pending state prosecution reflects negatively on state judges' ability and willingness to interpret and enforce federal constitutional rights; it is an affront to the state judiciary and is incompatible with parity. *See infra* Ch. XII, § II.C, at 269-270 *[R172]*.

(c) Allowing state courts to adjudicate the constitutionality of state laws provides more appropriate, presumably more substantial, deference to state policies, whether manifested in state legislation or in the discretionary activities of state executive officers. In one way, that contradicts parity. Parity assumes that state and federal courts are equally competent and willing to give federal law its due, but the Court's deference to state's entitlement to adjudicate constitutional challenges to state law implicitly denies that federal courts are equally competent and willing to give *state* law its due. [R220]

(d) Finally, *Younger* reflects the fear that wide federal-court injunctive authority could seriously disrupt smooth operation of state judicial processes. [R142]

(5) The Court did note that intervention might be appropriate (1) if the federal court's refusal to intervene would cause the state criminal defendant (the federal plaintiff) great, immediate, and irreparable harm *and* (2) if the state criminal defendant had no adequate remedy at law. Having to defend a single prosecution where the defendant can raise the constitutional challenge in defense *is* an adequate remedy at law, subject to an exception for bad-faith or harassing prosecutions. *See infra* § VII.G.4.b, at 212 *[R173]*. [R174]

(6) If *Younger* abstention is appropriate, the federal court dismisses the case, and the state courts adjudicate the federal issues, with possible United States Supreme Court review to follow, though it rarely does.

(7) In one way, *Younger* represents a liberalization of federal judicial policy with respect to exercising jurisdiction regarding state criminal prosecutions. Before *Younger*, the federal courts could *never* exercise jurisdiction in a case challenging a pending state criminal prosecution, and they could entertain cases involving threatened prosecution *only* if the federal plaintiff could satisfy the two conditions noted in

§ VII.G.3.c(5), *supra* at 211 *[R174]*. After *Younger*, satisfying the two conditions permitted a state criminal defendant a federal challenge to a *pending* prosecution, and the Court explicitly reserved decision about the circumstances that might justify federal judicial action in the face of a threatened prosecution. [R371]

4. Exceptions to *Younger*

   a. *Younger* recognized that there might be cases that justify federal injunctive relief. After noting possible examples, the Court said that other "unusual situations calling for federal intervention might also arise, but there is no point in our attempting now to specify what they might be." 401 U.S. at 54.

   b. First, if the state prosecutes in bad faith, or as part of a series of harassing prosecutions, federal courts should be able to enjoin. *Dombrowski* is an example. [R173]

   c. Second, absent bad faith and harassment, there may be "extraordinary circumstances" that would justify federal injunctive relief. The Court's example indicates how narrow this exception is: when state law is "flagrantly and patently violative of express constitutional prohibitions in every clause, sentence and paragraph, and in whatever manner and against whomever an effort might be made to apply it." 401 U.S. at 53-54, quoting *Watson v. Buck*, 313 U.S. 387, 402 (1941). So far, no law has qualified.

   d. *Gerstein v. Pugh*, 420 U.S. 103 (1975), mentioned a third situation that *Younger* did not: when the federal plaintiff cannot raise the federal issue in the state action. State prisoners there challenged Florida's delays in affording probable-cause hearings for pre-trial detainees. Florida had no procedure for hearing such claims, so the Court allowed the action to proceed. This is not surprising; it shows that there is no adequate remedy at law, a showing prerequisite to equitable relief generally.

   e. In sum, even when *Younger* otherwise appears to apply, the federal court may grant relief if there is bad faith, harassment, or some other extraordinary circumstance that justifies not deferring to the state judiciary. Such cases are rare.

Example: *Gibson v. Berryhill*, 411 U.S. 564, 578 (1973), found that the State Board of Optometry, which would have adjudicated the matter, was "so biased by prejudgment and pecuniary interest that it could not constitutionally conduct hearings looking toward the revocation of [plaintiff's] license to practice optometry." Thus, the Board was incompetent to adjudicate the issue, so the plaintiff had no adequate remedy at law. [R167] [R179]

5. Timing Federal Intervention

   a. The Distinction Between Future and Ongoing Prosecutions

      (1) *Younger* dealt with an injunction of a *pending* state criminal prosecution.

         (a) Many think that a federal injunction against an ongoing state proceeding is a greater invasion of state prerogative and a greater affront to the state-court system, than an injunction against *future* state-court proceedings.

         (b) An injunction against an ongoing proceeding stops state litigation—a direct interference with a state court. An injunction against a future proceeding merely stops parties (one of whom may represent the state's interest) from initiating a state-court proceeding.

         (c) On the other hand, it can be more difficult for a person subject only to *possible* state prosecution to have a case ripe enough to invoke federal judicial power.

      (2) *Steffel v. Thompson*, 415 U.S. 452 (1974), held that *Younger* abstention is *not* appropriate with respect to federal declaratory relief relating to *future* state prosecutions.

         (a) *Steffel* did not explicitly deal with whether a plaintiff could obtain injunctive relief against future prosecutions.

         (b) The Court emphasized that declaratory relief is less invasive than injunctive relief, directly contradicting its analysis in *Samuels v. Mackell*, 401 U.S. 66 (1971), *see supra* § G.2.a(3) at 208 *[R175]*.

         (c) Other portions of *Steffel* implied *Younger* might not limit federal power to issue any form of federal equitable relief (declaratory or injunctive) against future state-court prosecutions.

         (d) That is consistent with Anti-Injunction-Act precedent: the statute's restriction on federal injunctions applies only when a state proceeding is pending. The Anti-Injunction Act does not speak to federal power to enjoin future state-court proceedings. *See supra* § II.A.1.b at 185 *[R176]*.

         (e) *Steffel* makes sense. Without a pending state proceeding, there is no opportunity for the person to raise federal constitutional defenses in state court except by violating the statute. *Steffel* characterized the individual's choice as "plac[ing] the hapless plaintiff between the Scylla of intentionally flouting state law and the

Charybdis of forgoing what he believes to be constitutionally protected activity in order to avoid becoming enmeshed in a criminal proceeding." 415 U.S. at 462. Thus, assuming the individual has a justiciable case, the federal court should be available.

(3) *Hicks v. Miranda*, 422 U.S. 332 (1975), dealt with the difficult issue of delay in issuance of a federal injunction. California prosecuted a theater owner's employees under an obscenity statute. The owner sought a federal temporary restraining order (TRO) against his being prosecuted. The federal court denied the TRO but did convene a three-judge district court (then required by 28 U.S.C. § 2284) from which the owner sought an injunction against prosecution. By the time the federal court issued the injunction, however, the state prosecutor had amended the criminal case against the employees to name the owner as a defendant. Thus, when the theater owner began his federal case, there was no criminal case pending against him, but when the federal court issued the injunction, there was.

(a) The Court concluded that the federal court should have abstained after amendment of the state case to include the federal plaintiff, unless the federal court had already had "proceedings of substance on the merits" before the amendment. Denial of the TRO apparently was not such a proceeding.

(b) The Court gave no indication of the meaning of the quoted phrase, and its meaning remains ambiguous. For example, if the federal court had granted the TRO (which would mean the court found a likelihood of success on the merits), would that have been a proceeding of substance on the merits?

(c) Justice Stewart's dissent noted that after *Hicks*, when notified of a pending federal action for a declaratory judgment or injunction, a state prosecutor could render *Steffel* inoperative simply by filing a state prosecution instead of responding in the federal action. He also wryly noted:

> There is, to be sure, something unseemly about having the applicability of the *Younger* doctrine turn solely on the outcome of a race to the courthouse. The rule the Court adopts today, however, does not eliminate that race; it merely permits the State to leave the mark later, run a shorter course, and arrive first at the finish line. This

rule seems to me to result from a failure to evaluate the state and federal interests as of the time the state prosecution was commenced.

422 U.S. at 354.

(4) *Doran v. Salem Inn, Inc.*, 422 U.S. 922 (1975), held that at least *preliminary injunctive* relief could be appropriate against future state prosecution.

(5) *Wooley v. Maynard*, 430 U.S. 705 (1977), authorized permanent injunctive relief against future state prosecution. It was somewhat ambiguous, however, as to whether it represented a full extension of *Steffel* and *Doran* to permanent injunctive relief, or whether it merely fell within one of the exceptions recognized in *Younger*. Most commentators view the decision as a full extension of *Steffel* to injunctive relief. *See also Zablocki v. Redhail*, 434 U.S. 374 (1978).

b. Post-Trial Intervention

(1) Remember, *Younger* held that a federal court could not enjoin a *pending* state criminal proceeding.

(2) *Huffman v. Pursue, Ltd.*, 420 U.S. 592, 608 (1975), held, however, that even after the state proceeding has been completed in the state trial court, "a necessary concomitant of *Younger* is that a party . . . must exhaust his state appellate remedies before seeking relief in the District Court." (The Court did not discuss the apparent problem of a district court considering allowing relief from a state-court judgment, which the *Rooker-Feldman* doctrine prohibits. *See infra* Ch. XII, § III.C at 273-275 *[R177]*. Federal habeas corpus, an exception to *Rooker-Feldman*'s general rule, *see infra* Ch. XII, § III.C, at 273-275 *[R178]*, would not have been available because Pursue's loss in the state courts could not have resulted in incarceration or other criminal penalty.) Pursue leased a theater and was showing what the Court characterized as pornographic films. In that civil obscenity case, Pursue lost in state court, and the judgment closed the theater as a nuisance. Pursue then sought federal injunctive relief from enforcement of the state judgment, arguing that *Younger* did not apply because no state case was pending.

(a) The Court held that the federal courts could not issue relief. If a losing litigant in state court fails to appeal the state judgment, he can gain equitable relief from a federal court only by showing that the case fits one of the *Younger* exceptions. *See supra* § III.G.4, at 212-212 *[R179]*.

(b) "Virtually all of the evils at which *Younger* is directed would inhere in federal intervention prior to completion of state appellate proceedings, just as surely as they would if such intervention occurred at or before trial." 420 U.S. at 608.

(c) The Court could as easily disposed of the case under the *Rooker-Feldman* doctrine, which prohibits the inferior federal courts from reviewing state-court judgments. *See infra*, Ch. XII, § III.C, at 273-275 *[R180]*. [R181]

(3) *Wooley v. Maynard*, 430 U.S. 705 (1977), distinguished *Huffman*. There, the person seeking federal relief had been convicted three times for violating a state statute by covering the state motto on his license plates because of his religious beliefs. He presented his First Amendment defense (*pro se*) to the charge but did not appeal any of the convictions, instead seeking a federal injunction against future prosecution. The Court allowed him to proceed. Unlike the plaintiff in *Huffman*, Maynard did not seek to enjoin enforcement of a state judgment. Rather, he sought to enjoin future prosecutions. The five-to-four Court found the case indistinguishable from *Steffel*. The case did not fall under *Dombrowski* because there was no showing that the repeated prosecutions were in bad faith; the plaintiff claimed the statute as applied to him violated the First Amendment by compelling him to display a message with which he did not agree because of his religion.

6. *Younger* and Civil Proceedings

a. Background

(1) *Younger* applied only to a *criminal* proceeding, leaving unresolved the doctrine's applicability to purely civil proceedings. [R163]

(2) Some argued that "Our Federalism" should apply to state civil proceedings as well. They asserted that federal equitable relief against a state proceeding is just as intrusive and insulting to the state judiciary in a civil as in a criminal case.

(3) On the other hand, perhaps the state's substantive interest is not as compelling in civil proceedings—especially if entirely between private parties—as in criminal matters. [R164]

b. Post-*Younger* Developments

(1) In *Huffman v. Pursue, Ltd.*, *see supra* § III.G.5.b(2), at 215 *[R181]*, the plaintiff sought a federal injunction against state judicial enforcement of a public nuisance statute. Though

the state proceeding was not a criminal matter, the Court applied *Younger*.

(a) "[W]e deal with a state proceeding which in important respects is more akin to a criminal prosecution than are most civil cases," and noted that the federal injunction "has disrupted [the] State's efforts to protect the very interests which underlie its criminal laws. . . ." 420 U.S. at 604-05.

(b) Though *Huffman* extended *Younger* to quasi-criminal civil proceedings, it left the doctrine's applicability to purely civil proceedings unresolved.

(2) *Trainor v. Hernandez*, 431 U.S. 434 (1977), extended *Younger* to a state civil proceeding by the Illinois Department of Public Aid to recoup welfare payments allegedly obtained fraudulently. The state-case defendant sought federal equitable relief against use of the Illinois Attachment Act, arguing it was unconstitutional.

(a) *Younger* applied because the state was a party to the suit as administrator of public-assistance programs. The Court saw the suit and the accompanying writ of attachment as vindicating important state policies, including safeguarding the programs' fiscal integrity. (Note the shift from protecting state judiciaries from federal judicial interference to protecting substantive state-law policies. *See infra* § III.G.7.b.2.c at 219 *[R182]*.)

(b) The Court described extending *Younger* to civil cases as limited to suits by the State in its sovereign capacity.

(c) Justice Brennan's dissent argued that the case was simply another step on the road toward extending *Younger* to all state civil proceedings. [R165]

(3) *Juidice v. Vail*, 430 U.S. 327 (1977), applied *Younger* to a federal suit involving state contempt procedures, and *Moore v. Sims*, 442 U.S. 415 (1979), applied *Younger* to a federal suit to enjoin operation of the Texas rule for judicial protection of minors. It is not clear whether *Moore* intended to extend *Younger* to all civil proceedings.

(4) *Pennzoil Co. v. Texaco*, Inc. 481 U.S. 1 (1987), applied *Younger* to a civil suit in Texas state court between two private parties.

(a) The case challenged an allegedly prohibitive bond requirement Texas law imposed on a litigant seeking to prevent execution of a judgment during the appellate process.

(b) The Court reasoned that the federalism concerns underlying *Younger* "mandate[ ] application of *Younger* abstention not only when the pending proceedings are criminal, but also when certain civil proceedings are pending, if the State's interests in the proceeding are so important that the exercise of the federal judicial power would disregard the comity between the States and the National Government." 481 U.S. at 11. [R143]

(c) Four Justices, concurring in the judgment because they rejected the claim on the merits, disapproved the majority's application of *Younger*.

(d) Curiously, Texas "not a party to this appeal—expressly represented to the Court of Appeals that it 'has no interest in the outcome of the state-court adjudication underlying this cause,' except in its fair adjudication." *Id.* at 19 (Brennan, J., concurring in the judgment) (quoting Texas's brief in the Court of Appeals). [R355]

7. *Younger* and Non-Judicial State Action

a. State Executive Action

(1) *Rizzo v. Goode*, 423 U.S. 362 (1976), relied on *Younger*, at least in part, holding that a federal trial court erred by issuing an injunction to restructure the Philadelphia police department's disciplinary system. No state judicial proceeding was pending or even contemplated. Thus, principles of "Our Federalism" can apply to counsel federal abstention in cases seeking review of state executive decisions.

(2) Many lower courts construe *Rizzo* merely to require significant concern by the federal court for state executive-officer discretion but not invariably to require *Younger*.

b. State Administrative Action

(1) A litigant need not begin state administrative remedies before seeking relief in federal court under § 1983, *Patsy v. Board of Regents*, 457 U.S. 496 (1982), *see infra* Ch. XIV, § III.B.3.a, at 306-307 *[R183]*. (The Prison Litigation Reform Act, 42 U.S.C. § 1997e(a), partially overruled *Patsy*, mandating that prisoners exhaust administrative remedies in any § 1983 action challenging prison conditions.)

(2) *Younger* does, however, play some role with respect to certain types of on-going state administrative proceedings.

(a) In *Middlesex County Ethics Committee v. Garden State Bar Association*, 457 U.S. 423 (1982), an attorney claimed that a state disciplinary proceeding against him violated the First Amendment. He sought a federal injunction. The Supreme Court applied *Younger* and held federal injunctive relief inappropriate.

(i) The Court noted that the proceedings "bear a close relationship to proceedings criminal in nature, as in *Huffman*," and emphasized "the unique relationship" between the state supreme court and the local ethics committee. 457 U.S. at 432.

(ii) The Court also noted that before the attorney had filed his petition for certiorari, the Supreme Court of New Jersey had adjudicated the federal constitutional issues *sua sponte* and amended the disciplinary rules to allow interlocutory appeals of constitutional questions to that court. Thus, *Middlesex* may only apply when the administrative action and the state judicial process intertwine.

(b) *Hawaii Housing Authority v. Midkiff*, 467 U.S. 229, 238 (1984), refused extending *Middlesex* to administrative proceedings that "are not part of, and are not themselves, a judicial proceeding. . . ." Thus, *Younger* did not apply.

(c) On the other hand, *Ohio Civil Rights Commission v. Dayton Christian Schools, Inc.*, 477 U.S. 619 (1986), held that *Younger* applied and barred federal injunctive relief. The school sought the federal relief to prevent the state civil rights commission from exercising jurisdiction over a sex-discrimination complaint by a fired teacher. The school argued that the federal relief was necessary to protect its First Amendment right of religious freedom. Denying relief, the Court emphasized "that the elimination of prohibited sex discrimination is a sufficiently important state interest to bring the present case within the ambit of the cited authorities." 477 U.S. at 628. Thus, the Court saw *Younger* abstention as protecting against more than federal interference with on-going state processes; it also protected the underlying state substantive interest. [R182]

c. State Legislative Actions

(1) *New Orleans Public Service, Inc. v. Council of City of New Orleans*, 491 U.S. 350 (1989) (*NOPSI*), held that *Younger* did not bar an electric utility's federal challenge, on preemption grounds, to the results of a city council rate-making proceeding. *See supra* § III.E.2.f, at 203-204 *[R184]*.

(2) The Court stated that "it has never been suggested that *Younger* requires abstention in deference to a state judicial proceeding reviewing legislative or executive action." 491 U.S. at 368.

(3) Consistently with *NOPSI*, *Sprint Communications, Inc. v. Jacobs*, 571 U.S. 69 (2013), allowed a federal challenge to an Iowa Utilities Board rate decision, even though a state-court challenge was pending. The unanimous Court cautioned against overusing *Younger*:

> Circumstances fitting within the *Younger* doctrine, we have stressed, are "exceptional"; they include, as catalogued in *NOPSI*, "state criminal prosecutions," "civil enforcement proceedings," and "civil proceedings involving certain orders that are uniquely in furtherance of the state courts' ability to perform their judicial functions." Because this case presents none of the circumstances the Court has ranked as "exceptional," the general rule governs: "[T]he pendency of an action in [a] state court is no bar to proceedings concerning the same matter in the Federal court having jurisdiction."

571 U.S. at 73 (citations omitted). It is still too soon to tell whether *Sprint* presages a generally more restrained approach to *Younger* abstention. [R152] [R166]

H. *Colorado River* Abstention

1. The Case and Its Progeny

a. The most controversial and potentially most far-reaching doctrine takes its name from *Colorado River Water Conservation District v. United States*, 424 U.S. 800 (1976). The United States sued in Colorado federal court, seeking a declaration of its rights and the rights of Indian reservations to water. The Government also sought appointment of a special master to administer waters decreed to the United States. The suit named about 1,000 area water users as defendants.

(1) Colorado had a complex system of water allocation and adjudication of water claims. It had divided the state into water divisions and appointed referees and judges.

(2) The water in *Colorado River* was subject to allocation in a pending state proceeding, to which the United States was a party, in southeastern Colorado, about 300 miles from the federal court.

(3) The Supreme Court held that the federal district court correctly dismissed the federal proceeding.

b. The Court noted that none of the other bases of abstention—*Pullman*, *Burford*, *Thibodaux* or *Younger*—applied. (Some scholars have argued that the case really did fall within *Burford* abstention.) Nonetheless, considerations of "wise judicial administration" justified dismissal.

c. Ironically, the majority emphasized that abstention truly "exceptional," and that there is "a virtually unflagging obligation of the federal courts to exercise the jurisdiction given them," (citing, *inter alia* Chief Justice Marshall, *see supra* § II.A.3, at 194 *[R185]*) at the very moment it was announcing the new abstention doctrine.

d. Four factors determine whether "wise judicial administration" justifies abstention. None is necessarily determinative. Rather, the trial court is to address each to determine whether there is the "clearest of justifications" for dismissal.

   (1) The factors are: (1) whether either court had first assumed jurisdiction over property; that is, the Court analogized *Colorado River* to an *in rem* case; (2) inconvenience of the federal forum (apparently meaning geographical inconvenience); (3) desirability of avoiding piecemeal litigation; and (4) the order in which the state and federal courts obtained jurisdiction.

   (2) Applying the factors, the Court noted: (1) neither court had attached property; (2) the federal court was inconvenient—300 miles from the site of the water being allocated, while the state litigation was at the site; (3) federal legislation allowing the United States to be joined as a party in the state's water proceedings reflected Congress's desire to avoid piecemeal litigation, and (4) the state litigation was filed first, involved the same parties, and had progressed farther. Indeed, the federal court had invested little time or effort; it had done nothing, so dismissal wasted no effort.

e *Will v. Calvert Fire Insurance Co.*, 437 U.S. 655 (1978), upheld *Colorado-River* abstention in a very confusing context. A district judge stayed a federal antitrust action in deference to a state case involving federal antitrust issues the defense raised. The Seventh Circuit issued mandamus requiring the district judge to proceed. The Supreme Court reversed.

   (1) Some commentators see *Will* as an expansion of *Colorado-River* abstention.

   (2) Others read *Will* narrowly because it involved complicating factors such as mandamus, securities law, and antitrust claims, in which federal subject-matter jurisdiction is exclusive.

(3) The Court divided sharply; no majority opinion or rationale supported the holding that mandamus was improper.

f. *Moses H. Cone Memorial Hospital v. Mercury Construction Corp.*, 460 U.S. 1 (1983), emphasized abstention's extraordinary nature. Hospital sued Mercury in state court, seeking a declaration that (1) it owed the company nothing under a contract and (2) that Mercury had waived its right to arbitrate the dispute. Nineteen days later, Mercury sued Hospital in federal court, invoking diversity jurisdiction and seeking to compel arbitration.

(1) The federal trial court stayed proceedings under *Colorado River*, deferring to the previously-filed state case. The Supreme Court held that abstention was not justified under any of the extant *Colorado-River* factors and added some factors.

(2) *Colorado-River* factors

The Court noted: (1) neither court had obtained jurisdiction over property; (2) the federal and state forums were in the same city; (3) a stay was not necessary to avoid piecemeal (not duplicative) litigation; and (4) although the state court action came first by nineteen days, the state court had not invested significant effort in the case.

(3) Additional factors

Moses Cone also noted that the federal case, although invoking diversity jurisdiction, did involve a federal issue (whether the Federal Arbitration Act compelled arbitration) that counseled against abstention. Finally, it noted that the state-court proceeding might not protect Mercury's rights; it was not clear that the federal statute would require a state court to compel arbitration, although the Act did compel it to stay litigation.

g. A district court has greater discretion to abstain when the federal litigant seeks declaratory judgment. Then abstention does not require a showing of the *Colorado-River* exceptional circumstances. The Declaratory Judgment Act gives the district court greater discretion to determine whether to declare the rights of the parties. *Wilton v. Seven Falls Co.*, 515 U.S. 277 (1995). Thus, *Colorado River* and its progeny did not affect the holding of *Brillhart v. Excess Insurance Co.*, 316 U.S. 491 (1942) (district court has great discretion to refuse to declare rights of litigants under Declaratory Judgment Act).

2. Rationale and Requirements of *Colorado-River* Abstention

a. Unlike other bases of abstention, *Colorado River* abstention does not so clearly protect federalism. Instead, a desire to avoid duplicative litigation justifies it.

b. The doctrine flies in the face of the well-established doctrine that parallel *in personam* proceedings usually proceed independently. The mere pendency of an overlapping case ordinarily does not justify abstention or an injunction to avoid wasteful duplicative litigation. *See supra* § II.A.4.d, at 190 *[R186]*. Both cases proceed, though the first judgment may have claim- or issue-preclusive effect on the other case. [R149]

c. Though the Court went to great lengths to emphasize the extraordinary nature of its *Colorado River* holding, many commentators questioned whether the case was as "extraordinary" as Justice Brennan's majority opinion said. Some felt that the *Colorado River* Court might have ordered abstention on *Burford* grounds, because of the state's complex regulatory scheme for adjudication of water disputes; involvement of the federal courts might disrupt that system. But the Court rejected *Burford*.

d. *Moses Cone* did not formally change the *Colorado River* factors, but it did establish that the presence of a federal question makes abstention less appropriate.

e. Moreover, *Moses Cone*'s message seems to be that *Colorado-River* abstention is truly extraordinary. Duplicative litigation is wasteful, but *Colorado River* abstention is not a general tool for avoiding waste. [R359]

IV. Injunctions of Federal Judicial Proceedings

A. By a Federal Court

1. The Anti-Injunction Act sharply limits federal courts' power to enjoin *state-court* proceedings. It does not apply to federal injunctions of federal-court proceedings.

2. A federal court enjoining another federal action does not implicate federalism, nor does it affront state courts.

3. Thus, a federal court has discretion to determine whether to enjoin litigants from proceeding in a parallel *in personam* federal case. Alternatively, a federal court may stay its own proceedings to allow parallel litigation to proceed. Either avoids duplicative federal litigation.

4. *Kerotest Manufacturing Co. v. C-O-Two Fire Equipment Co.*, 342 U.S. 180 (1952), acknowledged a federal court's broad discretion to stay its own proceedings but did not definitively address its power to enjoin another federal court's proceedings. The lower federal courts generally speak of equitable considerations of wise judicial administration in determining whether to enjoin parties from engaging in parallel federal litigation or to stay litigation in favor of a parallel federal case.

   a. In general, federal courts follow the first-filed rule, which provides that the court in which the first of related cases was filed should proceed. That court may enjoin the parties from proceeding in parallel federal litigation

b. Generally, courts in which later duplicative cases are pending stay their own proceedings to allow the first-filed action to proceed to judgment.

c. The first-filed rule is merely a default rule, however, and circumstances may make it appropriate for a later-filed case to proceed, with that court enjoining parties from litigating parallel federal cases. *See, e.g., Semmes Motors, Inc. v. Ford Motor Co.*, 429 F.2d 1197 (2d Cir. 1970).

5. A federal court that has attached property, either as the subject of litigation or as a basis for *in rem* or *quasi-in-rem* jurisdiction may enjoin litigants from proceeding in another federal court (or state) concerning that property.

B. By a State Court

1. As a general rule, state courts cannot enjoin in personam proceedings in a federal court. *Donovan v. City of Dallas*, 377 U.S. 408 (1964).

2. However, a state court may enjoin a federal proceeding when the state court has already attached property and federal litigation would interfere with the state court's jurisdiction. *Donovan v. City of Dallas*, 377 U.S. 408 (1964)

Chapter X

CLAIM AND ISSUE PRECLUSION IN THE FEDERAL SYSTEM

■ ANALYSIS

I. Introduction

In Civil Procedure, you studied claim and issue preclusion, also known, respectively, as res judicata and collateral estoppel. Both preclude relitigation of components of a valid judgment in a prior case. That valid final judgment may have claim- or issue-preclusive effect. Claim preclusion prohibits a claimant, after a valid, final judgment on the merits, from asserting the same claim against the same defendant more than once and also excludes unasserted claims arising from the same transaction or occurrence. Issue preclusion prohibits re-litigation of an issue from a prior case provided that the court (1) actually litigated the issue, (2) decided it, and (3) that the decision of the issue helps to explain (majority approach) or is essential to (minority approach) the prior judgment. This chapter concerns applying claim and issue preclusion to a judgment from a different judicial system from the one adjudicating a subsequent case. This implicates constitutional and statutory principles of full faith and credit as well as common-law principles regarding finality of litigation. For discussion the interaction of federal courts with state-court judgments (the *Rooker-Feldman* doctrine), *see infra* Ch. XII, § III.C, at 273-275 *[R187]*.

II. Full Faith and Credit and Related Common-Law Doctrines

A. Constitutional Provision

1. Article IV, § 1, provides, in part, that "Full Faith and Credit shall be given in each State to the . . . judicial Proceedings of every other State."
2. This applies only to successive cases in state courts, not federal courts.
3. This generally means that the court of the second state (Forum-2) must apply the claim and issue preclusion rules of the state that entered the judgment in the first case (F-1).

Example: A Connecticut state court (F-1) enters a valid final judgment in a case between P and D. The parties litigate again in New Jersey (F-2), and the issue is whether the Connecticut judgment has a claim- or issue-preclusive effect in the pending in New Jersey case. Under the Full-Faith-and-Credit Clause, the F-2 court must apply the F-1 court's claim- and issue-preclusion rules. This ensures that New Jersey gives the same effect to the judgment that Connecticut, the judgment-rendering state, would.

B. Statute—The Full Faith and Credit Act

1. Title 28 U.S.C. § 1738, known as the Full-Faith-and-Credit Act, provides, in part, that "judicial proceedings" of a "State, Territory, or Possession of the United States" shall have "the same full faith and credit in every court within the United States and its Territories and Possessions as they have by law or usage in the courts of each State, Territory, or Possession from which they are taken."

2. This provision extends the full-faith-and-credit obligation to federal courts in the situation in which the first judgment is from a state court and the subsequent case is in a federal court.

   a. The federal court must give the state court judgment the same "full faith and credit" as would the state court that rendered the judgment.

   b. This generally means that the federal court in the second case must apply the claim- and issue-preclusion rules of the state that entered the judgment in the first case.

Example: A Connecticut state court in enters a valid final judgment in a case between P and D. The parties litigate again, this time in New Jersey federal court, and the issue is whether the Connecticut judgment has claim- or issue-preclusive effect in the federal case. It does; the federal court must apply Connecticut's preclusion rules.

3. Section 1738 occasionally leads to imponderable questions.

Example: Doctors sued a professional association in state court, alleging denial of membership in the association in violation of state law. After the state court entered judgment against them, the doctors sued in federal court, alleging that their exclusion violated federal antitrust laws. Federal antitrust claims have exclusive federal jurisdiction, and thus plaintiffs could not have asserted then in the state case. Nonetheless, the Supreme Court held that the federal court had to determine whether law of the judgment-rendering state would find that the doctors violated the rules of claim preclusion. It was a strange undertaking: state law had to govern whether failure to assert a claim over which the state court lacked subject-matter jurisdiction meant that the subsequent federal action was improper. *Marrese v. American Academy of Orthopaedic Surgeons*, 470 U.S. 373 (1985).

4. Section 1738 may result in preclusion on issues within the federal courts' exclusive jurisdiction.

Example: A plaintiff class action in Delaware state court asserted state-law claims arising out of a tender offer and corporate acquisition. Settlement of the class action included release of any federal claims concerning the tender offer and acquisition. The Delaware court approved the settlement and entered a valid final judgment incorporating it. Some of the class members filed a second case in federal court, asserting federal securities law violations, which are within the federal courts' exclusive jurisdiction. The Delaware court could not have adjudicated those claims. Nonetheless, the Supreme Court held that because Delaware law ascribed claim-preclusive effect to the settlement judgment, a federal court must also. Class members who had failed to opt out could not assert their federal claims in federal court. The Supreme Court emphasized that § 1738 required this result. *Matsushita Elec. Indus. Co. v. Epstein*, 516 U.S. 367 (1996). *Matsushita* shows that federal statutes do not supersede § 1738 unless they clearly so provide.

The result should not have surprised anyone. Causes of action are property. A person can agree to give up property as part of a settlement. A settlement is a contract between the disputing parties. In class actions, the contract must have the class-action court's approval, but it is a valid contract. The fact that federal law created some of the property that is the subject of the settlement is irrelevant; federal law also creates patents and copyrights, and a person can buy, sell, or give up those items as part of a settlement.

a. Federal securities laws did not supersede, even partially, § 1738; the state-court judgment releasing exclusively federal claims was entitled to full faith and credit. Nothing in federal law evinced congressional intent to contravene the rules of preclusion or to prevent state-court litigants from voluntarily releasing federal claims in approved settlements. *Id.* The state court in *Matsushita* never adjudicated anything with respect to federal securities law.

b. The Civil Rights Statute, § 1983, *see infra* Ch. XIV, at 301-330 *[R188]*, does not make an exception to and is not exempt from the Full Faith and Credit Act. In actions under § 1983, federal courts must give issue-preclusive effect to state judgments. *Allen v. McCurry*, 449 U.S. 90 (1980).

c. Similarly, a federal court in a § 1983 suit must give claim-preclusive effect to a state judgment on claims that plaintiff could have raised in the state court case but did not. *Migra v. Warren City School District Board of Education*, 465 U.S. 75 (1984). [R357]

C. Situations Covered by Neither Full Faith and Credit Provision

1. Neither the constitutional nor the statutory provisions for full faith and credit applies when the initial judgment is federal. Both apply to state judgments.

2. Nonetheless, it is clear that a second court—state or federal—must apply federal claim- and issue-preclusion law to a federal judgment on a federal-question claim. *Heck v. Humphrey*, 512 U.S. 477, 488 n.9 (1994).

3. Whether a second court must apply federal preclusion law if the first judgment was in a diversity case is a more difficult issue. Lower courts split; some applied federal preclusion law and others applied preclusion law of the state in which the federal court sat. *Semtek International, Inc. v. Lockheed Martin Corp.*, 531 U.S. 497 (2001), addressed this issue.

   a. A California federal court, exercising diversity jurisdiction, dismissed the case on the basis of the California statute of limitations. Plaintiff brought a second case in Maryland state court; under Maryland law it was still timely.

b. The question was whether Maryland should dismiss the case under claim preclusion—specifically, whether a limitations dismissal is "on the merits," a requirement for claim preclusion.

c. FED. R. CIV. P. 41(b), concerning involuntary dismissals, provides that such dismissals are "on the merits" unless they rest upon jurisdiction, venue, or indispensable parties. The *Semtek* dismissal rested on none of those; the defendant argued that the dismissal was "on the merits" and claim preclusive.

d. The Supreme Court held that Rule 41(b) simply states a rule for determining whether a case can be re-filed in federal courts and does not embody preclusion doctrine. (So much for textualism.)

e. Instead, federal common law governs the effect of a federal judgment in a diversity case.

f. Although federal common law governed the question, the Supreme Court, noting that there was no need for national uniformity on this question, held that the federal common law would adopt the law of the state in which that federal court sat. California law makes a limitations dismissal not "on the merits," so the federal judgment in California had no claim-preclusive effect.

g. The Court thus took advantage of its ability to defer to state law in diversity cases while retaining the option of annulling the adoption if state law became hostile to federal interests. *See infra* Ch. XI, § VI.D.1.f, at 248-249 *[R189]*. [R211]

Review Questions (Part II; Chapters IV-X)

True or False Questions

1. **T or F** The scope of the current federal-question statute, 28 U.S.C. § 1331, is co-extensive with the scope of the "arising under" jurisdiction provision of Article III, § 2.

2. **T or F** P sues two defendants, D-1 and D-2, in a single case. P's claim against D-1 arises under federal law. P's claim against D-2 arises under state law. The claims against D-1 and D-2 arise from the same transaction. P and D-2 are citizens of the same state. A federal court can adjudicate P's claim against D-2 only if the claim against D-1 invokes exclusive federal-question jurisdiction.

3. **T or F** The supplemental jurisdiction statute, § 1367(a), permits supplemental jurisdiction to the same extent in diversity cases as it does in federal-question cases.

4. **T or F** The Constitution mandates the complete-diversity rule, which requires that in a diversity case, all plaintiffs be of diverse citizenship from all defendants.

5. **T or F** For purposes of diversity jurisdiction, a corporation generally has at most citizenship in two states, while an unincorporated association may have citizenship in an unlimited number of states.

6. **T or F** A lower federal court cannot hear any case that falls within the Supreme Court's original (trial) jurisdiction.

7. **T or F** The adequate-and-independent-state-ground doctrine concerning the Supreme Court's appellate jurisdiction rests entirely on the prohibition of advisory opinions.

8. **T or F** In interpreting the final-judgment requirement for appellate jurisdiction under 28 U.S.C. § 1257, the Supreme Court has allowed appeals of orders that do not terminate all state-court proceedings in the case.

9. **T or F** To meet the amount-in-controversy requirement in a diversity case, a plaintiff must establish to a legal certainty that her claim is worth $75,000 or more.

10. **T or F** For a class action to invoke diversity jurisdiction, each member of the class must assert a claim meeting the amount-in-controversy requirement for a diversity case.

11. **T or F** P, a citizen of State A, sues D, also a citizen of State A, in state court, alleging that D breached a contract by failing to build an incinerator for P at P's lake home. P alleges that D will defend by saying that federal law prohibits incinerators within twenty miles of a National Park, and alleges further that this federal law does not apply because P's lake home is more than twenty miles from a National Park. D removes

the case to federal court. The federal court will remand the case to state court.

12. **T or F** P, a citizen of State A, sues D, a citizen of State B, in a state court in State B, alleging breach of contract under state law and demanding damages of $80,000. D removes the case to federal court. P moves to remand. Assume that the removal and the motion to remand were timely. The federal court denies the motion to remand. The federal court ruled correctly.

13. **T or F** P, a citizen of the Netherlands, sues D, a citizen of the United States domiciled in France, in federal court. P asserts a state-law claim of $80,000. The case invokes alienage jurisdiction, but not diversity jurisdiction.

14. **T or F** P, a citizen of State A, sues D, a citizen of State B, in federal court, alleging diversity jurisdiction. P asserts five separate and completely unrelated claims against D. No single claim exceeds $20,000, but they total $76,000. The federal court lacks diversity jurisdiction because a plaintiff may not aggregate transactionally unrelated claims against a defendant.

15. **T or F** Under the well-pleaded-complaint rule, a federal court has subject-matter jurisdiction under § 1331 if the plaintiff's claim or the defendant's counterclaim arise under federal law.

Essay Question

The legislature of State A enacted the following statute: "Any conduct that would violate federal antitrust laws if conducted in interstate commerce constitutes a violation of this statute when occurring solely within this state."

Paul, a citizen of State A, sues under this state statute in federal court, seeking recovery of $88,000. In Claim 1, Paul sues two defendants: Monster Corporation and Goliath Corporation, both of which are citizens only of State A. He alleges that the they conspired to interfere with his business. None of the parties conducts any business outside State A. In Claim 2 in the same case, Paul joins an unrelated state-law claim against Monster for fraud.

You are a law clerk to the federal judge hearing the case. She wants to know whether the federal court has subject-matter jurisdiction over Claim (1) or Claim (2). Explain fully.

PART THREE

Federal Courts, Federalism and the States

■ ANALYSIS

Chapter XI

FEDERAL COMMON LAW

■ ANALYSIS

I. Introduction

Federal common law exists. There is a widespread misconception that *Erie Railroad Co. v. Tompkins*, 304 U.S. 64 (1938), said there was none. It did not. It instead said, "There is no federal *general* common law." *Id.* at 78 (emphasis added). The italicized word is important, and the sequence of words is important; to think of "general federal common law" is misleading. When federal common law does exist, state and federal judges must apply it in preference to state law (whether statutory or common law); the Supremacy Clause, art. VI, cl. 2, demands that result. This Chapter concerns (1) when it is permissible for federal common law to exist, and (2) how federal courts go about making it. The areas in which federal common law exists are reasonably clear, but the courts' reasoning in finding an issue within or without the scope of permissible federal common law is often difficult to fathom, and the results are often quite challenging to reconcile.

II. The Difference Between Federal Common Law and "Federal General Common Law"

Federal common law may legitimately exist in areas where the Constitution creates federal power. Those are predominantly the areas that art. I, § 8, enumerates. The vice of federal *general* common law—what made it illegitimate—was that federal courts announced it in areas where the Constitution does not grant federal power.

III. English Common Law, Common-Law Method, and the Constitution

To understand federal common law, one must understand the common-law process that the United States inherited from England. Today, when we speak of common law, we mean judge-made law, but common-law judges in England who announced rules of common law were not *making* law under the legal theory of the time.

A. At the 1789 Outset: Common Law = Natural Law

1. What the United States Supreme Court later called "general common law" was not of human creation. It was a form of eternal natural law, the principles of which existed for common-law judges to discover.

2. When a common-law judge had to decide an issue, he took a mental excursion among the principles of general common law, "found" the applicable principle, and, as it were, brought it back to the courtroom to govern the case.

3. The eighteenth-century English legal world would have been appalled by the suggestion that judges *made* law. The common law simply existed. *Guaranty Trust Co. v. York*, 326 U.S. 99, 102 (1945) ("Law was conceived as a 'brooding omnipresence' of Reason, of which decisions were merely evidence and not themselves the controlling formulations.").

B. Sources of Law in the United States

1. When the United States began to emerge as a nation, there were already two sources of law: state law (largely inherited from colonial law) and common law.
2. After ratification in 1788, there were three sources: state law, common law, and federal law.
3. State law and common law antedated federal law and, before federal law existed, governed everything in the American legal system.
4. When federal law arrived, it displaced (because of the Supremacy Clause) some law states had previously used.
5. One of the major battles at the Constitutional Convention raged over how much the Constitution should allow federal law to displace state law and common law—the dispute over the division of power between the central government and the states.
6. At the beginning, state law and common law were the "default" sources of the law. They still are. State law (including state common law) governs unless federal law (including legitimate federal common law) displaces it. *See infra* § III.C.5, at 238-239 *[R190]*.

C. The Supremacy Clause and Vertical Choice of Law

1. When confronting any choice-of-law problem, the first step is *always* to isolate the precise issue as to which the court must make a choice of law.
2. It is absolutely critical to understand that choice of law operates on an issue-by-issue basis, not a case-by-case basis. It is quite common for different laws to govern different issues in a single case.
   a. In diversity cases, state law usually (but not always, *see infra* § VII.C, at 265 *[R191]*) governs substantive issues, such as the elements of a claim or a defense.
   b. But the Federal Rules of Civil Procedure govern most procedural issues in a diversity case. [R196]
3. "Vertical choice of law" refers to choosing between state and federal law.
4. "Horizontal choice of law" refers to choosing among the laws of different states and, in some cases, choosing between state or federal law and the law of another country.
5. The Supremacy Clause, art. VI, cl. 2, is a vertical choice-of-law rule.
   a. When state and federal law conflict, supremacy requires that federal law govern; state law yields.
   b. State and federal judges must use applicable federal law—the Constitution, a federal statute, some lesser form of federal regulatory material, or federal common law to the extent that it exists and is constitutional.

c. Vertical choice-of-law issues arise predominantly, though not exclusively, in diversity cases.

d. Most (but not all) Supreme Court discussion of federal common law occurs in diversity cases. [R190]

IV. Common Law in the United States, 1789 to 1938

A. The Judiciary Act of 1789, § 34

1. Today the Rules of Decision Act (RDA), is at 28 U.S.C. § 1652:

   a. "The laws of the several states, except where the Constitution or treaties of the United States or Acts of Congress otherwise require or provide, shall be regarded as rules of decision in civil actions in the courts of the United States, in cases where they apply." [R193]

   b. It appears to say that unless there is a constitutional provision, federal statute, or treaty on a particular point, "[t]he laws of the several states" govern.

2. The Supreme Court does not read RDA so literally.

   a. It has made clear that there are areas in which federal courts may make federal common law without violating the Constitution, RDA, or *Erie*.

   b. Principally, federal common law can exist to effectuate congressional intent or protect uniquely federal interests in areas in which the Constitution confers power on the federal government.

B. The Original Approach to Common Law in the Federal Courts: *Swift v. Tyson*, 41 U.S. (16 Pet.) 1 (1842)

1. The Supreme Court did not fully discuss common law in the federal courts for more than half a century. When it did, it interpreted RDA's reference to "laws of the several states" to concern only "the positive statutes of the state, and the construction thereof adopted by the local tribunals, and to rights and titles to things having a permanent locality, such as the rights and titles to real estate, and other matters immovable and intra-territorial in their nature and character." *Id.* at 18.

2. *Swift* was an ordinary commercial case from New York, raising the question of whether a pre-existing debt could constitute consideration.

   a. New York case law appeared to say that it could not.

   b. The Supreme Court differed, relying on long-established English interpretation of general commercial law, which viewed a debt as valid consideration, making the underlying contract good.

   c. Justice Story's majority opinion clearly conceived common law as a body of law independent of any government.

   d. Thus, he concluded that federal courts were entitled to have their own opinions of what the common law was.

C. *Swift*'s Mischief

1. Astute lawyers were quick to seize the opportunity *Swift* presented.

   a. They would elect to sue (or, representing defendants, elect to remove if removal was possible) depending on whether the state courts' or the federal courts' views of the common law were more favorable to their clients.

   b. That is good legal practice, but it caused case outcomes to turn on accidents of citizenship. And in one famous case, citizenship was no accident.

2. *Black & White Taxicab & Transfer Co. v. Brown & Yellow Taxicab & Transfer Co.*, 276 U.S. 518 (1928) (*Taxicab*), shined a harsh light on forum shopping.

   a. Brown & Yellow wanted to have an exclusive license to pick up passengers on the railroad-owned station in Bowling Green, Kentucky. Both taxi companies were Kentucky corporations.

      (1) Kentucky's view of common law forbade that sort of arrangement.

      (2) The federal view of common law permitted such contracts.

   b. Brown & Yellow unincorporated in Kentucky, reincorporated in Tennessee, and sued in diversity in a Kentucky federal court.

      (1) The federal court ruled for Brown & Yellow.

      (2) Brown & Yellow clearly would have lost in the Kentucky state courts.

      (3) The Supreme Court affirmed, relying on *Swift*.

   c. Understand that forum shopping is entirely lawful. It is a duty that counsel owes client (within the rules, of course), and everyone, lawyer or not, does it. Think back to your childhood: when you needed a parent's permission for something, how did you decide which parent to ask? [194]

V. *Erie* and the Jurisprudential Shift

A. *Swift*'s Reign

For ninety-six years, under *Swift*'s authority, federal courts in all cases reached their own conclusions about the content of common law, and those conclusions often clashed with states' interpretations.

1. *Swift* rested on the notion that there is only a single common law and that federal judges were just as competent as state judges to divine what it was.

2. The *Swift* Court expected (but could not require) the state courts to adopt the federal courts' views. Supremacy did not apply because the

general common law was *not* federal law. This is an important point to keep in mind.

3. This connoted a certain lack of respect for state judges, since they and federal judges were, in theory, looking at the same body of common law. Consider the parity implications. (On the other hand, perhaps it was the state judges showing lack of respect for the federal judges. Recall Justice Brandeis's lament in *Erie*: "Experience in applying the doctrine of *Swift v. Tyson*, had revealed its defects, political and social; and the benefits expected to flow from the rule did not accrue. Persistence of state courts in their own opinions on questions of common law prevented uniformity. . . ." [R221]

B. *Swift*'s Demise

1. *Erie Railroad Co. v. Tompkins*, 304 U.S. 64 (1938), overruled *Swift*.
2. *Erie*, citing no constitutional text, held that the *Swift* doctrine, which the Court had created ninety-six years earlier, was unconstitutional.
    a. "We *merely* declare that in applying the doctrine this Court and the lower courts have invaded rights which in our opinion are reserved by the Constitution to the several states." 304 U.S. at 80 (emphasis added).
    b. Thus, *Swift* was not only a doctrine of arrogance that created confusion, but also was an unconstitutional usurpation of state power by the Supreme Court.
    c. Justice Brandeis's opinion for the Court made clear that RDA was not unconstitutional. It did not make clear what constitutional provisions *Swift* offended.
        (1) Some commentators think Brandeis was obliquely referring the Tenth Amendment, which reserves power to the states.
        (2) On the other hand, *Erie* declared:

        > Congress has no power to declare substantive rules of common law applicable in a state whether they be local in their nature or 'general,' be they commercial law or a part of the law of torts. And no clause in the Constitution purports to confer such a power upon the federal courts.

        304 U.S. at 78. That may refer not to the Tenth Amendment, but rather to art. I, § 8, which does not confer any authority on the federal government to make law in areas we now view as predominantly state preserves: *e.g.*, contracts, property, and torts. [R205A] [R208]

3. More important, *Erie* represents a shift in the Court's jurisprudential thinking.

   a. It moved from a natural-law approach to a legal-positivism approach, quoting Justice Holmes's dissent in the *Taxicab* case to illuminate what the Court called *Swift*'s fallacy:

      > The doctrine rests upon the assumption that there is "a transcendental body of law outside of any particular State but obligatory within it unless and until changed by statute," that federal courts have the power to use their judgment as to what the rules of common law are; and that in the federal courts "the parties are entitled to an independent judgment on matters of general law"—:
      >
      > "But law in the sense in which courts speak of it today does not exist without some definite authority behind it. The common law so far as it is enforced in a State, whether called common law or not, is not the common law generally but the law of that State existing by the authority of that State without regard to what it may have been in England or anywhere else."

   304 U.S. at 79 (quoting *Black & White Taxicab & Transfer Co. v. Brown & Yellow Taxicab & Transfer Co.*, 276 U.S. 518, 533-34 (1928) (Holmes, J., dissenting)).

   b. Understanding these words is critical to understanding *Erie*. Having banished natural law, the "transcendental body of law" to which Justice Holmes had referred, *Erie* reduced the sources of law in the United States to two: state law and federal law. [R141]

   c. Justice Brandeis declared, "There is no federal *general* common law." 304 U.S. at 78 (emphasis added).

4. *Erie* was a tort/property case with two issues. One was whether, as Tompkins walked on a footpath paralleling Erie's tracks, he was a licensee or a trespasser, because that affected the scope of Erie's duty to him. The other was whether Erie had been negligent.

   a. Under state law Tompkins was a trespasser.

   b. The general common law that existed until *Erie* discarded it would have viewed him as a licensee.

   c. Because the Court said that there was no federal lawmaking power applicable to the issues in *Erie* (tort and property law), state law governed by default. [R206]

5. As a method of approaching *Erie* (vertical) choice-of-law problems, consider beginning with a rebuttable presumption that state law governs every issue in every case. The question then is whether some applicable provision of federal law displaces the state law by supremacy.

a. Constitutional principles obviously do.

b. Federal statutes that are constitutional do also.

c. The same is true of any federal regulatory material—*e.g.* agency regulations or the Federal Rules of Civil Procedure—within the scope of Congress's delegation of rule-making power. (Remember, though, that a provision of the FRCP must be "directly on point." That is, if one thinks about the issue as a question, the Federal Rule must directly answer the question.)

d. The difficult questions arise primarily when there is federal power in an area but no federal regulatory material exists.

(1) Chief Justice Warren referred to this situation as "the typical unguided *Erie* Choice." *Hanna v. Plumer*, 380 U.S. 460, 471 (1965).

(2) Then the issue is whether it is permissible for federal courts to create governing common-law principles.

e. Despite Chief Justice Warren's words, there is a guiding principle that explains the cases. *See infra* § VII, at 262 *[R192]*.

6. *Erie* did *not* say, "There is no federal common law" The same day, the Court decided *Hinderlider v. La Plata River & Cherry Creek Ditch Co.*, 304 U.S. 92 (1938), holding that federal common law controlled the issue of whether to apportion an interstate stream between two states, and Justice Brandeis again wrote for the Court.

a. Federal law had to resolve such disputes between states to avoid the friction that choosing one state's law over another's would cause.

b. Although Congress has now taken over such apportionment issues under the Federal Water Pollution Control Act Amendments of 1972, *Hinderlider*'s broader significance, confirming that federal common law continues to exist after *Erie*, remains undimmed.

c. *Erie* holds only that there is no federal ***general*** common law; it did not forbid all federal common law.

d. There are circumstances justifying creating federal common law, but the Court has not been entirely clear in defining those circumstances or in stating the justifications for federal common law.

7. Justice Jackson's concurring opinion in *D'Oench, Duhme & Co. v. Federal Deposit Ins. Corp.*, 315 U.S. 447 (1942), discussed the propriety of federal common law:

> The federal courts have no general common law, as in a sense they have no general or comprehensive jurisprudence of any kind, because many subjects of private law which bulk large in the traditional common law are ordinarily within the province of the states

> and not of the federal government. But this is not to say that wherever we have occasion to decide a federal question which cannot be answered from federal statutes alone we may not resort to all of the source materials of the common law, or that when we have fashioned an answer it does not become a part of the federal non-statutory or common law.

315 U.S. at 469 (Jackson, J., concurring).

8. Reflect for a moment on the jurisprudential shift in the federal courts that *Erie* represents.

Before *Erie*	Common law = Natural law
After *Erie*	Common law ≠ Natural law Common law = state common law + federal common law

C. Federal Common Law and the Rules of Decision Act

1. The Rules of Decision Act, 28 U.S.C. § 1652, *see supra* § IV.A.1.a, at 239 *[R193]*, which *Swift* and *Erie* interpreted, speaks to vertical choice of law.

2. Since the beginning, the question has been what Congress intended by "laws of the several states." *Swift* said that did not include state common law; *Erie* says that it does. More than that: *Erie* says that it *must*, as a matter of constitutional law, unless the Constitution grants the federal government power in the area *and* either Congress or the courts have displaced the state law that would otherwise govern.

D. *Erie*'s Policy Considerations

1. The *Taxicab* Case, *see supra* § IV.C.2, at 240 *[R194]*, starkly illustrated *Swift*'s forum-shopping legacy. *Erie* was, at least in part, a reaction to that.

2. Justice Brandeis noted *Swift* "rendered impossible equal protection of the law."

   a. That was not an oblique reference to the Fourteenth Amendment, which applies only to state, not federal, action. Nor was it a reference to the Fifth Amendment, which had no equal-protection component until the Court recognized one in *Bolling v. Sharpe*, 347 U.S. 497 (1954), a District of Columbia companion case to *Brown v. Board of Education*, 347 U.S. 483 (1954).

   b. Nonetheless, it was a major concern. A plaintiff from State A suing a citizen of State B on a state claim in a court located in State B could evaluate whether state or federal law was more favorable to his claim and could choose the court accordingly.

c. Because a citizen of the forum cannot invoke diversity jurisdiction as a ground for removal, *see supra* Ch. VII § III.D.2, at 157 *[R195]*, the plaintiff's choice of forum was final.

3. Later opinions spoke of the "twin aims of the *Erie* rule: discouragement of forum-shopping and avoidance of inequitable administration of the laws." *Hanna v. Plumer*, 380 U.S. 460, 468 (1965).

   a. In fact, those "twin aims" are merely two sides of the same coin; forum-shopping created the inequitable administration of the laws. (It would be more accurate, though not grammatically proper, to refer to the "twin *aim* of *Erie*.")

   b. The policy point is clear: to the extent possible, federal courts should adjudicate state claims using the same laws that the state courts would use to decide the rights and obligations of the parties. The object is not to have the result change merely because the forum changes. [R207] [R209]

   c. Justice Frankfurter's opinion for the Court in *Guaranty Trust Co. v. York*, 326 U.S. 99, 108 (1945), went so far as to say, "a federal court adjudicating a state-created right solely because of diversity of citizenship of the parties is for that purpose, in effect, only another court of the State. . . ."

VI. How, When, and Why Federal Common Law Exists

A. Method of Analysis

1. When a federal court faces a vertical choice-of-law decision as to any *issue*, *see supra* § III.C.2, at 238 *[R196]*, in a case, it first must ask whether there is some federal constitutional, statutory, other regulatory provision, or extant federal common law that applies. If there is, the Supremacy Clause demands that it control the issue.

2. If there is no such provision, the federal court must always engage in a two-step process.

   a. Step 1 is to decide whether state law or federal law must govern the issue. This step is the vertical (or *Erie*) choice-of-law decision.

   b. Step 2 depends on the Step-1 decision.

      (1) If Step 1 resulted in state law applying, the court must figure out what the relevant state law is. That is easy if there is a state constitutional provision, statute, or other state regulatory material on point, or if the state's highest court has recently declared the relevant state law. Absent one of those things, figuring out the state law can be quite challenging.

      (2) If Step 1 resulted in federal law applying, the court must either apply existing federal common law or create a new federal common-law rule, and things become far less definite.

B. Techniques Courts Use to Create Federal Common Law

1. Judge Henry Friendly of the United States Court of Appeals for the Second Circuit identified four ways the federal courts approach creating federal common law.

   a. Spontaneous generation occurs when federal courts confront issues that federal legislation does not address and that state law cannot address, such as the law of interstate boundary disputes or the law applicable to the foreign relations.

   b. Recognizing a private federal right of action occurs when a federal statute or constitutional provision creates an individual right but no explicit enforcement mechanism for the individual.

   c. Sometimes the Supreme Court construes a jurisdictional grant to be an implicit congressional command that the federal courts create a body of federal common law in the subject area.

   d. In many circumstances, what Judge Friendly called "the normal filling of statutory interstices" (and he could said "statutory and common-law interstices") occurs. Statutes rarely can explicitly cover all variations of a problem that may arise; courts routinely attempt to apply what they perceive as the underlying purpose of the statute, consistent with its wording, to the new variations. [R65]

2. At one time or another, the Supreme Court has used each of these techniques.

   a. However, they do not all have the same justifications.

   b. The Court clearly favors some over the others.

      (1) Recognizing rights of action in statutes and construing jurisdictional grants to authorize common law raise important separation-of-powers issues. Recognizing rights of action in constitutional provisions (*e.g.* the Bill of Rights) is different. When the nation ratified the Constitution and the Bill of Rights, the maxim *ubi jus, ibi remedium* (where there is a right, there is a remedy) governed. Congress and the states that ratified the Bill intended it would be self-executing. The Supreme Court has recognized that on several occasions but does not always follow it. [R271]

      (2) Whenever a federal court creates federal common law, there is a potential clash with state law that would otherwise govern, raising federalism concerns.

C. The Reach of Federal Common Law

1. When federal common law exists, the Supremacy Clause dictates that it governs in state and federal courts. *Banco Nacional de Cuba v. Sabbatino*, 376 U.S. 398, 425 (1964).

2. A claim that arises under federal common law is a federal-question claim within the meaning of 28 U.S.C. § 1331. [R275]

3. Congress can override federal common law, *New Jersey v. New York*, 283 U.S. 336, 348 (1931), [R288] [R292] [R339] except when it cannot. *Financial Oversight and Management Board for Puerto Rico v. Centro de Periodismo Investigativo, Inc.*, 598 U.S. 339 (2023), ruled that a statute conferring jurisdiction on the Puerto Rico district court (48 U.S.C. § 2126(a)) could not apply (but did not rule that either the statute or applying the statute in the case would have been unconstitutional). The Eleventh Amendment by its own terms did not apply, because it refers only to "one of the United States." The Court has extended that to include state-level agencies, but Puerto Rico is neither of those. The Court majority "assume[d] without deciding that Puerto Rico is immune from suit in federal district court, and that the Board partakes of that immunity." The majority faulted Congress for not being specific enough in the jurisdiction statute that it intended to discard the Court-assumed immunity. The Court has demanded a "super-strong clear statement" if Congress wants to overcome a state's Eleventh Amendment immunity, but had never before applied that approach to common law, much less common law that the Court simply assumed. [R210]

D. The Techniques in Action

1. Spontaneous generation

   a. *Clearfield Trust Co. v. United States*, 318 U.S. 363 (1943), involved a stolen federal check cashed on a forged endorsement.

      (1) The issue was whether state or federal law governed the effect of the federal government's long delay notifying banks in the endorsement chain of the forgery.

      (2) Under state law, unreasonable delay barred recovery.

      (3) The Court held that federal law governed the issue, requiring Clearfield Trust to show actual prejudice from the delay.

      (4) The Court distinguished *Erie*. "When the United States disburses its funds or pays its debts, it is exercising a constitutional function or power." *Id.* at 366.

         (a) The problem in *Erie* was that no branch of the federal government had constitutional authority to prescribe tort or property rules.

         (b) Article I, § 8, cl. 1, gives Congress power to pay debts and thus to define the rules of federal commercial paper.

   b. In addition to emphasizing the constitutional basis for federal law, the Court discussed why it was necessary to have a uniform rule governing federal checks in all states.

c. Many commentators have criticized *Clearfield* because one might read it to allow federal common law to dominate any area in which there is federal power, whether or not Congress has acted to displace state law that would otherwise govern.

d. Some also have questioned why, when the federal government is acting in an essentially commercial capacity, such as when it issues checks, it is any more entitled to uniform law than private enterprises, which routinely must deal with varying states' laws.

e. However, that federal law must govern an issue—presumably to forestall state hostility to federal interests (parity?)—does not always lead to a uniform federal rule.

   (1) The Court often adopts state law as federal common law, and Congress occasionally specifies state law as the content of federal law.

   (2) This lessens potential conflict between state and federal rules while still leaving the federal government able to protect itself if state law becomes manifestly inconsistent with federal policy.

f. *United States v. Kimbell Foods, Inc.*, 440 U.S. 715 (1979), reaffirmed *Clearfield*'s declaration that federal law governs the United States' rights under national programs.

   (1) But it also adopted state law.

Borrower took a loan from Private Lender. The loan agreement included a standard clause (a "dragnet" clause) identifying Borrower's assets as collateral to secure future advances from Private Lender. Borrower subsequently secured a loan from Bank, which accepted the same collateral as security. The Small Business Administration (SBA) guaranteed 90% of that later loan. Borrower used Bank's loan to repay its original debt to Private Lender, but Borrower's later loans from Private Lender fell into arrears. Borrower then defaulted on the SBA-guaranteed loan. Private Lender began state-court proceedings against Borrower. Meanwhile, Bank assigned its security interest to the SBA. Borrower sold its assets; the proceeds went into escrow because of the competing Private-Lender and SBA claims on the funds.

Private Lender then began a federal action to foreclose its lien, claiming its security interest was superior to the SBA's. The critical issue was whether state or federal law governed the question of priority. The district court ruled that federal law governed and that the SBA had priority, analogizing the SBA's interest to federal tax liens, which get special priority. The government won. The circuit court reversed. It agreed that federal law governed the issue. (Both courts were following clear Supreme Court precedent that federal law had to govern the federal government's rights under nationwide federal programs.) But the circuit court differed on content of the federal law, looking instead to the UCC for priority rules. Private Lender won on appeal.

The Supreme Court agreed with the lower courts that federal law had to govern the priority issue. But it diverged from them, ruling that the federal courts should adopt state law as the content of the federal common law. [R356]

(2) The Court set down a three-part balancing test to decide whether to adopt state law as the content of federal common law.

(a) the federal need for a uniform, nationwide federal rule,

(b) the danger that using state law would disrupt a federal program or frustrate its objectives,

(c) whether creating a federal rule would disrupt commercial relationships formed under and predicated upon state law. [R219] [R275] [R189] [R205] [R211]

g. *Kimbell Foods* might first appear to retreat from *Clearfield*, but the cases are distinguishable.

(1) The federal government issues checks *en masse*; it does not negotiate with each payee the applicable law if something goes wrong. That would be impossible because of volume.

(2) *Kimbell Foods* involved collateral for an SBA loan.

(3) The government does negotiate SBA loans individually and thus can protect itself, for example by asking pre-existing lienholders to subordinate their liens to the federal lien.

h. *United States v. Yazell*, 382 U.S. 341 (1966), had applied state law in a similar circumstance involving an SBA loan, but the Court there explicitly declined to explain *why* state law governed. "Although it is unnecessary to decide in the present case whether the Texas law of coverture should apply *ex proprio vigore*—on the theory that the contract here was made pursuant and subject to this provision of state law—or by 'adoption' as a federal principle, it is clear that the state rule should govern." The Court did not explain when it might be necessary to decide. Thirteen years later, *Kimbell Foods*, 440 U.S. 715, 728 & n.22 (1979), characterized *Yazell* as an adoption case. Justice White, who wrote *Yazell*, was a member of the unanimous *Kimbell Foods* Court and said nothing.

i. Federal proprietary law continues to exist. *West Virginia v. United States*, 479 U.S. 305 (1987), applied a federal common-law rule calling for prejudgment interest on delayed contract payments.

(1) The Court applied the *Kimbell-Foods* balancing test, finding a need for uniformity, harm to Congress's policy under the Disaster Relief Act if state law applied, and no underlying commercial relationships.

(2) Justice Marshall, author of *Kimbell Foods*, wrote for the Court.

j. *Kimbell Foods*' approach highlights the distinct stages of the vertical choice-of-law analysis. *See supra* § VI.D.1.f, at 248-249 *[R197]*.

(1) The Court decided that federal law had to govern the priority issue (the *Erie* (vertical) choice-of-law question). That was the first-stage inquiry, but no extant federal law spoke to the question.

(2) For the second-stage inquiry, the Court therefore had to create federal common law to deal with the new priority question.

(3) *Clearfield*, *Yazell* (as *Kimbell Foods* interpreted it), *Kimbell Foods*, and *West Virginia* all concern the second stage, not the *Erie*-choice-of-law question. Note that in all four, federal law governed the issue.

k. In *Clearfield*, *Yazell*, *Kimbell Foods*, and *West Virginia*, the federal government or a federal agency was a party. When there is no federal party, federal common law nonetheless applies . . . sometimes.

Example 1: A bank brought a diversity action against a private party for conversion of federal bonds it alleged were stolen. The United States had guaranteed payment on the bonds. One of the main issues was which party had the burden of proof on the issue of defendant's good faith presenting the bonds for payment. State law controlled that issue. On the other hand, federal law controlled the issue of whether the bonds were "overdue." *Bank of America National Trust & Savings Association v. Parnell*, 352 U.S. 29 (1956). The result makes sense. "Overdueness" is a characteristic of the federal bond itself. In a conversion case, however, the issue is rightful possession (usually, but not always, ownership), clearly an issue of state property and tort law. The fact that federal law created the property is no more reason for federal law to govern the ownership issue than for federal law to govern whether a pickpocket who takes someone else's currency is guilty of theft.

Example 2: Survivors of deceased air passengers brought a diversity case against a municipality, arguing that they were third-party beneficiaries of a contract between the municipality and the

Federal Aviation Administration. Under the contract, the municipality agreed only to conduct activities around the airport compatible with normal aircraft operations. The municipality breached the contract by maintaining a garbage dump near the airport. The dump attracted birds, and an aircraft's engines ingested some of them, causing the crash. State law governed the plaintiffs' potential rights as third-party beneficiaries of the contract and interpretation of the contract. The obviously substantial federal interest in regulating aircraft did not compel a federal common-law rule to govern the private actions. *Miree v. DeKalb County*, 433 U.S. 25 (1977).

Example 3: Plaintiff filed a libel suit against a former Navy officer because of an official report the officer had filed criticizing Plaintiff, then a civil employee of the Navy. The issue was whether the allegedly defamatory statements were privileged. Federal law controlled whether that issue because the case implicated important federal interests (military functioning) and filing the report was a part of the officer's duties. *Howard v. Lyons*, 360 U.S. 593 (1959).

Example 4: The estate of a United States Marine helicopter pilot, who drowned when his helicopter crashed, filed a diversity case alleging a state tort claim that the defendant, a private company that produced the helicopter under a contract from the federal government, had defectively designed the emergency escape-hatch system. The defendant invoked a new, federally recognized, common-law military-contractor defense, which preempted state tort law. *Boyle v. United Technologies Corp.*, 487 U.S. 500 (1988). *Boyle* seemed to establish a two-part inquiry: (1) whether the case involves a "uniquely federal interest," and, if so, (2) whether there is a significant conflict between the federal interest and state law that would otherwise apply.

Example 5: *Kamen v. Kemper Financial Services, Inc.*, 500 U.S. 90 (1991), involved a shareholder's derivative suit for securities fraud under federal law. The Court concluded that federal common law permitted the plaintiff to proceed without making a demand on the corporation if the demand would be futile and that federal law governed the issue of futility. Because the claim was federal, "any common law rule necessary to effectuate a private cause of action under that statute is necessarily federal in character." *Id.* at 98. However, corporate law is an area in which private parties expect state law to govern their relationship, so the Court adopted state law as the content of the federal common law, finding that adoption was not inconsistent with the federal policy underlying the claim.

l. The fact that a federal agency is a party does not guarantee that federal law governs. *O'Melveny & Myers v. Federal Deposit Ins. Corp.*, 512 U.S. 79 (1994), rejected the argument that federal common law should apply because the FDIC was a party to the litigation (acting as receiver for a failed bank). The Court found that applying state law could have no adverse impact on any federal policy or interest and left state law in place. *O'Melveny* may indicate a more restrictive view of federal common law in cases involving federal agencies that do not affect their day-to-day operations.

2. Recognizing Private Rights of Action

a. In statutes

Early English and American courts assumed that rights corresponded with remedies, so it was commonplace for courts to enforce rights without conceptualizing rights and remedies as distinct entities and without speaking separately of causes of action.

(1) This was in accord with the ancient maxim *ubi jus ibi remedium*: "[w]here there is a right, there is a remedy." One might sensibly ask what it means to have a "right" that is unenforceable. In 1799, the Supreme Court said, "[I]t is monstrous to talk of existing rights, without applying correspondent remedies."

Example: A switchman suffered an injury on the job and sued under the Federal Safety Appliance Acts because a defective handrail had caused him to fall and be injured. The Court made clear the reigning theory of the time:

> A disregard of the command of the statute is a wrongful act, and where it results in damage to one of the class for whose especial benefit the statute was enacted, the right to recover the damages from the party in default is implied * * * . This is but an application of the maxim, *Ubi jus ibi remedium.*

Texas & Pacific Railway Company v. Rigsby, 241 U.S. 33 (1916).

(2) During the twentieth century, the Supreme Court began separating the two. Eventually, the Court began to speak of rights, rights of action, and remedies as separate entities, leading to more restrictive approaches to recognizing remedies for violations of individual rights. Today's Court does not seem to think refusing a remedy is monstrous at all.

Example 1: Plaintiff-shareholder sued concerning a merger of the corporation, allegedly accomplished by use of false and misleading proxy statement. A federal statute made it unlawful to include fraudulent assertions in a proxy statement but did not explicitly provide a private right of action. The Supreme Court concluded that the plaintiff could proceed. A purpose of the statute was to protect investors from deceptive disclosures in proxy materials, "which certainly implies the availability of judicial relief where necessary to achieve that result." *J.I. Case v. Borak*, 377 U.S. 426, 432 (1964).

Example 2: A federal statute mandated criminal penalties for corporations that violated federal election laws. Plaintiff sought to assert a shareholder-derivative claim as a private right of action under the statute. The Court refused, based on four factors: (1) whether plaintiff is "one of a class for whose 'especial benefit' the statute was enacted"; (2) whether there is "any indication of legislative intent, explicit or implicit, either to create such a remedy or to deny one"; (3) whether an implied right of action would be consistent with the legislation's underlying purpose; and (4) whether the claim is one "traditionally relegated to state law, in an area basically the concern of the States, so that it would be inappropriate to infer a cause of action based solely on federal law." *Cort v. Ash*, 422 U.S. 66 (1975).

Example 3: Title IX of the Education Amendments of 1972 prohibits discrimination in education on the basis of sex. *Cannon v. University of Chicago*, 441 U.S. 677 (1979), applied the four *Cort* factors and found that Cannon, who asserted the University denied her admission to medical school because of her sex, had a private right of action.

Example 4: *California v. Sierra Club*, 451 U.S. 287 (1981), narrowed the focus. Justice White's majority opinion read the four *Cort* factors as bearing on the critical question of whether Congress intended there be a private right of action and, finding "no such indication," refused to recognize a claim. Justice Stevens's concurring opinion is noteworthy, because he believed the enacting Congress did intend there to be a claim, but nonetheless concurred in deference to the Court's *Cort* method.

Example 4: The Parental Kidnaping Prevention Act requires states to enforce child-custody decrees from other states provided the judgments are consistent with the Act. A California court decreed that Husband should have custody; a Louisiana court decreed that Wife should have custody. Husband sued in federal court and attempted to assert a claim under the Act. The Act contained no express right of action, and the Supreme Court refused to recognize one. *Thompson v. Thompson*, 484 U.S. 174, 187 (1988).

b. In constitutional provisions

Recognizing private rights of action in constitutional provisions has followed a similar arc. *Trustees of Dartmouth College v. Woodward*, 17 U.S. (4 Wheat.) 518 (1819), recognized that the Trustees could sue directly under art. I, § 10, cl. 1 (the Impairments Clause). In 1933, a unanimous Court recognized a private right of action in the Fifth Amendment under the Takings Clause, *Jacobs v. United States*, 290 U.S. 13 (1933), the opinion declaring "[s]tatutory recognition was unnecessary.") *Id.* at 16. The Court followed (but did not mention) *Jacobs* by recognizing private rights of action in three other Bill of Rights provisions in the 1970s and 1980s. Since then, the Court has become far more reluctant—hostile, really—to doing so and recently suggested it might have decided the three precedents differently had they arisen today.

(1) *Bivens v. Six Unknown Named Agents of the Federal Bureau of Narcotics*, 403 U.S. 388 (1971), *see infra* Ch. XIV, § V.B.1, at 324 *[R198]*, recognized a private damage remedy against federal officers for a violation of the Fourth Amendment's prohibition of unreasonable searches and seizures, even though (1) the Amendment makes no reference to any remedy, and (2) Congress has not provided one. (The search revealed nothing, and Bivens faced no charges.) **Terminology note:** It is now common to refer to most claims for individual relief for federal violation of constitutional provisions as "*Bivens* claims" whether or not they involve the Fourth Amendment.

(a) The Court concluded that the lack of congressional remedy was no bar to recognizing the damages claim when the judiciary concludes such a remedy is an appropriate means of enforcing a constitutional right.

(b) It seems likely that Bivens having no recourse at all without a damages claim influenced the Court. Injunctions are forward looking, offering no relief when the harm is complete, and Bivens probably could not have gotten one anyway, because the unconstitutional behavior was unlikely to recur.

(c) The Founders, who wrote the Constitution and the Bill of Rights, and the states that ratified them, were all quite familiar with English law; it was, after all, their background and heritage. A decade before the Revolution, the King's Bench had decided a significant constitutional case, *Entick v. Carrington*, (1765) 95 Eng. Rep. 807 (K.B.). At the direction of the Secretary of State, English officials conducted a search of a residence pursuant to what amounted to a general warrant. The homeowner sued everyone involved and received a handsome damages award. (In 2017 dollars, the damages amounted to roughly $80,000 against officials who executed the warrant and $320,000 against the Secretary of State.) The search had violated the (unwritten) English constitutional provision similar to our Fourth

Amendment. There was no mention of any sort of immunity in the opinion; the offending officials stood before the King's Bench not as the King's officials, but as individuals who had violated the King's law. Three other British cases from the 1760s are consistent with *Entick*. None are inconsistent.

(d) *Bivens* potentially raises a separation-of-powers issue, which Justice Harlan's concurrence addressed. Perhaps it is Congress's role, not the courts', to create rights of action to enforce constitutional guarantees. That is troubling; if Congress created the rights in the first place, it might be able to limit their scope, but it is unlikely that the Founders included the Bill of Rights in the Constitution but left their enforceability to the political winds of later Congresses. Justice Harlan concluded that the judiciary had authority to recognize a remedy in the case, noting that the judiciary had long recognized injunctive remedies against an officer who acted unconstitutionally, ordering the officer to cease the unconstitutional behavior or face contempt.

(e) A *Bivens* action lies against the individual federal actors and seeks to impose individual liability for damages in their personal capacities. The action is not against the United States, so it does not implicate the federal government's asserted sovereign immunity.

(f) Federal courts have subject-matter jurisdiction over *Bivens* claims under the federal-question statute, § 1331 and often under § 1343; there is no amount-in-controversy requirement in either, although § 1331 had the same one as diversity claims until 1980.

(g) *Bivens* mentioned two factors that might prevent implying a private right of action:

(i) "[S]pecial factors counseling hesitation in the absence of affirmative action by Congress" might preclude implying a private right of action on the *Bivens* model. *Bivens*, 403 U.S. at 396.

(ii) The absence of any "explicit congressional declaration that persons injured by a federal officer's violation of the Fourth Amendment may not recover money damages from the agents, but must instead be remitted to another remedy, equally effective in the view of Congress," influenced the Court. *Id.* at 397. This suggests that Congress could repeal or modify a *Bivens* claim, but seems to require a clear statement of congressional intent to do so.

(h) *Bivens* was a Fourth Amendment case. Some observers concluded that the Court might recognize a common law claim for damages for any constitutional violation deprivation under color of federal law. This raised the question of whether Congress might attempt to nullify or limit the *Bivens* claim and whether the Court might refuse to recognize *Bivens* claims in other circumstances. [R401].

(2) *Davis v. Passman*, 442 U.S. 228 (1979), recognized a *Bivens* claim against a Congressman for sex discrimination and treated *Jacobs* as settled law. *Id.* at 242. The allegations stated a violation of the equal-protection component of the Fifth Amendment that the Court had recognized in *Bolling v. Sharpe*, 347 U.S. 497 (1954), a companion case to *Brown v. Board of Education*, 347 U.S. 483 (1954).

(a) The Court recognized the claim even though Title VII of the Civil Rights Act of 1964 offered remedies for employment discrimination. Congress amended the statute in 1972 to permit most federal employees to sue, but it left congressional employees out.

(b) Although the statutory scheme arguably demonstrated that Congress had decided that a person in the plaintiff's situation should not have a claim under Title VII, the Court was undeterred, and seemed, according to some commentators, to imply that *Bivens* claims should exist for all constitutional rights.

(3) *Carlson v. Green*, 446 U.S. 14 (1980), permitted a federal prisoner to sue a federal prison official for alleged infliction of cruel and unusual punishment, an Eighth Amendment violation. The Court reiterated the two *Bivens* factors that could defeat a claim but concluded that they did not preclude the suit. A *per curiam* Court reaffirmed *Carlson* in November, 2020. On the other hand, *Correctional Services Corporation v. Malesko*, 534 U.S. 61 (2001), refused to allow a *Carlson* claim in an action against a private company running a federal correctional facility.

(a) Although Congress had recently amended the Federal Tort Claims Act (FTCA) to permit persons in the plaintiff's position to sue the United States, the Court rejected the notion that Congress had enacted a remedy it thought as effective as a *Bivens* claim.

(b) The *Bivens* claim gave the plaintiff several advantages not available under the FTCA. First, he could sue the officer rather than the United States. Second, he could recover punitive damages. Third, he had a right to jury trial. Fourth, he would not have to exhaust administrative remedies before suing. Thus, the Court concluded, a *Bivens* claim was a superior deterrent to unconstitutional behavior than the FTCA claim. [R288]

c. Since *Carlson*, however, the Court used congressional action and inaction as reasons for refusing to recognize additional *Bivens* claims. These cases recognize a broader legislative power to prevent private actions to enforce constitutional rights.

Example 1: In *Bush v. Lucas*, 462 U.S. 367 (1983), a federal employee, sued for First Amendment violation, alleging that he was demoted for making comments to the press about the facility where he worked that his superior alleged to be false. Congress had established an elaborate set of civil-service remedies. Although those remedies did not afford a jury trial or recovery for emotional distress, the Court noted that the claim arose from a government relationship controlled by comprehensive remedial provisions against the United States. These were "special factors counseling hesitation."

Example 2: *Schweiker v. Chilicky*, 487 U.S. 412 (1988), refused to permit a Fifth Amendment suit for unconstitutional denial of welfare disability benefits. Plaintiffs had succeeded in administrative review proceedings to have payments reinstated and to recover wrongfully withheld benefits. They could not, however, seek compensatory damages for harm the denial of benefits caused. The Court concluded that "Congress has provided *what it considers* adequate remedial mechanisms for constitutional violations" (emphasis added); that ended the matter, despite the majority's recognition that "[t]he trauma to respondents, and thousands of others like them, must surely have gone beyond what anyone of normal sensibilities would wish to see imposed on innocent disabled citizens." *Id.*, at 428-29. Thus, *Chilicky* makes clear that it is Congress's job, not the courts', to decide whether the congressional remedy is "equally effective." That seems to collide with *City of Boerne v. Flores*, 521 U.S. 507 (1977), which held that Congress cannot affect the scope of a constitutional provision. If Congress decides what is "equally effective," it does have a role in determining scope.

Example 3: "Special factors counseling hesitation" appear to preclude *Bivens* suits involving the military. *See United States v. Stanley*, 483 U.S. 669 (1987) (denying a right to sue for victim having been given LSD unknowingly, as part of an Army experiment on humans concerning the hallucinogenic drug); *Chappell v. Wallace*, 462 U.S. 296 (1983) (denying enlisted troops a right to sue for racial discrimination by officers). Without excessive elaboration, the Court found that claims involving military service, coupled with an absence of congressional remedy, counseled hesitation.

d. "Disfavored Activity"

Ziglar v. Abbasi, 582 U.S. 120 (2017), traced some of the history of recognizing private rights of action on statutes and constitutional provisions, noting that the criteria for such implication have substantially merged. It characterized judicial recognition of private rights of action in constitutional provisions as " 'disfavored' judicial activity." It did not, however, overrule *Bivens*, *Passman*, or *Carlson*, and it ignored *Jacobs v. United States*.

But as a practical matter, *Egbert v. Boulé*, 596 U.S. 482 (2022), overruled all four cases. The Court refused to allow a *Bivens* action over a palpable Fourth Amendment violation that resulted from a U.S. Border Patrol agent's visit to Boulé's home. There was no warrant. When Egbert arrived (following a phone call from Boulé about a visitor from Turkey who was arriving at Boulé's house), Boulé directed him to leave, and Egbert responded with violence. He determined that there was no illegal activity and left. The facts paralleled the facts in *Bivens* with two exceptions: (1) the locale was at the Washington/Canada border rather than New York City, and (2) the level of force in *Boulé* was greater. (Justice Sotomayor's dissent noted that *Boulé* was simply *Bivens* at the border.) The Court ordered the case dismissed. Harking back to *Ziglar v. Abbasi*, the majority stated, "[W]e have indicated that if we were called to decide *Bivens* today, we would decline to discover *any* implied causes of action in the Constitution." *Id.* at 502 (emphasis added). Thus, without quite saying so, the Court overruled *Jacobs*, *Bivens*, *Davis v. Passman*, *Carlson*, and *Bolling v. Sharpe*.

Boulé leaves no doubt that the Bill of Rights amendments will avail constitutional victims nothing against federal actors unless Congress decides to create a statutory right of action as it did with respect to state actors in 42 U.S.C. § 1983. The Court made no reference to the fact that several of the original states ratified the Constitution only on the understanding that individual-rights amendments—not mere statutes—would follow. And so, *Boulé* leaves at least two questions in its wake. First, why did some states insist on embedding certain rights in the Constitution rather than leaving the job of protecting them to future congresses? Second, did those who supported and ratified the Bill of Rights understand and intend that they would be toothless unless Congress acted? [R247] [R373A]

e. Procedural Issues in Cases Asserting *Bivens* Claims

(1) As in § 1983 cases, a *Bivens* plaintiff generally need not exhaust administrative remedies before suing. (The Prison Litigation Reform Act does apply in *Bivens* cases, so a federal prisoner must exhaust administrative remedies in accord with the Act. *See infra* Ch. XIV, § II.B.2, at 304 *[R199]*.) [R382]

(2) Title 42 U.S.C. § 1988(a) directs federal courts in several circumstances, including § 1983 cases, to look to state law when the federal law is deficient. *See infra* Ch. XIV § III.H.1, at 314 *[R200]*. But § 1988 does not apply to *Bivens* claims. Thus, federal common law, not state law, fills most of the law's gaps. There is no statute permitting a court to award attorney's fees to the prevailing party in a *Bivens* case, unlike in § 1983 cases. *See infra* Ch. XIV § III.G.4, at 314 *[R201]*.

(a) Federal common law governs limitations periods, although the court may adopt state law. *See infra* § VI.D.4 at 261-262 *[R202]*, Ch. XIV, § III.H.3 at 315 *[R203]*.

(b) Federal common law governs issues such as survival of the claim after death of a claimant.

(3) Immunities from suit are basically the same as in § 1983 litigation. *See infra* Ch. XIV § IV, at 316-323 *[R204]*; *Harlow v. Fitzgerald*, 457 U.S. 800 (1982) (discussing qualified immunity of executive officials in a *Bivens* case).

3. Construing jurisdictional grants and statutes that speak in general terms as commands or authorizations to create federal common law

a. In *Textile Workers Union v. Lincoln Mills*, 353 U.S. 448 (1957), a labor union sued to compel an employer to arbitrate a dispute under a collective bargaining agreement.

(1) Section 301 of the Labor Management Relations Act (a/k/a Taft-Hartley Act) granted federal subject-matter jurisdiction over suits for violations of such contracts, but provided no rules for determining the dispute.

(2) The Supreme Court held that the jurisdictional statute "authorizes federal courts to fashion a body of federal law for the enforcement of these collective bargaining agreements. . . ." 353 U.S. at 451.

b. The Court has developed other extensive bodies of federal common law as well (*e.g.* ERISA, antitrust), though not justifying them through jurisdictional statutes. For example, the Sherman Antitrust Act, 15 U.S.C. § 1 makes unlawful "[e]very contract, combination in the form of trust or otherwise, or conspiracy, in restraint of trade or commerce among the several States, or with foreign nations." There are no specifics. The Court has developed a vast area of federal common law interpreting the statute.

c. It is well established that federal courts have authority to develop a federal common law of admiralty.

(1) The source of that authority is unclear; perhaps Article III, § 2, extending the federal "judicial power" to "all cases of admiralty and maritime jurisdiction" undergirds it. If so, admiralty is another area in which the federal courts can create federal common law without statutory authorization.

(2) One may question, however, why the extension of the federal judicial power to admiralty supports the conclusion that federal courts can develop federal common law to furnish its substantive content, although art. I, § 8, cl. 10 may provide some faint support. The federal "judicial power" also extends to diversity, but *Erie* made clear that federal courts lacked authority to develop substantive common law in diversity cases except in areas in which the Constitution allows the federal government to exercise power.

(3) Originally, federal court authority to create a federal common law of admiralty did not apply to inland waterways. However, by 1851, the Supreme Court had extended the authority to include these waters.

(4) Federal courts do not develop a distinct federal common-law standard in every admiralty case. Rather, the Supreme Court uses a balancing test to decide whether federal common law should displace otherwise applicable state law. It is not clear how the Court has drawn the line in various cases; that has led to substantial confusion.

Example 1: *Southern Pacific Co. v. Jensen*, 244 U.S. 205 (1917), overturned a state workers' compensation award to relatives of a deceased stevedore because using state law would undermine the uniformity of federal maritime law. This view is no longer absolute, allowing state law a significant, albeit uncertain, role in the maritime area.

Example 2: State law requiring unemployment compensation contributions from employers of individuals working on navigable waters applies, even though federal common law could conceivably have controlled. *Standard Dredging Corp. v. Murphy*, 319 U.S. 306 (1943).

Example 3: On the other hand, federal common law, not state law, applied to a suit by a crew member's guest injured aboard a ship berthed in New York. *Kermarec v. Compagnie Generale Transatlantique*, 358 U.S. 625 (1959).

Example 4: Texas law applied to an insurance-coverage issue with respect to a houseboat fire occurring on an inland lake between Texas and Oklahoma, even though the case fell within the federal admiralty jurisdiction. *Wilburn Boat Co. v. Fireman's Fund Insurance Co.*, 348 U.S. 310 (1955).

Example 5: But federal common law applied to a diversity suit between a seaman and a ship-owner for breach of an oral agreement to assume liability for improper medical treatment. *Kossick v. United Fruit Co.*, 365 U.S. 731 (1961).

Example 6: *Exxon Corp. v. Central Gulf Lines, Inc.*, 500 U.S. 603 (1991), rejected a *per se* rule excluding agency contracts from admiralty jurisdiction. Instead, "lower courts should look to the subject matter of the agency contract and determine whether the services performed under the contract were maritime in nature." *Id.* at 612.

4. Filling in statutory interstices

Legislatures cannot anticipate all possible fact patterns or all possible applications of statutes. For centuries courts have interpreted statutes phrased in general terms to apply them in specific cases. Occasionally, a legislature even formally recognizes interstices' existence, the best example being 42 U.S.C. § 1988, which commands courts (state and federal) in cases where civil rights laws "are not adapted to the object, or are deficient in the provisions necessary to furnish suitable remedies and punish offenses against law" to extend and apply common law, using the common law of the state in which the federal court sits as a starting point.

Example 1**:** The Civil Rights Statute, 42 U.S.C. § 1983, creates a private right of action for violations of federal law "under color of state law" but specifies no limitations period for such claims. *Wilson v. Garcia*, 471 U.S. 261 (1985), directed federal courts to apply the personal-injury limitations period of the state in which the court sits. (Note that this also is an instance of adopting state law as the content of federal common law. *See supra* § VI.D.1.e, f, at 248-249 *[R205].*) One result of adoption is that § 1983 claims, which are federal, have a longer life-span in some states than in others. Congress could end that situation but has not, though it has provided a uniform federal statute of limitations for statutes it enacted after December 1, 1990. *See* 28 U.S.C. § 1658.)

Example 2**:** Some Chicago public schools suspended students without procedural due process. Section 1983 creates a cause of action for constitutional deprivations under color of state law, but says nothing about measures of damages. Reversing the Seventh Circuit's authorization of "substantial non-punitive damages" in the absence of any showing of actual harm from the violations, *Carey v. Piphus*, 435 U.S. 247 (1978), held that the students were entitled only to nominal damages (≤ $1.00) unless they showed specific harm. [R202]

VII. Deciding Whether to Create Federal Common Law: The Evolving Process

A. "Substantive" and "Procedural" Law

1. Much of the discussion of the *Erie* doctrine speaks of whether an issue is substantive or procedural, as if that were a neat dichotomy.
2. But those terms are neither self-defining nor neatly separated. The same issue may be substantive for one purpose and procedural for another—even in the same case. Some commentators view those adjectives as not analytically useful, but rather as labels pasted after the fact on decisions that actually rest on often unexpressed analysis.
3. The discussion appears to flow from the only appearance of "substantive" in *Erie*'s majority opinion: Justice Brandeis's declaration that Congress has no power to create substantive rules in non-federal areas. *See supra* §§ V.B.2.c(2) , at 241 *[R205A]*, V.B.4, 242 respectively *[R206]*.

B. Trying to Tell the Difference

1. *Erie* was an easy case to characterize. It had aspects of tort law (negligence) and aspects of property law (landowners' duties to persons on the land). No one would call those procedural issues.
2. Seven years later, the Court attempted to define "substantive" for *Erie* purposes.
   a. *Guaranty Trust Co. v. York*, 326 U.S. 99 (1945), revolved around a statute-of-limitations issue.
      (1) Under state law, the action was untimely.
      (2) Under the federal law of laches, it might survive.
      (3) There was no question that there could be federal law in the area; Congress certainly has the power to pass limitations periods for federal-court actions (and now has; *see* 28 U.S.C. § 1658).
      (4) That is why Justice Frankfurter's opinion for the Court spoke of *Erie*'s *policy*, *see supra* § V.D.3.b, at 245 *[R207]*, rather than its constitutional imperative. *See supra* § V.B.2, at 241 *[R208]*.
      (5) The Court noted that the issue was outcome-determinative, and, reflecting on *Erie*'s policy, *see supra* § V.D.3.b, at 245 *[R209]*, declared that since the state court would dismiss the case, the federal court should also. The statute-of-limitations issue was thus "substantive" for *Erie* purposes.

3. *York*'s outcome-determinative approach proved too much, and it began to prevent applying some of the Federal Rules of Civil Procedure in diversity cases. After all, violating any procedural rule may cause dismissal; that is about as outcome-determinative as possible. *York*'s test was simply too blunt an instrument.

4. *Byrd v. Blue Ridge Rural Electrical Cooperative, Inc.*, 356 U.S. 525 (1958), shifted course. When no regulatory material guides the court's path, it should weigh the state's interest in its common-law rule against the federal interest in having its own common-law rule. Outcome-determinativeness is a consideration (on the state side of the balance), but is not dispositive.

    a. *Byrd*'s issue was whether the judge (state law) or the jury (federal law) should decide if the plaintiff was a statutory employee and therefore limited to workers' compensation in place of a common-law remedy.

    b. The Court ruled that the distribution of functions within the federal courts was of enormous importance to the federal government and downplayed the possible importance of the state rule to the state. Having found the federal interest dominant, the Court applied the federal rule. [R192]

5. *Hanna v. Plumer*, 380 U.S. 460 (1965), split issues concerning the Federal Rules of Civil Procedure from the *Erie* line of cases. (Nonetheless, FRCP choice-of-law issues still come under the general rubric of "the *Erie* doctrine," which refers to all vertical choice-of-law situations.)

    a. RDA does not govern the FRCP or their applicability.

    b. The proper referent for questions concerning a Federal Rule's legitimacy or applicability is the Rules Enabling Act (REA), 28 U.S.C. § 2072.

    c. REA requires only that the FRCP "not abridge, enlarge or modify any substantive right." The Court has read that limitation narrowly, declining to declare a Federal Rule either inapplicable or illegitimate merely because applying it *affects* enforcement of some substantive right; virtually all procedural rules do.

    d. A Federal Rule of Civil Procedure governs if it is directly on point, that is, if it expressly answers the question the case poses. In *Hanna*, the question was how to make service of a summons on the executor of an estate. FED. R. CIV. P 4 specified a method, and plaintiff complied. State procedure called for a different method, with which plaintiff had not complied. Applying the state rule would have resulted in dismissal. The Court applied the federal rule, despite the fact that the choice of federal rather than state law was clearly outcome-determinative.

6. Subsequent cases in the *Erie* (non-FRCP) line exemplify *Byrd*'s approach.

   a. *Walker v. Armco Steel Co.*, 446 U.S. 740 (1980), applied state law to the issue of what stops the state statute of limitations from running out.

      (1) F.R. 3 is silent about statutes of limitations; it merely says that filing commences the case. The case involved a state tort claim.

      (2) There being no dominant federal interest in how long the state claim survived, the Court applied the state rule.

   b. *Gasperini v. Center for Humanities, Inc.*, 518 U.S. 415 (1996), exhibits interest-balancing cutting both ways.

      (1) Plaintiff won a substantial federal-court judgment on a conversion claim involving 300 transparencies he had lent to the Center. The jury awarded him $1,500 per transparency.

         (a) A New York statute directed appellate courts hearing appeals in a damages actions with itemized verdicts to "determine that an award is excessive or inadequate if it deviates materially from what would be reasonable compensation." That takes a traditional jury function and makes it an appellate-judge function. States can do that because the Court has never held that the Seventh Amendment applies to the states.

         (b) The Seventh Amendment sharply limits federal appellate review of jury-determined facts.

         (c) The Court subdivided the New York statute, recognizing that it had both substantive ("reasonable compensation") and procedural aspects (appellate-court factual review).

      (2) With respect to the substantive aspect, the Court agreed that damages should not vary from the range New York law prescribed ("deviates materially from . . . reasonable compensation"). There was no dominant federal interest in the amount of damages available on a state tort claim.

      (3) With respect to the procedural aspect, the situation was different. The Court was no more receptive to New York telling the federal judiciary how to distribute adjudicative functions than it had been in *Byrd*. It directed the district court to apply New York's deviates-materially standard on a motion for a new trial under FED. R. CIV. P. 59(a).

C. Substantive Federal Common Law in Diversity Cases

1. There is no bright-line test dictating that state substantive law (however defined or identified) necessarily governs every substantive issue in a diversity (or federal-question) case.

2. If there is a sufficiently dominant federal interest in a substantive issue, federal common law will govern. That is easy to say but hard to apply. There are cases in which there are federal interests but the Court decides that the federal interests are not important enough to displace state law.

3. *Banco Nacional de Cuba v. Sabbatino*, 376 U.S. 398 (1964), held that federal law, not state law, controls common-law issues implicating foreign relations of the United States.

    a. Federal common law applied in that diversity case to determine whether the act-of-state doctrine, which provides that courts in the United States will not inquire into the validity of a public act of a foreign sovereign within its own borders, protected Cuba's expropriation of a shipment of sugar.

    b. Though the claim asserted arose under state law, the act-of-state defense raised issues "that . . . are uniquely federal in nature." *Id.* at 424. The Court noted that if "state courts are left free to formulate their own rules, the purposes behind the doctrine could be as effectively undermined as if there had been no federal pronouncement on the subject." *Id.*

4. Though the Court recognized the federal common law's legitimacy in this area, it also acknowledged that decisions concerning foreign relations ultimately are for Congress and the Executive. Therefore, the political branches may supersede federal common law developed in the field of foreign relations, as they can in any other area of federal common law. *See supra* § VI.C.3, at 247-247 *[R210]*. [R191]

D. Claim- and Issue-Preclusion Effects of Federal Judgments

1. Neither the Full-Faith-and-Credit Clause, U.S. CONST. art. IV, § 1, nor the Full-Faith-and-Credit Act, 28 U.S.C. § 1738, addresses the claim- or issue-preclusive effect of a federal judgment. Federal common law governs.

2. *Semtek International, Inc. v. Lockheed Martin Corp.*, 531 U.S. 497 (2001), is the leading case. *See supra* Ch. X, § II.C.3, at 228-229 *[R211]*.

Chapter XII

STATE COURTS AND FEDERAL POWER

■ ANALYSIS

I. Introduction

This Chapter examines issues concerning state courts enforcing federal law and policy. First, consider the state courts' role in the federal system. Second, consider the state courts' authority to adjudicate federal claims. That depends on whether Congress has provided the federal courts with exclusive or concurrent jurisdiction (and what to do when Congress is silent). Third, when state courts may enforce federal rights, the question is whether state courts *must* do so. This implicates the Supremacy Clause. Fourth, can a state court issue an order, such as a writ of habeas corpus, binding on a federal officer? One of the most delicate themes of federalism—the proper relationship between state judicial systems and federal law—runs throughout this Chapter.

II. The Role of the State Courts in the Federal System

A. Constitutional Presumptions About State Courts

1. The Framers assumed that state courts would play an important role in adjudicating and enforcing federal law. *See supra* Ch. II, § III.A, at 60 *[R212]*.
2. First, the Constitution neither creates of lower federal courts nor requires Congress to do so. It guarantees only the Supreme Court, with original jurisdiction in two types of cases and appellate jurisdiction in all others within the federal judicial power. *See supra* Ch. VIII, §§ III-IV, at 166-181 *[R213]*.
3. Second, the Supremacy Clause, art. VI, cl. 2, expressly binds state courts to enforce federal law as "the supreme law of the land . . . anything in the Constitution or laws of any State to the contrary notwithstanding." [R148] [R226]
4. Thus, it is beyond dispute that state courts had to entertain cases arising under federal law, subject to the Supremacy Clause. This reflects the Framers' basic belief in the parity of state and federal courts. *See infra* § II.C, at 269-270 *[R214]*.

B. The Statutory Scheme: Concurrent and Exclusive Subject-Matter Jurisdiction

1. Although Congress created lower federal courts in 1789, it did not create a long-lasting federal-question until 1875. *See supra* Ch. IV, § III.A, at 97-98 *[R215]*. For over eighty years, the state courts were the only trial courts for most federal-question cases.
2. Congress has broad power to allocate jurisdiction over federal-question cases between state and federal courts. Even when Congress vested the lower federal courts with general federal-question jurisdiction, it did not make it exclusive. Congress has consistently assumed either state or federal trial courts can hear most cases arising under federal law. The two systems have concurrent subject-matter jurisdiction in that respect.

a. The plaintiff has the initial choice of forum. Often, however, the defendant may remove a state-court case to federal court. *See generally supra* Ch. VII, at 151-161 *[R216]*.

b. Congress occasionally chooses to give the plaintiff an absolute choice, as it has in the Federal Employers' Liability Act (FELA), which gives railroad workers a negligence claim enforceable in state or federal court but forbids removal. *See supra* Ch. VII, § III.C at 155-156 *[R217]*.

c. *Exclusive* jurisdiction means only federal courts may adjudicate; state courts have no jurisdiction. Congress is almost always explicit when it confers exclusive jurisdiction. *See, e.g.* 28 U.S.C. §§ 1333, 1334, 1338. *But see infra* § III.A.5, at 270-271 *[R218]*.

3. Congressional authority to exclude state courts from the adjudication of suits arising under federal law also derives from its Article I, § 8 powers and the Necessary and Proper Clause, art. I, § 8, cl. 18.

Example: Early on, Congress enacted a statute allowing patent holders to sue for patent infringement. It had that authority from its enumerated power to provide for patents. *See* art. I, § 8, cl. 8. It derives its authority to exclude state court jurisdiction (as 28 U.S.C. § 1338(a) does) from its power to do anything "necessary and proper" to the execution of its enumerated powers. *See* art. I, § 8, cl. 18.

C. A Recurring Theme: Parity

Concurrent jurisdiction over most federal actions connotes an assumption that state and federal courts are equally competent to adjudicate questions of federal law and equally receptive to arguments relying on federal law—an assumption known as parity. It could hardly be otherwise; imagine the increase in federal-state friction if the federal courts disdained state-court adjudications of issues of federal law. (Recall the Supreme Court's reaction when the Virginia Court of Appeals ruled that the Supreme Court could have no authority to review state-court judgments. *See Martin v. Hunter's Lessee*, 14 U.S. (1 Wheat.) 304 (1816).) There are some areas, of course, in which Congress has rejected parity by creating exclusive federal jurisdiction, presumably to encourage and facilitate development of federal judicial expertise in highly complex areas of intense federal interest: admiralty, bankruptcy, copyrights and patents, and some cases involving the Employee Retirement Income Security Act (ERISA), for example. More recently, Congress has implied lack of parity in large class action cases by passing the Class Action Fairness Act of 2005, which makes it possible for class-action defendants to avoid state court adjudication if the value of the case exceeds five million dollars and minimal diversity exists. That was Congress's reaction to the emergence of certain states as "magnet jurisdictions" for plaintiffs' class actions. Congress also implied a certain skepticism about parity when it allowed federal-officer removal. *See infra* § V.C, at 281-282 *[R219]*

The Supreme Court often lauds parity, particularly when explaining the common-law abstention doctrines it has created. *See supra* Ch. IX, § III.G.3.c(4)(b,c), at 211 *[R220]*; *see generally supra* Ch. XI, § V.A.3, at 241 *[R221]*. It is chary of permitting federal adjudication that might reflect adversely on state courts' ability and willingness to resolve matters including questions of federal law. It is a good idea to keep parity in mind when considering federal jurisdictional law and policy, whether coming from Congress or the courts. It is also a good idea to keep in mind that while the Supreme Court lauds parity, attorneys vote with their feet when choosing a forum. [R54] [R55] [R56] [R172] [R214] [R292]

III. State-Court Power to Adjudicate Federal Matters

A. The Presumption of Concurrent Jurisdiction and the Doctrine of Implied Exclusivity

1. When Congress creates a claim and provides exclusive federal jurisdiction, state courts cannot hear such claims. Congress has done so for bankruptcy proceedings, patent and copyright cases, cases brought under the Securities Exchange Act, and a few others.
2. Similarly, if Congress were expressly to provide concurrent jurisdiction, the courts would be bound by that as well.
3. A question might arise, however, when Congress is silent about exclusivity. Often, Congress creates a right and gives the federal courts jurisdiction to enforce it but says nothing about whether the jurisdiction is exclusive.
4. *Claflin v. Houseman*, 93 U.S. (3 Otto) 130, 136 (1876), the year after Congress enacted the predecessor to § 1331, created a rebuttable presumption for such situations. The Court held that a "state court has jurisdiction where it is not excluded by express provision, or by incompatibility in its exercise arising from the nature of the particular case." Thus, when federal law makes a claim possible, either by creating a claim or by being a critical part of a state-created claim, state or federal courts can adjudicate it. The Supreme Court adheres to that presumption. *See Tafflin v. Levitt*, 493 U.S 455, 460 (1990) (stating that exclusive federal jurisdiction exists if there is: "an explicit statutory directive, by unmistakable implication from the legislative history, or by a clear incompatibility between state-court jurisdiction and federal interests"); *Gulf Offshore Co. v. Mobil Oil Corp.*, 453 U.S. 473 (1981).
5. The Court has often repeated *Claflin*'s statement that unmistakable implication from a statutory directive may overcome the presumption of concurrent jurisdiction, but there are few examples. The Court has not been precise about what factors are relevant to the inquiry of an implied finding of exclusivity.
   a. Specifically (but, obviously, not specifically), the Court there suggested that "incompatibility" between federal interests and concurrent jurisdiction "from the nature of the particular case" could dictate exclusive federal jurisdiction. That is less than helpful.

b. *Charles Dowd Box Co. v. Courtney*, 368 U.S. 502 (1962), found concurrent jurisdiction for suits under § 301(a) of the Labor Management Relations Act, rejecting arguments that the statute's ambiguous scope and the need for uniform interpretation required exclusive federal jurisdiction. There were no references to exclusive jurisdiction in the legislative history. The Court thus seemed to limit consideration to the statute's language and legislative history.

c. More often, however, the Court has expressly considered pragmatic factors. In one case, it explained that "[t]he factors generally recommending exclusive federal-court jurisdiction over an area of federal law include the desirability of uniform interpretation, the expertise of federal judges in federal law, and the assumed greater hospitality of federal courts to peculiarly federal claims." *Gulf Offshore Co. v. Mobil Oil Corp.*, 453 U.S. at 483-84. One might reasonably ask, "But what of parity?" Possible follow-up questions might include, "when is uniformity in interpretation of federal law not desirable?"

d. The Supreme Court has inferred that federal jurisdiction is exclusive over antitrust claims arising under the Sherman and Clayton Acts, *see General Investment Co. v. Lake Short & M.S. Ry. Co.*, 260 U.S. 261, 287 (1922), and Congress appeared to confirm that inference in 15 U.S.C. § 15 by noting that persons having antitrust claims could "sue therefor in any district court of the United States in the district in which the defendant resides or is found or has an agent, . . ." as many of the inferior federal courts have confirmed. *See also Mercantile National Bank v. Langdeau*, 371 U.S. 555 (1961) (inferring exclusive jurisdiction in cases under the National Bank Act). [R218]

6. Commentators have criticized using pragmatic factors on separation-of-powers principles, noting that it is the legislature's job to determine when jurisdiction should be exclusive; thus, they argue, the Court should limit its assessment to statutory language and history.

7. Nonetheless, the Court continues to look to pragmatic factors. Usually, such factors buttress the presumption of concurrent jurisdiction.

a. *Tafflin* found concurrent jurisdiction for suits under the Racketeer Influenced and Corrupt Organizations (RICO) Act. It rejected arguments that a supposed need for uniform federal interpretation overcame the presumption of concurrent jurisdiction; indeed, the Court expressed "full faith in the ability of state courts to handle the complexities of civil RICO actions." 493 U.S. at 465. Parity smiled.

b. *Yellow Freight System, Inc. v. Donnelly*, 494 U.S. 820, 826 (1990), found concurrent jurisdiction for suits alleging discrimination under Title VII. The Court recognized that most legislators drafting the law expected that there would be exclusive federal court jurisdiction. It concluded, though, "that such anticipation does not overcome the presumption of concurrent jurisdiction that lies at the core of our federal system." [R231] [R352]

B. State-Court Adjudication of Issues Normally Arising in Cases of Exclusive Federal Jurisdiction

1. On occasion, state courts face federal issues that would form the basis for a suit within the federal courts' exclusive jurisdiction. For example, federal courts have exclusive jurisdiction over a case "arising under any Act of Congress relating to patents, plant variety protection, copyrights and trademark. . . ." 28 U.S.C. § 1338(a). Nonetheless, patent issues can arise in contract cases in state court.

Example 1: Patentee (P) gives a license to A to manufacture the patented product. A manufactures and sells the product but fails to pay royalties to P. P sues A in state court for breach of contract. As a defense, A claims that P's patent is invalid. Unless the case is removable on diversity grounds, the state court must decide the issue of the patent validity, because P's claim sounds in contract (similar to the Mottleys' claim, *see supra* Ch. IV, § III.B.3, at 99 *[R222]*), not under the patent laws.

Example 2: The same situation occurs when plaintiff sues in state court for breach of contract and the defendant claims that the contract violated federal antitrust law.

2. State courts can decide such questions. *See, e.g., Lear, Inc. v. Adkins*, 395 U.S. 653 (1969) (contract case raising patent issues).

3. State courts determining such issues might appear incongruous. If the state courts can decide these questions, state courts will adjudicate *issues* of federal law even though unable to adjudicate *claims* for recovery under the same law. (But remember that legislatures confer jurisdiction over claims, not issues.) On the other hand, if the state courts cannot decide these matters, the litigation must either (a) proceed entirely in federal court or (b) in both courts, with the federal court adjudicating only the federal issue and the state court adjudicating the rest of the matter (a very messy way to handle a case), or (c) proceed in state court, depriving the defendant of the invalidity defense entirely. Were Congress to authorize the first alternative, it might swamp the federal courts and would undermine the well-pleaded-complaint rule, *see supra* Ch. IV, § III.B, at 98-102 *[R223]*. A defense based on an area of exclusive jurisdiction would be enough to support removal. The second alternative is unworkable. The third might have a rationale: the state court might say to the licensee, "when you signed the license contract, you implicitly acknowledged the validity of the patent," and estop the licensee from claiming invalidity.

C. The *Rooker-Feldman* Doctrine

State-court judgments are sometimes subject to federal judicial review, but with the exception of habeas corpus, *see infra* Ch. XV, at 331-346 *[R224]*, federal review comes only in the Supreme Court. Congress has given the inferior federal courts no appellate jurisdiction with respect to state-court judgments other than habeas. The Supreme Court had long characterized habeas as review of the legality of the *custody* rather than the judgment underlying the custody, but discarded that fiction in *Exxon Mobil Corp. v. Saudi Basic Industries Corp.*, 544 U.S. 280, 292 n.8 (2005), acknowledging that Congress has granted the inferior courts appellate jurisdiction with respect to habeas. [R145]

No competent attorney would explicitly ask a lower federal court to review a state-court judgment, but two types of cases have attracted the Supreme Court's attention, giving rise to the *Rooker-Feldman* doctrine: (1) federal-court cases in which attorneys have tried a variety of ways to disguise *de facto* appellate review, and (2) federal-court cases preceded by a state-court judgment involving the parties but in which the federal plaintiff is not asking the federal court to review the state-court judgment. Distinguishing between those two case patterns is not always easy.

1. The Doctrine's Origins

   a. *Rooker v. Fidelity Trust Co.*, 263 U.S. 413 (1923), involved a state-court loser who unsuccessfully sought review by the United States Supreme Court because of failure to show a reviewable issue under the predecessor of 28 U.S.C. § 1257. She then filed a constitutional challenge to the state-court judgment in a federal district court, which dismissed for lack of subject-matter jurisdiction. The Supreme Court affirmed. "The jurisdiction possessed by the District Courts is strictly original." Although the federal complaint alleged constitutional errors in the state judgment, the Court unsurprisingly ruled that Rooker should have made her constitutional challenge in the state-court proceedings.

   b. *District of Columbia Court of Appeals v. Feldman*, 460 U.S. 462 (1983), was more complex. Applicants to take the District of Columbia bar examination who had not attended ABA-approved law schools sought waiver of that requirement from the District of Columbia Court of Appeals—the District's equivalent of a state appellate court that is a non-Article III court. The case turned on whether refusal of the waiver was a judicial or an administrative act.

      (1) The Supreme Court made a critical distinction. The federal courts had no jurisdiction to hear the applicants' challenge to the D.C. court's denial of the waiver because that was a judicial decision.

(2) However, the applicants' more general challenge to the District of Columbia rule requiring bar applicants to have attended an ABA-approved law school was not seeking review of a prior judicial decision in a case. In establishing rules for admission to the D.C. bar, the District of Columbia Court of Appeals was not acting in a judicial capacity, so the federal district court did have jurisdiction to entertain that challenge.

(3) Thus the Court distinguished between challenges to rules—permissible—and challenges to rulings—impermissible.

2. Variations on a Theme

Rooker-Feldman problems come in four flavors. Courts consider (1) whether the injury the federal plaintiff asserts comes from an independent act or the state-court judgment, (2) the type of relief the plaintiff seeks, (3) whether the federal case is really an appeal, a collateral attack, or an independent action, and (4) whether federal plaintiff has standing to challenge a general rule or whether the state and federal cases are so intertwined that such a challenge is effectively a challenge to the state-court judgment.

a. The Injury Plaintiff Asserts

Exxon Mobil Corp. v. Saudi Basic Industries Corp., 544 U.S. 280 (2005), involved parallel state and federal litigation. Saudi Basic (SABIC) sought royalties from Exxon Mobil in state court. In a federal court, Exxon Mobil sought damages for SABIC's overcharging and also included that claim as a counterclaim in the state action. The state action went to judgment first, and the Third Circuit ruled that *Rooker-Feldman* required dismissal of the federal action. A unanimous Supreme Court reversed, declaring *Rooker-Feldman* inapplicable because it applies only to challenges to state-court judgments that are final before federal proceedings commence. In *Exxon Mobil*, preclusion principles governed the effect of the state judgment on the federal action. The Court cautioned against overuse of *Rooker-Feldman*, noting that it is not a substitute for preclusion.

b. The Type of Relief Sought

This distinction relates back to the difference between challenging a rule and challenging a ruling, as *Feldman* illustrated. In *Centifanti v. Nix*, 865 F.2d 1422 (3d Cir. 1989), a disbarred attorney seeking reinstatement challenged the procedural rules that the Pennsylvania Supreme Court had promulgated covering readmission of disbarred attorneys. That Court had already rejected his application for readmission, but he was entitled to reapply. The Third Circuit likened the case to Feldman's challenge to the District of Columbia's approved-law-school rule and ruled that the federal district court had jurisdiction.

c. Appeal, Collateral Attack, or Independent Action

When unhappy class members mounted a federal-court challenge to an approved (and reaffirmed) settlement in a state-court class action, alleging lack of personal jurisdiction and fraud on the state court, the Seventh Circuit had to decide whether *Rooker-Feldman* barred the federal action. A sharply split Circuit denied rehearing en banc after a panel had affirmed dismissal. The majority's reasoning was that deciding the action would require the federal court to examine exactly the same issues that the state court had considered. The minority analogized the case to a collateral attack on a default judgment on grounds of lack of personal jurisdiction and would have permitted the district court to hear the case. *Kamilewicz v. Bank of Boston Corporation*, 92 F.3d 506, *reh. denied*, 100 F.3d 1348 (7th Cir. 1996).

d. Standing

A Colorado resident bounced a check. After receiving notice of the check's rejection, he paid the debt by money order. Thereafter, a collection agency began a state-court action to recover on the bounced check, and the defendant defaulted, apparently believing that the money order had resolved the matter. The state court entered judgment against him. He began a federal action, challenging a state rule that a debtor show a meritorious defense in order to have a court vacate a default judgment. The Tenth Circuit ruled alternatively. First, it ruled that there was no federal-court jurisdiction to set aside the default judgment; that would directly violate *Rooker-Feldman*. Second, the Circuit found that the federal plaintiff lacked standing to challenge the meritorious-defense rule because it was entirely speculative whether he would ever be subject to the rule again. *Facio v. Jones*, 929 F.2d 541 (10th Cir. 1991). [R27] [R178] [R180] [R187]

IV. State Courts' Obligation to Adjudicate Federal Claims

A. The Traditional Rule

1. *Martin v. Hunter's Lessee*, 14 U.S. (1 Wheat.) 304 (1816), made clear to any recalcitrant state courts that the Supreme Court does indeed have appellate jurisdiction to review state-court decisions of federal law. *See generally supra* Ch. VIII, § IV.A-F at 168-180 *[R225]*. (The Virginia Supreme Court had refused to acknowledge that the Supreme Court had such power. Justice Story's majority opinion enlightened Virginia.) Thus, it has long been clear that state courts must acknowledge applicable federal law in adjudicating state claims. Supremacy demands no less.

2. That left the question, however, of whether a state court has to open its doors to permit enforcement of a federal claim. That is: when federal law

creates a claim and does not mandate exclusive federal jurisdiction, must a state court hear the claim if the plaintiff files there?

3. The answer is plainly yes. *Mondou v. New York, N.H. & H.R.R.*, 223 U.S. 1 (1912), held that claims arising under the Federal Employers' Liability Act (FELA) are enforceable in state court.

   a. The Court relied on the Supremacy Clause. *See supra* § II.A.3, at 268 *[R226]*.

   b. The Court rejected the argument that the state court could decline to enforce a federal right if it found that right inconsistent with state policy. The Supremacy Clause operates to ensure that the federal policy trumps state policy. "Federal law is enforceable in state courts . . . because the Constitution and laws passed pursuant to it are as much laws in the States as laws passed by the state legislature." *Howlett v. Rose*, 496 U.S. 356, 367 (1990).

4. On the other hand, the Supreme Court has allowed state courts may refuse to enforce federal claims in limited circumstances—if they have "valid excuses." *See infra* § IV.B, at 276-279 *[R227]*.

5. Many observers thought that a state court would have a valid excuse to refuse to enforce a federal penal law. There has long been a school of thought in Conflicts of Law that one jurisdiction is under no obligation to enforce the penal laws (laws that enforce a penalty rather than providing damages actions, not limited to provisions of criminal law) of another jurisdiction.

Example: The Rhode Island Supreme Court refused a case arising under the Emergency Price Control Act (EPCA). EPCA authorized suits for treble damages for violations of the Act, which fixed prices that sellers could charge during World War II. The Rhode Island Supreme Court concluded that the treble-damages provision made the statute penal and held that it had no obligation to enforce such a law from a "foreign" government (the United States).

The Supreme Court unanimously reversed. Rather than simply holding that EPCA was remedial (and thus not penal), the Court drove home the point that the United States is not a foreign government. The Supremacy Clause required Rhode Island to apply federal law, regardless of whether it considered the law penal.

The Rhode Island courts did enforce multiple-damages claims under state law. The Supremacy Clause prevented them from *discriminating* against federal law. *Testa v. Katt*, 330 U.S. 386 (1947). [R228] [R229] [R232]

B. The Valid-Excuse Doctrine

1. The Supremacy Clause generally requires state courts to enforce federal claims. The Supreme Court has moderated this principle, however, by

recognizing that state courts may have a "valid excuse" not to apply federal law.

2. The Court has never offered a full justification for the valid-excuse doctrine. Commentators have suggested two possibilities.

   a. First, some argue that it stems from the Constitution. In *National League of Cities v. Usery*, 426 U.S. 833 (1976), *overruled by Garcia v. San Antonio Metropolitan Transit Authority*, 469 U.S. 528 (1985), the Court recognized a Tenth Amendment protection against disruption of important state functions. That recognition lasted only nine years.

   b. Second, some commentators assert that the valid-excuse doctrine may rest on inferred congressional intent. The idea appears to be that had Congress foreseen a particular situation it would not have intended to burden the state courts with jurisdiction and so would have made federal jurisdiction exclusive. This clashes with the presumption of concurrent jurisdiction and requires the courts to become mind-readers, which clashes with *Clafin* and *Yellow Freight.* Worse, by conceding that Congress had not foreseen the situation, the idea compels the federal court to figure out what Congress *would have thought* if it had thought about it. The courts should enforce the laws Congress does write, not laws it might have written if it had greater foresight. Otherwise the courts look like they are ruling on the wisdom of legislation rather than its interpretation or constitutionality. The Supreme Court recognizes the impropriety of courts doing that. *See, e.g., Day-Brite Lighting, Inc. v. Missouri*, 342 U.S. 421, 423 (1952) ("[W]e do not sit as a super-legislature to weigh the wisdom of legislation nor to decide whether the policy which it expresses offends the public welfare.").

   c. Justification for the valid-excuse doctrine becomes important only in the unlikely event that Congress attempts to overturn judicial recognition of a particular excuse. If the rationale is solely an inference of congressional intent, Congress could do so. On the other hand, if the Constitution underlies the doctrine, Congress lacks any power to overturn the decision. The Court has never suggested that the Constitution does . . . or that it does not.

3. The Supreme Court has recognized two excuses that permit a state court to refuse to enforce a federal claim. There is also a third situation in which a state court has refused to enforce a federal claim in circumstances that the Supreme Court seems likely to approve.

   a. If the state court has limited subject-matter jurisdiction under state law that does not extend to the federal suit, wholly apart from its federal nature

Example: *Herb v. Pitcairn*, 324 U.S. 117 (1945), allowed a city court in Illinois to decline jurisdiction over a claim under the Federal

Employers' Liability Act (FELA). Under the Illinois Constitution, the city court lacked competence to adjudicate a claim (state or federal) that arose outside its city limits. The FELA claim arose outside the city. A contrary ruling would allow the federal law to interfere with the state court system's allocation of subject-matter jurisdiction.

b. The doctrine of *forum non conveniens* applies if the forum would apply the doctrine in a similar situation to a state law claim

Example: Plaintiff brings a FELA case in state court. State law allows dismissal of any claim (state or federal) in which no party resides in the state. Because no party to the FELA case was a resident of the state, dismissal was permissible. *Missouri ex rel. Southern Ry. v. Mayfield*, 340 U.S. 1 (1950).

c. The critical thing in both examples is that the state court is not discriminating against the federal claim by treating it differently from the way it would treat a similar state-law claim.

d. The third possible valid-excuse situation arises when a parallel suit between the same parties is pending in federal court. *Barnett v. Baltimore & Ohio Ry.*, 200 N.E.2d 473 (Ohio Ct. App. 1963), upheld dismissal of an FELA claim pending in federal court on an identical complaint. The Ohio court stressed that it was not discriminating against federal law because Ohio courts would also dismiss state-law claims in similar circumstances. Once again, there was no discrimination against federal law. The United States Supreme Court has never spoken to this situation (and no other federal court can speak to it except in *dictum*, because the inferior federal courts cannot hear appeals of a state-court dismissals). On the other hand, since the key factor for the Supreme Court appears to be whether the state courts have discriminated against federal law, one may expect, if the issue ever reaches the Court, that it will affirm the state court's power to dismiss.

4. Some commentators suggest recognizing a valid excuse when the state does not recognize a state-law right analogous to the federal right being asserted.

   a. The concept finds some backhanded support in several Supreme Court opinions. Notably, in *Testa v. Katt*, 330 U.S. at 394, *see supra* § IV.A.5, at 276 *[R228]*, the Court required Rhode Island courts to enforce a federal penal (in the conflict-of-laws sense) law. In the opinion, the Court said: "It is conceded that this same type of claim arising under Rhode Island law would be enforced by that State's courts. . . . Under these circumstances the State courts are not free to refuse enforcement of the petitioners' claims." By negative implication, a state might be free in the opposite situation.

b. The Supreme Court first used the phrase "analogous right" in *FERC v. Mississippi*, 456 U.S. 742, 760 (1982), requiring Mississippi courts to enforce a federal claim. A state administrative commission "ha[d] jurisdiction to entertain claims analogous to those granted by [the federal act], and it can satisfy [that act's] requirements simply by opening its doors to claimants. . . ." However, the Court has never expressly adopted this form of the valid-excuse doctrine.

c. Some commentators argue against such recognition. First, requiring a state court to enforce a federal claim without an analogous right in state law does not seem unduly burdensome. Second, allowing a state to invoke such an excuse gives the Supremacy Clause insufficient weight .

5. It is clear that a state may not simply reject federal law. In *McKnett v. St. Louis & San Francisco Ry.*, 292 U.S. 230 (1934), Alabama courts refused to entertain a FELA claim because a state statute permitted claims against foreign corporations only based upon state law, not federal law. The Supreme Court noted: "The denial of jurisdiction by the Alabama court is based solely upon the source of the law sought to be enforced. The plaintiff is cast out because he is suing to enforce a federal act. A state may not discriminate against rights arising under federal laws." 292 U.S. at 234. Thus, *McKnett* did not involve a valid excuse; it was, instead, blatant discrimination against federal law, violating supremacy. [R227] [R367]

C. State Courts' Obligation to Employ Federal Procedures in Adjudicating Federal Claims

1. State courts have a general obligation to enforce federal claims. But must state courts also adopt federal procedures related to those claims?

2. Two important principles clash. First, the state courts, as independent systems, obviously are entitled to adopt their own procedures. But second, adequate protection of federal interests may require that a state adhere to federal dictates on procedures for enforcing federal claims.

3. *Dice v. Akron, Canton & Youngstown R.R. Co.*, 342 U.S. 359 (1952), held that a state court adjudicating a suit under the Federal Employers' Liability Act (FELA) had to allocate decision-making authority between judge and jury as a federal court would. Specifically, state law would have allowed the judge to determine whether a release was invalid because of fraud. *Dice* held that the jury had to decide the issue.

a. The reasoning is not entirely clear, but it seems the Court relied on: (a) ensuring an important role for the jury was essential to the achievement of Congress's substantive FELA goal, and (b) requiring state courts to follow the federal allocation of responsibility would not unduly burden the state judicial system since it routinely conducted jury trials anyway.

b. The Court distinguished *Minneapolis & St. Louis R. Co. v. Bombolis*, 241 U.S. 211 (1916), in which it held that a state court need not employ a unanimous-verdict requirement in adjudicating FELA cases, even though federal courts do. Presumably, the Court felt that requiring unanimity might significantly burden and delay state courts' functioning and was not essential for FELA. Congress appears to have thought that it was, leaving the question of whether the *Bombolis* Court acted properly.

4. Similarly, in an FELA case the state court may not adhere to its general pleading rule of construing a pleading strictly against the pleading party. Instead, it must construe pleadings liberally in favor of the pleading party. *Brown v. Western Ry. of Alabama*, 338 U.S. 294 (1949).

5. Some commentators suggest that *Dice* applies only to FELA cases. Most seem to agree, however, that it does not and that Congress may create other claims for which state courts must use at least some federal procedure. [R255]

V. State-Court Power to Control Federal Officers

A. Writs of Habeas Corpus

1. In *Ableman v. Booth*, 62 U.S. (21 How.) 506, 516 (1859), a state court issued a writ of habeas corpus to compel the release of a federal prisoner. The Court held that the state court lacked power to issue the writ. The state courts simply could not interfere with the federal government's workings because the federal government was "another and independent Government."

2. *In re Tarble*, 80 U.S. (13 Wall.) 397 (1871) (*Tarble's Case*) reiterated and extended *Abelman*. A state court issued a writ of habeas corpus to compel release of a soldier allegedly under the required age for service. The Supreme Court reversed; the state court lacked power to issue the writ.

a. *Tarble's Case* relied heavily on *Ableman* and stressed that state courts cannot interfere with federal-government operations. "In many exigencies the measures of the National government might . . . be entirely bereft of their efficacy and value." *Tarble's Case*, 80 U.S. at 409.

b. The Court could have limited *Ableman* to comity situations—in which the state writ interfered with federal litigation. *Tarble's Case* by clear implication rejects such a limitation, however, and seems to embrace the broader principle that state courts lack judicial power to interfere with federal officers' activities.

c. Some have suggested that these holdings should apply only to situations involving national emergency or some vital federal interest, such as military functioning, as in *Tarble's Case*. The courts recognize no such limitation, which probably would be too nebulous to apply consistently.

3. Some commentators see *Tarble's Case* as inconsistent with the traditional view, *see supra* § IV.A, at 275-276 *[R229]*, that state courts must enforce federal law as federal courts would, viewing *Tarble's Case* as evincing insufficient faith in parity and state courts' fealty to supremacy.

4. Other commentators argue the traditional view substantially disregards fundamental changes in the relations between state courts and the federal government and the general philosophy of federalism growing out of the Civil War and post-Civil War constitutional amendments.

   a. Federal-officer removal, *see infra* § C, at 281-282 *[R230]*, implies that Congress does not see state courts as equal to federal courts in applying and enforcing federal law. Perhaps this is a blow to parity, but it is nonetheless within Congress's power.

   b. One might see *Tarble's Case* as recognizing implied exclusivity under *Claflin*, *see supra* § III.A, at 270-272 *[R231]*, subject to express congressional reversal, but no court has suggested that.

5. Whatever its merits, *Tarble's Case* is still the law. It provides a clear rule: state courts lack judicial power to issue writs of habeas corpus to federal officers.

6. Note, however, that Tarble was free to seek *federal* habeas corpus, as the Court noted. *Tarble's Case*, 80 U.S. at 411. Because art. I, § 9, cl. 2, guarantees the right of habeas corpus, there must be some avenue—either in federal or state court—to seek it. [R25]

B. Mandamus and Injunctions

1. *Ableman* and *Tarble's Case* held that state courts may not issue a writ of habeas corpus to a federal officer. Query whether that ban applies to state court authority to issue mandamus or an injunction to a federal officer.

2. For mandamus, the answer is clear. Long before the habeas cases, *McClung v. Silliman*, 19 U.S. (6 Wheat.) 598 (1821), held that state courts lack authority to issue mandamus to federal officers.

3. The Court has never decided whether *Tarble's Case* extends to state injunctions against federal officers.

   a. The lower federal courts have split, the majority concluding that state injunctions are also impermissible.

   b. It is difficult to reconcile *Tarble's Case*'s continued vitality with a conclusion that state courts can enjoin federal officers; an injunction would interfere with federal sovereignty as much as a writ of habeas corpus or mandamus.

C. Relevance of Federal-Officer Removal

1. 28 U.S.C. § 1442(a)(1) allows federal-officer removal. A federal officer sued or prosecuted in her personal or official capacity "for any act under

color of such office" may remove the case without the consent of other defendants, provided the officer raises a federal defense.

2. Some commentators argue that Congress's broadening federal-officer removal in 1948 makes *Tarble's Case* irrelevant today.

    a. Once the state habeas cases against the federal officer commences, according to this argument, she can simply remove the case to federal court.

    b. On the other hand, without *Tarble's Case*, a state court might restrain operation of a federal program before the federal officer could remove, so *Tarble's Case* removes almost any danger of even limited state judicial interference.

3. Federal-officer removal traces back to early in United States history, though Congress sharply limited it, first to federal customs officers and later to federal revenue officers more generally. Even at an early date, there was concern that state courts might be hostile to federal programs and federal officers. This contradicts commentators' argument that *Tarble's Case* is inconsistent with a traditional view that state and federal courts are fungible for the enforcement of federal rights—in other words, in parity. *See supra* § IV.A, at 275-276 *[R232]*. That may be the traditional view, and it may be good practical policy to reduce friction between state and federal judiciaries, but the Constitution does not command that view. Early in the nation's history, Congress obviously entertained doubts about state courts' willingness to enforce federal law. [R219] [R230]

Chapter XIII

STATE SOVEREIGN IMMUNITY AND THE ELEVENTH AMENDMENT

■ ANALYSIS

I. Introduction

The Eleventh Amendment's words, reacting to a case that upheld federal jurisdiction over a debt action against a state, removes federal judicial power over actions by a citizen of a state against another state. The Supreme Court also interprets the Amendment to bar cases by a citizen against her own state, despite the wording. The Amendment embodies sovereign immunity and has come to stand for the proposition that certain plaintiffs cannot sue a state in federal court. Despite narrow literal terms, the Supreme Court has interpreted the Amendment broadly. It is clear, for instance, that it applies in most (but not all, *see infra* § IV.A at 290-294 *[R233]*) cases in which the state is not a named party but is the real party in interest.

Plaintiffs may be able to avoid the Amendment, however, by invoking one of three well-established but narrow exceptions. The Amendment and the exceptions raise important questions of federalism—whether a citizen ought to be able to seek justice from a state in a federal court. Many criticize the idea that a state should not have to answer in federal court when it commits an actionable wrong, particularly when the plaintiff's claim sounds in federal law.

II. Background and History of the Eleventh Amendment

A. The Evolving Concept of Sovereign Immunity

1. Sovereign immunity generally means that a sovereign—the state—cannot be held liable. It may derive from modern (but inaccurate) understanding of the medieval English dictate that "the king can do no wrong," which in turn may derive from the precept that no man could be sued in his own court without his consent.

2. Some commentators have suggested that that "the king can do no wrong" meant originally was that the king *could not* violate his own law. Certainly, one may question the logic of applying such a principle, developed in a monarchy, to a democratic society, particularly one whose Constitution created and limits the government. [R235]

3. Others take the position that the phrase means that the king *would* do no wrong, so that if an official acted illegally, the act was not attributable to the sovereign, and the officer stood before the court as an individual defendant. That is clearly the position of English law and has been at least since the Stuart dynasty. It also crops up in cases long antedating the Stuarts.

4. Nevertheless, the Supreme Court has long asserted that the Framers contemplated some form of state sovereign immunity. That elides the question of whether the people or the government is the sovereign. The Framers probably thought that states could insulate themselves from liability under their own laws. It is at least questionable that they also thought that states could insulate themselves from liability under *federal* law that the Framers—in contrast to the ill-fated Articles of Confederation—had just declared supreme.

5. For generations, the Supreme Court treated the Amendment's principle as ensuring that a federal court could never hold a state liable. The Court saw the Eleventh Amendment's primary goal as protecting state treasuries. *See, e.g., Hess v. Port Authority Trans-Hudson Corp.*, 513 U.S. 30 (1994) (protecting state treasuries from federal judgments is the most "salient" factor in determining when an action is against a state).

6. More recently, the Court has emphasized a broader immunity, based on the Court's perception of states' dignity interests, seeing the Amendment as freeing states from being subjected to litigation based on federal law at all, even in their own courts. *Alden v. Maine*, 527 U.S. 706 (1998). Thus, the Eleventh Amendment, though clearly worded as a forum immunity, now has a muscular substantive component as well.

B. *Chisholm* and Ratification of the Amendment

1. Article III, § 2, which lists the classes of cases falling within the federal juridical power, provides jurisdiction over cases "between a State and Citizens of another State," as one form of diversity jurisdiction.

   a. At the Constitutional Convention, some worried that the clause might permit suits against a state, ignoring sovereign immunity.

   b. Various delegates responded that the provision would not apply to suits with states as defendants. They thought that the clause only allowed diversity cases with states as plaintiffs.

2. Nonetheless, *Chisholm v. Georgia*, 2 U.S. (2 Dall.) 419 (1793), upheld diversity jurisdiction. A citizen of South Carolina sued Georgia to recover on a state Revolutionary War debt. The Court exercised original (trial) jurisdiction over Georgia's claim of immunity.

3. *Chisholm* caused public uproar and led to rapid ratification of the Eleventh Amendment: "The judicial power of the United States shall not be construed to extend to any suit in law or equity, commenced or prosecuted against one of the United States by citizens of another state, or by citizens or subjects of any foreign state."

III. Interpreting the Eleventh Amendment

A. Narrow Literal Terms Have Not Limited the Amendment's Application

1. The Eleventh Amendment's language is quite specific: it purports to remove federal judicial power only over cases "commenced or prosecuted against one of the United States by Citizens of another State, or by Citizens or Subjects of any Foreign State." Thus, it bars suits by a citizen of one state against another state, and by a foreign citizen or subject against a state. *Principality of Monaco v. Mississippi*, 292 U.S. 313 (1934), also read it to bar a suit by a foreign government against a state.

2. On its face, the Amendment appears not to bar a federal suit by a citizen against her own state. Nonetheless, *Hans v. Louisiana*, 134 U.S. 1

(1890), upheld dismissal in that situation on the basis of its inference that the Founders never intended such suits. It specifically disclaimed the Eleventh Amendment as the basis of the decision. Nonetheless, the Supreme Court subsequently read and now views *Hans* as an Eleventh Amendment decision. *But see infra* § III.C.2, at 287 *[R234]*.

3. The Amendment also bars suits by Indian tribes against a state, by a municipality against a state, and even suits against territories, though they are not states. *See, e.g., Puerto Rico Aqueduct Auth. v. Metcalf & Eddy, Inc.*, 506 U.S. 139 (1993). In *Financial Oversight and Management Board for Puerto Rico v. Centro de Periodismo Investigativo, Inc.*, 598 U.S. 339 (2023), the Court "assume[d] without deciding that Puerto Rico is immune from suit in federal district court, and that the Board partakes of that immunity," *id.*, at 346, though the majority never mentioned the Amendment. (The Court apparently finds adjudication much easier when it begins by assuming its conclusion.)
4. The Court's refusal to read the Amendment literally, in accord with its terms, reflects the Court's notions of federalism and state power but abandons the Court's oft-stated fidelity to textualism.

B. The Amendment, Even Broadly Construed, Does Not Bar All Suits Against States

1. For instance, the United States can sue a state in federal court. *See United States v. Mississippi*, 380 U.S. 128 (1965). The Court has not interpreted the Amendment to forbid such actions.
2. Also, because the Amendment speaks only of the federal judicial power, it does not in terms forbid suits sounding in federal law against a state in state court. However, *Alden v. Maine*, 527 U.S. 706 (1998), recognized a state constitutional immunity to private actions in state courts based on at least some federal laws Congress enacted under Article I, § 8.
3. The Amendment does not prevent the Supreme Court from exercising appellate jurisdiction over a state-court case against a state. *Nevada v. Hall*, 440 U.S. 410 (1979).

C. The Amendment Bars Specified Suits in Federal Court Regardless of Jurisdictional Basis

1. For close to a century after ratification, some judges and commentators thought that it barred only diversity cases against a state. After all, *Chisholm v. Georgia* had construed the diversity-jurisdiction clause, leading to adoption of the Amendment. The logical consequence of that approach is that the Amendment does not bar federal-question actions against states, regardless of the plaintiff's citizenship.
   a. In support of the theory, some argued that extending state immunity to federal-question suits would be inconsistent with the Constitutional Convention's plan—supremacy: the notion that

states ceded their sovereignty to the extent that they ratified Article I's vesting legislative authority in Congress.

b. The greatest problem with the diversity theory of the Amendment is that the language does not suggest that it is so limited. The amendment bars "any suit" against a state by a citizen of another state, drawing no distinction on the basis of federal subject-matter jurisdiction. That reading, however, leads to the apparent anomaly (as *Hans* pointed out) of a state citizen being able to bring a federal claim against the state while a non-citizen with an identical claim—perhaps even arising from the same incident—cannot.

2. *Hans v. Louisiana*, 134 U.S. 1 (1990), affirmed dismissal of a federal-question suit by a Louisiana citizen. Justice Bradley's opinion for the Court strongly implied that the Eleventh Amendment did *not* dictate the result but found other reasons to dismiss. The Court has subsequently read *Hans* as an Eleventh Amendment case. *See supra* § III.A.2 at 284 *[R235]*. [R234]

3. It is now clear that the head of subject-matter jurisdiction is not important, with one exception.

   a. The Amendment bars diversity suits against a state.

   b. It bars federal-question suits against a state.

   c. It bars supplemental-jurisdiction claims against a state.

   d. It bars admiralty-jurisdiction suits against a state.

   e. *Cory v. White*, 457 U.S. 85 (1982), held that the Amendment barred a claim asserted against a state by interpleader.

   f. ***However,*** *Central Virginia Community College v. Katz*, 546 U.S. 356 (2006), held that the Eleventh Amendment does not protect states from being unwilling participants in bankruptcy proceedings, the Court's theory being that the states agreed to such proceedings when they ratified Article I's Bankruptcy Clause. *Allen v. Cooper*, 589 U.S. 248 (2020), declined to extend *Katz*'s rationale to copyright cases. [R251] [R290]

D. Nature of the Eleventh Amendment Defense

1. If the Amendment applies, the federal court will dismiss an action that began in federal court. It used to be the law that the would remand an action that the defendants removed. However, *Lapides v. Board of Regents*, 535 U.S. 613 (2002), held that because all defendants must consent to removal, the state defendant's consent was also consent to federal-court jurisdiction, waiving any Eleventh Amendment objection.

2. The Amendment's words, however, sound distinctly like a restriction on federal subject-matter jurisdiction. If that were so, two things would follow: (1) courts would have to raise the issue *sua sponte*, and (2) the state could never waive the defense, because doing so would create subject-matter jurisdiction.

3. The Supreme Court has sent conflicting signals as to whether the defense is jurisdictional in this sense.

   a. The Court allows a state to raise the defense at any time, even on appeal. That is consistent with raising a subject-matter-jurisdiction defense. *Edelman v. Jordan*, 415 U.S. 651, 679 (1974) (Douglas, J., dissenting).

   b. On the other hand, the Court also has said that an appellate court need not raise the issue, *see, e.g., Patsy v. Board of Regents of Florida*, 457 U.S. 496, 515 n.19 (1982), which is inconsistent with the way courts treat subject-matter jurisdiction, and there is no doubt that the state can waive the Eleventh Amendment defense and thereby consent to federal suit, although it must be remarkably specific about doing so. This is contrary to the approach for subject-matter jurisdiction. *See infra* § IV.B, at 294 *[R236]* (methods of waiver).

4. Some courts refer to the Eleventh Amendment defense as a "personal privilege" of the state that the state must timely assert or suffer waiver. *See, e.g., Agua Caliente Band of Cahuilla Indians v. Hardin*, 223 F.3d 1041 (9th Cir. 2000).

5. That a state may be immune from suit in state court does not necessarily mean that it has Eleventh Amendment immunity in federal court.

E. What Constitutes a State for Eleventh Amendment Purposes?

1. The Amendment bars suits in federal court against a "State." Clearly, then, it bars claims naming the state as a defendant.

2. Few cases name the state as a defendant, but many involve some state political subdivision, agency, or individual. Whether such a defendant is an "arm of the state" and entitled to immunity is an often difficult question.

3. The Supreme Court has made it clear that the case will almost always be considered against a state, and therefore barred, even if the state is not a named party but is the real party in interest. *But see infra* § IV.A at 290-294 *[R237]*. The court must look to the "essential nature and effect of the proceeding" to determine whether the case is in fact against the state. *Ford Motor Co. v. Dept. of Treasury of State of Indiana*, 323 U.S. 459, 464 (1945). *See also Edelman v. Jordan*, 415 U.S. 651 (1974). (*Ford Motor* had also ruled that a state could raise the Eleventh Amendment defense even if its attorney-general had apparently waived it by litigating on the merits, because *state law* did not allow officials to waive. *Lapides v. Board of Regents of Univ. Sys.*, 535 U.S. 613 (2002), overruled that part of *Ford Motor Co.*)

4. The burden is on the defendant to establish that it is an arm of the state and thus entitled to immunity under the Amendment.

5. Federal law determines whether a political entity is part of the state for Eleventh Amendment purposes. Though the federal court will consider whether the state views the entity as an arm of the state, the state's view does not bind the federal court.

6. The state is usually considered the real party in interest if the action seeks recovery from the state treasury. *Quern v. Jordan*, 440 U.S. 332 (1979).

7. That test is rough, however, and the courts also look to other factors to determine whether the defendant is entitled to immunity. For instance, courts look at the defendant's autonomy, whether it is enforcing statewide rather than local rules, and state funding. Cases are often difficult to reconcile, but there are some general rules.

   a. Municipalities and municipal agencies usually are not arms of the state, and thus do not have Eleventh Amendment immunity. *See, e.g., Jinks v. Richland County*, 538 U.S. 456 (2003).

   b. Public-school districts are not arms of the state, though state educational departments and agencies are.

   c. Cases are split on whether state universities, correctional facilities, highway departments, and bar associations are arms of the state.

8. The Court has emphasized legal liability, rather than whether the plaintiff seeks to collect from the state treasury. In *Regents of the University of California v. Doe*, 519 U.S. 425 (1997), the federal government would have indemnified the state for any judgment against the state university, so the case could have no impact on the state treasury. Nonetheless, the Court held that the Eleventh Amendment barred the action because it sought to impose legal liability on the state university.

9. However, the state cannot *create* immunity by agreeing to indemnify a political entity that is not otherwise an arm of the state. Thus, if the defendant is not an arm of the state, the Amendment does not bar the case; the state's agreement to indemnify does not convert the case into one against the state notwithstanding the impact on the state treasury.

10. Even a suit against an individual may be barred because it is in fact against the state. If the plaintiff seeks a money judgment that the state treasury would have to pay, the Eleventh Amendment bars the action. *Ford Motor Co. v. Dept. of Treasury of State of Indiana*, 323 U.S. 459 (1945) (suit by state taxpayer against state officers to recover refund of taxes allegedly illegally imposed deemed to be against the state).

    a. The Amendment does not bar suits against a state officer in her individual capacity, to impose personal liability. *Scheuer v. Rhodes*, 416 U.S. 232 (1974).

b. Individual state officers are subject to suit under 42 U.S.C. § 1983. *See infra* Ch. XIV, § II.A.1 at 303 *[R238]* and § III.D.2 at 307 *[R239]*.

c. Suits against a state officer often implicate the doctrine of *Ex parte Young*. *See infra* § IV.A at 290-299 *[R240]*. [R246]

IV. Avoiding the Eleventh Amendment

There are three ways for a plaintiff to avoid the Amendment and sue a state (or an arm or officer of the state) in federal court: (1) through the common-law doctrine of *Ex parte Young*, *see infra* § A, (2) if state conduct (including, but not limited to, legislation) waives the immunity, *see infra* § B, at 294-295 *[R241]*, and (3) if Congress properly abrogates Eleventh Amendment immunity. *See infra* § C, at 295-299 *[R242]*.

A. The Doctrine of *Ex parte Young*

Ex parte Young, 209 U.S. 123 (1908), provides an important way to avoid the Eleventh Amendment. *Young* sometimes permits a plaintiff to sue a state *actor* in federal court for equitable relief that effectively prevents the *state* from doing something illegal.

1. The Case

a. In a federal district court, the plaintiff sued Young, Minnesota's attorney-general, seeking an injunction against his enforcing a state law requiring railroads to reduce their rates. Plaintiff argued that the state law was confiscatory, violating due process. The injunction would stop the state from enforcing its statute. Thus, the case appeared effectively to be against the state, in conflict with the Eleventh Amendment. The lower federal court issued the injunction and held the attorney-general in contempt when he began a state-court enforcement action the very next day.

b. The Supreme Court upheld the contempt citation. It reasoned that the officer's illegal action, "stripped" him of the state's Eleventh Amendment immunity. After all, said the Court, the state could not instruct an officer to violate the Constitution. Thus, the maverick state official did not act for the state, making the case simply against a private individual rather than the state.

c. The Eleventh Amendment did not bar the case. Two stripping theories vie for attention in *Young*, and Justice Peckham's opinion for the Court does not make clear which is dominant. First, the Court relied on supremacy for stripping Young of his immunity as a state officer:

> If the act which the state attorney general seeks to enforce be a violation of the Federal Constitution, the officer, in proceeding under such enactment, comes into conflict with the superior authority of that Constitution, and he is in that case stripped of his

> official or representative character and is subjected in his person to the consequences of his individual conduct.

Second, there are echoes of the ancient maxim that "the king can do no wrong."

> [T]he officer is simply prohibited from doing an act which he had no legal right to do. An injunction to prevent him from doing that which he has no legal right to do is not an interference with the discretion of an officer. . . .
>
> It is simply an illegal act upon the part of a state official in attempting, by the use of the name of the state, to enforce a legislative enactment which is void because unconstitutional.

Young, 209 U.S. at 159.

In England, from the thirteenth century on, if a crown official did an act the law forbade, the courts would not attribute the act to the sovereign. The official then stood before the court as an individual, unable to claim the protection of the sovereign for his act. In *Young*, either theory avoids the Eleventh Amendment bar. The difference becomes important in other cases. *See infra* § IV.A.5.b, at 291-292 *[R243]*.

2 Some argue that *Ex parte Young* is analytically flawed, characterizing the case as result-oriented, logically indefensible, unprincipled, and resting on a fiction that an official's act can simultaneously be state action and not state action.

a. On one hand, the Court held that the illegal acts of a state officer do not constitute state action for Eleventh Amendment purposes.

b. On the other hand, the Court held that the very same acts did constitute state action for Fourteenth Amendment purposes.

3. Others have argued that there is nothing unusual about legal terms meaning different things in different contexts. One may, for example, be incompetent to defend a criminal charge but competent to make a will or handle financial affairs.

4. Despite considerable criticism, *Ex parte Young* remains vital and provides an important vehicle for federal-court challenges to the constitutionality of state statutes under which state officers act.

5. Development of Current Doctrine on Specific Issues

a. First, the state-officer defendant must have a duty to enforce the challenged state law. Though the challenged statute need not state the duty, it must be more than a mere general duty to enforce the law. *Ex parte Young* is not available to challenge the state officer's discretionary acts or tasks .

b. Second, it now is clear that the state action must violate *federal* law. Often, the federal law will be the Constitution, but a federal statute is sufficient. The point is that *Ex parte Young* is not a vehicle for challenging violations of state law. *Pennhurst State School & Hospital v. Halderman*, 465 U.S. 89 (1984) (Eleventh Amendment barring federal court from ordering state officials to conform their conduct to state law). *Pennhurst* makes clear that the Court has adopted *Ex parte Young*'s supremacy-stripping theory. Justice Stevens vigorously dissented, arguing that, as in England, an act violating the (state) sovereign's law, cannot be the sovereign's act for Eleventh Amendment purposes. [R243]

c. Third, only federal law—not state law that federal law merely authorizes—justifies supremacy stripping.

Example: A state adopts a federal program such as Medicaid. If the program requires the state to adhere to federal guidelines, then those guidelines are supreme. By contrast, if the federal program permits the state to set its own guidelines, they are state, not federal, law, even though federal law authorizes them generally. They are not enforceable under *Ex parte Young*.

d. Fourth, the Court has recently narrowed *Ex parte Young* by holding that it is not available if federal law provides such intricate remedies that it is clear that Congress did not intend to allow *Ex Parte Young* cases. In other words, if a federal law sets up its own remedial scheme for violation of the federal law, the court may infer that Congress meant to foreclose using *Ex parte Young*. *Seminole Tribe of Florida v. Florida*, 517 U.S. 44, 75 (1996) (because Indian Gaming Regulatory Act contained a "carefully crafted and intricate remedial scheme," Congress did not intend *Ex parte Young* to apply).

e. Fifth, *Idaho v. Coeur d'Alene Tribe of Idaho*, 521 U.S. 261 (1997), held that the *Ex-Parte-Young* theory is not available if it would interfere with special state sovereignty interests, such as those involved in quiet-title actions to real property. [R244]

6. Development of Current Doctrine Concerning Remedies

a. The question of what remedies are available under the *Ex parte Young* has generated more discussion and confusion than have its requirements. *See supra* § IV.A.5, at 291-292 *[R244]*.

b. In *Ex parte Young*, plaintiff sought an injunction against the enforcement of the state law. On the other hand, it was already clear that the Eleventh Amendment barred recovering damages from the state treasury. Therefore, some suggested that the dividing line for *Ex parte Young* relief was whether the plaintiff sought damages (impermissible) or equitable relief (permissible). This distinction, however, proved to be too facile.

c. *Edelman v. Jordan*, 415 U.S. 651 (1974), altered the focus. Plaintiffs sought a mandatory injunction requiring state officials to comply with a federal program's time limits concerning processing applications for aid to disabled persons and to pay back benefits wrongfully withheld.

(1) The Court rejected the Seventh Circuit's conclusion that the payment was permissible as "equitable restitution" rather than damages. "We do not read *Ex parte Young* . . . to indicate that any form of relief may be awarded against a state officer, . . . out of the state treasury, so long as the relief may be labeled 'equitable' in nature." *Id.* at 655-66.

(2) The Court recognized, however, that appropriate relief, such as the injunction in *Ex parte Young* itself, may have an ancillary future effect on the state treasury. Such an effect is acceptable if a prospective remedy, such as an injunction or declaratory judgment, causes it.

(3) On the other hand, an award from the state treasury based on past state conduct—even if not labeled "damages"—is impermissible.

d. The dissent and some commentators have criticized *Edelman*'s prospective-versus-retrospective approach, but it retains vitality.

e. Thus, federal courts may grant prospective injunctive and declaratory relief in cases brought under *Ex parte Young*, including injunctions requiring expenditure of state funds to comply with federal law, so long as the order is prospective.

Example: An order requiring state officials to desegregate schools in Detroit at a cost billions of dollars was proper, because it was prospective. Thus, the effect on the state treasury was "ancillary" and acceptable. *Milliken v. Bradley*, 433 U.S. 267 (1977). [R365]

f. Because only prospective relief is possible, suits must concern ongoing violations of federal law. If the violations have ceased and cannot recur, the only available remedy would be damages, which the Eleventh Amendment bars.

g. The Court has permitted monetary recovery from the state in limited circumstances, when the court's order to pay was ancillary to prospective relief.

(1) *Hutto v. Finney*, 437 U.S. 678 (1978), upheld an award of attorney's fees against the state for bad-faith failure to comply with a court order.

(2) *Quern v. Jordan*, 440 U.S. 332 (1979), permitted a court order notifying class members of their right to pursue retroactive relief in a state forum.

(3) But *Green v. Mansour*, 474 U.S. 64 (1985), restricted *Quern*. Plaintiffs in *Green* sought prospective relief that became

moot when Congress changed relevant statutes during the case's pendency. They sought a *Quern* order giving notice to class members of the possibility of pursuing retroactive relief in a state forum. The Court affirmed dismissal; "notice relief" is appropriate only when accompanying other prospective relief, to which the notice relief can be "ancillary." [R233] [R237]

B. Waiver by the State

1. The Traditional Waiver Rule

   a. It is old law that a state may waive its sovereign immunity and allow suit.

   b. This applies to the Eleventh Amendment. A state may waive its Eleventh Amendment protection in several ways. *See infra* § B.2.

   c. Because the Amendment accords constitutional protection, however, the courts will not infer waiver. Unequivocal actions or language must support it. *Port Authority Trans-Hudson Corp. v. Feeney*, 495 U.S. 299 (1990).

   d. This section addresses waiver by state conduct, which may include state constitutional provisions, legislation, or actions in litigation. Contrast this with a doctrine of implied congressional abrogation of Eleventh Amendment immunity, which the Court has now repudiated. *See infra* § IV.C, at 295-299 *[R245]*.

2. Actions by the State Constituting Waiver

   a. A state may waive Eleventh Amendment immunity by statute. For example, *Port Authority Trans-Hudson Corp. v. Feeney*, the Supreme Court held that a state venue statute waived the state's immunity because it "expressly indicat[ed]" the state's consent to federal suit. The waiver must be express.

   b. A state may waive its immunity expressly by constitutional provision. This waiver also must be express; a state constitutional provision waiving state-sovereign immunity without mention of *federal* actions is insufficient. *Atascadero State Hospital v. Scanlon*, 473 U.S. 234 (1985). [R247]

   c. A state may waive its immunity by giving express consent in a particular federal case.

   d. A state may waive its immunity by litigation conduct. *Lapides v. Board of Regents of Univ. Sys.*, 535 U.S. 613 (2002), held that the state joining in removal to federal court waives the Eleventh Amendment immunity by invoking federal jurisdiction. Though the Court emphasized that its holding involved only removal on the basis of diversity jurisdiction, it clearly seems to apply to any case a state removes.

e. There may be a question about who is empowered to waive the state's immunity. *Lapides* held that the state attorney general's office waived the immunity by removing. The state argued that the attorney general's waiver was ineffective unless a state statute conferred authority to do so. The Court rejected the argument, overruling that part of *Ford Motor Co. v. Department of Treasury of Indiana*. *See supra* § III.E.3, at 288-290 *[R246]*.

f. State consent to state-court suits does not compel the conclusion that it has waived Eleventh Amendment immunity from federal suit. *Florida Department of Health and Rehabilitation Services v. Florida Nursing Home Association*, 450 U.S. 147 (1981) (*per curiam*); *Atascadero State Hospital v. Scanlon*, *supra* § IV.B.2.b, at 294 *[R247]*. [236] [R241]

C. Congressional Abrogation

1. Background on Congressional Abrogation

a. Can Congress abrogate Eleventh Amendment immunity and, if so, how?

b. Direct abrogation involves Congress passing a statute under the final sections of the Thirteenth, Fourteenth, and Fifteenth Amendments that explicitly allows federal actions against the states for violating it. It is possible, though in recent years, the Supreme Court, while bringing increased clarity to the area, has narrowed the circumstances in which Congress can do this. *See infra* §§ IV.C.2, 3, at 295-298 *[R248]*.

c. Indirect abrogation involves federal legislation providing that state participation in a federal program waives Eleventh Amendment immunity. Some refer to this as constructive waiver. This wing of abrogation theory is now moribund. *See infra* § IV.C.4, at 298 *[R249]*. [R353]

2. Direct Abrogation

a. There is substantial scholarly opinion that Congress may abrogate states' Eleventh Amendment immunity by proper legislation.

b. There has been serious question, however, about what parts of the Constitution permit Congress to do that. Only if Congress acts under an appropriate constitutional provision will abrogation be effective.

c. Some commentators argued that the Fourteenth Amendment automatically overrode Eleventh Amendment immunity because ratification came after the Eleventh. Thus, they argued, any claim under the Fourteenth Amendment against a state can proceed in federal court.

d. It is now clear that the Fourteenth Amendment does not automatically abrogate Eleventh Amendment immunity, but Congress can override the immunity by legislating pursuant to § 5 of the Fourteenth Amendment.

e. Section 5 empowers Congress to enforce the Fourteenth Amendment through "appropriate legislation." The Supreme Court insists upon a clear statement of congressional intent. *See infra* § IV.C.3, at 296-298 *[R250]*.

f. Lower courts had found congressional abrogation under other constitutional provisions. Though the Supreme Court embraced this theory one time, it has since rejected it.

(1) In *Pennsylvania v. Union Gas*, 491 U.S. 1 (1989), *overruled by Seminole Tribe of Florida v. Florida*, 517 U.S. 44 (1996), a sharply-split Court with no majority theory held that Congress can abrogate immunity by legislating under the Interstate Commerce Clause.

(2) Only seven years later, *Seminole Tribe* overruled *Union Gas*, holding that neither the Interstate Commerce Clause nor the Indian Commerce Clause supports direct abrogation.

(3) *Seminole Tribe* means that Congress may abrogate Eleventh Amendment immunity only with legislation under amendments post-dating the Eleventh; abrogation cannot rest upon Article I powers. *But see Central Virginia Community College v. Katz*, 546 U.S. 356 (2006) (upholding jurisdiction under the Bankruptcy Clause, art. I, § 8, cl. 4). *See also Alden v. Maine*, 527 U.S. 706 (1999) (Congress cannot abrogate state immunity in state court using its Article I powers.). *Allen v. Cooper*, 589 U.S. 248 (2020), appears to reject applying *Katz*'s reasoning to other Article I powers, even if cases arising under those powers qualify for exclusive federal jurisdiction. *See supra* § III.C.3.f, at 287 *[R251]*. [R363]

g. After wrestling with the issue in a series of cases, the Court finally held that Congress did not intend 42 U.S.C. § 1983 to abrogate state' Eleventh Amendment immunity. *Will v. Dept. of State Police*, 491 U.S. 58 (1989). *See infra* Ch. XIV, § III.D.1 at 307 *[R252]*.

3. Determining Whether Congress Intended Direct Abrogation

a. Simply enacting a statute under § 5 of the Fourteenth Amendment does not abrogate Eleventh Amendment immunity. The statute must state expressly that it permits federal actions against states.

(1) Title VII of the Civil Rights Act of 1964 properly authorizes damages suits against states. *Fitzpatrick v. Bitzer*, 427 U.S. 445 (1976).

(2) On the other hand, the Education of the Handicapped Act did not abrogate immunity because it contains no clear statement making states amenable to federal suit. The Court will not find abrogation on the basis of legislative history. *Dellmuth v. Muth*, 491 U.S. 223 (1989). *See also Blatchford v. Native Village of Noatak & Circle Village*, 501 U.S. 775, 785 (1991) (Congress must speak with "unmistakable clarity.").

b. *City of Boerne v. Flores*, 521 U.S. 507 (1997), clarified the issue of determining congressional intent in upholding federal suit against a state for violating the Voting Rights Act. The Court established two inquiries.

(1) First, because § 5 is remedial, legislation can only enforce provisions of the Fourteenth Amendment rather than creating new rights. The Court struck Title I of the Age Discrimination in Employment Act in part because Congress improperly used § 5 to pass substantive legislation. *Kimel v. Florida Bd. of Regents*, 528 U.S. 62 (2000). [R253]

(2) Second, there must be "congruence and proportionality," which means that Congress must tailor the legislation to remedy a particular constitutional violation; it must not be overly broad. In situations of widespread and pervasive violation by states, broad measures such as the Voting Rights Act may be appropriate. (Note, however, statutes once appropriate may become inappropriate because of passage of time and changed conditions. *See, e.g., Shelby County v. Holder*, 570 U.S. 529 (2013) (setting aside Voting Rights Act's coverage formula).) The Court has not ruled on whether passage of time can make a statute appropriate again.

(3) Note that although § 5 bears some resemblance to the Necessary and Proper Clause, art. I, § 8, cl.18. The Court has allowed Congress far more leeway under the latter. [R364]

c. *Board of Trustees of the University of Alabama v. Garrett*, 531 U.S. 356 (2001), applied *City of Boerne* to strike Title I of the Americans With Disabilities Act because Congress failed to demonstrate a widespread pattern of irrational state discrimination against the disabled. Thus, the legislation was not "appropriate" within the meaning of § 5.

d. Similarly, *Florida Prepaid Postsecondary Education Expense Board v. College Savings Bank*, 527 U.S. 627 (1999), applied *City of Boerne* and held that the Patent Remedy Act exceeded congressional authority under § 5 of the Fourteenth Amendment because nothing in the legislative record showed a pattern of state patent violations for which the states provided constitutionally insufficient remedies. (Bear in mind, however, that Congress has committed adjudication of patent claims exclusively to the federal courts. *See* 28 U.S.C. § 1338.)

e. *Kimel v. Florida Board of Regents*, 528 U.S. 62 (2000), applying *City of Boerne*, also held that Title I of the Age Discrimination in Employment Act did not validly abrogate Eleventh Amendment immunity. States may permissibly discriminate on the basis of age if it is rationally related to a legitimate state interest, so the legislation unduly restricted state behavior. Congress failed to show that such discrimination by states was a widespread problem that justified abrogation. Moreover, Congress had improperly used § 5 to pass substantive legislation. *See supra* § IV.C.3.b.(1), at 297 *[R253]*.

f. *Nevada Department of Human Resources v. Hibbs*, 538 U.S. 721 (2003), again applied *City of Boerne*, upholding provisions of the Family Medical Leave Act. Congress addressed gender discrimination by states, which triggers heightened scrutiny, making it "easier for Congress to show a pattern of state constitutional violations" justifying the legislation. In addition, the remedy Congress chose—the family-care leave provision—was congruent and proportional to the targeted violation. However, *Coleman v. Court of Appeals of Maryland*, 566 U.S. 30 (2012), held that the legitimacy of congressional allowance of damages in family-leave cases did not extend to similar actions under the Act's self-care provisions. [R248] [R250]

4. Indirect Abrogation (Constructive Waiver)

a. Occasionally, the Supreme Court has held that states waived Eleventh Amendment immunity by participating in federal programs if Congress conditioned such participation upon states waiver. In other words, Congress can provide that a state's mere participation in such a federal program is a waiver.

b. *Parden v. Terminal Railway*, 377 U.S. 184 (1964), is the best example. The Court held that Alabama waived its immunity by operating an interstate railroad after passage of the Federal Employers Liability Act, which explicitly made railroad *employers* (not mentioning states specifically) amenable to federal suits for negligence.

(1) The Court presumed that when the state chose to operate the interstate railroad, it was aware of the condition Congress set for doing so—amenability to suit in federal court.

(2) Some criticized *Parden* for conflicting with the unconstitutional-conditions doctrine, which provides that the government may not condition receipt of a benefit upon surrender of a constitutional right. Others, however, questioned whether the doctrine's logic (which the Court developed to

protect individuals against the state) had any place in defining the relationship between federal and state governments.

(3) *Parden* did not last long. The Court eroded the impact of its holding and finally overturned it.

c. *Edelman v. Jordan*, 415 U.S. 651 (1974), held that inferring indirect abrogation or constructive waiver is improper. It is appropriate only if Congress *expressly* conditions state participation in a federally-funded program upon consent to federal suit.

d. Other cases cut *Parden* back further. *Welch v. State Dept. of Highways and Public Transportation*, 483 U.S. 468 (1987), rejected indirect abrogation under the Jones Act because the statute lacked express language conditioning participation in a federal program upon consenting to suit in federal court. It overruled *Parden* to the extent that it was inconsistent with the *Edelman*'s clear-statement principle.

e. Finally, *College Savings Bank v. Florida Prepaid Postsecondary Educ. Expense Bd.*, 527 U.S. 666 (1999) overruled what was left of *Parden*. The Court held that constructive waiver has no place regarding constitutional rights such as Eleventh Amendment immunity. The majority rejected an argument that it should recognize a difference between conduct a state can choose to abandon, such as a business venture, and conduct that it cannot abandon, such as its police power. [R22] [R30] [R106] [R111] [R132] [R240] [R242] [R245] [R249] [R268] [R354]

Chapter XIV

ACTIONS TO VINDICATE FEDERAL CIVIL RIGHTS

■ ANALYSIS

I. Introduction

Following ratification of the Thirteenth, Fourteenth, and Fifteenth Amendments, Congress enacted statutes permitting individuals to sue to enforce federal rights. Some of these Reconstruction-era statutes are quite specific, but the most important of them—the major focus of this Chapter—is fairly broad: 42 U.S.C. § 1983 creates a private right of action for violation of one's federal rights under color of state law. Section 1983 remains an important and widely studied tool for vindicating civil rights; §§ II through IV of this Chapter focus on it. Section V discusses the extent to which there is a right to sue for deprivation of constitutional rights by federal officials. Section VI returns to another Reconstruction-era statute, which allows removal of civil and criminal cases if, *inter alia*, the state court will not protect a litigant's rights of racial equality.

II. Principal Civil Rights Statutes

A. "The" Civil Rights Act—Section 1983

1. Title 42 U.S.C. § 1983:

    > Every person who, under color of any statute, ordinance, regulation, custom, or usage, of any State or Territory or the District of Columbia, subjects, or causes to be subjected, any citizen of the United States or any other person within the jurisdiction thereof to the deprivation of any rights, privileges, or immunities secured by the Constitution and laws, shall be liable to that party injured in an action at law, suit in equity, or other proper proceeding. . . .

    [R159] [R238] [R246] [R287]

2. Several parts of the statute—"person," "color of state law," "rights, privileges, or immunities"—have caused uncertainty, and their meanings continue to develop.
3. The statute creates *no* substantive rights. Rather, it supplies a private right of action for vindicating "rights, privileges, or immunities" federal law secures in some other provision—constitutional or statutory. Thus the plaintiff must prove a deprivation of some cognizable federal right found elsewhere. *See infra* § III.F, at 310-313 *[R254]*.
4. Before the 1960s, there were few § 1983 cases. They now number in the tens of thousands annually. The increased use of the statute reflects modern expanded recognition of constitutional and other federal rights and liberal interpretations of § 1983 itself.
5. Section 1983 does not create subject-matter jurisdiction either. Federal courts have subject-matter jurisdiction over § 1983 cases under 28 U.S.C. §§ 1331, 1343. When Congress passed § 1983 in 1871, before there was a general federal-question statute, it also provided a jurisdictional statute, now codified at 28 U.S.C. § 1343(a)(3).

a. Until 1980, § 1331 had the same amount-in-controversy requirement as the diversity statute, § 1332. Then Congress eliminated that requirement, so § 1343(a)(3) is now redundant.

b. At one time, some thought that § 1343(a)(3) granted jurisdiction only over claims for violation of personal rights not easily subject to monetary valuation, on the theory that cases involving proprietary rights—those capable of valuation—could come to federal court under § 1331. *Lynch v. Household Finance Corp.*, 405 U.S. 538 (1972), rejected this distinction, so § 1331 and § 1343(a)(3) now have identical jurisdictional reach in civil-rights cases.

6. Federal jurisdiction over § 1983 cases is not exclusive; state courts may hear § 1983 claims. *Maine v. Thiboutot*, 448 U.S. 1, 3 n.1 (1980). Indeed, state courts *must* entertain § 1983 claims if they would hear analogous claims under state law. *Howlett v. Rose*, 496 U.S. 356 (1990). *See supra* Ch. XII, § IV at 275-280 *[R255]*. [R264]

B. Contrast With Habeas Corpus

1. Habeas corpus, *see infra* Ch. XV, at 331-346 *[R256]*, allows state prisoners to challenge the legality of their incarceration in federal court. Unlike the § 1983 plaintiff, a habeas petitioner is not suing for damages or other relief against officers who violated his federal rights. Rather, he is arguing that he should be released from custody because of some constitutional infirmity with the fact or duration of his imprisonment.

2. Habeas petitioners, unlike most § 1983 plaintiffs, must exhaust state remedies before seeking the writ from the federal court. (The Prison Litigation Reform Act now also requires exhaustion § 1983 cases by prisoners challenging the conditions of confinement. *See infra* Ch. XV, § III.B.2, at 335 *[R257]*.) [R199]

3. Moreover, while the general rules of claim and issue preclusion apply in § 1983 litigation (*see infra* § III.H.7, at 316 *[R258]*), they used to apply less stringently in habeas proceedings, but the Anti-Terrorism and Effective Death Penalty Act of 1996 (AEDPA) changed that. *See infra* Ch. XV, § II.C, at 333-334 *[R259]*. Thus, the fact that a state court decided an issue adversely to the habeas petitioner did not previously bar him from raising the issue again in the habeas proceeding. Now it does. The § 1983 plaintiff, on the other hand, never could raise the issue again. *See infra* § III.H.7, at 316 *[R260]*.

C. Other Reconstruction-Era Civil Rights Statutes

1. 42 U.S.C. § 1981 provides that "[a]ll persons within the jurisdiction of the United States shall have the same right in every State and Territory to make and enforce contracts, . . . and to the full and equal benefit of all laws and proceedings for the security of persons and property as is enjoyed by white citizens. . . ."

a. This prohibits racial discrimination in making and enforcing wholly private contracts. *Runyon v. McCrary*, 427 U.S. 160 (1976). Section 1981(c), which Congress enacted in 1991, codifies *Runyon*.

b. A contract for education is a "contract" under this statute. A state university's freshman admissions policy violated § 1981 because its use of race was not narrowly tailored to achieve the university's interest in diversity. *Gratz v. Bollinger*, 539 U.S. 244, 276 n.23 (2003) ("[P]urposeful discrimination that violates the Equal Protection Clause of the Fourteenth Amendment will also violate § 1981."). *Students for Fair Admissions, Inc. v. President and Fellows of Harvard College*, 600 U.S. 181 (2023), appears to doom affirmative action, at least in higher-education cases.

2. 42 U.S.C. § 1982 provides that "[a]ll citizens of the United States shall have the same right, in every State and Territory, as is enjoyed by the white citizens thereof to inherit, purchase, lease, sell, hold, and convey real and personal property." This is a valid exercise of legislative power under the Thirteenth Amendment and bars private and public racial discrimination in the sale or rental of real property. *Jones v. Alfred H. Mayer Co.*, 392 U.S. 409 (1968).

3. 42 U.S.C. § 1985(3) permits recovery for private conspiracies to deny equal protection of the laws or to interfere with civil rights.

4. 42 U.S.C. § 1988(a) provides that when a civil rights statute is "deficient in the provisions necessary to furnish suitable remedies," the federal courts are to apply "the common law, as modified and changed by the constitution and statutes of the State wherein the court having jurisdiction . . . is held," at least so long as such law is not "inconsistent" with federal law. The Supreme Court has found § 1983 "deficient" in several particulars, as to which federal courts will apply state law. *See infra* § III.H.2, at 342 *[R261]*. [R278]

D. Modern Civil Rights Statutes

1. Congress has passed many civil rights statutes in since 1960, including the Civil Rights Act of 1964, the Voting Rights Act of 1965, the Americans with Disabilities Act, the Violence Against Women Act of 1994, and Title IX of the 1972 Education Amendments to the Civil Rights Act. Detailed listing, let alone consideration, of such legislation is beyond the scope of this book.

2. As important as these statutes are, most Federal Courts courses focus on § 1983, which, though it creates no rights, is a vehicle for enforcing a panoply of federal rights guaranteed elsewhere. *See infra* § III.F, at 340-313 *[R262]*.

3. The Attorney's Fees Award Act of 1976, 28 U.S.C. § 1988(b), is worth special focus. It now permits a court to allow "the prevailing party" to

recover a reasonable attorney's fee from another party. The statute explicitly applies to cases brought "to enforce a provision" of specific statutes, including § 1983.

a. The general American rule is that each party bears its own attorney's fees, and a court without statutory authorization ordinarily cannot order one party to pay another's attorney's fees. Section § 1988(b) is such an authorization.

b. Questions of when one is a "prevailing party" who may qualify for an attorney's fee award and what fee is "reasonable" have generated considerable litigation, especially under § 1983. *See infra* § III.G, at 341-342 *[R263]*. [R277]

III. Litigation Under § 1983

A. Section 1983 Was Little Used Until 1961

1. Congress passed § 1983 during Reconstruction. *See supra* §§ I, II.A, at 303-304 *[R264]*. Although the statute clearly provides a remedy for one suffering deprivation of federal rights under color of state law, it sat essentially unused for generations. One study found only nineteen reported cases construing or applying the statute in its first sixty-five years.

2. By contrast, in calendar 2020, private plaintiffs filed over 40,000 civil rights cases in the federal courts; most of those were undoubtedly § 1983 cases. (Note: federal jurisdiction in civil rights cases is not exclusive.) The stunning increase in § 1983 cases traces, at least in large measure, to a single 1961 case. [R183]

B. *Monroe v. Pape* Invigorated the Statute

1. *Monroe v. Pape*, 365 U.S. 167 (1961), arose when Chicago Police Department officers, without a warrant, burst into Monroe's house in the early morning, forced him and his family out of bed, and made Monroe stand naked in the living room while they searched the house. They arrested Monroe and took him to the police station, where they held him for ten hours on "open charges," not allowing him to call his lawyer. Police questioned him about a two-day old murder. He was never arraigned, though a magistrate was available. The city never prosecuted him for anything.

2. Monroe sued the individual police officers and the City of Chicago, seeking damages. Specifically, he asserted that the warrantless search was unreasonable and violated the Fourth Amendment, which applies to the states through the Fourteenth Amendment's Due Process Clause.

3. The Supreme Court upheld Monroe's right to sue under § 1983, establishing three critical points that continue to apply in § 1983 litigation. (The Court also held that municipalities were not persons within the meaning of § 1983, and thus not proper defendants. *Monell v. Department of Social Services*, 436 U.S. 658 (1978), overruled that holding.) *See infra* § III.D, at 307-309 *[R265]*.

a. First, § 1983 plaintiff need not exhaust state remedies (such as tort suits or administrative claims within the police department) before filing under § 1983. (In 1995, Congress added an exhaustion requirement for § 1983 actions challenging prison conditions of confinement. Prison Litigation Reform Act (PLRA), 42 U.S.C. § 1997e(a), *see infra* Ch. XV, § III.B.2, at 335 *[R266]*. The Court made clear that the § 1983 claim supplements any remedy under state law. Thus, it is no defense to a § 1983 case to say that the plaintiff could have sued in state court or sought administrative relief under state law. *Patsy v. Florida Bd. of Regents*, 457 U.S. 496 (1982) (§ 1983 plaintiff need not exhaust administrative remedy before commencing suit). [R183] [R274] [R380]

b. Second, the officers' actions in *Monroe* were "under color" of state law, as § 1983 requires, even though their actions violated state law. The under-color requirement looks to whether the defendant had some badge of authority to enforce state law, not to whether state law authorized the actions. *See infra* § III.E, at 309-310 *[R267]*. [R273]

C. Plaintiff Must be a Citizen or Person Within U.S. Jurisdiction

1. Section 1983 uses "person" twice, and it is important to keep "plaintiff persons" and "defendant persons" separately in mind. Section 1983 permits suit by "any citizen of the United States or other person within the jurisdiction thereof," subject to the ordinary requirements of justiciability such as standing, ripeness, and mootness.

2. Thus, aliens may pursue § 1983 actions on the same basis as citizens. Corporations are also "persons" for purposes of the Due Process and Equal Protection Clauses, so they may maintain § 1983 actions. Thus, "person" includes corporations generally..

D. Defendant Must be a "Person"

1. A state is not a § 1983 person and thus is not subject to suit under the statute in state or federal court. *Will v. Michigan Dept. of State Police*, 491 U.S. 58, 66 (1989). *See also Lapides v. Board of Regents of State Univ. System*, 535 U.S. 613, 617 (2002). This construction of the statute avoids the question of whether § 1983 would constitute sufficiently clear abrogation of a state's Eleventh Amendment immunity from suit in federal court. *See supra* Ch. XIII § IV.C, at 295-299 *[R268]*. Given the Court's current Eleventh Amendment approach, it almost certainly would not. [R252]

2. Officers sued in their official capacities are also not § 1983 persons. *Will*, 491 U.S. at 71. On the other hand, officers sued in their personal capacities are § 1983 persons for acts in their official capacity. *Hafer v. Melo*, 502 U.S. 21, 26 (1991).

Example: Plaintiff has a claim that Sergeant Joe Friday of the Los Angeles Police Department violated his constitutional rights while on duty. Plaintiff may not properly file a § 1983 case naming "Joe Friday, in his capacity as an Officer of the Los Angeles Police Department," but he may file a § 1983 case against "Joe Friday, in his personal capacity" and sue for the deprivation of rights Sergeant Friday's on-duty behavior allegedly caused. [R239] [R374]

3. Many § 1983 cases now assert claims against municipalities—cities and counties. The Supreme Court has changed positions on whether municipalities are § 1983 persons, but the law now seems clear that they are.

    a. *Monroe v. Pape*, 365 U.S. 167 (1961), interpreted the legislative history of § 1983 as dictating that a municipal corporation is not a § 1983 person, at least not for damages claims. Later, the Court extended the holding to claims for equitable relief. *City of Kenosha v. Bruno*, 412 U.S. 507 (1973), and held that a county is not a § 1983 person either. *Moor v. County of Alameda*, 411 U.S. 693 (1973).

    b. But seventeen years after *Monroe*, *Monell v. Department of Social Services*, 436 U.S. 658 (1978), exhaustively analyzed § 1983's legislative history (which *Monroe* had not done) and held that a municipality *is* a § 1983 person, but only for "a policy statement, ordinance, regulation, or decision officially adopted and promulgated by that body's officers" or for a "governmental 'custom' even though such a custom has not received formal approval through the body's official decision-making channels."436 U.S. at 690-91.

    c. Under *Monell* municipalities are not subject to *respondeat-superior* liability. They are liable only if some municipal policy or custom caused the deprivation.

Example: Assume that Sergeant Friday of the Los Angeles Police Department violated Plaintiff's federal rights by using excessive force while on duty. As above, Plaintiff can sue Sergeant Friday personally—in his private capacity. But Los Angeles is not liable under § 1983 simply because its officer committed a tort, even a constitutional tort. To proceed against the City, Plaintiff would have to show that the City had some policy or custom of hiring or continuing to employ police officers while consciously disregarding a high risk that officers would use excessive force. *Board of County Commissioners v. Brown*, 520 U.S. 397 (1997). That is an extraordinarily difficult showing to make. [R375]

    d. Regardless of the existence of a policy or custom, a municipality is not liable under for punitive damages § 1983. *City of Newport v. Fact Concerts, Inc.*, 453 U.S. 247 (1981). [R101] [R102] [R276]

4. A private corporation is a § 1983 "person," basically along the same lines as a municipality.

5. Be sure to keep in mind that a proper defendant may be entitled to immunity—absolute or qualified—from a § 1983 suit. *See infra* § IV, at 316-323 *[R269]*. [R265]

E. Defendant Must Have Acted "Under Color" of "State Law"

1. *Monroe v. Pape* established that a defendant satisfies this requirement even when acting contrary to state law or if state law does not authorize his action. Thus, the *Monroe* officers acted under color of state law because they committed the violations while wielding governmental power.

   a. The acts were under color of state law even though they were (1) unconstitutional and (2) state law did not authorize them .

   b. Thus, § 1983 does not cover only cases involving official regulations, policies, or customs that violate constitutional norms. It also addresses abuse of power by one "who is a repository of state power." It reaches those "who carry a badge of authority of a State and represent it in some capacity, whether they act in accordance with their authority or misuse it." *Monroe*, 365 U.S. at 172. [R372]

2. Of course, a plaintiff suing for a violation of the Fourteenth Amendment must show state action.

   a. If the constitutional requirement of state action exists, the case also satisfies the statutory under-color requirement. *See Lugar v. Edmondson Oil Co.*, 457 U.S. 922, 929 (1982) ("[I]n a § 1983 action brought against a state official, the statutory requirement of action 'under color of state law' and the 'state action' requirement of the Fourteenth Amendment are identical.").

   b. Moreover, a § 1983 action may vindicate other constitutional and even statutory rights that do not require a showing of state action; nonetheless, in such cases the plaintiff still must show that the defendant acted under color of state law, because § 1983 demands that.

3. The under-color requirement is rarely a problem when the acts are by state or local officers exercising their authority or appearing to exercise their authority.

Example: Barney Fife, a deputy sheriff, moonlights off-duty as a security guard. While doing so, he wears his deputy's uniform. He accosts a suspected shoplifter in an unconstitutional manner. His acts may be under color of state law, making him susceptible to a § 1983 case. *See, e.g., Lusby v. T.G. & Y Stores, Inc.*, 749 F.2d 1423 (10th Cir. 1984).

4. On the other hand, not every act of a state officer is under color of state law.

Example: Barney Fife, while on duty as a deputy sheriff, accosts his cousin Virgil over a debt. Barney probably does not act under color of state law because the fact that he is an officer had nothing to do with the stop.

5. Private actors—those who do not "carry a badge of authority of a State"—may be § 1983 defendants if they nonetheless act under color of state law.

Example: Private individuals attach P's property under a state attachment statute. P sues the individuals, alleging that the statute is unconstitutional, denying P due process. The individuals acted under color of state law, because they engaged in joint activity with the state in seizing the property. *Lugar*, 457 U.S. at 941.

Example: Private individuals conspire with a state judge to have them win pending litigation. The private individuals acted under color of state law, because they engaged in joint activity with a state actor in depriving the other party of a constitutional right. The private individuals are proper § 1983 defendants even though the judge is immune from suit. *Dennis v. Sparks*, 449 U.S. 24 (1980). *See infra* § IV, at 316-323 *[R270]*.

6. On the other hand, not all private actors having some relationship with a state act under color of state law.

Example: State University imposes discipline against Coach pursuant to regulations and recommendations by the National Collegiate Athletic Association. NCAA did not act under color of state law, since the University's acceptance of the NCAA regulations did not transform them into state rules. *NCAA v. Tarkanian*, 488 U.S. 179 (1988). [R280]

7. "State law," within the meaning of § 1983, includes "any statute, ordinance, regulation, custom, or usage, of any State or Territory, or the District of Columbia."

   a. In 1979, Congress added a sentence to § 1983 providing that any congressional act "applicable exclusively to the District of Columbia shall be considered to be a statute of the District of Columbia."

   b. Section 1983 does not apply if the defendant acts under color of federal law. A *Bivens* action may be available for those cases. *See supra* Ch. XI.VI.D.2.b.1, at 246 *[R271]*. *See infra* § V.A, at 323 *[R272]*. [R267]

F. Defendant Must Have Deprived Plaintiff of a Federal Right

1. The gravamen of a § 1983 case is that the defendant has deprived the plaintiff of any "rights, privileges, or immunities secured by the Constitution and laws."

2. The statute creates *no* substantive rights; it creates a private right of action for enforcing some substantive right found elsewhere in federal law. Not all rights are federal; suits for deprivation of state rights—even

state constitutional rights that parallel the federal Constitution—are not proper under § 1983. [R376]

3. Not all provisions of the Constitution confer enforceable rights. *Chapman v. Houston Welfare Rights Organization*, 441 U.S. 600 (1979), held, for instance, that the Supremacy Clause does not confer such rights, and a Court unanimous on this point confirmed that rule. *Armstrong v. Exceptional Child Center, Inc.*, 575 U.S. 320 (2015). Neither is there a First Amendment right to provide legal assistance to fellow inmates. *Shaw v. Murphy*, 532 U.S. 223 (2001).

4. Clearly, however, the Reconstruction-era Amendments, including the Equal Protection and Due Process Clauses of the Fourteenth Amendment and those portions of the Bill of Rights applicable to the states (First, Second, Fourth, some Fifth, Sixth, and Eighth Amendment rights), are enforceable in § 1983 cases. The Commerce Clause also creates such a right. *Dennis v. Higgins*, 498 U.S. 439 (1991) (allowing § 1983 claim that local regulation unduly burdens interstate commerce or discriminates against it).

5. *Trustees of Dartmouth College v. Woodward*, 17 U.S. (4 Wheat.) 518 (1819), allowed a claim directly under the Impairment Clause, art. I, § 10.

Example: Prisoner claims that prison officers took intentionally harmful acts with deliberate indifference to his rights. He states a proper claim for violation of his Eighth Amendment right to be free from cruel and unusual punishment. *Estelle v. Gamble*, 429 U.S. 97 (1976).

Example: Monroe, *see supra* § III.B, at 306-307 *[R273]*, claimed that the police officers made an unreasonable search and seizure. He stated a Fourth Amendment claim. *Graham v. Connor*, 490 U.S. 386 (1989).

6. The Supreme Court distinguishes between what some commentators call "fundamental rights" and "non-fundamental rights," an important distinction. Fundamental rights include those the Bill of Rights protects and substantive-due-process rights (including those related to reproductive choice (*but see Dobbs v. Jackson Women's Health Organization*, 597 U.S. 215 (2024)) guarantee. Non-fundamental rights include deprivations of property and perhaps even liberty. Bear in mind that state law may create property or liberty interests (*e.g.* public education and drivers' licenses) to which due-process and equal-protection requirements then attach.

   a. Plaintiffs asserting fundamental rights may proceed in a § 1983 cases and, generally, need not exhaust any available state court remedies. *See supra* § III.B.3.a, at 307 *[R274]*.

   b. There is no right to proceed under § 1983 in non-fundamental-rights cases if the state provides an appropriate opportunity for hearing.

Example: Prison officials lose Prisoner's hobby kit, worth $23.50. Prisoner sues under § 1983, asserting that the officials deprived him of his property without due process of law. State law provides a mechanism by which Prisoner can recover the value of the hobby kit from the state. Prisoner could not proceed under § 1983 because a pre-deprivation remedy for negligence is not possible, and the state provided a meaningful post-deprivation remedy. *Parratt v. Taylor*, 451 U.S. 527 (1981).

Some observers conclude that *Parratt* imposed a rule, contrary to *Monroe v. Pape*, that the plaintiff exhaust state remedies. The better way to interpret the case, however, is that state negligence law did not deprive Prisoner of a constitutional right, since the availability of the post-deprivation remedy meant that there was no deprivation of property *without due process*. The state negligence action is the process that was due.

Daniels v. Williams, 474 U.S. 327 (1986), overruled *Parratt*, stating that a negligence claim never states a claim for deprivation under the Fourteenth Amendment's Due Process Clause. Thus, apparently, even if the state provides no meaningful post-deprivation remedy, negligence will not support a § 1983 claim. The Court thus distinguishes, for purposes of § 1983, between intentional and unintentional torts.

Example: A fellow inmate beat Prisoner after Prisoner had warned officials that he was in danger of attack from the inmate. Negligence of prison guards made the beating possible. Prisoner could not proceed under § 1983 even though it seemed clear that state law afforded him no remedy. *Davidson v. Cannon*, 474 U.S. 344 (1986). Mere negligence by state officials does not implicate due process.

Even intentional torts may not support § 1983 claims.

Example: A school principal repeatedly struck a student, meting out corporal punishment without a hearing in advance. The student sued under § 1983, seeking damages for a denial of liberty without due process. The student could not proceed under § 1983 because he could proceed against the principal in tort in state court after the punishment. *Ingraham v. Wright*, 430 U.S. 651 (1977).

The Court seems to be saying there is no due-process deprivation, even of a liberty interest and even if a pre-deprivation hearing is possible, as long as the state makes available a post-deprivation remedy. As the Court likes to say, the post-deprivation remedy may be the process that is due. But a pre-deprivation hearing may be necessary when the risk of an erroneous deprivation outweighs the government's interest in speed. *Mathews v. Eldridge*, 424 U.S. 319 (1976). In such a case, denial of a pre-deprivation hearing could be the basis of a damages claim under § 1983. Neither *Parratt* nor *Ingraham*, said the Court, involved such a situation.

7. Section 1983 applies not only to deprivations of federal constitutional rights but also to deprivations of rights, privileges, and immunities secured by "the laws" of the United States. Thus, deprivation of federal statutory rights may be the basis of a § 1983 claim. *Maine v. Thiboutot*, 448 U.S. 1 (1980) (permitting § 1983 case for violation of Social Security Act). But *Thiboutout* is less extensive than one might think.

   a. The Supreme Court once seemed more willing than it is now to permit enforcement of federal statutory rights through § 1983. *Compare, e.g., Wright v. Roanoke Redevelopment & Housing Auth.*, 479 U.S. 418 (1987) (allowing suit by tenants to recover overcharges under a rent-ceiling provision of the Public Housing Act) *with Suter v. Artist M.*, 503 U.S. 347 (1992) (rejecting § 1983 suit to enforce provision of Adoption Assistance and Child Welfare Act of 1980 requiring states receiving funds for adoption assistance to have a plan to make reasonable efforts to keep children out of foster homes).

   b. *Gonzaga University v. Doe*, 536 U.S. 273 (2002), revisited the issue and may have clarified the standard. The Court likened the inquiry, at least in one respect, to deciding whether a statute creates a private right of action, concluding that a statute is enforceable under § 1983 only if Congress indicates "an unambiguously conferred right." Thus, even if a statute does not create a private right to sue, it may be enforceable through § 1983 if Congress *clearly* indicated that the statute created both a private right and a private remedy, not just a general interest. (If this distinction seems less than pellucid to you, you are paying appropriately close attention.) The Court held that provisions of the Family Educational Rights and Private Act (FERPA) prohibiting federal funding of educational institutions that release educational records to unauthorized persons did not create a personal right enforceable under § 1983. The Court noted (1) that FERPA's language was insufficiently specific to create an enforceable private right and remedy and (2) that Congress has explicitly committed FERPA enforcement to the Secretary of Education, noting that the customary remedy for state violation of legislation under the Spending Clause of art. I, § 8, cl. 1, is withholding federal funds. The Court inferred, therefore, that Congress had not intended to create a privately-enforceable right. *See supra* Ch. XI, § VI.C.2, at 247 *[R275]*. [R254]

G. Remedies, Including Attorney's Fees

1. Section 1983 expressly provides that the defendant "shall be liable to the party injured in an action at law, suit in equity, or other proper proceeding for redress."

2. Most § 1983 cases are damages claims. Because the § 1983 claim is in the nature of tort, the damages should compensate the plaintiff for the

harm done. Compensatory damages do not consider the abstract value or importance of the constitutional right. *Memphis Community Sch. Dist. v. Stachura*, 477 U.S. 299, 310 (1986).

a. Punitive damages may also be available from individual defendants, but not from municipalities. *See supra* § III.D.3.d, at 308 *[R276]*.

b. Showing that the defendant acted with ill will or malice is sufficient for punitive damages but not prerequisite. Punitive damages are also appropriate for callous or reckless indifference to the denial of rights. *Smith v. Wade*, 461 U.S. 30 (1983).

3. Equitable remedies, including declaratory judgments and injunctions, are available in appropriate circumstances.

a. Under the Prison Litigation Reform Act, injunctive relief is appropriate only if the court finds that the relief is narrowly drawn, extends no further than necessary to correct the violation, and constitutes the least intrusive means needed to correct the violation. 18 U.S.C. § 3626(a)(1).

b. The defendants can move to terminate a PLRA order of prospective relief if the court did not make such express findings in its order. 18 U.S.C. § 3626(b)(2).

4. Title 42 U.S.C. § 1988(b), permits the court to award an attorney's fee in a reasonable amount to the prevailing party in § 1983 litigation. *See supra* § II.D.3, at 305-306 *[R277]*.

a. A party prevails by obtaining relief on the merits of the claim that "materially alters the legal relationship between the parties by modifying the defendant's behavior in a way that directly benefits the [party]." *Farrar v. Hobby*, 506 U.S. 103, 111-12 (1992).

b. Such fees may be appropriate even if the plaintiff won only nominal damages, provided (1) the amount recovered is not outrageously less than what he sought, (2) the case raised significant legal issues, and (3) the case served the public goal of the suit. *Murray v. City of Onawa*, 323 F.3d 616, 619-20 (8th Cir. 2003) (upholding award of $7,428 in attorney's fees for plaintiff who won $1 in damages). [R201]

H. Miscellaneous Litigation Issues

1. Title 42 U.S.C. § 1988(a), *see supra* § II.C.4, at 305 *[R278]*, applies to § 1983 suits in federal court. It directs the court to apply "the common law, as modified and changed by the constitution and statutes of the State wherein the court is held" whenever § 1983 is "deficient." [R200]

2. Section 1983 may be deficient when it fails to address a particular issue.

a. The statute says nothing about whether a claim survives the death of the plaintiff. The Supreme Court has held that this falls within § 1988(a) and requires the federal court to apply state law. *Robertson v. Wegmann*, 436 U.S. 584 (1978).

b. Section 1988(a) also allows the court to ignore state law if applying it would be inconsistent with policies underlying § 1983. *Robertson* concluded that the state law—directing dismissal because the plaintiff left no close relatives—was not inconsistent with such policies because few cases would involve a plaintiff with no close relatives.

3. Congress never prescribed a statute of limitations or a rule for tolling a limitations period for § 1983 cases.

a. These deficiencies do require that the federal courts apply state statutes of limitations, including state tolling periods. *Board of Regents v. Tomanio*, 446 U.S. 478 (1980).

b. Specifically, the court looks to the state statute "governing an analogous cause of action under state law." *Wilson v.* Garcia, 471 U.S. 261, 271 (1985). The problem, of course, is that § 1983 claims might have different state-law analogs. For instance, a claim that police officers beat the plaintiff may implicate a statute of limitations different from the one applicable to a claim that the defendant fired plaintiff on the basis of race. *Wilson* indicated that there should be a single statute of limitations for cases arising in a particular state, generally that for a personal injury claim.

c. If state law has more than one statute of limitations for personal injury cases, the federal court applies "the general or residual statute for personal injury actions" from state law. *Owens v. Okure*, 488 U.S. 235, 250 (1989). [R203]

4. Although § 1983 does not create a right to jury trial, parties to a § 1983 case in federal court have the same Seventh Amendment right to jury trial as litigants in other federal civil cases. *City of Monterey v. Del Monte Dunes at Monterey, Ltd.*, 526 U.S. 687 (1999). (Recall that the Court has ruled that the Fourteenth Amendment does not incorporate the Seventh Amendment, so it does not apply in state courts.)

5. Some lower courts imposed heightened pleading requirements for specificity in § 1983 cases. *Leatherman v. Tarrant County*, 507 U.S. 163 (1993), rejected the practice, noting that nothing in the Federal Rules of Civil Procedure permitted courts to impose anything more than the typical "notice" requirements for pleadings in § 1983 cases. (Be aware, though, that *Ashcroft v. Iqbal*, 556 U.S. 662 (2009), and *Bell Atlantic Corp. v. Twombly*, 550 U.S. 544 (2007), appear to establish more rigorous pleading standards under FED. R. CIV. P. 8(a)(2) generally, in what some commentators see as a step back toward code-pleading requirements.) *Leatherman* left open whether a court might impose more rigorous pleading requirements on defendants raising a defense of qualified immunity. *See infra* § IV.C, at 318-323 *[R279]*.

6. Reacting to a large number of frivolous § 1983 and Federal Tort Claims Act claims by prisoners, Congress passed the 1995 Prison Litigation Reform Act (PLRA). As one court explained, Congress intended "to reduce the number of frivolous cases filed by imprisoned plaintiffs, who have little to lose and excessive amounts of free time with which to pursue their complaints." *Napier v. Preslicka*, 314 F.3d 528, 531 (11th Cir. 2002). To that end, it imposes various restrictions, including:

   a. Unlike other § 1983 plaintiffs, a prisoner cannot file a proceeding concerning prison conditions until he has exhausted administrative remedies. This requirement "applies to all inmate suits about prison life, whether they involve general circumstances or particular episodes, and whether they allege excessive force or some other wrong." *Porter v. Nussle*, 534 U.S. 516 (2002).

   b. A prisoner who has filed at least three previous civil actions or appeals that a federal court dismissed as frivolous, malicious, or failing to state a claim may not again seek civil relief *in forma pauperis* "unless the prisoner is under imminent danger of serious physical injury." 28 U.S.C. § 1915(g). (Several circuits and district courts have ruled that § 1915(g) does not violate either the First Amendment right to petition for redress or the Fourteenth Amendment right to equal protection, because it does not prohibit further litigation but merely imposes a procedural rule requiring the prisoner to pay filing fees.)

   c. A convicted felon may not sue for mental or emotional injury suffered in custody without showing physical injury. 42 U.S.C. § 1997e(e). R381]

7. As a general rule, principles of claim and issue preclusion (res judicata and collateral estoppel respectively) apply in § 1983 litigation. *Allen v. McCurry*, 449 U.S. 90 (1980) (applying issue preclusion to issue litigated and determined against § 1983 plaintiff in state proceedings if the state court system would apply preclusion); *Migra v. Warren City School District*, 465 U.S. 75 (1984) (discharged public-school teacher's state-court damages suit would bar subsequent federal action against the same defendants on § 1983 claim not raised in state litigation if state law would preclude). [R258] [R260]

IV. Immunity for Violating Individuals' Constitutional Rights

A. Preliminary Note

1. All but one of the immunity doctrines are species of federal common law and therefore could fit logically in Chapter XI. (The single exception is the legislative immunity the Constitution provides in art. I, § 6, cl. 1.) But since they deal predominantly with cases asserting constitutional civil-rights violations, we present them here.

2. The Supreme Court began developing the immunity doctrines in the context of cases under 42 U.S.C. § 1983, but they apply equally in cases against federal officials.

B. Background and Definitions

1. Section 1983 says nothing about immunity, and the Constitution provides limited immunity only for members of Congress. Nonetheless, the Supreme Court has consistently ruled that some defendants should be immune from § 1983 litigation. The Court routinely asserts that there is a long history of immunity for certain official acts and refuses to believe that Congress intended to override it in § 1983 without some clear statement to that effect. *Tenney v. Brandhove*, 341 U.S. 367 (1951). English law in the late eighteenth century, however, recognized immunity only for legislators (in the English Bill of Rights of 1689, and participants in judicial proceedings (under English common law), not for executive officials. The Founders were well aware that several British cases in the 1760s had rejected the idea of executive immunity and adjudicated damages actions in hefty amounts against the King's officials, including the English Secretary of State.

2. Generally, immunity protects the official against the lawsuit itself, not merely against liability. (In this respect, it resembles the Fifth Amendment's Double-Jeopardy Clause.) Consequently, the courts have endeavored to mold immunity rules applicable near the outset of litigation, so that if immunity exists, the court can dismiss promptly. Thus, the factors that go into finding immunity should be ascertainable without having to get deeply involved in litigating the underlying dispute. If a defendant can only determine whether she is immune by litigating the underlying suit, the immunity fails to serve part of its purpose—sparing the defendant from having to go through trial. [R286]

3. Generally, immunity is from a suit *damages*. Ordinarily, someone immune from a damages suit is *not* immune from suit for equitable relief—an injunction or declaratory judgment—an obvious inconsistency.

4. Immunity is usually available only to state actors, but a private individual may act under color of state law if acting in concert with a state official in depriving the plaintiff of a federal right. *See supra* § III.E.5, 6, at 310 *[R280]*.

   a. Although the state official may be entitled to immunity, generally the immunity is "not transferable to private parties." *Wyatt v. Cole*, 504 U.S. 158, 168 (1992). *See also Dennis v. Sparks*, 449 U.S. 24 (1980) (judge immune but private party with whom he acted to deny plaintiff's federal rights was proper § 1983 defendant).

   b. Sometimes private parties act in lieu of a local government. For example, an increasing number of localities contract with private corporations to run prison facilities. Arguably, employees of such facilities ought to be able to claim the same sort of immunity as an officer in a public prison, but *Richardson v. McKnight*, 521 U.S. 399 (1997), withheld it.

5. There are two types of immunity.

   a. Absolute immunity, as the name implies, protects the defendant from suit without exception. Only certain officials are entitled to absolute immunity, and only while performing certain types of tasks. *See infra* § IV.C, at 318-321 *[R281]*.

   b. Qualified immunity (sometimes misleadingly called "good-faith" immunity) protects a state actor from suit only if she acted in an objectively reasonable manner. The question is intimately connected with whether the right was well established at the time the claim arose. *See infra* § IV.C, at 318-321 *[R282]*. When the Supreme Court created the qualified-immunity doctrine, it had a good-faith component, but *Harlow v. Fitzgerald*, 457 U.S. 800 (1982), eliminated it. [R284]

C. Absolute Immunity

1. Judges are absolutely immune from suit for damages for acts taken in their judicial capacity—no matter if the judge was wrong, unreasonable, or even corrupt—as long as she was performing a judicial function. Courts tend to find that an act is judicial unless taken with a "clear absence of all jurisdiction." *Stump v. Sparkman*, 435 U.S. 349, 356 (1978). Even a judicial act with no legal basis qualifies for immunity.

Example: In *Stump*, a state judge in a court of general jurisdiction granted Mother's petition to have minor Daughter (whom Mother's affidavit characterized as "somewhat retarded") sterilized. He granted the order without a hearing and without notice to Daughter, then fifteen. Pursuant to the order, physicians sterilized Daughter. Later, then-married Daughter found she could not have children, discovered why, and sued several persons, including the judge who issued the order. Although no state law permitted a parent to consent to sterilization or provided for such an order, the judge was absolutely immune from suit. Although acting in excess of his legal authority, he had performed a judicial function.

Example: State court judge for County A enters an order affecting persons in County B. Under state law, the judge has no authority in County B. "For a judge to assume authority outside the geographic bounds of his office is the kind of clear judicial usurpation which cannot be condoned by any grant of immunity." *Maestri v. Jutkofsky*, 860 F.2d 50, 53 (2d Cir. 1988).

2. The Supreme Court justifies absolute judicial immunity as necessary (1) to keep judges free from suits by disappointed litigants and (2) to ensure that judges act without fear of adverse personal consequences.

3. Judges are *not* absolutely immune in two circumstances.

a. Claims for equitable relief, even for judicial acts.

Pulliam v. Allen, 466 U.S. 522 (1984). Although *Pulliam* held that a judge could be held liable for attorney's fees by the prevailing party in such a case, four years later Congress overruled that portion of the holding and prohibited fee awards against judges "unless such action was clearly in excess of such officer's jurisdiction." 42 U.S.C. § 1988(b).

b. Acts taken in a non-judicial (*i.e.* administrative) capacity. Non-judicial acts entitle a judge only to qualified immunity.

Example: Judge allegedly engaged in sex discrimination in demoting and firing a probation officer. Because this was an administrative, not a judicial, act, the judge was not absolutely immune from a damages claim. He could claim only qualified immunity. *Forrester v. White*, 484 U.S. 219 (1988).

4. Jurors and witnesses in litigation are absolutely immune from damages claims. This rule clearly is necessary to enable them to act without fear of reprisal. *See Briscoe v. LaHue*, 460 U.S. 325 (1983) (civil immunity for witnesses alleged to have given perjured testimony). English common law recognized this immunity before the United States existed.

5. Prosecutors are absolutely immune from damages claims based on traditional advocacy functions. As with judicial immunity, however, when prosecutors perform administrative functions, they receive only qualified immunity. *See Kalina v. Fletcher*, 522 U.S. 118 (1997) (preparing and filing documents charging a crime protected by absolute immunity, but executing certificate for probable-cause determination was not a traditional advocacy function but rather was investigatory and therefore absolute immunity unavailable); *Buckley v. Fitzsimmons*, 509 U.S. 259 (1993) (alleged misconduct in course of investigation was administrative, eligible for qualified immunity only). [R283]

6. Legislators are absolutely immune for actions taken "within the sphere of the legitimate legislative activity." *Supreme Court of Virginia v. Consumers Union of United States*, 446 U.S. 719, 732 (1980). Nearly a century before the United States existed, the English Bill of Rights had codified such an immunity.

   a. This immunity applies to claims for damages and claims for equitable relief.

   b. Federal legislative immunity rests upon the Speech and Debate Clause. U.S. CONST., art. I, § 6, cl. 1.

   c. Thus no action lies against a legislator for legislation that turns out to be unconstitutional or for anything said in legislative debate.

d. This immunity also applies to officials who, while not legislators, are engaged in a legislative function. For example, a state supreme court that promulgates attorney-discipline rules acts performs a legislative function. *Supreme Court of Virginia*, 446 U.S. at 734.

e. The immunity does not apply, however, to employees of the legislative body.

7. Presidential Immunity

a. The President of the United States had absolute immunity, at least from suits for damages for actions in her official capacity. *Nixon v. Fitzgerald*, 457 U.S. 731 (1982).

b. The President is not immune, however, from damages suits for acts before becoming President, even if the suit is filed during the presidency. *Clinton v. Jones*, 520 U.S. 681 (1997).

c. On July 1, 2024, the Court decided *Trump v. United States*, 603 U.S. 593 (2024), greatly expanding and complicating presidential immunity. The 6-3 majority ended up creating a three-tier structure.

(1) There is absolute privilege from civil and criminal liability for actions with the president's "core and exclusive" powers (such as the pardon power and control of the military).

(2) There is a presumptive absolute privilege for official actions within the "outer perimeter" of presidential power.

(3) Unofficial actions by the president receive no privilege.

d. The majority left many things unclear, such as how to distinguish official from unofficial presidential acts. It left those problems for the lower courts on remand.

e. The opinion is remarkable for the things it did not say.

(1) Although the Court spoke of "presumptive immunity," contrasting it with absolute immunity, it did not discuss what showing would rebut the presumption, though it did make clear that the government has the burden of proof in a criminal case against a former president.

(2) The Court made no attempt to rest the immunity upon any constitutional language, relying instead on "our constitutional structure of separated powers. . . ."

(3) Although the Court noted the Framers' desire for a vigorous executive, it did not mention the Framers' intent with respect to presidential immunity. In THE FEDERALIST No. 70 (Hamilton), upon which the majority relied, Hamilton made clear that he favored a unitary executive over a plural executive *because* it would make the executive more accountable

under the law, an odd position for someone favoring presidential immunity.

(4) The Court did not comment on the significance of the Framers' including only one immunity—legislative immunity in art. I, § 6—in the Constitution.

(5) The Court did not comment on the absence of immunity for executive officials in England, as demonstrated by the four famous English cases from the 1760s.

f. The Court did make clear that it, not the Constitution, was creating the immunity: "We conclude that under our constitutional structure of separated powers, the nature of Presidential power requires that a former President have some immunity from criminal prosecution for official acts during his tenure in office." The Court did not mention why, if the necessity was so clear, it escaped the Framers' notice or why that conferred on the Court authority to finish the Framers' work. [R279] [R281] [R282]

D. Qualified Immunity

1. Most § 1983 cases name state or local officials, such as governors, mayors, or police officers, as defendants. They do not enjoy absolute immunity. In addition, some state actors—prosecutors and judges—are entitled to absolute immunity only when performing particular functions; when acting outside those functions, they have only qualified immunity. *See supra* § IV.C.3, 5, at 318-319 *[R283]*.

2. Such defendants may benefit from qualified immunity, which courts occasionally call good-faith immunity (mistakenly, because there is no longer a subjective component to the test, *see supra* § IV.B.5.b at 318 *[R284]*). The basic notion is that the defendant should not be liable for damages if she acted reasonably. *Harlow v. Fitzgerald*, 457 U.S. 800 (1982). (*Harlow* was not a § 1983 case; it was an action against a federal official. But the Supreme Court embraced the *Harlow* approach in § 1983 cases. *See Davis v. Scherer*, 468 U.S. 183 (1984)). But "good faith" is misleading, because it connotes a subjective test. *Harlow* diverged from *Wood v. Strickland*, 420 U.S. 308 (1975), on precisely that point. *Wood* described a combined subjective/objective standard. *Harlow* prescribed an objective standard only, and it is now absolutely clear that the court evaluates defendant's "good faith" *objectively* (whatever that may mean).

   a. The question is not whether the defendant actually knew what he did violated the plaintiff's constitutional rights. Rather, it is whether a "reasonable official would have known." *Harlow v. Fitzgerald*, 457 U.S. at 800.

b. The crux of whether one "would have known" of a constitutional violation is whether the right was "clearly established." More specifically, the law must have been clear when the alleged misconduct occurred. *Hope v. Pelzer*, 536 U.S. 730 (2002).

c. This does not mean that there must be case law specifically holding that the precise conduct at issue is unconstitutional.

Example: Confining an inmate "in a pair of shockingly unsanitary cells . . ." violated the Eighth Amendment, and "no reasonable correctional officer could have concluded that, under the extreme circumstances of this case, it was constitutionally permissible to house Taylor in such deplorably unsanitary conditions for such an extended period of time." *Taylor v. Riojas*, 592 U.S. 7 (2020) (*per curiam*).

Example: Notwithstanding lack of case law specifically addressing a claim that sexual harassment in the classroom was a deprivation of equal protection, clear authority concerning sexual harassment in the workplace as a denial of equal protection places a reasonable teacher on notice that sexual harassment denies equal protection. *Sh. A. ex rel. J.A. v. Tucumcari Mun. Schools*, 321 F.3d 1285 (10th Cir. 2003).

d. The Court justifies qualified immunity as necessary to permit state actors to exercise their discretion boldly. If they were subject to suit every time their acts caused an arguable constitutional deprivation, officers would be hesitant to do anything close to the hazy constitutional line. With qualified immunity, officers can exercise their discretion with less concern. Even if they cross the line and commit an unconstitutional act, they are not liable to suit for damages if a reasonable official would not have known that the act was a violation. (In Fourth Amendment cases, which turn on whether a search or seizure is "unreasonable," this leads to the oxymoron of an official being reasonably unreasonable.) [R285]

Example: Police Officer arrested Plaintiff, who was heckling the governor at a speech. Plaintiff sued Officer under § 1983, seeking damages for Officer's excessive force in effecting the arrest. Even if the force was excessive—and therefore unconstitutional—a court might determine that Officer has qualified immunity because a reasonable officer might have thought such force was necessary to protect the governor. *See Saucier v. Katz*, 533 U.S. 194 (2001).

3. The Supreme Court has attempted—without much success or consistency—to clarify the sequence a court should use to adjudicate qualified-immunity claims. *Saucier v. Katz*, 533 U.S. 194 (2001). (Although *Saucier* was against a federal official, the Court almost certainly would apply it in § 1983 cases; *see supra* § IV.D.2.d, at 322 *[R285]*). Because

qualified immunity is immunity from being sued, courts endeavor to determine the issue before trial, often on summary judgment. *See supra* § IV.B.2, at 317 *[R286]*.

a. Under *Saucier*, the court first asked: "[t]aken in the light most favorable to the [plaintiff], do the facts alleged show the officer's conduct violated a constitutional right?" 533 U.S. at 201.

b. If the answer to that question is no, "there is no necessity for further inquiries concerning qualified immunity" because the plaintiff states no actionable wrong.

c. If the answer to that question is yes, however, then a court should ask whether the right was clearly established when the claim arose. If so, qualified immunity does not apply, and the case proceeds to trial. If not, qualified immunity protects the defendant, and the court dismisses.

Saucier's continuing vitality is at least questionable. *Pearson v. Callahan*, 555 U.S. 223 (2009), made the *Saucier* sequence optional. Courts may follow that sequence but need not. And in what may provide a powerful incentive for courts to abandon the *Saucier* sequence, *Camreta v. Greene*, 563 U.S. 692 (2011), was an appeal from a Ninth Circuit decision that, following *Saucier*, had ruled that the defendant had violated the Fourth Amendment but also was immune, so the court dismissed. The Supreme Court, permitting the officer to obtain review on the Fourth Amendment *issue*, declared the case moot and vacated the Ninth Circuit's finding of a Fourth Amendment violation. Thus, it seems that judges who follow the *Saucier* sequence open themselves to reversals of decisions on constitutional issues that they could avoid by simply ruling on the immunity issue first.

Nonetheless, the Supreme Court still follows the *Saucier* sequence on occasion. *See Plumhoff v. Rickard*, 572 U.S. 765 (2014) (when the *Saucier* approach is "beneficial"). Regrettably, the Court articulated no *indicia* of when it would be beneficial. Note that *Pearson* and *Plumhoff* were all unanimous opinions (although Justices Ginsburg and Breyer, concurring on the sequence of inquiry, did not join some other parts of *Plumhoff*). In *Saucier*, all Justices supported the result, though Justice Souter would have remanded for qualified-immunity examination. [R204] [R269] [R270]

V. Deprivations Under Color of Federal Law: *Bivens* Claims

A. Section 1983 Does Not Apply to Federal Actors

1. Section 1983's express language applies only to deprivations of federal rights by persons acting under color of *state* law. *See supra* § II.A.1, at 303 *[R287]*. A person acting under color of federal law is not a proper § 1983 defendant. *See, e.g., Rockefeller v. Court of Appeals, Tenth Circuit Judges*, 248 F. Supp. 2d 17, 24 (D.D.C. 2003) (federal judges not amenable to suit under § 1983, because they act under color of federal law).

2. There is no analog of § 1983 that allows suit against federal actors.

3. Other statutes, however, provide remedies for acts of federal officials in limited circumstances. For example, the Federal Tort Claims Act, 28 U.S.C. § 2680(h), allows suit against the United States for many torts federal officers commit. As amended in 1974, it now permits recovery for officers' intentional torts, but the suit lies against the United States, not against the officers, a reversal of the common-law limitation of *respondeat-superior* liability in torts. [R373]

B. Remedies for Federal Actors' Unlawful Conduct Exist

1. In 1933, the unanimous Supreme Court recognized a right of action directly against the United States under the Fifth Amendment's Takings Clause. *Jacobs v. United States*, 290 U.S. 13 (1933). Although the Fifth Amendment contains no explicit private right of action, the Court was unequivocal: "The form of the remedy did not qualify the right. It rested upon the Fifth Amendment. Statutory recognition was not necessary." The Supreme Court has also recognized a right of action directly against an individual federal actor—a "*Bivens* claim."

Example: Officers entered Plaintiff's apartment, handcuffed him, and threatened his family with arrest. The officers tore up the apartment, ostensibly searching for illegal drugs. Although the officers arrested Plaintiff, subjected him to a strip search at the federal courthouse, and charged him with narcotics violations, the Government never prosecuted him. Plaintiff claimed that the warrantless search was without probable cause and with excessive force, violating the Fourth Amendment.

Variation One: If the officers were from the local police department, therefore acting under color of state law, Plaintiff could have sued them under § 1983.

Variation Two: If they were federal officers, Plaintiff could not sue under § 1983, and, at the time, the Federal Tort Claims Act provided no remedy because it exempted intentional torts.

Variation Two is *Bivens v. Six Unknown Named Agents of Federal Bureau of Narcotics*, 403 U.S. 388 (1971), which held that a plaintiff may sue federal officers to recover damages for an unconstitutional search and seizure, using a right of action the Court recognized in the Fourth Amendment.

2. The Court has recognized similar claims under other the Fifth and Eighth Amendments, though its willingness to do so has declined noticeably, and it now says it regrets even those three decisions. *See supra* Ch. XI, § VI.D.2.b, at 253-257 *[R288]*. [R198] [R272] [R373]

VI. The Civil-Rights Removal Statute

A. Background and the Provision for Civil-Rights Removal

1. The civil-rights removal statute, 28 U.S.C. § 1443, like garden-variety removal, *see supra* Ch. VII, at 151-161 *[R289]*, allows a defendant in state trial court litigation to move a case to a federal trial court.

a. The statute's roots are in Reconstruction. The original version was part of the Civil Rights Act of 1865. It implemented the Thirteenth Amendment, and Congress seemed clearly to intend African-Americans to have access to the federal courts, presumably more sympathetic to their newly enfranchised status than state courts. Parity wept.

b. In two ways, civil-rights removal is broader than garden-variety removal: (1) it permits removal of criminal as well as civil cases, and (2) remand orders in civil-rights-removal cases are appealable.

c. In another way, however, civil-rights removal is narrower than garden-variety removal because it permits removal only under circumstances that raise some question about whether the state court will protect a party from discrimination on the basis of race.

2. The current version of the statute provides:

> Any of the following civil actions or criminal prosecutions, commenced in a state court, may be removed by the defendant to the district court of the United States for the district and division embracing the place wherein it is pending:
>
> > (1) Against any person who is denied or cannot enforce in the courts of such state a right under any law providing for the equal civil rights of citizens of the United States, or of all persons within the jurisdiction thereof;
> >
> > (2) For any act under color of authority derived from any law providing for equal rights, or for refusing to do any act on the ground that it would be inconsistent with such law.

3. The statute contains three main clauses, each describing a situation authorizing removal:

a. The denial clause in subsection (1), which allows removal when an actor denies an individual the benefit of an equal-rights law or the individual cannot enforce in state court some right under an equal-rights law;

b. The authority clause in subsection (2), where a defendant faces a civil suit or prosecution for performing an act under an equal-rights law; and

c. The refusal clause in subsection (2), where the individual fails or refuses to perform an act inconsistent with an equal-rights law and consequently faces a civil suit or criminal charge.

4. Most reported cases have involved the denial clause, but today there are very few cases under the statute as a whole.

5. In 1875, Congress revised the original statute significantly.

   a. Under the original version, removal could occur either before or after trial in the state court. Post-trial removal permitted the federal court to review the entire record to determine whether the state court denied some civil right of racial equality. (The Supreme Court had not yet created the *Rooker-Feldman* doctrine. *See supra* Ch. XII, § III.C, at 286-275 *[R290]*.)

   b. The 1875 legislation, now codified at 28 U.S.C. § 1446(b), eliminates post-trial removal, though it apparently had been the 1865 Congress's understanding that post-trial removal would be the primary means of enforcing the Act. [R293]

   c. Since a case is removable only before trial, removal decisions under the denial clause rest on a prediction that the state court will deny the defendant a civil right of racial equality.

   d. Because removal is thus based upon a prediction of unconstitutional behavior by a state court, the statute creates great potential for friction between the federal and state court systems.

6. To avoid the unseemliness of predicting that a state court will behave in an unconstitutional way, the Supreme Court has interpreted § 1443, especially the denial clause, narrowly. Very few cases have avoided remand.

B. "Equal Rights" Interpreted Narrowly

1. Clause 1 of § 1443 permits removal when a party cannot enforce a law providing for the "equal civil rights" of United-States citizens. Clause (2) refers to cases involving actions under a law providing for "equal rights," where the defendant faces prosecution for performing a protected act or for refusing to perform an act inconsistent with an equal-rights law.

2. The Supreme Court has concluded that § 1443 applies not only to civil rights in existence in 1875 (when Congress enacted the current version of the statute), but also to civil rights recognized later. On the other hand, the Court ruled that the equal rights the statute implicates are only those involving racial equality. *Georgia v. Rachel*, 384 U.S. 780 (1966).

   a. Thus, First Amendment free-speech rights and Fourteenth Amendment due-process rights do not come under § 1443.

   b. Even constitutional rights concerning equality based upon factors other than race provide no basis for § 1443 removal.

   c. Commentators have criticized the Court's limitation as inconsistent with the text and the purpose of the statute, but *Johnson v. Mississippi*, 421 U.S. 213 (1975), reaffirmed the point the last time the Court spoke to it. [R362]

C. Distinguishing State Statutes from State Practices

1. *Strauder v. West Virginia*, 100 U.S. 303 (1879), was a state murder prosecution of an black defendant. He unsuccessfully attempted to remove the prosecution from state court to federal court, arguing that the state court would deny his rights because state law permitted only white men to serve on juries. (***N.B.*** Remember that until 1948, defendants had to petition the *state* court for removal. *See supra* Ch. VII, § IV.A.2, at 159 *[R291].*)

2. The Supreme Court held that pretrial removal was necessary. The defendant demonstrated that he would be unable to enforce his equal civil rights in state court because the state's juror-selection statute violated the Fourteenth Amendment.

3. The same day, however, the Court decided *Virginia v. Rives*, 100 U.S. 313 (1879). The black state-court criminal defendants had argued that the state court would deny their equal rights because Virginia had never permitted blacks to serve on county juries in trials involving a black defendant. The difference from *Strauder* was that the rule excluding blacks from jury service was not in a statute; it was, instead, simply a practice the state followed.

4. The Supreme Court denied removal in *Rives*, relying upon the absence of a statute. In *Strauder*, the statute outlawing black participation compelled the trial court to exclude black citizens from the jury. In *Rives*, the absence of a statute meant that the state courts were not bound.

5. The Court's distinction, known generally as the *Strauder-Rives* doctrine, is questionable at best, and commentators have criticized it.

    a. The Supremacy Clause binds state courts to enforce federal law, including the Constitution. Thus, assuming parity, there should have been no reason in *Strauder* to assume the state courts would hold the exclusion statute constitutional, thus failing to enforce the Fourteenth Amendment.

    b. Besides, if state courts will not invalidate state statutes that clearly violate the Fourteenth Amendment, why would they invalidate an unconstitutional non-statutory state practice?

    c. *Strauder*'s holding, which exposes inherent mistrust of a state court's ability or willingness to invalidate a plainly unconstitutional state statute (*i.e.* and thus assumes the state court will not honor the Supremacy Clause) hardly reduces friction between the two judicial systems. It does illustrate that the presumption of parity, *see supra* Ch. XII, § II.C, at 269-270 *[R292]*, is stronger at some times than at others.

    d. The dichotomy the two cases created shows that it was unfortunate that Congress decided, in 1875, to make post-trial removal unavailable. *See supra* § VI.A.5.b, at 326 *[R293]*. Had post-trial removal been available, as under the original civil-rights-removal statute in 1865, Rives could have removed the case after he was tried in state court by a jury that included no black members.

D. The Modern Era

1. Statutory limitations on the right to appeal cases denying removal meant the Supreme Court had few opportunities to review denials of 28 U.S.C. § 1443 removal before 1948, the year that Congress made removal automatic, rendering denial impossible. *See supra* Ch. VII, § IV.A.2, at 159 *[R294]*. Similarly, although remand orders were originally appealable, Congress removed that possibility in 1887.

2. In 1964, Congress liberalized the Supreme Court's ability to review remand orders in § 1443 removal cases by making them appealable. 28 U.S.C. § 1447(d). Two years later the Court decided two cases in which it reexamined, and in some ways changed, longstanding principles.

3. In *Georgia v. Rachel*, 384 U.S. 780 (1966), Blacks who had sought service at certain hotels and restaurants faced indictments under a trespass statute for refusing to leave when requested. The Court upheld removal at an interlocutory stage, under § 1443(1)'s denial clause, emphasizing that the defendants asserted a right to equal service at public accommodations, which the 1964 Civil Rights Act expressly guaranteed. The Court's ruling allowed the defendants the opportunity to prove that their prosecutions resulted from their refusal to leave places of public accommodation after being ordered to do so. (Had they failed to make that showing, remand was still possible.)

   a. The defendants had a right not merely to avoid conviction, but to avoid *prosecution* in state court. "It is no answer in these circumstances that the defendants might eventually prevail in the state court. The burden of having to defend the prosecutions is itself the denial of a right explicitly conferred by the Civil Rights Act of 1964." *Rachel*, 384 U.S. at 805.

   b. Because prosecution on the basis of race denies a federal right, the Court had no problem recognizing, subject to proof, that there might have been denial of the federal right in state court; filing the indictments was the denial.

   c. *Rachel* is significant because the Court found a denial of equal rights in the absence of a discriminatory state statute.

4. By authorizing pre-hearing removal, Congress arguably showed less than complete respect for the state courts. Removal at that stage is inconsistent with *Rives*.

   a. The *Rachel* prosecutions violated the Civil Rights Act only if the defendants had been asked to leave the premises and thereafter charged with trespass *because of* their race. It is possible, however, that the defendants were asked to leave for other reasons—for example, they were being rowdy or the store was closing—in which case the state-court prosecution would not have violated a law concerning equal rights.

b. Thus, some court would have to hold a hearing concerning the complaining witness's motivation before determining whether removal under § 1443 was proper. A state court could hold that hearing just as readily as a federal court.

c. By permitting removal before such a hearing (*i.e.* effectively transferring the hearing to a federal court), Congress seems to have signaled its distrust that state courts would engage in meaningful factual hearings on the complaining witnesses' motivations.

d. This conclusion, however, is contrary to *Rives*'s implicit message—that the state courts are trustworthy and will do the right thing under the Constitution and laws of equal rights. The parity implications are striking.

5. In *City of Greenwood v. Peacock*, 384 U.S. 808 (1966), decided the same day as *Rachel*, civil rights workers in Mississippi removed cases charging them with obstructing the public streets, assault, disturbing the peace, creating a public disturbance, and inciting a riot. They asserted that they were being prosecuted because of their efforts to register black voters, and argued that removal was proper under § 1443(1) and § 1443(2). *See supra* § VI.A.2, at 159 *[R295]*. The Supreme Court directed remand.

   a. With respect to subsection (2), the Court affirmed the Fifth Circuit's order, holding that "the second subsection of § 1443 confers a privilege of removal only upon federal officers or agents and those authorized to act with or for them in affirmatively executing duties under any federal law providing for equal civil rights." 384 U.S. at 824 (footnote omitted).

   b. With respect to subsection (1), the Court noted that the civil rights statute in *Peacock* contained no protection from a state's attempt to prosecute. By contrast, the *Rachel* defendants relied upon the public accommodations provision of the Civil Rights Act, which included protection even from attempted prosecution in violation of equal rights. The Court also distinguished *Rachel* by noting that "no federal law confers an absolute right on private citizens . . . to obstruct a public street" or commit any other of the violations with which the defendants were charged.

6. Thus, after *Rachel* and *Peacock* (both majority opinions by Justice Stewart), civil-rights removal continues to receive a narrow construction.

   a. The *Strauder-Rives* dichotomy remains generally in force, so only in the extremely rare instance in which a state *statute*, rather than a state practice, denies equal rights in state judicial procedures is civil-rights removal possible.

b. *Rachel* is a very limited exception to this rule, apparently applicable only when the state prosecution is for conduct a federal right protects against the state even initiating prosecution, such as in the public-accommodations provision of the Civil Rights Act. Even then, although removal is automatic, the federal court will remand the case unless the defendants can demonstrate "that their prosecutions had resulted from orders to leave places of public accommodation 'for racial reasons.' " 384 U.S. at 785. [R121] [R123] [R188]

Chapter XV

FEDERAL HABEAS CORPUS

■ ANALYSIS

I. Introduction

The writ of habeas corpus permits a federal court to inquire into the legality of detention of someone in government custody and to order release if appropriate. (Traditionally, granting the writ merely launched the judicial inquiry; the court might end up either granting or denying release. In modern parlance, "granting the writ" has—colloquially at least—come to mean granting relief to the prisoner.) Release is appropriate only if the prisoner's custody violates federal law, usually the Constitution. The prisoner ("petitioner") usually alleges that her conviction and incarceration violated or are violating some constitutional right. A federal court order releasing a state prisoner raises significant federalism and comity concerns. Some commentators consider it the greatest source of friction between the federal courts and the states. In the last several decades, both Congress and the Supreme Court have restricted habeas corpus relief. In 1996, Congress imposed notable restrictions. That legislation is controversial; some argue it goes too far. Others contend, however, that further restrictions on habeas are necessary in the interests of federalism and finality of state-court judgments. The Constitution, art. I, § 9, cl. 2, protects only against complete suspension of the writ. [R300]

II. Background, Origins of the Writ, and Overview of Current Statutes

A. The Concept of Habeas Corpus

1. "Habeas corpus" is the colloquial name of the writ of "*habeas corpus ad subjiciendum*." Courts frequently refer to it simply as "the Great Writ." By whatever name, it provides a means for the judiciary to test the legality of a person's detention by government authority.
2. The writ thus provides an important vehicle for preventing government lawlessness and protecting individuals from secret and unjustified restraint.
3. Though habeas corpus applies to any government detention, it most often appears in cases seeking release of prisoners incarcerated pursuant to state criminal convictions.
4. Issuance of the writ commands the government authority to respond to judicial inquiry into the legality of the detention. The court may subsequently grant relief to the prisoner, usually by releasing the prisoner, either permanently or temporarily.
   a. Release may be complete, ending incarceration entirely.
   b. Or, release may be for a limited purpose, such as commanding the custodian to bring the prisoner to court to be a witness.

B. History of the Writ

1. The judiciary developed the writ in England, and the Habeas Corpus Act of 1679 codified it.

2. Article I, § 9, cl. 2, protects the writ: "The privilege of the writ of habeas corpus shall not be suspended, unless when in cases of rebellion or invasion the public safety may require it."

3. Section 14 of the Judiciary Act of 1789 first provided federal jurisdiction to issue the writ.

4. Congress expanded habeas corpus in federal courts in 1867 by authorizing issuance "in all cases where any person may be restrained of his or her liberty in violation of the constitution, or of any treaty or law of the United States."

   a. This provision plainly made federal habeas relief available for persons restrained illegally by state authorities.

   b. Though Congress has amended the statutory grants of federal habeas authority several times since 1867, the writ still permits a federal court to order the release of someone held under state authority.

C. Overview of Current Statutes, as Amended by the Antiterrorism and Effective Death Penalty Act of 1996 (AEDPA)

1. This section provides an overview of the statutes, followed in separate sections by detailed discussions of their most important provisions. Statutes on habeas corpus in the federal courts appear at 28 U.S.C. §§ 2241-2255.

2. The Antiterrorism and Effective Death Penalty Act of 1996 (AEDPA) contains the most sweeping changes to the habeas provisions in over a generation. AEDPA significantly restricts federal habeas relief.

3. Section 2241 contains important basic provisions about who may issue a writ of habeas corpus and the circumstances under which a court may grant the writ and relief.

   a. Section 2241(a) provides that "[w]rits of habeas corpus may be granted by the Supreme Court, any justice thereof, the district courts and any circuit judge within their respective jurisdictions." Section 2441(b) permits those courts and judges to decline habeas relief and transfer the application to the federal district court having jurisdiction over the matter.

   b. Section 2441(c) lists five circumstances in which the writ may issue concerning "a prisoner." The writ issues only if at least one of them exists:

      (1) the prisoner "is in custody under or by color of the authority of the United States or is committed for trial before some court thereof," or

(2) the prisoner "is in custody for an act done or omitted in pursuance of an Act of Congress, or an order, process, judgment or decree of a court or judge of the United States," or

(3) the prisoner "is in custody in violation of the Constitution or laws or treaties of the United States;" or

(4) the prisoner is a citizen of a foreign state and is domiciled there, but is in custody for an act done under her government's authority, which international law governs, or

(5) "It is necessary to bring [the person] into court to testify or for trial."

c. Of these five provisions, the third has caused the most difficulty and will be the focus of discussion. It applies to state prisoners challenging the legality of their confinement.

4. AEDPA changed habeas law in four respects. Sections 2242, 2243, and 2245 through 2252 concern procedural matters for a federal court's entertaining the application for the writ. For example, § 2242 provides that the application for habeas corpus must be in writing, signed, and verified, and §§ 2245-2249 address evidentiary matters for the habeas hearing.

a. Section 2244, as amended, contains important provisions regarding the finality of habeas determinations. *See infra* § III.D, at 336-338 *[R296]*.

b. Section 2254, as amended, addresses habeas corpus sought by persons in state custody. *See infra* § III, at 334-342 *[R297]*.

c. Section 2255, as amended, addresses habeas corpus sought by persons in federal custody. *See infra* § V, at 345-346 *[R298]*.

d. The AEDPA added a new chapter to the habeas provisions of Title 28, codified at §§ 2261-66. These provisions apply only to state prisoners subject to the death penalty. *See infra* § III.H, at 342 *[R299]*. [R25] [R146] [R259]

III. Habeas Corpus for State Prisoners

A. Basic Statutes

1. Section § 2254 governs writs of habeas corpus for "a person in custody pursuant to the judgment of a State court." Section 2254(a) provides that the writ may be issued for such a person "only on the ground that he is in custody in violation of the Constitution or laws or treaties of the United States."

2. This use of habeas raises profound questions of federalism. *See supra* § I, at 332 *[R300]*.

B. Statutory Requirement of Exhaustion of State Remedies

1. Section 2254(b) imposes an exhaustion requirement for anyone seeking federal habeas concerning state incarceration. Before the writ may issue, one of the following must be true:
   a. "that the applicant has exhausted the remedies available in the courts of the State," or
   b. that "there is an absence of available State corrective process," or
   c. "circumstances exist that render such process ineffective to protect the rights of the applicant."
2. *Ex parte Royall*, 117 U.S. 241 (1886), began judicial development of the exhaustion requirement. Congress codified it in 1948. With respect to suits involving prison conditions, the Prison Litigation Reform Act, 42 U.S.C. 1997e(a), expands the exhaustion requirement to § 1983 actions. [R257] [R266]
3. The exhaustion requirement serves federalism interests and "give[s] the State the initial 'opportunity to pass upon and correct' alleged violations of its prisoners' federal rights." *Wilwording v. Swenson*, 404 U.S. 249, 250 (1971).
4. Some early commentators concluded that a state prisoner could never exhaust state remedies, and thus could never seek federal habeas relief, if the state permitted successive applications for post-conviction relief. *Brown v. Allen*, 344 U.S. 443 (1953), rejected that view, holding that the statutory exhaustion principle does not require multiple state-court applications. The petitioner had raised federal constitutional issues on appeal from his conviction in the state system; he did not have to request collateral relief from the state courts before seeking federal habeas relief.
5. Exhaustion thus requires that the state prisoner pursue his federal argument to the highest possible state court once, either by appeal or collateral attack. This applies even if an intermediate state court of appeals has exercised discretionary review. *O'Sullivan v. Boerckel*, 526 U.S. 838 (1999).
6. The prisoner satisfies the requirement by seeking review by the state's highest court, even if that court refuses review or reviews the case without discussing the federal issues.
7. If a state prisoner combined both exhausted and non-exhausted claims in one habeas corpus petition, *Rose v. Lundy*, 455 U.S. 509 (1982), originally required the court to dismiss. However, with AEDPA's passage, Congress imposed strict time limits on a prisoner's entitlement to seek federal habeas relief. Recognizing that AEDPA's interplay with *Rose* would cause significant difficulties, *Rhines v. Weber*, 544 U.S. 269 (2005), allows lower federal courts to stay (rather than dismiss) mixed

habeas petitions so that petitioners can return to the state courts to exhaust state remedies.

8. The habeas applicant has the burden of showing exhaustion. Failure to do so causes denial of the petition. [R301] [R383]

C. State Waiver of the Exhaustion Requirement

1. The federal courts had recognized exceptional circumstances constituting constructive waiver of the exhaustion requirement. In those rare circumstances, the federal court can adjudicate the habeas petition even if the applicant had not exhausted state remedies.
2. In AEDPA, Congress for the first time codified the possibility that a state can waive the exhaustion requirement. It permits waiver, however, *only* in one situation: when the state, through its lawyer, "expressly waives the requirement."
   a. Thus, courts are no longer free to determine other circumstances in which the state may be deemed to have waived the exhaustion requirement.
   b. In this and other ways, the AEDPA restricts federal habeas relief.

D. Review of State Court Findings

1. The habeas petitioner must exhaust state remedies before seeking habeas corpus relief from a federal court. *See supra* § III.B, at 335-336 *[R301]*. Thus, by the time an applicant brings the question of the legality of his confinement to federal court, a state court will have addressed the merits, absent an explicit waiver of exhaustion.
2. Then what is the effect of the state-court determination of the issue?
3. Traditional principles of claim and issue preclusion generally did not apply to federal habeas for state prisoners, *see Brown v. Allen*, 344 U.S. 443 (1953), because giving preclusive effect to state-court findings on the relevant issues could render federal habeas relief meaningless. Thus, the fact that a state court had determined an issue did not bar the federal habeas court from determining the question afresh.
4. On the other hand, a federal court is not free simply to ignore state court findings of fact.
   a. *Brown v. Allen* requires the federal court to accept state-court findings of fact unless there were "unusual circumstances" or a "vital flaw" in the state-court proceedings.
   b. *Townsend v. Sain*, 372 U.S. 293 (1963), held that a federal habeas court must re-examine state factual findings if the state court did not afford the applicant a "full and fair hearing" at trial.
5. These phrases did not provide clear guidance for lower federal courts, leading Congress in 1966 to codify when a federal court hearing a habeas case can review state-court determinations of fact. The result, 28 U.S.C.

§ 2254(d), was that the federal court had to presume state findings were correct unless one of the following conditions existed:

a. the state proceeding did not resolve the merits of the factual dispute;

b. the state's fact-finding procedure was inadequate to afford a full and fair hearing;

c. "the material facts were not adequately developed at the State court hearing";

d. the state court lacked subject-matter jurisdiction;

e. the applicant, an indigent, did not have counsel;

f. the applicant did not receive a full and fair hearing;

g. "the applicant was otherwise denied due process of law in the State court proceeding"; or

h. if the federal court concludes that the state court's factual determination "is not fairly supported by the record. . . ."

6. AEDPA changed this dramatically. The relevant provision is now § 2254(e)(1).

   a. "[A] determination of a factual issue made by a State court shall be presumed to be correct."

   b. Significantly, the state court determination need not have been made pursuant to "a hearing on the merits," as the 1966 codification required.

   c. Even more important is that the new statute contains no list of circumstances that overcome the presumption.

   d. Rather, it provides that the applicant "shall have the burden of rebutting the presumption of correctness by clear and convincing evidence." [R377]

7. But § 2254(d)(2) provides that if the state decision was "based on an unreasonable determination of the facts in light of the evidence presented in the State proceeding," the federal court may grant relief. It is not clear how to reconcile that provision with the presumption of correctness in § 2254(e)(1). [R378]

8. Section 2254(d) added a significant restriction on habeas for state prisoners by providing that the court shall not grant relief "with respect to any claim that was adjudicated on the merits in State court proceedings" unless the applicant shows either:

   a. That adjudication resulted in a decision contrary to, or unreasonably applying, clearly established law as determined *by the Supreme Court*, or

b. That adjudication resulted in a decision based upon an unreasonable determination of the facts in light of the evidence in state court.

9. AEDPA added a provision permitting a federal court to *deny* habeas corpus on the merits even if the applicant failed to exhaust state remedies. 28 U.S.C. § 2254(b)(2).

10. AEDPA also added a provision that incompetence or ineffectiveness of counsel— in either state or federal post-conviction proceedings—cannot be a basis for habeas relief. 28 U.S.C. § 2254(i). *See infra* § IV.A.4.e, at 343-344 *[R302]*.

11. Section 2254(e)(2), concerning cases involving an applicant who failed "to develop the factual basis of a claim in State court proceedings," forbids a federal evidentiary hearing unless the petitioner shows both:

a. That her claim relies upon (1) a new rule of constitutional law that *the Supreme Court* made retroactive to cases on collateral review, or (2) a factual predicate that petitioner could not have previously discovered through the exercise of due diligence, *and*

b. That the facts underlying the claim would establish by clear and convincing evidence that but for constitutional error, no reasonable finder of fact would have found the applicant guilty of the underlying crime. [R296] [R304]

E. Deprivations Cognizable in Federal Habeas Corpus Proceedings

1. Habeas corpus is a vehicle for reviewing the legality of a state prisoner's conviction and deprivation of liberty. It does not follow, however, that federal habeas corpus can remedy *every* constitutional deprivation.

2. Federal habeas does not lie to review claims that the state court improperly admitted evidence obtained through Fourth Amendment violations. Criminal defendants can seek review of such issues only on appeal and, if state procedure permits, through state collateral review. *Stone v. Powell*, 428 U.S. 465 (1976). Specifically, the Court held that a federal habeas court could not review the claim by a state prisoner that evidence used against him in the criminal trial was illegally seized and should have been excluded from the trial. The reason for barring federal review was that the state court had afforded the criminal defendant "an opportunity for a full and fair" consideration of the claimed illegal seizure.

a. The Court focused on the exclusionary rule's costs, because evidence the state obtains by violating the Fourth Amendment may nevertheless be probative. *Stone* held that while the rule should still apply at trial, its costs did not justify further use in a habeas corpus proceeding.

b. According to the *Stone* Court, the exclusionary rule does not create a personal right in the criminal defendant. Rather, it is a judicial remedy to be employed in the criminal trial and cognizable there and on appeal from the criminal judgment. The Court identified the rule's purpose as deterring unlawful police conduct—a societal value but not a right personal to the criminal defendant—and reasoned that habeas relief usually comes so long after the criminal trial that there is little possibility of deterrence.

c. *Stone* is noteworthy because it barred federal review on a question of law, not just a determination of fact by the state court.

d. Though *Stone* remains good law, the Court has not provided meaningful guidance on what constitutes "an opportunity for a full and fair" consideration of the Fourth Amendment issue.

3. Justice Brennan dissented, expressing concern that *Stone* presaged "drastic withdrawal of federal habeas jurisdiction, if not for all grounds of alleged unconstitutional detention, then at least for claims—for example, of double jeopardy, entrapment, self-incrimination, *Miranda* violations, and use of invalid identification procedures—that this Court later decides are not 'guilt related.'" 428 U.S. at 517-18 (Brennan, J., dissenting).

   a. Some commentators echoed Justice Brennan's concern that *Stone* marked the beginning of significant restrictions in the availability of federal habeas relief generally.

   b. For the most part, however, that has not happened. The Court has not expanded *Stone* beyond the Fourth Amendment's exclusionary rule. It does not, for example, prevent habeas review of Fifth Amendment claims that the trial court improperly admitted a confession into evidence.

Example: Applicant seeks federal habeas corpus, alleging that the state court improperly denied his claim of racial discrimination in the selection of the grand jury that issued the indictment. *Stone v. Powell* does not preclude federal review of the state court ruling. *Rose v. Mitchell*, 443 U.S. 545 (1979). *See also Vasquez v. Hillery*, 474 U.S. 254 (1986) (reaffirming *Rose*). If the standard to be employed were whether the constitutional challenge might go to the issue of guilt or innocence, it is unclear whether racial discrimination in selecting the grand jury would satisfy it.

4. *Jackson v. Virginia*, 443 U.S. 307 (1979), refused to extend *Stone* to a claim that the evidence supporting conviction was constitutionally insufficient.

5. *Withrow v. Williams*, 507 U.S. 680 (1993), refused to extend *Stone* to bar habeas review of a claim that the defendant's confession was obtained in violation of his *Miranda* rights. Even though a "full and fair" hearing in state court addressed the *Miranda* claim and suppression of the confession, the federal habeas court can also address the issue.

6. *Stone* thus appears to take only Fourth Amendment claims out of the realm of federal habeas corpus. There is, however, one additional and very significant limitation on what federal habeas corpus can do. From time to time, the Supreme Court announces new rules of constitutional law, *see, e.g. Mapp v. Ohio*, 367 U.S. 643 (1961) (applying Fourth Amendment exclusionary rule to state criminal proceedings); *Miranda v. Arizona*, 384 U.S. 436 (1966) (rules governing custodial interrogation by police), and one question that always arises is whether such rules are applicable retroactively. In criminal prosecutions, the rule had long been that new constitutional rules were applicable to cases then on trial and to cases in the appellate stages of direct review of convictions. The question was what rule of retroactivity should govern the applicability of new constitutional rules announced after the direct review process was completed. *Teague v. Lane*, 489 U.S. 288 (1989), declared the Court's approach. Justice Harlan had earlier suggested that only new rules "implicit in the concept of ordered liberty" should receive retroactive application in federal habeas cases. The *Teague* Court made clear that only "watershed rules of criminal procedure" should receive retroactive application on habeas review.

   For more than thirty years after *Teague*, no new rule the Court announced passed the watershed test. Finally, *Edwards v. Vannoy*, 535 U.S. 255 (2021), over three dissents, interred the never-used watershed exception, the majority declaring that no new rule of criminal procedure ever could satisfy the exception. The three-decade track record made it clear that *Edwards* would have no practical effect; it simply declared a state of habeas law that had existed *de facto* since *Teague*.

F. Statute of Limitations and Limitations on Successive Applications for Federal Habeas Relief

1. AEDPA imposes a one-year limitation on a state prisoner's application for federal habeas relief. 28 U.S.C. § 2254(d)(1).

   a. The year runs from the latest of: (1) the date the judgment becomes final, or (2) the date of removal of an unconstitutional impediment to filing an application that state action created, or (3) the date the Supreme Court first recognized the constitutional right, provided that *the Supreme Court* made the newly-recognized right applicable retroactively, or (4) the date the factual predicate for the claim was discoverable through exercise of due diligence.

   b. The time during which a proper application for state post-conviction review runs its course tolls the one-year period.

2. AEDPA also imposes important restrictions on successive applications for habeas relief by state prisoners.

   a. A claim previously presented in a habeas application under § 2254 "shall be dismissed." 28 U.S.C. § 2254(b)(1).

b. A claim *not* presented in a previous habeas application under § 2254 gets dismissed unless the applicant shows either (1) that the claim relies on a new rule of constitutional law, made retroactive to cases on collateral review *by the Supreme Court*, or (2) the factual predicate for the claim was not previously discoverable through due diligence *and* those facts, if proven and viewed in light of the evidence as a whole, would establish by clear and convincing evidence that no reasonable finder of fact would have found the applicant guilty. 28 U.S.C. § 2254(b)(2). The upshot is that failure to raise a claim at the earliest possible time may end up being constructive waiver, even of an underlying constitutional right.

3. Under AEDPA, a second or successive application is improper until the applicant obtains an order from the court of appeals authorizing the district court to consider the application. 28 U.S.C. § 2244(b)(3)(A).

a. The court of appeals will grant the order if the petitioner makes a *prima facie* showing that the case satisfies the standard. 28 U.S.C. § 2244(b)(3)(C).

b. The district court must nonetheless dismiss the claim unless the applicant demonstrates that she has satisfied the standard. 28 U.S.C. § 2244(b)(4). (Presumably the showing this section requires goes beyond a mere *prima facie* showing. Several courts have characterized the burden as "clear and convincing evidence," *see e.g.*, *McLeod v. Peguese*, 337 Fed. Appx. 316, 327 (4th Cir. 2009), although the burden in habeas cases generally is preponderance of the evidence. *See, e.g.*, *United States ex rel. Brennan v. Fay*, 353 F.2d 56 (2d Cir. 1965)).

c. The circuit court's decision granting or denying authorization to file a second or successive application is final and not subject to Supreme Court review by writ of certiorari. 28 U.S.C. § 2244(b)(3)(E). [R262] [R303] [R309]

G. Appellate Review of Federal Habeas Decisions

1. Section 2253 governs appellate review of federal habeas decisions. Before AEDPA, a state prisoner could appeal a denial of habeas relief only if she obtained a "certificate of probable cause" from the court of appeals.

2. Under AEDPA, a state prisoner may appeal a denial of federal habeas relief only if "a circuit justice or judge issues a certificate of appealability." 28 U.S.C. § 2253(c)(1)(B).

3. Such a certificate issues only if the applicant makes a "substantial showing of the denial of a constitutional right." The showing must be specific. 28 U.S.C. § 2253(c)(2)-(3).

H. Special Provisions for Capital Cases

1. AEDPA added a new chapter to the habeas corpus provisions of 28 U.S.C.: §§ 2261-65. They deal with cases involving state prisoners incarcerated "subject to capital sentence."
2. The chapter applies only to federal courts in states that "opt in" by adopting a rule concerning appointment and compensation of competent counsel for state post-conviction proceedings brought by indigent prisoners when the state's highest court has upheld the capital convictions and sentences on direct appeal. 28 U.S.C. § 2261(b).
   a. If the state has such a rule, the provisions apply to any state prisoner under a death sentence.
   b. The state's mechanism must provide for entry by a state court of an order either appointing counsel to represent the applicant if she is indigent or finding that the applicant has rejected the offer of counsel or is not indigent. [R261]
3. Entry of such an order automatically stays the order of execution pending the prisoner's application for federal habeas relief under § 2254.
   a. The stay expires, however, if (1) the prisoner fails to file a timely habeas application, (2) waives the right to file an application, (3) makes the application but fails to make a substantial showing of a denial of a federal right, or (4) the federal court denies habeas relief.
   b. If any of those things has occurred, no federal court may thereafter enter a stay of execution unless the applicant qualifies to file a second application under § 2244(b). *See supra* § III.F, at 340-341 *[R303]*.
4. Section 2263 addresses the timing of the habeas application. Section 2264 addresses the scope of federal review. Section 2265 provides specific rules applicable in states that allow a defendant to raise issues on direct appeal that he can also raise on collateral attack. And § 2266 provides detailed time limits for federal-court action. [R263] [R297] [R299]

IV. "Abortive State Proceedings"—The Problem of Adequate and Independent State Grounds

A. Background: Case Law Through *Wainwright v. Sykes*

1. The federal habeas court's role in reviewing state-court determinations of fact appears *supra*, § III.D, at 336-338 *[R304]*. "Abortive state proceedings" are situations where the petitioner lost in state court because she failed to comply with state procedures for presenting her claim.
2. In *Daniels v. Allen*, 344 U.S. 443 (1953), the applicant filed his appeal in the highest state court one day late. The Supreme Court held that this failure barred the applicant's efforts to seek federal habeas relief. *Daniels* thus imported the adequate-and-independent-state-ground doctrine

(which the Supreme Court has long applied to its appellate jurisdiction to review state court decisions, *see supra* Ch. VIII, § IV.E, at 174-179 *[R305]*) to habeas corpus cases. Under that doctrine, a federal court would not review a federal issue from a state case if the state court declined to decide the issue because the litigant failed to comply with a legitimate state procedural requirement.

3. *Fay v. Noia*, 372 U.S. 391 (1963), abandoned *Daniels*. The Court held that a state defendant's noncompliance with state procedural requirements did not preclude federal habeas review unless the defendant had deliberately by-passed his state judicial remedies. Inadvertent failure to comply with state procedures did not bar federal consideration of a constitutional challenge even when the state rule served a legitimate state interest.

4. *Wainwright v. Sykes*, 433 U.S. 72 (1977), turned away from *Noia*. The Court held that a state defendant's failure to object contemporaneously to admission of evidence precluded federal habeas review, even though the failure was not a deliberate by-pass of a state judicial remedy.

   a. After *Sykes*, before federal habeas will lie, the habeas applicant must establish (1) cause for his failure to object and (2) prejudice from admission of the challenged evidence.

   b. Thus, *Sykes* shifted the focus from "deliberate bypass" to "cause and prejudice."

   c. *Sykes* relied heavily on *Francis v. Henderson*, 425 U.S. 536 (1976), which effectively applied the adequate-and-independent-state-ground doctrine, *see supra* Ch. VIII, § IV.E at 174-179 *[R306]*, in habeas corpus without addressing *Fay v. Noia*.

   d. Though *Sykes* did not expressly overrule *Noia*, it criticized the that case, throwing serious doubt on its continued validity.

   e. *Coleman v. Thompson*, 501 U.S. 722 (1991), finally overruled *Noia*, holding that failing timely to appeal denial of collateral relief in a state habeas proceeding forfeited federal habeas review. *Coleman* also ruled that because there is no constitutional right to have an attorney in state post-conviction proceedings, an ineffective-assistance-of-counsel claim would not lie, *Martinez v. Ryan*, 566 U.S. 1 (2012), modified that aspect of *Coleman*, holding that ineffective assistance of post-conviction counsel at the initial collateral review stage "may establish cause for a prisoner's procedural default of *a claim of ineffective assistance at trial*." [Emphasis added.]

   But *Shinn v. Ramirez*, 596 U.S. 366 (2022), sharply limits *Martinez*'s scope, disallowing district courts from conducting evidentiary hearings unless the petitioner can satisfy 28 U.S.C. § 2254(e)'s strict requirements for getting an evidentiary hearing. That is likely to happen only rarely, if at all. It is not clear why the 7-2 Court did not simply overrule *Martinez*, despite its recent vintage. [R302] [R379]

B. Subsequent Developments

1. *Engle v. Isaac*, 456 U.S. 107 (1982), held that failure to object to a jury instruction at trial barred federal habeas relief for error in the instruction, rejecting an argument that *Sykes* should apply only to errors unrelated to fact-finding at the criminal trial.

2. *Smith v. Murray*, 477 U.S. 527 (1986), held that *Wainwright* applies in capital as well as non-capital cases.

3. *Reed v. Ross*, 468 U.S. 1 (1984), held that the defendant had shown cause to excuse his failure to raise an issue in state proceedings. The case involved a "constitutional claim so novel that its legal basis is not reasonably available to counsel." *Id.* at 16. The defendant's state criminal trial occurred six years before the Court announced the constitutional rule that made Ross's argument possible and eight years before the Court announced that the rule was retroactive. When the state tried Ross, the constitutional rule had been the opposite.

4. *Murray v. Carrier*, 477 U.S. 478 (1986), held that mere mistake by the petitioner's lawyer in the state trial is not "cause" under *Sykes*. To constitute cause, the error must amount to ineffective assistance, and, under the exhaustion doctrine, petitioner must first have presented the issue in the state court.

5. In addition to showing cause, the applicant must also satisfy the "prejudice" requirement under *Sykes* to avoid dismissal.

   a. The Court measures prejudice in the context of the entire trial.

   b. Moreover, showing possible prejudice is insufficient. The applicant must demonstrate that the mistake "worked to his *actual* and substantial disadvantage, infecting his entire trial with error of constitutional dimension." *United States v. Frady*, 456 U.S. 152, 170 (1982).

6. *Michigan v. Long*, 463 U.S. 1032 (1983), *see supra* Ch. VIII, § IV.E, at 174-179 *[R307]*, addressed the adequate-and-independent-state-ground requirement with respect to Supreme Court appellate jurisdiction. *Harris v. Reed*, 489 U.S. 255 (1989), extended *Long*'s plain-statement requirement to habeas cases.

   a. *Long* held that an independent and adequate state ground exists only if the state court expressly indicates that state law compelled the decision.

   b. Thus, under *Harris*, state procedural default bars consideration by a federal habeas court *only* if the state court expressly stated that its judgment rested upon a state procedural bar.

   c. *Harris* (borrowing from *Long*) thus creates a presumption that a state decision rests upon federal law, and thus is reviewable on federal habeas. Only a plain statement of reliance on state law overcomes the presumption.

d. *Coleman v. Thompson*, 501 U.S. 722, 735 (1991), however, held that the *Harris* presumption applies only when "the decision of the last state court to which the petitioner presented his federal claims . . . fairly appears to rest primarily on federal law or to be interwoven with federal law."

e. *Coleman* appears to increase the number of cases in which federal courts will find a procedural bar to habeas relief, because it permits federal courts to proceed only if the state court opinion appears to rest *primarily* on federal law or be interwoven with it.

f. It is difficult to reconcile *Coleman* with *Harris*, which permitted a federal habeas court to proceed so long as there was no plain statement that the state court based its ruling *only* upon state law. By the same token, *Coleman* appears to be inconsistent with *Michigan v. Long*. *See supra* Ch. VIII, § IV.E.10, at 178-179 *[R308]*. *Coleman* came later, but subsequent opinions continue to cite *Long*'s articulation. *See, e.g,, Florida v. Powell*, 559 U.S. 50, 56 (2010); *Ohio v. Robinette*, 519 U.S. 33, 37 (1996).

V. Habeas Corpus for Federal Prisoners

A. Statutes

1. Federal habeas relief is available for persons held by a state for an act done under federal authority. 28 U.S.C. § 2241(c)(2). Such cases are removable, however, under 28 U.S.C. §§ 1442 and 1442a. Thus, there is little need for federal habeas relief in such situations.

2. Federal habeas relief is also available to test the legality of holding a person in federal custody. 28 U.S.C. § 2241(c)(1).

3. Section 2255 permits a prisoner in federal custody "under sentence of a court" to make a motion to vacate, set aside, or correct her sentence, based upon various grounds, including that the sentence violates the Constitution or a federal statute. That section permits second or successive applications only if the petitioner can persuade a panel of a court of appeals that there is newly discovered evidence that "if proven and viewed in light of the evidence as a whole, would be sufficient to establish by clear and convincing evidence that no reasonable factfinder would have found the movant guilty of the offense," or if the Supreme Court announced a new rule of constitutional law applicable to cases on collateral review.

   a. The section sets forth procedures by which the prisoner must make the motion.

   b. There is a one-year statute of limitations and a limitation on second or successive motions similar to the limitation § 2244 imposes on state prisoners. *See supra* § III.F, at 340-341 *[R309]*.

   c. An application for habeas relief "shall not be entertained" if the prisoner did not request relief from the sentencing court or if the court denied the motion, unless "the remedy by motion is inadequate or ineffective to test the legality of his detention."

4. For many years, persons in custody of the United States Immigration and Naturalization Service challenged custody by seeking federal habeas relief. The Illegal Immigration Reform and Immigrant Responsibility Act of 1996 (IIRIRA) largely has removed that use of the writ.
   a. The Supreme Court held, however, that resident aliens subject to deportation under IIRIRA because of criminal activity may challenge their convictions in federal habeas proceedings.
   b. Moreover, by statute, aliens seized at the border may seek federal corpus relief.
5. Suspected terrorists subject to trial in special military tribunals established by presidential order in the wake of the attacks of September 11, 2001, have access to federal habeas relief. *Boumediene v. Bush*, 553 U.S. 723 (2008).

B. Some Specific Issues Concerning Habeas Corpus by Persons in Federal Custody

1. Obviously, a writ of habeas corpus from a federal court to a federal officer does not implicate federalism concerns.
2. Habeas corpus is useful, however, in several non-criminal situations. For example, it may challenge commitment to a federal mental hospital or conscription into the military. [R26] [R225] [R256] [R298]

Review Questions (Part III; Chapters XI-XV)

True or False Questions

1. **T or F** When Congress is silent on the issue of whether state courts shall have jurisdiction to enforce claims created by a federal statute, the presumption is that state and federal courts have concurrent jurisdiction.

2. **T or F** A state's participation in federal programs may constitute the state's waiver of Eleventh Amendment immunity.

3. **T or F** The doctrine of *Younger v. Harris* applies only to ongoing state criminal proceedings.

4. **T or F** When the federal government exercises one of its constitutional powers, federal law governs any issue arising in a suit concerning the exercise of those powers that is not controlled by statute.

5. **T or F** The Constitution requires a federal court to give full faith and credit to a valid final judgment of a state court.

6. **T or F** Under all forms of abstention, the plaintiff may ultimately return to federal court for a final adjudication.

7. **T or F** The civil-rights-removal statute permits removal of a state prosecution to federal court if the state prosecution will preclude the defendant from enforcing any federal right.

8. **T or F** Congress may abrogate the Eleventh Amendment immunity of states directly only by legislation it enacts under § 5 of the Fourteenth Amendment.

9. **T or F** Under *Ex parte Young*, a federal court may enter an order having an adverse impact on the treasury of a state, so long as the order is prospective in nature.

10. **T or F** A federal court may issue an injunction prohibiting someone from instituting litigation in state court without satisfying one of the exceptions of the Anti-Injunction Act.

11. **T or F** Though generally state courts must adjudicate suits under federal law, the Supreme Court has recognized valid excuses, which allow the state courts to decline jurisdiction of such suits.

12. **T or F** Though § 1983 is silent as to whether a federal court can issue an injunction against state court proceedings, the Supreme Court held that it constitutes an expressly authorized exception to the Anti-Injunction Act.

13. **T or F** The in-aid-of-jurisdiction exception to the Anti-Injunction Act permits federal courts to enjoin parallel state court cases and thus avoid overlapping *in personam* litigation in the state and federal courts.

14. T or F Because § 1983 is an express exception to the Anti-Injunction Act, a federal court may issue an injunction against state court proceedings whenever the equitable requirements for an injunction are satisfied.

15. T or F A plaintiff who alleges that federal law enforcement officers burst into her home without a warrant and subjected her home to an illegal search and seizure in violation of the Fourth Amendment may sue the officers in their individual capacity under § 1983.

16. T or F A plaintiff who alleges that municipal law enforcement officers burst into her home without a warrant and subjected her home to an illegal search and seizure in violation of the Fourth Amendment may sue the officers in their official capacities and may sue the municipality that employed them.

17. T or F Section 1983 does not authorize a claim that officers acting under color of state law violated the plaintiff's state law rights.

18. T or F In a federal habeas corpus proceeding in which a state prisoner challenges her confinement, the federal court is free to ignore state court findings of fact whenever the federal court disagrees with the state court's findings based upon the record.

19. T or F Under current habeas corpus doctrine, a state prisoner's failure to satisfy a state procedural basis for asserting her claim in state court will bar federal habeas relief only if the prisoner deliberately bypassed the state remedy.

20. T or F Plaintiff is a state prisoner. If she sues under § 1983 for deprivation of federal rights, she need not exhaust state remedies, but if she seeks federal habeas, she must.

Essay Question

A public school fired a tenured teacher for teaching the use of birth control devices in a high school sexual-education class. The firing rested upon a state statute providing that a tenured teacher is removable for "teaching matter not in the best interests of the students." The statute provides that the school's principal makes the initial removal decision and that an appeal lies to an administrative review board, consisting of several state-appointed educators. The review board's decision, according to the statute, may receive only very limited judicial review in the state courts.

Instead of pursuing the state statutory procedure, the teacher filed suit in federal district court, challenging the state statute as a violation of his First Amendment right of free expression because it was unconstitutionally vague. He seeks a mandatory injunction ordering the principal to reinstate him. The lawyer for the principal asserts that the federal court should abstain on grounds of *Pullman*, *Burford* and *Younger* abstention. Discuss how the court should rule on each of these contentions.

APPENDIX A

Answers to Review Questions

■ PART I (CHAPTERS I-III)

1. False. The plaintiff has not suffered injury-in-fact, which is a prerequisite for standing. See Chapter I, § IV.B at 35-40 *[R310]*.

2. False. Because the plaintiff has actually been threatened with prosecution, there is a live controversy. The plaintiff need not wait until the prosecution has actually been filed to bring a federal court challenge to the constitutionality of such a prosecution. The case is fit for judicial decision, and it would cause hardship on the individual to withhold judicial consideration of the issue. *See supra* Chapter I, § V.B, at 47-49 *[R311]*.

3. True. The political-question doctrine does not apply to questions concerning the constitutionality of state governmental action, which is involved in this question. The doctrine applies only to political questions involving the federal government. Thus, the case can proceed. *See supra* Chapter I, § VII.A.4, at 53 *[R312]*.

4. False. However broad Congress's Article III power may be, other provisions of the Constitution, particularly those contained in the amendments, can limit it. The law in question would clearly violate the Fifth Amendment's Due Process Clause, which incorporates an equal-protection component. Thus, a statute denying certain groups access to the federal courts would be unconstitutional. *See supra* Chapter II, § VI.A, at 67-68 *[R313]*.

5. False. Though Article III mandates the Supreme Court's existence, its appellate jurisdiction is subject to Congress's power to impose regulations and make exceptions. *See supra* Chapter II, § II.A, B, at 59-60 *[R314]* and § V.A, at 65 *[R315]*.

6. True. Separation of powers means that even though Congress may exclude the jurisdiction of the Article III federal courts completely, it may not undermine their integrity by ordering them to act in an unconstitutional manner. *See supra* Chapter II, § VI.C, at 68-71 *[R316]*.

7. False. The Supreme Court has viewed administrative agencies simply as adjuncts to the Article III federal courts. Because the ultimate judicial power remains in an Article III court, adjudication by administrative agencies does not run afoul of constitutional limitations. *See supra* Chapter III, § IV.B, at 80-87 *[R317]*.

8. True. Though the Supreme Court has not addressed this specific question, it has said that the political-question doctrine will apply to prevent a federal court from possibly embarrassing the executive branch in the conduct of foreign policy. *See supra* Chapter I, § VII.C.2, at 54 *[R318]*.

9. False. An organization's special interest in an area is insufficient for standing. To have standing, a plaintiff must have suffered some injury-in-fact. On the facts of this question, there is no such injury. *See supra* Chapter I, § IV.A, at 33 *[R319]*.

10. True. Though the mootness doctrine probably derives from the Article III requirement of a case or controversy, the Supreme Court has on occasion developed exceptions, largely because of the public interest in having the legal issue resolved. *See supra* Chapter I, § VI.B, at 50-52 *[R320]*.

11. True. Under *Crowell v. Benson*, separation of powers dictates that some Article III court have final power to rule upon constitutional questions. While the Court has undermined *Crowell*, that is largely because the case concerned property rights, which have less weight today than at the time of the decision. The general principle remains sound. Note, however, that the Article III review of constitutional facts need not be *de novo* review. *See supra* Chapter III, § III.C.6, at 84-85 *[R321]* and § IV.B.2, at 86-87 *[R322]*.

12. False. While there is language in *McCardle* that seems to justify broad congressional power over the Supreme Court's appellate jurisdiction, the Court there also emphasized that Congress had not totally removed all procedural avenues to obtain Supreme Court review. *Felker v. Turpin*, 518 U.S. 651 (1996), reaffirmed the principle. *See supra* Chapter II, § V.B, at 66 *[R323]*.

13. False. Though the Due Process Clause usually requires an independent forum prior to the deprivation of property or liberty, the Supreme Court has never construed it to require appellate review. *See supra* Chapter II, § VI.B.3, at 68 *[R324]*.

14. False. Although three justices in *Tidewater* accepted this view, a majority of the Court rejected it. *See supra* Chapter II, § VII.D.2, at 74-75 *[R325]*.

15. True. Such a practice would violate the case-or-controversy requirement of Article III. *See supra* Chapter I, § III.A, at 33 *[R326]*.

Essay Question

Proposal 1: Of all the proposals, this is the most clearly unconstitutional. While Article III may grant Congress power to limit federal court jurisdiction, it says nothing about congressional authority to employ its jurisdiction-curbing authority to overrule Supreme Court constitutional determinations. Under *Crowell v. Benson*, the courts, independent of political pressures, must make the final determination of the meaning of constitutional provisions.

Proposal 2: Under traditional thinking, this proposal would be constitutional. Many think that because Congress need not have created lower federal courts, it may abolish them. Therefore, Congress may take the lesser step of limiting the lower federal courts' jurisdiction. Similarly, Congress has broad power under the Exceptions Clause of Article III to regulate the Supreme Court's appellate jurisdiction. The due-process right to an independent forum is intact, because the state courts remain available. However, certain modern theories, such as the essential-functions thesis, would render the proposal unconstitutional.

Proposal 3: Such a statute would be unconstitutional because it deprives all judicial fora of their function as enforcers and interpreters of the Constitution and constitutional rights.

Proposal 4: This statute poses difficult questions concerning the interrelation of due process and separation of powers. Traditionally, the courts have assumed that while due process requires an independent adjudicator, such independence need not include the Article III protections of judicial tenure and salary. Thus, it is conceivable that a non-Article III legislative court could meet the due process requirement of independence. While of course such a court does not meet the requirement of Article III independence, it is questionable whether that Article requires an Article III court. *Crowell v. Benson* does seem to require such a result (or at least the use of state courts), but the basis in Article III for such a position remains unclear.

■ PART II (CHAPTERS IV-VIII)

1. False. Although the operative language of the statutory and constitutional provisions is identical, Supreme Court has interpreted the statutory language more narrowly. The relatively narrow construction of the statute avoids inundation of the federal courts with federal-question cases. *See supra* Chapter IV, § II.A, at 94-95 *[R327]*, and § III, at 97-109 *[R328]*.

2. False. Every claim in federal court must have a basis of federal subject-matter jurisdiction. The claim against D-1 invokes federal-question jurisdiction. The claim against D-2 does not invoke federal-question jurisdiction (because it arises under state law) and does not invoke diversity jurisdiction (because P and D-2 are citizens of the same state). Nonetheless, the claim against D-2 arises from the same transaction as the federal-question claim against D-1 and thus invokes supplemental jurisdiction under 28 U.S.C. § 1367(a). Nothing in that section limits its application to exclusive federal-question cases. *See supra* Chapter VI, § I, at 134 *[R329]* and § IV.B, at 141-143 *[R330]*.

3. False. Section 1367(a) appears to grant supplemental jurisdiction to the full extent of Article III. However, § 1367(b) cuts back on that grant in diversity cases. Thus, supplemental jurisdiction is narrower in diversity cases than in federal-question cases. The restrictions on supplemental jurisdiction in diversity cases are to avoid undermining the complete-diversity rule. *See supra* Chapter VI, §§ IV.B, C, at 141-146 *[R331]*.

4. False. In establishing the complete diversity requirement in *Strawbridge v. Curtiss*, Chief Justice John Marshall was clearly construing the diversity statute as applied to the facts of the case. The Court stated no opinion on a closely related state of facts, presumably under the statute. The opinion never mentions the Constitution. In 1967, the Supreme Court has made it absolutely clear that the requirement is a matter of statutory (and not constitutional) construction. Congress, therefore, can overturn it. *See supra* Chapter V, § III.A.3, at 117 *[R332]*.

5. True. By statute, 28 U.S.C. § 1332(c)(1), a corporation is a citizen of the states in which it is incorporated and the one state in which it has its principal place of business. Because most corporations incorporate in only one state and because there can never be more than one principal place of business, a corporation generally is a citizen of, at most, two states. *See supra* Chapter V, § III.C, at 121-122 *[R333]*. On the other hand, as recently as 1990, the Supreme Court reaffirmed the longstanding rule that an unincorporated association has the citizenship of each of its members. Thus, for example, if a partnership had members who were citizens of all fifty states, the partnership would be a citizen of all fifty states. *See supra* Chapter V, § III.D, at 122-123 *[R334]*.

6. False. The lower federal courts may adjudicate all matters falling within the Court's original jurisdiction except cases between two or more states, pursuant to 28 U.S.C. § 1251. Article III, § 2, while specifying the Supreme Court's original jurisdiction, says nothing about exclusivity. *See supra* Chapter VIII, § II.B, at 165-166 *[R335]*, § III.B., at 167-168 *[R336]*.

7. False. While the Supreme Court's refuses to review non-federal substantive bases for a state decision reflects its desire to avoid advisory opinions, the *procedural* branch of the adequate-and-independent-state-ground doctrine rests upon comity and federalism. *See supra* Chapter VIII, § IV.E, at 174-179 *[R337]*.

8. True. Under the collateral-order doctrine of *Cohen v. Beneficial Industrial Loan Corp.*, the Court has authorized appeals from state-court decisions that are not final because the state court has not completed adjudicating the case. Also, *Cox Broadcasting Corp. v. Cohn*, described four categories of cases in which appeal lies although the order below is not final. *See supra* Chapter VIII, § IV.D, at 171-174 *[R338]*.

9. False. There are two significant problems with this statement. First, the legal-certainty test does not apply to the plaintiff. She need not show to a legal certainty that her claim meets the amount in controversy. Rather, after the plaintiff makes a good faith allegation that her claim meets the requirement, the burden is on the defendant to show to a legal certainty that the plaintiff cannot recover that much. *See supra* Chapter V, § IV.B, at 125 *[R339]*. Second, 28 U.S.C. § 1332 requires that the amount in controversy *exceed* $75,000. The question says "$75,000 or more." That is wrong; a claim for $75,000 does not satisfy the statutory requirement. *See supra* Chapter V, § IV.A, at 124 *[R340]*.

10. False. *Zahn v. International Paper Co.* required that each member of the class claim more than $75,000. On the other hand, the Court now has interpreted the supplemental-jurisdiction statute, § 1367, to abrogate that requirement and to permit the class to proceed if the class representative's claim exceeds $75,000 (regardless of the value of the other class members' claims). *See supra* Chapter VI, § IV.F.2.e, at 148-149 *[R341]*.

11. True. The starting point is the general rule that the defendant can remove a case to federal court if the case qualifies for federal subject-matter jurisdiction. *See supra* Chapter VII, § III.B, at 155 *[R342]*. This case fails to invoke any basis of federal subject-matter jurisdiction, however, and therefore is not removable. It does not invoke diversity jurisdiction because P and D are citizens of State A. *See supra* Chapter V, § III.A, at 116-119 *[R343]*. It does not invoke federal-question jurisdiction because P's claim does not arise under federal law. The federal issue appears in the complaint only by P's anticipation of a federal defense. Under the well-pleaded-complaint rule, the case does not arise under federal law and does get federal-question jurisdiction. *See supra* Chapter IV, § III.B, at 98-102 *[R344]*.

12. False. The general rule is that the defendant can remove a case to federal court if the federal court has subject-matter jurisdiction over the case. This case does invoke diversity jurisdiction, because the plaintiff is diverse from the defendant and the amount in controversy exceeds $75,000. *However*, the general rule is subject to significant exceptions. One exception, under 28 U.S.C. § 1441(b), is that a case is not removable on the basis of diversity jurisdiction if any defendant is a citizen of the forum. Defendant D is a citizen of State B, the forum (the state in which the case is pending). Thus, even though the case would satisfy diversity jurisdiction if originally in federal court, it is not removable. *See supra* Chapter VII, § III.D.2, at 157 *[R345]*.

13. False. The case invokes neither alienage nor diversity jurisdiction. First, note that the amount-in-controversy requirement for either diversity or alienage is sufficient because the claim exceeds $75,000. *See supra* Chapter V, § IV.A, at 124 *[R346]*. Second, however, an alienage case must be between an alien and a citizen of a state in the United States. *See supra* Chapter V, § II.B.4, at 114 *[R347]*. Though P is an alien, D is not a citizen of a state. To be a citizen of a state, a U.S. citizen must be domiciled in that state. *See supra* Chapter V, § III.B, at 119-121 *[R348]*. D is not domiciled in a state at all, so is not a citizen of a state. (D is also not an alien; she is still a citizen of the U.S.) Third, a diversity case must be between citizens of different states of the United States. Here, neither P nor D is a citizen of a state of the United States. *See supra* Chapter V, § III.B, at 119-121 *[R349]*.

14. False. Under the principles of aggregation, when a case is by one plaintiff against one defendant (as here), the plaintiff may add together (aggregate) all claims that she has against the defendant, even if the claims are unrelated factually, transactionally, and legally. In this case, the amount in controversy exceeds $75,000, and the plaintiff is diverse from the defendant. Thus, the case properly invokes diversity jurisdiction. *See supra* Chapter V, § IV.C, at 127-128 *[R350]*.

15. False. The well-pleaded-complaint rule requires that the federal ingredient be part of the *plaintiff's claim*—in other words, not part of an anticipated defense (as in Question 11). *Holmes Group v. Vornado Air Circulation*, 535 U.S. 826 (2002), made clear that this rule applies also to counterclaims. Thus, even if the defendant asserted a counterclaim that clearly arose under federal law, it would not invoke federal-question jurisdiction. The plaintiff's claim alone must do so. *See supra* Chapter IV, § III.A.7, at 98 *[R351]*.

Essay Question

1. There is no federal subject-matter jurisdiction over Claim 1. Federal courts have limited subject-matter jurisdiction. The two principal types of cases that federal courts can hear are diversity and federal-question cases.

For diversity jurisdiction, all plaintiffs must be diverse from all defendants, and the amount in controversy must exceed $75,000. Here, the claim against both defendants fails to qualify for diversity jurisdiction for two reasons. First, the claim is for $55,000 and thus does not exceed $75,000, as 28 U.S.C. § 1332 requires. Second, all parties are citizens of State A. The facts indicate clearly that P is a citizen of State A. The defendants are corporations. Under § 1332(c)(1), a corporation is a citizen of the state in which incorporated and the state in which it has its principal place of business. The facts indicate that both Monster and Goliath are incorporated and have their PPB in State A. There is no diversity.

To invoke federal-question jurisdiction under § 1331, the case must arise under federal law. The claim here appears in P's well pleaded complaint—it is not an anticipated defense. The question is whether the federal ingredient in the claim is sufficiently important to invoke federal-question jurisdiction. The Supreme Court has embraced differing tests for this element. One, set forth in *American Well Works*, is whether federal law created the cause of action. Here, however, state law created the cause of action, so the case does not invoke federal-question jurisdiction under that test. Under *Smith*, the test is whether the right to relief depends upon the construction of federal law. Arguably, that is so here, because the statute invites courts to look at what behavior constitutes a violation of *federal* antitrust law.

On the other hand, in *Merrell Dow*, *Grable*, and *Gunn*, the Court seems to have stated a nebulous substantiality standard, indicating that federal-question jurisdiction might exist for state-created claims when some important issue of federal law exists. In the present case, only matters of state law are ultimately at stake. No federal statute is on point, since the state statute has an impact only upon *intrastate* commerce—an area that Congress has no constitutional power to regulate. Moreover, federal law did not create a private right of action for intrastate cases. Since interpretation of the state law can have no effect on any federal interests, there is no justification for invoking federal court power. This is so even though the state has chosen to incorporate the federal standard by reference.

2. There is no federal subject-matter jurisdiction over Claim 2. First, there is no diversity jurisdiction over this claim because P and Monster are citizens of the same state. Second, there is no federal-question jurisdiction over this claim because the claim sounds in common law (state) fraud. Finally, there is no supplemental jurisdiction over this claim for two reasons. First, supplemental jurisdiction is appropriate only when some claim in the same case invokes a basis of federal subject-matter jurisdiction. Here, as in Part 1, the first claim fails to qualify for subject-matter jurisdiction. Second, supplemental jurisdiction is proper under § 1367(a) only by a claim that shares a common nucleus of operative fact with a claim that does have federal subject-matter jurisdiction. Thus, even if Claim 1 did have federal-question jurisdiction, supplemental jurisdiction would not attach to Claim 2 because it is factually unrelated to Claim 1 and thus cannot satisfy the common-nucleus test.

■ PART III (CHAPTERS 9-17)

1. True. This is the rule of *Claflin v. Houseman*. Note, however, that under *Claflin*, this presumption is rebuttable, as has happened in suits to enforce the federal antitrust laws. *See supra* Chapter XII, § III.A.4-7, at 270-272 *[R352]*.

2. False. The Supreme Court initially upheld this constructive-waiver notion. The leading case was *Parden v. Terminal Railway*. More recently, however, the Court has rejected the concept. Today it is clear that *Parden* is dead and that constructive waiver has no role to play regarding Eleventh Amendment immunity. *Florida Prepaid Postsecondary Education Expense Bd. v. College Savings Bank*. *See supra* Chapter XIII, § IV.C.1.c, at 295 *[R353]*, § IV.C.4, at 298-299 *[R354]*.

3. False. The *Younger* doctrine started in such instances, and still has its greatest force in the area of ongoing state criminal proceedings. Nonetheless, the Supreme Court used *Younger* to prevent federal judicial interference with certain state civil proceedings in *Pennzoil Co. v. Texaco, Inc. See supra* Chapter IX, § III.G.6.b(4), at 217-218 *[R355]*.

4. True. This is the rule of *Clearfield Trust*, which, though criticized, is still good law. Note, however, that while federal common law always applies in those cases, today the Supreme Court will often choose to adopt state law as the federal common-law standard. *See supra* Chapter XI, § VI.D.1, at 247-252 *[R356]*.

5. False. It is true that a federal court must give full faith and credit to a state court judgment, but the Constitution does not compel that result. The constitutional provision requires a state court to give full faith and credit to the valid final judgment of another state's court. It is the Full-Faith-and-Credit Statute, § 1738, that requires a federal court to give full faith and credit to a state-court judgment. *See supra* Chapter X, § II.A & B, at 226-228 *[R357]*.

6. False. This is true of *Pullman* abstention; the *England* procedure, by which the federal court stays pending litigation in state court, applies without question in *Pullman* abstention. *See supra* Chapter IX, § III.D, at 195-201 *[R358]*. It may also be true in *Colorado River* abstention, in which the federal court stays the action pending return from state court. *See supra* Chapter IX, § III.H, at 220-223 *[R359]*. In *Thibodaux* abstention, though the Supreme Court upheld a stay of federal proceedings, it is not clear that there is any issue left for the federal court to litigate. *See supra* Chapter IX, § III.F, at 205-207 *[R360]*. But in *Burford* abstention, the statement in Question 6 clearly is not true. The federal court dismisses the case, and the parties go to the state system for ultimate adjudication. *See supra* Chapter IX, § III.E.2.g.1, at 204 *[R361]*.

7. False. The civil-rights-removal statute covers only federal rights of racial equality. *See supra* Chapter XIV, § VI.B.2, at 326 *[R362]*.

8. False. This statement is underinclusive. It is clear that it may abrogate Eleventh Amendment immunity under amendments adopted after the Eleventh. *Seminole Tribe of Florida v. Florida. See supra* Chapter XIII, § IV.C.2.f at 296 *[R363]*. The phenomenon has occurred thus far only under the Fourteenth Amendment, but the Thirteenth and Fifteenth Amendments have identical enforcement clauses. Remember, however, that legislation under an enforcement clause does not automatically abrogate Eleventh Amendment immunity. Congress must (1) expressly indicate its intent that states be amenable to suit in federal court and (2) tailor the statute to remedy a particular constitutional violation; the Court talks of this second point as the requirement for "congruence and proportionality." *See supra* Chapter XIII, § IV.C.3.b, at 297 *[R364]*.

9. True. So long as the case satisfies *Ex parte Young*'s requirements, the fact that the state must expend funds to satisfy an equitable order does not make the order invalid. Relief requiring state expenditures, such as in *Milliken v. Bradley* (requiring state officials to desegregate schools), is acceptable if ancillary to prospective equitable orders. *See supra* Chapter XIII, § IV.A.6.e, at 293 *[R365]*.

10. True. The Anti-Injunction Act applies only when state court proceedings are already under way. Thus, it does limit a federal court's power to enjoin someone from instituting suit in state court. Because the statute does not apply, the federal court need not satisfy one of the exceptions. As long as the equitable requirements for an injunction exist, the court may enter it. This was the holding in *Dombrowski v. Pfister*. *See supra* Chapter IX, § III.G.3.b, at 209-210 *[R366]*.

11. True. The Court has recognized two valid excuses, though their theoretical bases are unclear. First, if the state court has limited subject-matter jurisdiction and cannot hear the claim, then notwithstanding the claim's federal nature, the state court need not enforce the federal claim. Second, if the state court would dismiss under the doctrine of *forum non conveniens*, it need not entertain the federal claim. *See supra* Chapter XII, § IV.B, at 276-279 *[R367]*.

12. True. This is the holding of *Mitchum v. Foster*. The case stands for the proposition that Congress can invoke the expressly-authorized exception to the Anti-Injunction Act without specifically referring to that statute. The Court has had difficulty applying *Mitchum* more recently, and it seems likely that the Court will not find an unexpressed express authorization so readily in other circumstances. *See supra* Chapter IX, § II.B.2, at 209 *[R368]*.

13. False. Despite arguments by commentators that the in-aid-of-jurisdiction exception extend to avoid overlapping federal and state *in personam* litigation, the Supreme Court has interpreted the exception narrowly. Generally, it applies to permit injunctions against state cases only in *in rem*, *quasi-in-rem*, and other cases involving federal-court attachment of property. *See* Chapter IX, § II.A.4, at 189-190 *[R369]*. Though some lower courts have expanded use of the exception, the expansion has been limited, and it clearly does not permit federal courts to enjoin overlapping *in personam* cases in the interest of avoiding duplicative litigation.

14. False. Though the Anti-Injunction Act does not restrict the federal court's power in this regard, "Our Federalism," embodied in *Younger v. Harris*, does. *See supra* Chapter IX, § III.G, at 207-209 *[R370]*. That case stands for the proposition that a federal court may not enjoin pending state-court criminal proceedings absent exceptional circumstances, such as bad faith or harassment. *See supra* Chapter IX, § III.G.3-4, at 207-212 *[R371]*.

15. False. Section 1983 allows suing persons who violate the plaintiff's federal rights under color of state law. Here, the officers allegedly violated her rights under color of federal law. Thus, § 1983 does not apply. *See supra* Chapter XIV, § III.E.1, at 309 *[R372]*, § V.A, at 323. The plaintiff may proceed against the officers by asserting a *Bivens* claim, which is available for violations under color of federal law. *See* Chapter XIV, § V, at 323-324*[R373]*. But remember the Court's current hostility to *Bivens* actions *[R373A]*. *See supra* Ch. XI, § VI.D.2.d, at 258-258 *[R373A]*.

16. False. Plaintiff may sue the officers only in their individual capacities, not in their official capacities. *See supra* Chapter XIV, § III.D.2, at 307-308 *[R374]*. Officers in their official capacities are not persons under § 1983; officers in their individual capacities are. The municipality is not liable under *respondeat superior*, but is liable only if the deprivation resulted from some official municipality policy or custom. *See supra* Chapter XIV, § III.D.3.b-c, at 308 *[R375]*.

17. True. Section 1983 vindicates only certain federal rights. Deprivation of state-law rights is not within the statute. *See supra* Chapter XIV, § III.F.2, at 310 *[R376]*.

18. False. The federal courts have always been more deferential to state fact-finding than the standard this question states. Under recent revisions to § 2254 under AEDPA, a state-court factual determination is presumptively correct, and the federal court can ignored it only if the petitioner can rebut the presumption by clear and convincing evidence. *See supra* Chapter XV, § III.D.6, at 337 *[R377]*. Another section of the AEDPA, however, authorizes habeas if the state decision rested upon an unreasonable determination of the facts in light of the evidence presented in the State proceeding. *See supra* Chapter XV, § III.D.7, at 337 *[R378]*. It is not clear how these two provisions interact, but each clearly requires more deference to the state-court findings than the standard this question mentions.

19. False. This was true under *Fay v. Noia*, but it is no longer good law in light of *Wainwright v. Sykes*. *See supra* Chapter XV, § IV.A.3-4, at 343-344 *[R379]*.

20. True. There is generally no exhaustion-of-state-remedies requirement under § 1983. *See supra* Chapter XIV, § III.B.3.a, at 307 *[R380]*. (The Prison Litigation Reform Act does require exhaustion of administrative remedies by federal prisoners proceeding under a *Bivens* claim. *See supra* Chapter XIV, § III.H.6, at 316 *[R381]*.) In contrast, the state prisoner who seeks federal habeas must exhaust state remedies before proceeding in federal court. *See* Chapter XI, § VI.D.2.e.1, at 259 *[R382]*. *See also* Chapter XV, § III.B, at 335-336 *[R383]*.

Essay

1. *Pullman* Abstention.

The argument in support of *Pullman* abstention is that the state statute is ambiguous and therefore the state courts should be given the opportunity to construe the statute narrowly to avoid the constitutional issue.

Arguably, however, *Pullman* abstention is inappropriate. The fact that the state statute may be unconstitutionally vague does not mean that it is ambiguous for purposes of *Pullman* abstention. When there is a small number of ways to interpret a statute, *Pullman* abstention may be appropriate. But an unconstitutionally vague statute lends itself to multiple interpretations as individual cases arise, so the state court cannot simply offer one interpretation that is authoritative; it would need many cases to give more discernible meaning to the statute. Moreover, the case involves First Amendment free-speech rights, where delay in ultimate vindication of the federal right may increase the chilling effect.

On the other hand, many federal judges might wish to provide the state court the opportunity to narrow the statute.

2. *Burford* Abstention.

At least a plausible argument could be made to support *Burford* abstention in this case. Public education is a matter of great importance to the state, and, as in *Burford*, the state has established a complex network of administrative and judicial review. On the other hand, a federal court could decide that *Burford* should be limited to truly complex matters of state law, and not apply to cases in which the central issue is a matter of federal constitutional law.

3. *Younger* Abstention.

Younger abstention traditionally applied to cases of state criminal prosecutions. The Supreme Court has invoked it, however, in certain state civil proceedings implicating important state interests. In the present case, the federal interference would not be with an ongoing judicial proceeding of any kind, but rather one that is—at least at now—administrative. Though state judicial review exists, it is only after the administrative process is completed, which may unduly delay vindication of First Amendment rights. While the basic assumption of *Younger* is that state courts are constitutionally and historically capable of enforcing federal rights, the same cannot be said of state administrative agencies.

Middlesex County Ethics Committee v. Garden State Bar Association held that *Younger* barred federal injunctive relief against a state attorney disciplinary proceeding that plaintiffs challenged on First Amendment grounds. The Court did note the important state interest involved, which arguably renders the case relevant to this one. The case might be distinguishable, however, because the Court emphasized the unique relationship between the administrative ethics committee and the state supreme court, which appointed and supervised it. This seemed to indicate that *Middlesex* applies only to such instances of close judicial and administrative interaction, a view *Hawaii Housing Authority v. Midkiff* confirmed.

APPENDIX B

Model Examination

QUESTION 1

In response to concern over what some people consider undue interference by the federal judiciary in the operation of federal prisons, Congress has enacted and the President signed into law the Judicial Prison Review Act of 2004. The Act provides:

> Section 1. No federal district court may review the constitutionality of decisions by federal prison officials regarding the confinement or discipline of prisoners.
>
> Section 2. Any prisoner may seek review of a decision by federal prison officials in the Federal Prison Review Board, which is to be comprised of three individuals, appointed by the President and confirmed by the Senate, who sit at the discretion of the President.
>
> Section 3. Decisions of the Federal Prison Review Board are not subject to review in any federal court.

Write a memorandum discussing the constitutionality of the Act.

QUESTION 2

P, a citizen of Illinois, sued in federal district court two defendants: X, a citizen of Venezuela, and Y Corp., a Delaware corporation. P's claim rests upon state law, and she claims that X and Y Corp., as joint tortfeasors, caused her personal injuries of $100,000. Y Corp. has its headquarters in Chicago, Illinois, where it makes corporate decisions. It manufactures all of its products in Tucson, Arizona.

X asserted a state-law counterclaim against P. The counterclaim arose from the same transaction as that alleged by P in her complaint. X claimed damages of $55,000. In addition, Y Corp. asserted a counterclaim against P. Its counterclaim also arose from the transaction that P alleged in her complaint. Y Corp.'s claim against P arises under federal law.

X and Y Corp. then move to dismiss the entire case for lack of subject-matter jurisdiction. Assume that the motion is timely, because subject-matter jurisdiction is in issue throughout the proceedings.

The district court held (1) that P's claims against X and Y Corp. failed to invoke federal subject-matter jurisdiction, but that (2) it had subject-matter jurisdiction over the case because Y Corp.'s claim against P invoked federal-question jurisdiction, and (3) that X's counterclaim against P failed to invoke federal subject-matter jurisdiction.

Write a memorandum discussing the correctness of each of the district court's rulings.

QUESTION 3

A sued B in state court under state unfair-competition law. A and B are citizens of the same state. B answered, arguing that its alleged unfair competition was proper because of its interest in protecting its patent.

The state court denied defendant's motion for summary judgment, holding that because the federal courts have exclusive jurisdiction over patent cases, it lacked authority to rule upon the relevance of defendant's patent as a justification for its actions. Under state law, interlocutory appeals run directly to the state supreme court. B took such an appeal to the state supreme court, which affirmed. B then sought review in the United States Supreme Court, which agreed to hear the case and reversed the state courts' conclusion that they could not consider the relevance of B's patent.

Write a memorandum considering the correctness of each judicial ruling.

ANSWER TO MODEL EXAMINATION

■ QUESTION 1

All conceivable constitutional objections to the Act flow either from Article III or from the Fifth Amendment's Due Process Clause.

ARTICLE III

The clear impact of the Act is to exclude the Article III federal courts (including the Supreme Court) from review of significant constitutional issues. Under traditional thinking, Congress need not vest the federal judicial power in any Article III court. It need not vest the judicial power in the lower federal courts, because Article III expressly allowed Congress not to create lower courts, and so Congress could abolish such courts. If Congress has power to abolish them, the argument proceeds, it has power to take the lesser step of curbing their jurisdiction. The argument that Congress could exclude Supreme Court appellate jurisdiction turns on Article III's Exceptions Clause, which allows Congress to make exceptions to the Supreme Court's appellate jurisdiction.

Several arguments, however, would preclude all or part of Congress's action. Most suspect is the limitation of Supreme-Court jurisdiction. The Exceptions Clause has never received a definitive interpretation, and some commentators argue that Congress may not make exceptions that interfere with performance of the Court's essential functions. Though there is little linguistic or historical basis to support such a thesis, if accepted it would invalidate Congress's exclusion of Supreme Court appellate jurisdiction.

Other commentators have adopted a type of floating essential-functions thesis—a theory that since Article III provides that the federal judicial power "shall be vested," the Article requires that *some* federal court (*either* the Supreme Court or a lower federal court) exercise the judicial power. Under this theory, the Act is invalid because it removes *both* lower court *and* Supreme-Court jurisdiction. However, these theories have never received judicial acceptance.

Crowell v. Benson did indicate that separation-of-powers principles dictate that the judiciary have the final say on the meaning of the Constitution, but it is not clear whether Supreme-Court review of state-court decisions could satisfy that requirement. State-court review is also relevant to the due process concern.

DUE PROCESS

Due process requires an independent forum for adjudication of constitutional rights. At least in regard to actions of the federal government, state courts—which the Supremacy Clause requires to enforce the Constitution—meet this independence requirement. However, under *Tarble's Case*, state courts may not directly control federal officials' actions.

If the rule of *Tarble* were held applicable even when Congress has closed the federal forum (not the case in *Tarble*), it is conceivable that the Act's exclusion of federal judicial review would be unconstitutional. The question would then come down to whether a hearing before the newly created review board satisfies due process. However, if *Tarble*'s *Case's* limit on state-court jurisdiction were to fall, that would satisfy *Crowell*'s requirements of due process and separation-of-powers.

■ QUESTION 2

1. *P's claims against X and Y Corp.* Because P's claims against X and against Y Corp. rest only upon state law, P cannot invoke federal-question jurisdiction. P can, however, proceed in federal court if the action satisfies the requirements for diversity or alienage jurisdiction.

For diversity (28 U.S.C. § 1332(a)(1)) and alienage (28 U.S.C. § 1332(a)(2)) jurisdiction, the amount in controversy must exceed $75,000. In determining the amount in controversy, a plaintiff may not aggregate separate claims against multiple defendants. Here, however, the claims against the two defendants allege liability as "joint tortfeasors." With allegations of joint liability, the amount in controversy is the amount of the claim against them. Here, that claim is for $100,000. Thus, it exceeds $75,000 and satisfies the amount in controversy requirement.

In addition to the amount in controversy, alienage jurisdiction requires suit between a citizen of a state in the United States and a citizen of a foreign country. The claim by P against X satisfies this requirement, because P is a citizen of Illinois and X is a citizen of Venezuela. Thus the district court was erroneous in concluding that it lacked subject-matter jurisdiction over P's claim against X.

In addition to the amount in controversy, diversity jurisdiction requires suit between citizens of different states. This statutory requirement means that every plaintiff must be of diverse citizenship from every defendant. Here, again, P is a citizen of Illinois. Under 28 U.S.C. § 1332(c)(1), Y Corp., because it is a corporation, is a citizen of both the state of its incorporation and the state in which it has its principal place of business. Y Corp. is incorporated in Delaware, so is a citizen of that state and is diverse from P.

But if Y Corp.'s principal place of business is in Illinois, it will be a co-citizen of P, and thus diversity jurisdiction will fail. A corporation's principal place of business is its headquarters, where its officers make corporate decisions. For Y Corp., that place is Chicago, so Y Corp. is a citizen of Illinois and there is no diversity between it and P. Before the Supreme Court decided *Hertz Corp. v. Friend*, some courts regarded the place of operations, —where the corporation does most of its activity—as its principal place of business. Here, that would have been where Y Corp. has its sole manufacturing plant—Arizona. If this were the principal place of business, there would be diversity between P and Y Corp. Thus, the district court was correct in concluding that there was no diversity jurisdiction over P's claim against Y Corp.

2. Y's counterclaim against P. There is no question that Y's counterclaim against P qualifies for federal subject-matter jurisdiction. Specifically, there is federal-question jurisdiction under 28 U.S.C. § 1331. The citizenship of the parties and the amount in controversy are irrelevant. The claim invokes federal-question jurisdiction, and thus is proper in the pending case by P against X and Y Corp., if P's case qualifies for alienage or diversity jurisdiction.

The district court concluded, however, that P's original claims did not qualify for federal subject-matter jurisdiction. But the court ruled that it had jurisdiction over the suit under federal-question jurisdiction because of the federal-question counterclaim. The court erred. *Holmes Group v. Vornado Air Circulation* held that a federal court does not have subject-matter jurisdiction simply because counterclaim arises under federal law. If the plaintiff's claims did not qualify for federal subject-matter jurisdiction, the court must dismiss. Stated another way, federal-question jurisdiction is available only through a well-pleaded complaint, not through a counterclaim.

3. X's counterclaim against P. X's counterclaim against P arises under state law, and thus fails to invoke federal-question jurisdiction. Federal-question jurisdiction attaches only to claims that arise under federal law. X's counterclaim against P also fails to invoke alienage jurisdiction under 28 U.S.C. § 1332(a)(2). Though it is brought by a citizen of a foreign country (X) against a citizen of a state of the United States (P), and thus satisfies that requirement for alienage, it does not satisfy the amount-in-controversy requirement. For alienage jurisdiction, the claim must exceed $75,000. X's claim does not. Thus the district court was correct insofar as it concluded that there is no *independent* basis of federal subject-matter jurisdiction over X's counterclaim.

The counterclaim would have qualified for supplemental jurisdiction if the court had had subject-matter jurisdiction over plaintiff's case. Supplemental jurisdiction permits asserting claims in federal court that do not have an independent basis of federal subject-matter jurisdiction such as federal-question, diversity, or alienage. 28 U.S.C. § 1367(a) grants supplemental jurisdiction to claims that involve a common nucleus of operative fact as a claim over which there is federal subject-matter jurisdiction. Here, the facts make clear that X's counterclaim arises from the same transaction as P's claims against X and Y Corp., but supplemental jurisdiction fails because the court has no subject-matter jurisdiction over plaintiff's case. Thus, § 1367(a) does not grant supplemental jurisdiction over X's counterclaim.

■ QUESTION 3

1. State Court Power to Adjudicate the Patent Defense: The state courts were incorrect and the Supreme Court correct on the issue of state court power to adjudicate the federal patent claim. While it is true that under 28 U.S.C. § 1338 federal jurisdiction for suits under the patent laws is exclusive, the Supreme Court held in *Lear, Inc. v.*

Adkins that state courts must adjudicate defenses under the patent laws. This is because the opposite conclusion would threaten enforcement of federal patent law policy.

2. *Appealability:* 28 U.S.C. § 1257 allows Supreme Court review of only final decisions of the state's highest court. Since the state supreme court here reviewed a denial of a summary judgment motion, its decision is not final.

Though the Court has recognized a number of exceptions to the strict finality requirement, particularly in *Cox Broadcasting Corp. v. Cohn*, none of those exceptions applies to this case. Therefore the Supreme Court incorrectly agreed to review the state supreme court's decision.

APPENDIX C

Glossary

A

Abstention. A judge-made doctrine authorizing federal courts to relinquish jurisdiction over an action in favor of the state courts in order to further important interests of federalism. The doctrine is sub-divided into specific categories. *See Pullman* Abstention, *Burford* Abstention, *Thibodaux* Abstention, *Colorado River* Abstention, and *Younger* Doctrine.

Adequate-and-Independent-State-Ground Doctrine. A judge-made principle that prevents the Supreme Court from reviewing a state court decision when the decision is premised, at least in part, on grounds of state law, so that even if the Supreme Court were to alter the disposition of the federal issue in the case, the result would remain the same.

Alienage Jurisdiction. A form of federal subject-matter jurisdiction for cases between a citizen of a foreign country and a citizen of a state of the United States and the amount in controversy exceeds $75,000. 28 U.S.C. § 1332(a)(2).

Ancillary Jurisdiction. A judge-made doctrine allowing a federal district court to exercise jurisdiction over claims that lack an independent basis of subject-matter jurisdiction, such as federal-question or diversity jurisdiction. The concept is now subsumed under the generic principle of supplemental jurisdiction, which is codified at 28 U.S.C. § 1367.

Anti-Injunction Act. A federal statute providing that a federal court may not enjoin state proceedings unless expressly authorized by Congress, or where necessary in aid of its jurisdiction, or to protect or effectuate its judgment. 28 U.S.C. § 2283.

Appeal. Review of the decision of a lower court by a higher court.

Article I Courts. *See* Non-Article III Courts

Article III Courts. Federal courts whose judges receive the protections of salary and tenure provided by Article III of the Constitution. Matters heard by them include the following types of cases: those arising under the Constitution and the laws and treaties of the United States, those to which the U.S. is a party, and those between states and between citizens of different states.

B

***Burford* Abstention.** A form of judge-made abstention that authorizes a federal court to defer to a state's review system when the subject matter is better adjudicated under a complex regulatory scheme and concerns predominantly local factors in sensitive areas of state concern.

C

Certification. A procedure, authorized by state law, allowing a federal court to submit unsettled issues of state law to a state's highest court for determination while retaining jurisdiction over the action. This procedure can be used instead of abstention, but certification is not available in all states.

Certiorari. A statutorily-provided means of obtaining Supreme Court review. The Supreme Court uses its discretion in choosing whether to review a lower court's proceedings. The votes of four Justices are required. A denial of certiorari by the Supreme Court is not a decision on the merits.

Civil-Rights Removal. A statute, 28 U.S.C. § 1443, authorizing the removal of a case from state to federal court in any of the following circumstances: 1. where a person has been "denied or cannot enforce" a civil right of equality in a state court; 2. where a person is being sued or prosecuted for performing "any act under color of authority derived from any law providing for equal rights;" or 3. where a person is the subject of suit for refusing to perform an act that would be inconsistent with a law providing for equal rights. The denial clause has been narrowly construed to permit removal only when a state statute or constitutional provision invades a federal civil right, or when a federal statute immunizes from prosecution the very conduct for which a person is being prosecuted.

Claim Preclusion. The principle that a final judgment by a court of competent jurisdiction is an absolute bar to a subsequent action involving the same cause of action between the same parties or their privies.

Collateral Estoppel. See Issue Preclusion.

***Colorado River* Abstention.** A category of judge-made abstention under which a federal court may in extreme circumstances abstain due to concurrent state judicial proceedings in order to avoid harassment of the parties or duplication of effort.

Comity. The notion that the federal system will operate best if the states are allowed to perform their legitimate functions without undue interference from federal courts. Federal judicial deference to state courts. This principle was used in part to justify the *Younger* doctrine.

Complete Diversity. The requirement that the federal courts exercise the diversity jurisdiction only when *all* plaintiffs are citizens of different states from *all* defendants. Developed originally by Chief Justice Marshall in *Strawbridge v. Curtiss*, the rule was held in 7 to derive from the diversity statute, rather than Article III, allowing Congress to modify the rule if it so desires. The Federal Interpleader Act is an example of congressional provision for only "minimal" diversity (*i.e.*, at least one plaintiff is a citizen of a state different from the state of *at least* one defendant).

Concurrent Jurisdiction. A situation in which tribunals of more than one system have jurisdiction over a case. For example, the federal and state courts have concurrent jurisdiction in diversity actions.

Constitutional Facts. A constitutional doctrine, deriving from separation-of-powers principles, that provides that the Article III federal courts are not bound by an administrative agency's findings of facts when such findings have constitutional implications. Though today the federal court may not conduct a *de novo* proceeding to make its own findings regarding such facts, it still is supposed to make an independent inquiry on the basis of the preexisting record.

D

Declaratory Relief. A procedure allowing a litigant to seek a binding decision to settle a controversy prior to engaging in conduct that may lead to legal liability. The procedure is authorized in federal court by federal statute. However, the procedure is limited by the constitutional requirement of case or controversy.

Diversity jurisdiction. A form of federal subject-matter jurisdiction in which the case is between citizens of different states and the amount in controversy exceeds $75,000. 28 U.S.C. § 1332(a)(1).

Domicile. A human being's one true, fixed, permanent location. It is established by a person's physical presence in a place combined with the subjective intent to make it her permanent home. Though a person may have more than one "residence," she cannot have more than one domicile at a time.

E

***England* Procedure.** A procedure, devised in *England v. Louisiana St. Bd. of Medical Examiners*, providing that after a federal court has referred issues of state law to a state court under *Pullman* abstention and the state court has adjudicated the state law issues, a litigant has the right to return to federal court for adjudication of federal constitutional issues.

Erie Doctrine. A principle, derived from *Erie Railroad Co. v. Tompkins*, governing whether a federal court in a diversity case must apply state law to determine an issue. In *Erie*, the Court held that the federal courts are bound by the constitutional limits of Congress's power to prescribe statutory law for such suits and by the statutory limits prescribed for the courts by the Rules of Decision Act and the Rules Enabling Act.

Exceptions Clause. A provision of Article III authorizing Congress to make exceptions and regulations to the Supreme Court's appellate jurisdiction.

Exhaustion of Remedies. This doctrine requires that relief must be sought in one forum before entering another. Exhaustion of state administrative or judicial remedies may be required before a federal court will adjudicate a case. A state criminal defendant must exhaust his state judicial remedies before obtaining federal habeas corpus relief. The Supreme Court has held, however, that generally a federal civil rights plaintiff, suing under 42 U.S.C. § 1983, need not first exhaust state administrative or judicial remedies.

Expressly Authorized Exception. An exception to the bar of the Anti-Injunction Act providing that a federal court may issue an injunction to stop litigants from proceeding in a state court when such an injunction has been expressly authorized by an act of Congress. 28 U.S.C. § 2283. Courts have found such an authorization in such laws as the Securities Exchange Act and the Civil Rights Act, 42 U.S.C. § 1983.

F

Federal Common Law. A body of decisional law developed by the federal courts. The application of this body of common law is limited by the *Erie* doctrine and by the Rules of Decision Act, which provides that except for cases governed by the Constitution, the treaties of the United States, or acts of Congress, federal courts are to apply state law. Areas in which federal common law have been developed include federal "proprietary" interests, admiralty and foreign relations.

Federal-question jurisdiction. A form of federal subject-matter jurisdiction for cases arising under federal law. 28 U.S.C. § 1331.

Final Judgment. A decision that terminates the action. An appeal to a higher court must ordinarily be from a final judgment.

Forum Non Conveniens. The discretionary power of a court to decline jurisdiction when, in the interest of justice, the action should proceed in another forum. This power is usually used when another forum would be more convenient for the parties because the parties, witnesses, or evidence is located in that forum.

Full Faith and Credit. The enforcement of one jurisdiction's law or judgments in the court of another forum. Under the Constitution, a state must give the judgment of a court of another state the authority that would be accorded it by the courts in the state in which the judgment was rendered. Under the Full Faith and Credit Act, 28 U.S.C. § 1738, the federal courts must recognize the judgments of state courts.

H

Habeas Corpus. A writ used to test the legality of a person's detention by the government, but not to determine his innocence or guilt. It is a Latin expression meaning "you have the body."

I

"In Aid of Jurisdiction" Exception. An exception to the Anti-Injunction Act authorizing a federal court to issue an injunction to stay litigants from proceeding in a state court where such an injunction is necessary in aid of the federal court's jurisdiction. 28 U.S.C. § 2283. This exception has generally been limited to cases that are *in rem*, in which the federal court has acquired jurisdiction of the subject property prior to the state court action.

Injunction. An equitable remedy that prohibits a party from performing a particular act. Injunctions may be either temporary or permanent.

Issue Preclusion. A rule that provides that when an issue of fact or mixed law and fact has been decided in a previous action brought under a different cause of action between the same parties or their privies, it cannot be relitigated.

J

Johnson Act of 1934. A statute providing that federal district courts cannot enjoin an order issued by a state administrative body affecting rates charged by a public utility. 28 U.S.C. § 1342.

Judicial Review. The principle that courts may examine the constitutionality of the actions of the executive and the legislative branches of government. Courts will decline to rule on those issues that are purely political questions. *See* Political Question.

Jurisdictional-Amount Requirement. The dictate that a case may be heard in federal court only if the dispute involves a specified amount in controversy. The most important such requirement is found in 28 U.S.C. § 1332, which requires that diversity and alienage cases involve an amount in excess of $75,000, exclusive of interest and costs.

L

Legal Certainty Test. The test for determining whether the amount-in-controversy requirement is met. It provides that the amount claimed in the complaint will control unless it appears to a "legal certainty" that the claim could not be for more than $75,000.

Legislative Court. *See infra* Non-Article III Court

M

Manufactured Diversity. The improper or collusive creation of diversity for the sole or primary purpose of obtaining federal court jurisdiction. Such a practice is prohibited by 28 U.S.C. § 1359.

Mootness. The principle that when the matter in dispute has already been resolved, there is no actual controversy that would be affected by a judicial decision, and federal courts will not exercise their jurisdiction. Though federal courts will not hear any case that has been mooted, they may exercise their jurisdiction when the behavior is likely to recur but to continually evade review.

N

Non-Article III Court. A federal court whose judges lack constitutional protections for salary and tenure. Congress forms such courts not under its authority in Article III, but usually under its authority under Article I and the "necessary and proper" clause. Congress has the power to make all laws necessary to execute such courts' functions, and it may require such courts to perform non-judicial activities. Examples of non-Article III courts include are the Territorial Courts, the Tax Court and the local courts of the District of Columbia. A court that Congress creates pursuant to its powers under Article I or Article IV. Judges of non-Article III courts do not enjoy the Article III protections of tenure and non-reduction of salary.

O

Our Federalism. *See* comity. *See Younger* Doctrine.

P

Pendent Jurisdiction. A judge-made doctrine allowing a federal district court to exercise jurisdiction over claims that lack an independent basis of subject-matter jurisdiction, such as federal-question or diversity jurisdiction. The concept is now subsumed under the generic principle of supplemental jurisdiction, which is codified at 28 U.S.C. § 1367.

Pendent-Party Jurisdiction. The exercise of supplemental jurisdiction to allow a federal court to hear a claim over which there is no independent basis of subject-matter jurisdiction and that is by or against a party as to whom no claim has an independent basis of subject-matter jurisdiction. The concept is codified in 28 U.S.C. § 1367(a), which grants supplemental jurisdiction to the full extent of Article III and, in its last sentence, makes clear that this grant applies to claims involving additional parties. This statute overruled the result in *Finley v. United States* and other cases in which the Supreme Court had refused to permit pendent parties jurisdiction.

Political Question. The principle that a federal court will refuse to decide issues that it determines are committed to other branches of the government by the Constitution, or for which no judicially discoverable and manageable standards can be found, or where judicial determination may create enforcement difficulties or institutional conflicts.

***Pullman* Abstention.** The judge-made doctrine that a federal court may stay a case involving a federal constitutional question to give the state courts the opportunity to interpret an ambiguous state law that can be construed in a manner that will render it constitutional, although unconstitutional constructions are also possible. *See also* *England* Procedure.

R

Removal. The process authorizing a case to be transferred from state to federal court before a final decision occurs. *See also* Civil-Rights Removal.

Res Judicata. *See* Claim Preclusion.

Ripeness. The principle that the federal courts require an actual, present controversy, and therefore will not act when the issue is only hypothetical or the existence of a controversy merely speculative.

Rules of Decision Act. A statute that provides that state law shall be regarded as the rules of decision in a federal court unless the federal Constitution, a treaty of the United States, or an act of Congress otherwise requires or provides. 28 U.S.C. § 1652.

S

Standing. The principle that only one with a tangible and legally protectable interest has the capacity to obtain judicial resolution of a controversy. The plaintiff must be able to show that she has suffered or will suffer actual injury and that there is a causal nexus between the injury suffered and the conduct complained of. A taxpayer who challenges the constitutionality of a federal action must establish a logical link between his status as a taxpayer and the type of federal action she is challenging. She must also prove that there is a nexus between her "status and the precise nature of the constitutional infringement alleged." *Flast v. Cohen*, 392 U.S. 83 (1968). Within the limits of the case-or-controversy requirement of Article III, Congress may grant an express right of action to those who would otherwise meet these requirements. *See* Third-Party Standing.

State Sovereign Immunity. The principle that there can be no legal action against a state unless it has consented to the suit. The doctrine has a common law basis and, to an undefined extent, may have received some level of constitutional protection in the Eleventh Amendment. Congress may abrogate a state's Eleventh Amendment protection under § 5 of the Fourteenth Amendment. In addition, a state may waive its Eleventh Amendment protection, either expressly or by litigation conduct.

Supplemental Jurisdiction. The authority of the federal courts to hear claims that do not satisfy an independent basis of federal subject-matter jurisdiction, such as federal-question or diversity. The concept is codified in 28 U.S.C. § 1367. Section 1367(a) grants supplemental jurisdiction to the full extent of Article III, which codifies the result in *United Mine Workers v. Gibbs*. That case permitted such jurisdiction over claims sharing a "common nucleus of operative fact" with a claim that invoked an independent basis of federal subject-matter jurisdiction. The last sentence of § 1367(a) provides that the grant applies even as to claims involving additionally joined parties and intervenors, thus establishing the propriety of what had been called "pendent-party jurisdiction." Section 1367(b), however, imposes significant restrictions on the grant of supplemental jurisdiction that apply only in cases brought in federal court under § 1332, which includes diversity. Section 1367(c) provides discretionary grounds on which a court with supplemental jurisdiction might decline to exercise it.

Supremacy Cl. Article VI, cl. 2, of the Constitution, providing that the Constitution, treaties and laws of the United States are the "supreme law of the land; and the Judges in every State shall be bound thereby, any Thing in the Constitution or laws of any State to the contrary notwithstanding."

T

Tax Injunction Act of 1937. A statute that mandates that federal district courts not interfere with the assessment or collection of any state tax where a plain, speedy and efficient remedy is available in the state courts. 28 U.S.C. § 1341.

Taxpayer Standing. *See* Standing.

Thibodaux **Abstention.** The judge-made principle that a federal court has the discretion to abstain to allow state courts to decide difficult issues of public importance that, if decided by the federal court, could result in unnecessary friction between state and federal authorities.

Third-Party Standing. The assertion of one individual's right by another. Traditionally, third-party standing has not been allowed in federal court. On occasion, however, the practice is allowed, to protect important interests that might otherwise be undermined. The classic example of such a case involves the First Amendment overbreadth doctrine, which allows an individual who could constitutionally be prosecuted for his conduct to challenge a statute on its face because it reaches constitutionally protected, as well as unprotected conduct.

V

Venue. The particular place within a judicial system in which a court may adjudicate a cause of action. In the federal courts, the term refers to the federal district in which suit is brought. The venue statute for civil actions in federal district courts is 28 U.S.C. § 1391, which generally allows plaintiff to lay venue in any federal district in which all defendants reside or in which a substantial part of the claim arose.

W

Well-pleaded-complaint rule. The principle that the federal courts have federal-question jurisdiction only when the plaintiff's complaint, properly drawn, establishes the presence of a controlling issue of federal law. Though the general federal-question statute, 28 U.S.C. § 1331, makes no explicit reference to the requirement, the Supreme Court has construed the statute to impose the requirement.

Y

Younger **Doctrine.** The principle, developed by the Supreme Court in *Younger v. Harris* and other cases, that federal courts should not interfere with an ongoing state criminal proceeding, either by injunction or declaratory relief, unless the prosecution has been brought in bad faith or as harassment. The *Younger* doctrine has also been applied in civil actions where the state is a party and important state substantive goals are implicated.

APPENDIX D

Table of Cases

APPENDIX E

Index